Fringe Finance

The most recent conversations about financial instability in International Political Economy (IPE) have addressed the ongoing financial chaos of the past five years; a global financial spasm unleashed by the 2008 subprime debacle, ongoing Eurozone instability, and general price volatility in securities markets globally.

Alongside and as part of these broader spasms, however, has been another key trend – the intensifying reach of the global financial market into and among those populations which live at its very edges. There are increasing, and increasingly profitable, experiments which are explicitly targeted at those without regular access to full or formalized financial practices. This book places the practices of fringe finance in critical context by situating them within a larger set of discussions in the field. Most importantly, this book is part of a much broader attempt in IPE to rethread the study of finance to questions of cultural and social theory in a meaningful manner. Finance is increasingly subjected to innovative forms of social inquiry influenced by a range of diverse methods including governmentality, actor-network theory and cultural economy. By drawing on several strands of social theory, this book contributes to this broader movement in IPE and helps open more space for the continuation of these interdisciplinary conversations.

This work will be of great interest to students and scholars of IPE, development studies and economic sociology.

Rob Aitken is Associate Professor of International Relations and International Political Economy at the University of Alberta, Canada.

RIPE Series in Global Political Economy

Series Editors: Jacqueline Best (University of Ottawa, Canada), Ian Bruff (Manchester University, UK), Paul Langley (Durham University, UK) and Anna Leander (Copenhagen Business School, Denmark)

This series, published in association with the Review of International Political Economy, provides a forum for current and interdisciplinary debates in international political economy. The series aims to advance understanding of the key issues in the global political economy, and to present innovative analyses of emerging topics. The titles in the series focus on three broad themes:

- the structures, processes and actors of contemporary global transformations
- the changing forms taken by governance, at scales from the local and everyday to the global and systemic
- the inseparability of economic from political, social and cultural questions, including resistance, dissent and social movements.

The RIPE Series in Global Political Economy aims to address the needs of students and teachers. Titles include:

Transnational Classes and International Relations
Kees van der Pijl

Globalization and Governance
Edited by Aseem Prakash and Jeffrey A. Hart

Nation-States and Money
The Past, Present and Future of National Currencies
Edited by Emily Gilbert and Eric Helleiner

Gender and Global Restructuring:
Sightings, Sites and Resistances
Edited by Marianne H. Marchand and Anne Sisson Runyan

The Global Political Economy of Intellectual Property Rights
The New Enclosures?
Christopher May

Global Political Economy
Contemporary Theories
Edited by Ronen Palan

Ideologies of Globalization - Contending Visions of a New World Order
Mark Rupert

The Clash within Civilisations
Coming to Terms with Cultural Conflicts
Dieter Senghaas

Capitalist Restructuring, Globalisation and the Third Way
Lessons from the Swedish Model
J. Magnus Ryner

Transnational Capitalism and the Struggle over European Integration
Bastiaan van Apeldoorn

World Financial Orders
An Historical International Political Economy
Paul Langley

Global Unions?
Theory and Strategies of Organized Labour in the Global Political Economy
Edited by Jeffrey Harrod and Robert O'Brien

Political Economy of a Plural World
Critical Reflections on Power, Morals and Civilizations
Robert Cox with Michael Schechter

The Changing Politics of Finance in Korea and Thailand
From Deregulation to Debacle
Xiaoke Zhang

Anti-Immigrantism in Western Democracies
Statecraft, Desire and the Politics of Exclusion
Roxanne Lynn Doty

The Political Economy of European Employment
European Integration and the Transnationalization of the (Un)Employment Question
Edited by Henk Overbeek

A Critical Rewriting of Global Political Economy
Integrating Reproductive, Productive and Virtual Economies
V. Spike Peterson

International Trade and Developing Countries
Bargaining Coalitions in the GATT & WTO
Amrita Narlikar

Rethinking Global Political Economy
Emerging Issues, Unfolding Odysseys
Edited by Mary Ann Tétreault, Robert A. Denemark, Kenneth P. Thomas and Kurt Burch

Global Institutions and Development
Framing the World?
Edited by Morten Bøås and Desmond McNeill

Contesting Globalization
Space and Place in the World Economy
André C. Drainville

The Southern Cone Model
The Political Economy of Regional Capitalist Development in Latin America
Nicola Phillips

The Idea of Global Civil Society
Politics and Ethics of a Globalizing Era
Edited by Randall D. Germain and Michael Kenny

Global Institutions, Marginalization, and Development
Craig N. Murphy

Governing Financial Globalization
International Political Economy and Multi-Level Governance
Edited by Andrew Baker, David Hudson and Richard Woodward

Critical Theories, International Relations and 'the Anti-Globalisation Movement'
The Politics of Global Resistance
Edited by Catherine Eschle and Bice Maiguashca

Resisting Intellectual Property
Debora J. Halbert

Globalization, Governmentality, and Global Politics
Regulation for the Rest of Us?
Ronnie D. Lipschutz, with James K. Rowe

Neoliberal Hegemony
A Global Critique
Edited by Dieter Plehwe, Bernhard Walpen and Gisela Neunhöffer

Images of Gramsci
Connections and contentions in political theory and international relations
Edited by Andreas Bieler and Adam David Morton

Global Standards of Market Civilization
Edited by Brett Bowden and Leonard Seabrooke

Beyond Globalization
Capitalism, territoriality and the international relations of modernity
Hannes Lacher

Global Public Policy
Business and the countervailing powers of civil society
Edited by Karsten Ronit

The Transnational Politics of Corporate Governance Regulation
Edited by Henk Overbeek, Bastiaan van Apeldoorn and Andreas Nölke

Critical Perspectives on Global Governance
Rights and Regulation in Governing Regimes
Jean Grugel and Nicola Piper

National Currencies and Globalization
Endangered Specie?
Paul Bowles

Conflicts in Environmental Regulation and the Internationalization of the State
Contested terrains
Ulrich Brand, Christoph Görg, Joachim Hirsch and Markus Wissen

Beyond States and Markets
The challenges of social reproduction
Edited by Isabella Bakker and Rachel Silvey

Governing International Labour Migration
Current Issues, Challenges and Dilemmas
Edited by Christina Gabriel and Hélène Pellerin

The Industrial Vagina
The Political Economy of the Global Sex Trade
Sheila Jeffreys

The Child in International Political Economy
A Place at the Table
Alison M.S. Watson

Capital as Power
A Study of Order and Creorder
Jonathan Nitzan and Shimshon Bichler

Global Citizenship and the Legacy of Empire
Marketing Development
April Biccum

The Global Political Economy of Intellectual Property Rights,
Second Edition
The New Enclosures
Christopher May

Corporate Power and Ownership in Contemporary Capitalism
The politics of resistance and domination
Susanne Soederberg

Savage Economics
Wealth, Poverty and the Temporal Walls of Capitalism
David L. Blaney and Naeem Inayatullah

Cultural Political Economy
Edited by Jacqueline Best and Matthew Paterson

Development, Sexual Rights and Global Governance
Resisting Global Power
Amy Lind

Cosmopolitanism and Global Financial Reform
A Pragmatic Approach to the Tobin Tax
James Brassett

Gender and Global Restructuring
Second Edition
Sightings, Sites and Resistances
Edited by Marianne H. Marchand and Anne Sisson Runyan

Variegated Neoliberalism
EU Varieties of Capitalism and International Political Economy
Huw Macartney

The Politics of European Competition Regulation
A Critical Political Economy Perspective
Hubert Buch-Hansen and Angela Wigger

The Political Economy of Global Remittances
Gender and Governmentality
Rahel Kunz

A Critical History of the Economy
On the Birth of the National and International Economies
Ryan Walter

The International Political Economy of Transition
Neoliberal Hegemony and Eastern Central Europe's Transformation
Stuart Shields

The Global Political Economy of Trade Protectionism and Liberalization
Trade Reform and Economic Adjustment in Textiles and Clothing
Tony Heron

Transnational Financial Associations and the Governance of Global Finance
Assembling wealth and power
Heather McKeen-Edwards and Tony Porter

The Capitalist Mode of Power
Critical Engagements with the Power Theory of Value
Edited by Tim Di Muzio

The Making of Modern Finance
Liberal Governance and the Gold Standard
Samuel Knafo

The State of Copyright
The Complex Relationships of Cultural Creation in a Globalized World
Debora J. Halbert

Transnational Financial Regulation after the Crisis
Edited by Tony Porter

The Political Economy of Global Capitalism and Crisis
Bill Dunn

Global Capitalism
Selected Essays
Hugo Radice

Debtfare States and the Poverty Industry
Money, Discipline and the Surplus Population
Susanne Soederberg

Currency Challenge
The Euro, the Dollar and the Global Financial
Miguel Otero-Iglesias

Fringe Finance
Crossing and Contesting the Borders of Global Capital
Rob Aitken

Fringe Finance

Crossing and contesting the borders of global capital

Rob Aitken

Routledge
Taylor & Francis Group
LONDON AND NEW YORK

First published 2015 by Routledge

2 Park Square, Milton Park, Abingdon, Oxfordshire OX14 4RN
52 Vanderbilt Avenue, New York, NY 10017

Routledge is an imprint of the Taylor & Francis Group, an informa business

First issued in paperback 2020

British Library Cataloguing in Publication Data
A catalogue record for this book is available from the British Library

Library of Congress Cataloging in Publication Data
Aitken, Rob.
Fringe finance : crossing and contesting the borders of global capital / Rob Aitken.
pages cm. – (RIPE series in global political economy)
Summary: "This work will be of great interest to students and scholars of IPE, development studies and economic sociology"– Provided by publisher.
Includes bibliographical references and index.
1. Finance–Social aspects. 2. International finance–Social aspects. I. Title.
HG101.A357 2015
332'.042–dc23
2014030098

ISBN: 978-0-415-72889-8 (hbk)
ISBN: 978-0-367-59964-5 (pbk)

Typeset in Times New Roman
by Taylor & Francis Books

Contents

List of illustrations
Acknowledgments xiii

1 Finance at its centre and its edges 1

PART I
Sites of conversion 31

2 Mapping the logics of expansion: The globalization of payday lending 33

3 The financialization of micro-credit 65

4 Bodies at/of risk: Micro-insurance and the vulnerable life course 91

PART II
Fringe finance as a social practice 127

5 Making regular: Fringe-lending as a formal practice 129

6 From 'inclusion' to adverse incorporations 160

7 Economies of social practice: Creating alternative circuits of financial incorporation 198

Index 233

List of illustrations

1.1 *Non Credited Americans* (Study) 2
1.2 *The Counterfeiters of Coin and the Counterfeiters of Securities* 9
2.1 *Intercontinental Ballistic Microfinance* 34
2.2 *Stock Ticker Orbital Comparison* 34
2.3 Our Customer Base is Large and Growing 54
3.1 Highways of Empire 66
4.1 *Life Insurance Map Showing Extra Premiums for Residence in Various Countries* 92
7.1 P2P Gift Credit Card 200
7.2 *The People's Bailout* 220

Acknowledgement

In Chapter 7 of this book I make reference to Judith Butler's claim that 'we are, even as located, always elsewhere, constituted in a sociality that exceeds us.' Butler's contention offers a unique way of figuring debt—a kind of mechanism of entanglement which immerses us into the social world in ways that both expose us to fragility but make us possible in the first place. This kind of indebted being, this constitutive elsewhere, is also an apt metaphor for the writing of this book, an achievement made possible only through the kindness, support and assistance—the sociality—of the many others who have generously enabled it. Although debt is an impossibility that can never be acknowledged in some kind of final manner, some easy settling of accounts, I do want to note the importance of those who have helped advance this project in innumerable ways: Yasmeen Abu-Laban, Jacquie Best, Phil Cerny, Michael Chu, Chris Clarke, David Cooper, Mark Davidson, Michael Dartnell, Joe Deville, Sara Dorow, Marion Fourcade, Elizabeth Friesen, Tim Gannon, Thomas Gokey, Marieke de Goede, Lois Harder, Dwight Haase, Trevor Harrison, Eric Helleiner, Daniel Henrie, Ali Howell, Amin Husain, Suzan Ilcan, Emilian Kavalski, Stan Keyes, Uriah King, Anita Lacey, Marie Langevin, Sue Lott, Philip Mader, Johnna Montgomery, Ben Muller, James Muir, David Mutimer, Taylor Nelms, Mat Patesron, Daniel Pierre-Antoine, Dan Preece, Alisdair Rogers, Chris Rogers, Andrew Ross (for conversation and inspiration), Herman Schwartz, Greg Seigworth, Elizabeth Smythe, Anil Sud, Marcus Taylor, Michael Thompson, Lauren Tooker, William Walters, Bob Whitelaw, and Magdalena Zolkos. A special note of thanks is due to Paul Langley who has long been supportive and patient and Jacquie Best who continued to ask even when it appeared remote. Randall Germain provided advice and support at a crucial moment—a debt I'm particularly grateful to incur. Monty Bal provided research assistance at various moments and suffered throughout the duration. Mikael Hellstrom and Satish Joshi also provided research assistance. Hajar Amidian stepped in at the last minute and contributed her immense efficiency and grace under fire. Finally, a special acknowledgement of my U of A comrades (you know who you are) for conversations and support of all kinds.

The research for this book was supported, in part, by a Standard Research Grant from the Social Sciences and Humanities Research Council of Canada. I also gratefully acknowledge the additional support of the Rockefeller Archive Center in Sleepy Hollow, New York as well as the Faculty of Arts, University of Alberta. I also want to acknowledge the support and professionalism of everyone at Routledge, a team that has been patient with my requests in ways that have made this process as seamless as possible: Paola Celli, Peter Harris, Nicola Parkin, Alex Quayle and Kris Wishenkamper.

The sociality that makes this book possible is marked most importantly by my indebtedness to Gita Sud and her own enabling support (acknowledged here if not always in kind). Finally, if there is an 'elsewhere' for this book it is Anokhi, who was born during the book's own strange gestation. Although she would likely recognize it only as a debit, and not at the same time as the credit extended to me that it was, my borrowings from her, of time and gratitude, cannot be repaid. American poet Sophie Cabot Black writes that 'to be in debt is to remain awake', a resonant distillation of my life with Anokhi —awake but indebted to her in measures not previously thought possible.

1 Finance at its centre and its edges

> Boundaries, borders and limits must express both inner and outer edges … The modern political imagination is profoundly indebted to specific spatiotemporal topologies of inclusion and exclusion regulated by idealized accounts of lines that seem to do no more than distinguish presence from absence, here from there and now from then … I especially want to draw attention to the work that is done both within lines and between lines: within lines that may seem to have zero width … but which nevertheless host the most intense practices … that are both internal and external.
>
> (R.B.J. Walker 2010: 53)

For three weeks during the spring of 1981, feminist conceptual artist Lynn Hershman mounted an installation in the windows of Wanamaker's Department Store in Philadelphia. *Non Credited Americans* consisted of a conventional storefront window divided so that 1/3 of the surface was painted black, punctuated by the phrase 'Economy and Income: The Great Divide'. In the remaining transparent space, Hershman installed a mannequin dressed glamorously and equipped with a credit card that seemingly attracted objects with its own magnetic force field. A second window, by contrast, featured 'a headless mannequin dressed in anonymous work clothes, grasping unsuccessfully for a feathered credit card that flew just out of reach' (Tromble 2005: 52). The head of this mannequin was occupied by a screen on which was projected 'the faces of dispossessed Americans' who narrated their own stories (projected via a repeating audio tape) of credit denial. Hershman's intervention sought to disrupt everyday practices of consumption by placing them alongside the kinds of dislocations and disenfranchisements they often entail – see Figure 1.1 (Horyn 2012). Hershman's installation also explicitly situates her audience in a unique space precisely at the borders of mainstream credit. By placing the indulgence of credited consumption alongside the spectre of credit dispossession, Hershman invites her audience to move between the spaces of credit availability and refusal. Moreover, the unique space the installation occupies – both a part of the street yet deeply internal to the closed circuit of credit consumption – enacts borders not as lines of strict separation but as zones of complicated and thick confrontation.

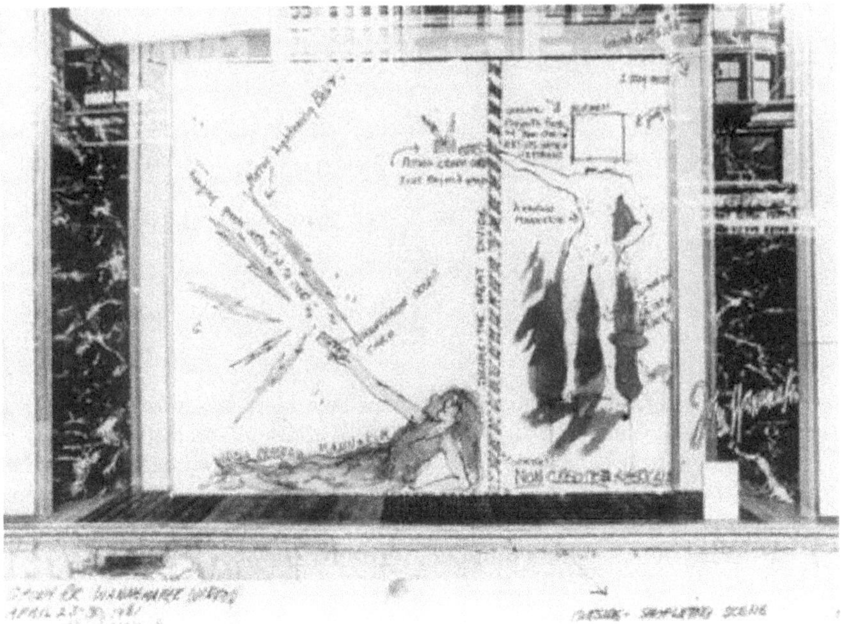

Figure 1.1 Non Credited Americans (Study)

The borders of mainstream credit are not, in Hershman's conception, marked by straight lines. Rather her installation reworks these borders into deeply resonant spaces of critical and artistic exploration and confrontation. Hershman's critical gesture prefigures borders not as 'lines of zero width' as Rob Walker has put it, but as sites that 'host the most intense practices', not easily designated as fully 'internal' or 'external'.

Fringe Finance takes Hershman's critical gesture and Walker's reminders as provocations to explore the borders of global finance as spaces which host 'the most intense practices'. Conventionally, International Political Economy (IPE) has been wedded to conceptions of borders as lines of zero width. Most striking are the ways in which capital is often figured in these terms. Capital has often been drawn as if it transcends borders seamlessly; a kind of 'end of geography' in which capital crosses borders with ease and agility (O'Brien 1992). Perhaps more important are depictions or assumptions which figure capital itself as a well-bounded category, the borders of which are either unproblematic or assumed as given. This is evident, for example, in analyses which have painted capital as an expansive force. As Susan Strange has noted, a key characteristic of global finance is its expansive size and scope: 'the sheer size of these markets, the volume traded, the variety of possible deals to be done, the number of new financial centres, the men and women employed directly or indirectly in the business of international finance' (Strange 1998: 9). Although the intensity with which global finance has expanded has attracted enormous scholarly attention, its borders are often assumed as lines which unproblematically follow or contain that expansion. By contrast, borders are an important, if somewhat implicit feature in the wealth of research which details the local specificities with which finance is experience as a lived reality. This work has examined the particularities with which finance is rooted in specific geographies and in particular experiences (Leyshon and Thrift 1997; Sassen 2005; Zaloom 2006; McDowell 2010).

Questions precisely about the borders of finance and the complexities with which the borders of finance are made, remade or performed lie at the core of *Fringe Finance*: Where and what are the edges of capital? What kinds of lines (legal, cultural, and political) have been drawn around finance? Perhaps most importantly, what are the fates of the human bodies that exist at or beyond the borders of global capital? These questions build upon an emergent body of research which has begun asking questions about the very 'making up' of finance as a category. A range of work relating to the social studies of finance, to cultural studies and to economic sociology have begun to inquire into the ways in which financial categories are constituted. This work is part of a growing body of research in IPE increasingly keen to frame mundane and everyday practices as irreducibly significant to the typical focus in conventional forms of IPE: the pressure of macro-structural forces; the power and authority of elite actors; or the work of specialized economic agents abstracted from any sense of their connections to those living on or beyond the edges of the global political economy. Recent work recasts finance and its boundaries not as given or unproblematic, but as objects that can be subjected to critical examination. For Alex Preda, for example, the legitimacy of finance is only possible once its borders have been inscribed (Preda 2009: 12). Far from accepting the actors or objects that populate the financial world as given, this recent work has trained attention precisely on the practices that constitute finance in the first instance. At the core of this recent work is a keen interest in the 'meticulous details' with which financial practices are reshaped over time – attention to the actual ways in which what counts as 'finance' has varied across time and space. As Marieke de Goede has noted, this approach inverts common representations which depict finance and capital as categories with assumed, coherent and stabilized boundaries:

> The reification of capital as a unitary, sovereign and (all-)powerful agent (or system) does little to clarify the precise ways in which value and entitlements are created … Images of global finance … homogenise financial institutions and markets and assume unproblematic boundaries to the system … the assumption of capital as a fundamental driving force … prohibits … enquiring more meticulously into the meanings and measurements of this concept …. The questions prompted … include: what is capital? … what or where are 'capital's markets' … These questions are not meant to make the concept of capital disappear; they are rather intended to come to a more detailed understanding of modern financial practices.
>
> (De Goede 2003: 82–83)

Building on this work, *Fringe Finance* argues that the borders of global finance are increasingly in flux, are contested across a range of sites and, most importantly, host intense practices. To make this kind of claim, I pay particular attention in this book to the set of intense practices which increasingly dominate the edges of global capital: the specific set of formalized financial practices systematically designed to extract value from the very borders of global finance and the vulnerable bodies that exist at those edges. As I argue in this book, there are increasingly profitable efforts to extend financial services of some description to those who populate the world's poorest communities, those who have been marginalized by traditional banking services or those who find themselves unwilling or unable to access mainstream financial practices. Although estimates are notoriously complicated, one recent study suggests that 2.4 billion adults (just over half of the world's adult population) do not use formal financial services. The vast majority of these populations (2.2 billion) live in Africa, Asia, Latin America and the Middle East (Chala *et al.* 2009: 2; Federal Deposit Insurance Corporation 2009). This is echoed in the Global Findex database compiled by the World Bank which reports that 50% of adults worldwide have no relationship to any formalized financial account (Demirguc-Kunt and Klapper 2012: 2). Financial unevenness also characterizes those spaces at the core of global financial markets. The Federal Deposit Insurance Corporation, for example, concludes that there are now 17 million Americans residing in 'unbanked' households and a further 43 million adults in households which are 'underbanked'; figures that when combined indicate that almost 25% of Americans are unable to fully access mainstream financial practices.[1]

The diverse populations which live at or beyond edges of global finance have increasingly become an object of knowledge and intervention; attracting the *organized* attention of some of the largest agents and institutions in today's global financial markets. An astonishing variety of novel credit and financial practices now profitably seek out 'financially excluded' populations in ways designed to enmesh those populations within the spaces of formal credit and finance: payday lending, home-credit, commercialized micro-credit, micro-insurance, peer-to-peer lending and all variety of profitable micro-lending around the world. Taken together, these diverse practices constitute what I refer to as *fringe finance.* By fringe, I do not mean to suggest that these practices are somehow unimportant or secondary. Rather, fringe refers to the ways in which, despite their stark differences, these credit practices remain preoccupied with the very edges – the very fringes – of the global financial system. A major claim made in this book is that the practices of fringe finance are an increasingly important link between the 'centre' of global finance and those populations that exist at its edges. By extension they offer a particularly useful glimpse into the under-examined practices that predominate on the edges of global finance; the practices that, at the same time, often emanate from global finance at its core. Fringe finance is an increasingly important *diagram* of the logics that lay at the very heart (as well as at the edges) of global finance.

Diagramming fringe finance

Because this book addresses the very borders of finance, and the conditions in which those borders become important as sites of intervention, it places particular emphasis on geographical and spatial metaphors. The main argument focuses on a particular kind of geography of finance, about the (shifting) spaces it occupies, the borders that bound it and the bodies that comprise its various populations. The emphasis I place on spatial metaphors draws on Foucault's insistence that objects are constituted at the intersection of space, knowledge and power. Invoking geographical metaphors, Foucault notes that his analytics are designed 'to trace the forms of implantation, delimitation and demarcation of objects ... the organization of domains means the throwing into relief of processes ... of power' (Foucault 1980: 70). Our contemporary language of financial markets is deeply reliant on spatial vocabularies which emphasize mobility, flows, and (de)territorializations. As French et al. have noted, finance and 'financialization' must 'be understood as profoundly spatial phenomenon' (French, Leyshon and Wainwright 2011: 800). In order to take this claim that finance is a 'profoundly spatial' practice seriously, I draw on a particular kind of geographical language developed from Deleuze as a template for the conceptual framework this book develops. I draw, in particular, on the concept of *diagram*, a particular kind of cartography which Deleuze transposes from Foucault's contention that a 'diagram or abstract machine [is] ... a functioning abstracted from any obstacle ... or friction [which] must be detached from any specific use' (Deleuze 2006: 34). This 'abstract machine' is a delineation of the basic language, ordering coordinates and architecture with which practices are to be organized. The diagram does not refer to any specific configuration of relations – any specific policy or particular practice – but, rather, is a map of abstract relations ('abstracted from any friction') which are always taken up in diverse and diffuse ways in practice. The diagram, according to Deleuze, maps 'the relations between forces, or power relations ... microphysical, strategic, multipunctual and diffuse ... The diagram or abstract machine is the map of relations between forces, a map of destiny, or intensity, which proceeds by primary non-localizable relations' (Deleuze 2006: 36). Diagrams are the idealized ambitions and mappings with which clusters of particular practices are imagined and rationalized. 'Diagrams', affirms William Walters, 'are abstractions, not expressions of a sociological reality ... diagrams are not to be confused with particular policies. Instead, they delineate certain political and organizational *a priori* operating at a level that usually places them beyond our apprehension' (Walters 2006). Because they are 'detached' from any actual practice, diagrams are abstract designs and idealized conceptions of how practices could be (re)organized and of the particular spaces they could come to occupy.

Deleuze's notion of the diagram offers particular kinds of map; not singular representations that correspond seamlessly to some particular reality.

Although diagrams are often represented as perfect or parsimonious designs, they are riddled with ambiguity and instability. Diagrams, notes Deleuze, are 'unstable, formless and fluctuating' (Deleuze 2006: 36). Diagrams do not only map out clean, unambiguous or well-bounded types of spaces. They are also maps, as Foucault puts it, of 'places' and 'non-places'. Diagrams both map out idealized relations and foreground points of rupture, ambiguity and interruption, a cartography not only of geometric borders and well-integrated spaces but points of movement not easily captured or territorialized. 'There is no diagram', implores Deleuze, 'that does not also include, besides the points which it connects up, certain relatively free or unbound points, points of creativity, change and resistance … each diagram testifies to the twisting line of the outside … without beginning or end, an oceanic line that passes through all points of resistance' (Deleuze 2006: 35–44). It is in these terms that the strategic importance of Deleuze's notion of diagram lies in the ways that it allows both a way to map a particular abstraction – as 'diffused' relations between forces – and a way to place that map in critical context.

Diagrams and maps are apt metaphors for the processes through which capital is extended beyond its own edge. Conceiving of fringe finance as a diagram places at the centre of analysis a process that entails the reordering of spatial relations. The language that has accompanied this extension is riddled with spatial metaphors: dis-aggregations, combinations, insertions, inclusions, mediations, circuits and circulation. Transcribing Deleuze, this book argues that fringe finance is a particular diagram of financial power and practice. This is not to suggest that fringe finance is a well bounded map issued in the name of a singular project but, rather, a series of distinctive but linked mappings assembled by a range of actors often pursuing heterogeneous objectives. The diverse network of actors who have shaped the diagram of fringe finance consists of banks, investment houses, non-governmental organizations, development agencies, international organizations, accountants, financial consultants, academics and all variety of creditors big and large. Despite this diversity, the diagram that links the diverse practices of fringe finance maps the edges of the financial system as a site where financial value can be extracted. This is not to imply that those populations have not, historically, been able to access capital in various ways. As Taylor (2014) notes, 'marginal' populations have often been saturated in credit and financial relations of all variety. What I argue in this book is that over the last two decades in particular, the edges of global finance have become objects of financial knowledge and intervention (Kunz 2011) in ways that are uniquely consolidated, institutionalized and globalized.

Linking diverse and varied experiments, this diagram maps the edges of the global financial economy as a fertile space. These edges are diagrammed not as inert or unreachable, but as spaces which, in particular kinds of conditions, could be transformed into sources of profit and value. This diagram also offers various ways in which the populations living at the financial edges could be transported across the lines which separate formal from informal economy, banked from unbanked, mainstream from illicit finance. In these terms, fringe finance is a diagram of expansion; a version of a longstanding map which sketches finance as a practice that could fill new territories and engage new populations outside of its reach.

Deleuze's fluid concept of diagram facilitates a series of unique questions regarding the specific ways in which financial spaces are constituted. It foregrounds borders as constantly shifting lines that require empirical investigation. This, in turn, directs attention to the specific mechanisms and practices that constitute spaces and which shape and reshape borders over time. If fringe finance is a diagram which maps the financial edges as fertile sites, what specific mechanisms have been used to reach those sites? What particular kinds of practices have been deployed to remake the edges of the financial system into sources of financial value and profit? These questions address what Paul Langley has described as the 'specific calculative tools … the devices and techniques through which the future uncertainties of saving and borrowing are measured' (Langley 2008: 15). The critical intent of this book is twofold: both to document *and* disrupt this diagram. As I will catalogue throughout this book, the diagram of fringe finance pivots on three broad clusters of practices each of which addresses the edges of the financial world, and the populations that exist at and across those edges, in diverse types of ways. These three clusters of practices include the processes of conversion, formalization and incorporation.

Conversion

As Leyshon and Thrift have noted, global finance is constituted not in dramatic moments of speculation or financial convulsion. Rather, at the heart of what they describe as 'financial capitalism' is the mundane 'prospecting' for new asset streams. For Leyshon and Thrift, financialization is not possible without an incessant search for objects – some quite distant from the world of 'high finance' – which can be converted into financial assets. The 'bedrock of financial capitalism', they implore, 'is not the spectacular system of speculation but something more mundane; that is financial capitalism is dependent on the constant searching out, or construction of, new asset streams' (Leyshon and Thrift 2007: 98). This construction of new asset streams entails processes of *conversion*; complicated mechanisms and devices which transform objects into sources of financial value.

Conversion, I argue, is at the heart of both *financialization* and the diagram of fringe finance; a diagram which maps the edges of the global economy as a zone that is *convertible,* a fertile zone from which new financial asset streams could be generated. As the various chapters of the book attest, the edges of the financial economy are increasingly subjected to an astonishing variety of techniques – mergers/acquisitions, share transfers, securitizations, initial public offerings, structured finance arrangements, and countless little financializations in the 'cramped spaces' of everyday practice – designed to facilitate the flow of finance capital into and across the edges of finance. Through these techniques, fringe finance is increasingly situated within the spaces of global finance and increasingly reliant on the techniques, expertise, and technical infrastructure associated with that world. The examples of fringe finance explored in this book, and in Part 1 in particular, are sites at which seemingly inert objects are converted into sources of financial value.

Conversion has long been at the heart of financial markets. Preda, for example, emphasizes the ticker as a novel socio-technical device of the late-nineteenth century which was able to convert disparate, often fragmented strands of information into a homogenous stream of price data. 'The ticker made market exchanges visible as they happened, disentangled them from local conversations, and transformed them into something that is both abstract and visible to everybody at once … single, continuous, homogenous, nearly real-time price variations' (Preda 2006: 775). But conversion has often implied a much broader ambition – the transformation of particular kinds of social objects and relations (even particular kinds of human bodies) into objects capable of generating financialized income streams. Historian Edward Baptist, for example, has written an account of the panic of 1837 that focuses on the intersection of slavery and financial innovation. Developing a focus on the 'mechanics of historical financial crises', Baptist (2010) describes a credit bubble deeply enmeshed in the international webs of the slave trade. Key to the panic was a set of innovations which accomplished what Baptist calls the 'securitization of human [slaves] … turning persons into numbers and paper bonds, and so dividing them up and recombining them' (Baptist 2010). The financial innovations (facilitated by some of the largest international financial houses such as Baring Brothers) allowed slave owners and traders to mortgage slaves. Financial claims associated with these mortgaged slaves were then bundled into financial instruments held by distant, sometimes overseas, investors. The proceeds generated by these manoeuvres were often leveraged or re-invested in slave and cotton trades, creating a 'real' economy perched perilously on top of murky layers of financial innovation. At the height of the credit bubble that preceded the panic, 'a quarter million people were moved by force, sold, mortgaged, collateralized, securitized, sold again 3,000 miles from where they actually toiled' (Baptist 2010). In Baptist's retelling, the financial innovations of the 1837 panic were essentially techniques of conversion capable of rendering slaves into financialized objects that were then inserted into complex webs of profitable international financial exchange.

As a diagram of the financial edge, fringe finance places similar emphasis on mechanisms of conversion designed to render objects at or outside of the edges of global finance into financial chains or streams of income. This is not to suggest any kind of easy equivalency between the securitizations Baptist narrates and the kinds of financial practices described in this book. These examples each exist within particular political-cultural contexts and are enabled by unique financial devices. Nonetheless, the securitization that Baptist documents shares with the practices of fringe finance a preoccupation with expanding the sites of financial value. Moreover, these practices connect the edges of global finance to a range of financialized assets that are so central to – what Leyshon and Thrift call the 'bedrock' of – the global financial system. Part 1 of this book narrates three particular if diverse sites of conversion, each of which opens dense linkages between global capital and its own edges.

Formalization

In 1910, Puck Magazine, Joseph Keppler's iconoclastic source of inventive political caricature, published a series of cartoons targeted toward Wall Street and the webs of financial corruption in which it was implicated. One of his caricaturists, Alan Young, published an image which explicitly juxtaposed Wall Street financiers and 'counterfeiters of coin' (see Figure 1.2). By setting these two worlds alongside each other, Young disrupts any easy distinction we might want to make between the realm of Wall Street ('high up and legal') and its 'low down and illegal' other: 'what is the difference morally between making and circulating valueless paper in the guise of money, and making and circulating valueless paper in the form of securities?' (Young 1910). Although finance is often depicted as a rational and legitimate ('high up and legal') category, this is a relatively recent (and contestable) representation. As Young's image underscores, and as a wealth of research on the cultural history of finance now confirms, the moral, cultural and political status of finance was deeply contested throughout the eighteenth, nineteenth and early twentieth centuries. The lines that separate 'rational' finance (in culture, law

Figure 1.2 The Counterfeiters of Coin and the Counterfeiters of Securities (Young 1910)

and politics) from the dubious spaces of illegitimate and criminal intent have historically been the source of intense political contestation. The sedimentation of these lines, and the depiction of finance as a respectable and rational domain, was not the product of some inherent rationality, but an intensely political achievement. Of particular importance in these disputes were contests over where the lines between gambling and finance should be drawn (see De Goede 2005; Mackenzie 2006; Preda 2009). The constitution of finance as a legitimate category involved, in addition, a broad set of struggles to re-imagine financial exchange as a rational practice: the reconfiguration of finance as an object that could be knowable in statistical and quantitative analysis; the 'discovery' of a science of investor analysis and portfolio management; and the marketing of finance to working class and 'mass' audiences as a legitimate tool of everyday economic security (Harmes 2001; De Goede 2004; Aitken 2007; Preda 2009; Stäheli 2013).

The drawing of lines that separate legitimate finance from its illegitimate others, however, has not been a once-and-for-all achievement. As Deleuze argues in his discussion of Foucault,

> lines … do not outline or surround systems which are each homogenous in their own right … but follow directions, trace balances which are always off balance, now drawing together and then distancing themselves from one another. Each line is broken and subject to *changes in direction,* bifurcating and forked, and subject to *drifting.*
>
> (Deleuze 1988: 159, emphasis in original)

In these terms, drawing lines that bound finance is not a static but an ongoing, and 'off balanced' project. This book argues that fringe finance is precisely one set of sites where the lines that bound finance – where the borders of what counts as legitimate and formally permissible financial practices – continues to be reshaped and contested in our present; the financial edges not only as sites of conversion, but also as spaces that could be *formalized.* Fringe finance is a diagram which sketches a redrawn and expanded border around what might count as formally legitimate finance. Put simply, fringe financial providers often seek both to re-settle where the borders of finance lie and to move their practices across those borders. This is, in part, a response to the ways in which fringe financial services have often been confronted by political, cultural and legal claims which frame them as dubious, unethical or predatory. These pressures have a particular resonance in the American context where the practices of payday lending have been confronted not only with civil litigation but increasingly a range of new legal and regulatory limits.

In reaction to these pressures, the commercial interests associated with fringe finance have increasingly struggled to establish new mechanisms of *formal* legitimacy. This has entailed both legal and regulatory devices which, in quite diverse ways, have sought to secure a settled sense of legal legitimacy. These devices include licensing mechanisms, oversight rules, interest regulations, disclosure regimes, registration requirements and complex audit or compliance procedures. This has been a common practice in Canada, some American states and in the United Kingdom where regulatory or legislative devices have actually settled the status of fringe lending as a permissible form. Although these devices often impose some cost on the fringe lending sector they also establish a kind of formal legitimacy which insulates the sector from the kinds of legal and political risk it has confronted over the past two decades. It is in this sense that fringe finance constitutes a diagram which maps the murky practices of high-cost financial services as forms which can be unambiguously transported across the lines which separate formal from informal; a zone where the borders of global finance are visibly negotiated and reworked.

There are, however, limits to techniques of formalization. As I argue in Chapter 5, contestation is internal to the practices of formalization – not a reaction to some more primary impulse but a constitutive element of the techniques of formalization. The ambition to transform fringe lending into settled legal practice is, in some important ways, a response to the waves of activism that have cast legal and regulatory shadows over their claims to legitimacy. These contestations have taken diverse form in different contexts. In the USA, at both the State and Federal levels, anti-poverty, consumer rights, and Occupy activists have mounted successful campaigns framing fringe lending as predatory, unfair and, in some contexts, a deeply racialized practice. These campaigns have helped enact a range of consumer rights protections and, in some jurisdictions, effective prohibitions or interest rate caps. In other contexts, notably Hungary and Australia, serious regulatory barriers have been established partly in response to pressures brought to bear by those concerned with fringe lending and the costs it exerts on vulnerable populations at the very edges of the financial system. Viewed from this perspective, formalization, although key to the diagram of fringe finance, and central to the political ambitions of fringe lenders, remains an unfinished and deeply contested project (see Aitken 2013).

Incorporation

A third cluster of practices mapped in the diagram of fringe finance relate to *incorporation*. If conversion is preoccupied with the remaking of the edge as a financialized space and if *formalization* is concerned with the legal legitimacy of the practices that result, both of these processes imply an additional ambition; the absorption of disenfranchised populations into the formal spaces of global finance. All programmes of fringe finance are framed by a dream that seeks to transport the populations who live beyond its reach into organized financial spaces. In doing so, fringe finance is a diagram intimately concerned with the relationship between capital and vulnerable bodies.

The conventional language of political economy has often framed the bodies at the edges of capital as surplus populations. Drawing on Marx, surplus populations are those bodies that lie outside of or are not immediately absorbed into the processes of capital accumulation. This 'mass of human material' is, however, at the same time, a latent force central to capital accumulation. As a potential source of labour, the production and maintenance of surplus populations, in Marx's words, 'furnishes to capital an inexhaustible reservoir of disposable labour power' (Marx 1999 [1887]: 444). Surplus populations constitute a

> lever of capitalist accumulation ... a condition of existence of the capitalist mode of production. It forms a disposable industrial reserve army that belongs to capital quite as absolutely as if the latter had bred it at its own cost ... it creates ... a mass of human material always ready for exploitation.
>
> (Marx 1999 [1887]: 438)

Surplus populations provoke questions of serious political urgency, especially crucial in a context in which 'capital incorporates some places and peoples, and ejects and rejects others' (Li 2009: 68). However, transposing a nineteenth-century conceptual apparatus poses some important challenges. Some, for example, have noted the overly functional language with which Marx delineates surplus populations – a mechanistic view of an essentialized role surplus labour occupies in the broader reproduction of capitalist development. As Li has noted, to 'assume a link between dispossession, and the (re)production of a labour reserve is not just too linear, it is dangerously complacent' (Li 2009: 70). Moreover, Marx's delineation of surplus labour as a key mechanism in production and 'industrial' development invokes an overly narrow conception of economic life, one that ignores the relationship between finance and the populations on the edges of the global economy.

In this book I approach the question of bodies at or beyond the reach of capital – what Gavin Smith (2011) refers to as a relationship between 'capital and ordinary people' – in a slightly different manner. I make both an empirical and a conceptual argument (see Chapter 6 in particular). Empirically, I am interested not in the places where finance capital renders populations surplus, but its inversion – places where those outside of its reaches are incorporated into the spaces of global finance. Increasingly, as this book argues, those outside of or on the edges of capital, are targeted by financial institutions as bodies that could be enrolled within mainstream global finance. This is not to suggest that there are not large populations without any link to finance capital. Indeed, the conditions of existence for fringe finance are constituted in the swelling ranks without access to financial services or without any meaningful kind of financial account. Rather, my claim is that to ignore the complex ways in which financial agents address those outside of its reach, and to focus on the relations of absence, is to occlude one of the key empirical dynamics associated with global finance. Ever expansive, what defines global finance is not only (or perhaps even primarily) the large populations surplus to its needs, but, rather, the populations outside of its reach (or only partially in its grip) that it increasingly seeks to address, enrol and instrumentalize.

At a conceptual level, this is an argument for a focus that moves beyond overly general ways of understanding the populations that live at or beyond the borders of capital. In contrast to those who paint these populations and their relationship to capital in general terms – as an instance of 'hegemony' or in terms of some simple rubric of 'inclusion' and 'exclusion' – I want to stress a different focus. The focus I take up in this book is not a general approach (as Li reminds us, to 'assume a link' between dispossession and capital writ large in some general way is misplaced). Rather I want to adopt a more concrete and situated approach which trains analytical attention not on generalized schemas, but on the actual mundane techniques and practices of *incorporation* – the actual mechanisms that facilitate incorporation and the terms and conditions those mechanisms facilitate. As du Toit argues, 'what defines marginality is not exclusion (or even imperfect inclusion!) but the terms and conditions of incorporation' (du Toit 2004: 1003). This entails questions not about some single pathway from 'inclusion' to 'exclusion' or about some generalized pressure exerted by Capital in the singular, but about the actual terms and processes of incorporation, especially those that lead to instances of *adverse* incorporation: How are unbanked populations incorporated into mainstream financial practices? What kinds of incorporations do these mechanisms facilitate?

In addressing these questions, I complicate the ways in which fringe finance operates as a diagram of incorporation. Lenders, consultants, financial firms and advocates often stress fringe finance as a set of practices that can enact straight lines of inclusion; a set of (profitable) practices capable of drawing new populations across the lines that mark financial exclusion. It is a central argument of this book, however, that the incorporations that result are more complex and ambiguous than often represented. As Deleuze reminds us, diagrams do not map straight lines but mark the 'twisting line of the outside'. This language offers an apt framing of the complexity of ways in which fringe financial practices incorporate the populations they target. In contrast to a diagram which imagines a series of straight-forward moves from spaces unambiguously outside (exclusion) to practices clearly inside (inclusion) of global finance, fringe financial practices position the populations they target in more complicated ways. The practices of fringe finance, for example, enact grids that both include and exclude, that simultaneously incorporate vulnerable populations more fully into formal financial markets but do so in ways that can deepen or entrench existing forms of inequality. Moreover, and as the experiences associated with fringe finance increasingly underscore, economic disenfranchisement is not only the result of exclusion from, but also of adverse incorporation within, newly formalized financial arrangements. Incorporation, to put it simply, can deepen forms of economic disenfranchisement. Although the diagram which underpins fringe finance stresses a simple language – of 'inclusion' and 'exclusion' – the argument at the core of this book disrupts any easy claim that might separate those two conditions; a caution against maps of everyday economic security which sketch clear or distinct lines.

Neither is this to suggest that incorporation is exclusively a practice authored by capital. Although most instances of incorporation are facilitated by private financial institutions, incorporation is a malleable political technology available to a wide range of interests and intentions. As Chapter 7 suggests, there is now a network of activist and non-governmental organizations which have mounted their own experiments in incorporation in the form of social or peer-to-peer lending. These experiments seek alternative forms of incorporation, the terms of which are crafted not by finance capital but by a network of interests operating, at least in part, to the side of that logic.

The genealogies of finance

> But for me this is precisely the point at issue, both in historical analysis and in political critique. We aren't, nor do we have to put ourselves, under the sign of a unitary necessity.
>
> (Foucault 1991: 78)

Although each of the chapters in this book is oriented around its own discrete conceptual commitments, the connective tissue of the argument as a whole relates to genealogy as a method and practice. Genealogy, via Foucault, is a method organized around the importance of discontinuity and heterogeneity. Genealogy does not assume that practices or objects have a linear history but, in contrast, purposely places emphasis on the unintended and diverse ways in which objects are formed. In narrating the formation of particular practices in these ways, genealogy seeks to de-familiarize those practices, to disrupt the ways in which particular practices are imagined as somehow given. As Foucault noted, genealogy is a method designed to fragment categories that are conceived as homogenous, unproblematic or necessary. Genealogy seeks to 'show the heterogeneity of what was imagined consistent with itself' (Foucault 1984: 82). Genealogy is an analytical strategy that eschews easy or smooth historical narratives by attending 'to the breaks that punctuate history' (Shiner 1982: 387). Attending to these breaks often requires interrogating objects for the surprising ways in which they were formed; not as histories that are 'completed' seamlessly but as diverse processes with endless and contingent moments of intersection. As Walters suggests this is an imminently empirical task of uncovering the detailed and concrete ways with which objects that we now conceive as whole or given were actually constituted. One of the intents of this style of genealogy, argues Walters, 'is to decompose what otherwise appears integral and complete; to identify seams and stitches that were initially hidden from view; to reveal that a final product is actually a hodge podge of bits and pieces, each of which has its own history' (Walters

2012: 118). An act of 'decomposition', genealogy places into focus the concrete and twisting 'lines of descent' that make up objects not as whole bodies but as 'bits and pieces'.

The 'decomposition' genealogy accomplishes is an attempt neither to compile additional knowledge, nor to add empirical refinement to the history of particular objects, but rather, to undo those objects and the ways in which they are often understood. Genealogy does not seek pure or untainted stories, but rather purposely discontinuous accounts designed to disturb what was considered 'consistent with itself'. This strategy, claims Walters, 'uses historical knowledge to reveal that who and what we are is not fixed or eternal, not a matter of destiny or grand design, but a series of contingent becomings … to unsettle the boundaries and encrusted shapes we inhabit' (Walters 2012: 115–118). In Foucault's terms, unsettling 'the encrusted shapes we inhabit' is a strategy of 'dispersion'; a very particular kind of historical writing committed to disruption by foregrounding the brokenness with which objects are formed and shaped:

> Genealogy does not pretend to go back in time to restore an unbroken continuity that operates beyond the dispersion of forgotten things; its duty is not to demonstrate that the past actively exists in the present … On the contrary, to follow the complex course of descent is to maintain passing events in their proper dispersion; it is to identify the accidents, the minute deviations … the errors, the false appraisals, and the faulty calculations that gave birth to those things that continue to exist.
>
> (Foucault 1977: 81)

In lieu of categories conceived as given or continuous, genealogy offers purposely disjointed histories in an effort to unsettle – to insert a stutter into – the ways in which we relate to or understand the practices that make up our present. Genealogy is 'effective' to the degree that 'it introduces discontinuity into our very being … It will uproot its traditional foundations and relentlessly disrupt its pretended continuity. This is because knowledge is not made for understanding; it is made for cutting' (Foucault 1977: 88).

This focus on knowledge for cutting is particularly important in fields of inquiry – such as IPE – which have traditionally worked with categories of analysis that are often treated as given. The basic language and analytical categories of IPE (capital, production, labour, work, economy) are often framed as universal or material categories somehow outside of or prior to their representations. (See, for example, Mitchell 2002.) Although much attention, especially in strands of critical IPE, has been paid to the ways in which capital has been assembled historically or transformed over time, capital is still often represented as a bounded and implacable kind of force. Once historically constituted, capital exerts a monolithic, disciplinary or even determinant pressure on the global political economy. (For one example see Gill 1995.) Put in the language of genealogy, work in IPE often neglects the discontinuities of capital, the remakings of capital over time. As Foucault reminds us, however, genealogy requires redrawing categories, like capital, not as universalizing machines, but as complex and plural categories, the boundaries of which shift over time. Universalization is not an assumption to guide analysis, but is itself a depiction, a way of mapping a category, that has its own detailed histories. Genealogy, argues Foucault, 'means rediscovering the connections, encounters, supports, blockages, plays of forces, strategies and so on which at a given moment establish what subsequently counts as being self-evident, universal and necessary' (Foucault 1991: 76). In genealogical terms, framings that rely on consistency, universalism, unity, or coherence need to be explained (and disrupted) not assumed as given.

> Against beliefs of unifying structure, its task is to … fragment the cohesion of objects and to deliberately oppose comparisons of 'necessary sameness' (that the 'now' is necessarily like the 'then'; that the 'here' of the analytical context is necessarily like the 'there' of that being analyzed).
> (Hook 2005: 11)[2]

As Timothy Mitchell has noted, economic categories have tended to resist the styles of critical analysis, like genealogy, which are now common across the social sciences and humanities (Mitchell 2002). Nonetheless, approaches to IPE drawing on these broader forms of critical, cultural and social theory have been quickly accumulating over the past decade. (See Best and Paterson 2009.) Genealogies of finance, in particular, capitalize on their own debt to the work of Marieke de Goede who has helped open space for histories of the present of capital (de Goede 2003, 2004, 2005, 2007). For de Goede, although finance was deeply contested as a dubious practice in the nineteenth century, and as recently as the 1930s, it is now most commonly framed as a scientific and legitimate pursuit. To disturb this image, de Goede has narrated both the earlier contestations that marked finance as a socially controversial practice as well as the complex work required to recast finance. This is an approach, as she describes it, that aims

> to disturb the depoliticized nature of finance theory and practice through a genealogical reading of the historical struggles, debates, controversies, insecurities, and ambiguities that had to be purged from nascent credit practices in order to produce the image of today's coherent and – largely – rational global financial sphere … finance as a legitimate, rational, and, above all, *natural* practice.
> (de Goede 2005: x, emphasis in original)

This purging of finance from its others was accomplished in a range of ways (Mackenzie 2006; Preda 2009). The most important of these strategies, however, were various attempts to refashion the discourse of finance as a scientific endeavour. Assembled from a range of directions – from econometrics and statistics, from new techniques of visual display and charting borrowed from demographics and economics, from the crucible of practical experimentation – finance was slowly, but haphazardly, transformed into an object that could be understood in a language of statistical analysis and display. This entailed the codification of risk not as a random or uncontrollable force, but as an object with properties that could be managed, known and charted. One key step in this transformation, for de Goede, occurs in the nineteenth-century invention of financial averages and charting – indices of financial prices made visible as scientific, and politically legitimate, movements. 'The virtues associated with statistics', she argues, 'provided one way in which the moral superiority of speculators became articulated in the face of political critiques' (de Goede 2005: 89; see also Preda 2009). Rooted in empirical analysis, a central focus of genealogies of finance is the contention that the settling of finance as a rational – and, hence, legitimate – sphere of practice, was a recent and uncertain achievement.

Fringe Finance is deeply indebted to and located within the space opened by these types of analyses. Most importantly, I argue that fringe financial practices are situated in the genealogies of finance, one site where the un/settling of finance is made particularly visible. The attempts to recast finance as a legitimate realm in the face of depictions which frame it as dubious or politically controversial, and the innovation of complex practices designed to resettle what finance is, are not a residue of some overcome past, but an *ongoing* set of processes; a description not of some prehistory of financial exchange but of the contemporary contests which characterize the very edges of finance. The rationalization of finance has a long history encompassing eighteenth-century associations with games of chance and lotteries, nineteenth-century innovation of statistical analysis, and the twentieth-century enrolment of finance in the codified sciences of financial economics and economic modelling. This history continues to be enacted, however, in the practices that convert the edges of the financial system into sources of financial value, in the processes that formalize legally questionable and politically dubious credit practices, and in the diverse methods which incorporate the 'poorest of the poor' into mainstream financial spaces. Because it is a zone where global finance is visible not as a settled world, but a world that is shifting, ambiguous and contested, the edges of the financial world are uniquely relevant to the genealogies of finance.

The particular version of genealogy I develop in this book operates along two different lines. On one hand, and in ways that echo many other critiques, I sketch finance as a force that is often typified by its desire to expand; a version of a longstanding map which sketches finance as a practice that could fill new territories beyond its reach. On the other hand, however, I paint this expansiveness not as an effect of some implacable or inevitable force, but as a mundane capacity enabled by specific mechanisms and techniques. Put in Deleuze's terms, expansion is a diagram not a 'reality'. When translated into concrete practices, and when viewed from the very edges they seek to overcome, ambitions of expansion often encounter friction and unanticipated corrosions. *Fringe Finance* is concerned with finance as an expansive ambition. This is an expansiveness, however, that is marked not 'as an unbroken continuity' but as a contested and shifting set of edges. This implies that finance is not an already-existing or unproblematic category, but a set of objects attached to their own historical and *social* surfaces of emergence.

Finance as a 'social' practice

Although finance has always been a relevant theme in traditions of critical political economy, it has now become the object of creative new avenues of analysis in a wide range of disciplinary settings, especially sociology, anthropology and the social studies of technology/science. This larger set of interdisciplinary conversations has, in part, coalesced as an emergent field of inquiry known as the 'social studies of finance'. Although it is too diverse to gesture at here, I want to note some of the important ways in which *Fringe Finance* is indebted to and situated within certain strands of this broader work.

First, and most immediately apparent in the chapters of Part 1, this book is deeply shaped by the focus in the social studies of finance on the material and technical worlds that finance inhabits. The social studies of finance are preoccupied with the material and concrete devices which inscribe financial knowledge in practices. This contrasts sharply with approaches which construe financial markets in overly abstract terms, as macro-structural forces or as a 'fictitious' or 'imaginary' form of capital. Anthropologists, for example, have largely been attracted to finance as a space that could be narrated in relation to the concrete and often messy practices which it forms. 'The starting premise of an anthropological approach', notes Riles, 'is that markets are not abstract machines to be reduced to a few equations or theorems, but messy contexts, full of contradictory forces and elements, actors, languages, institutions, ways of living and knowing … assemblages of many forms of expertise and many kinds of technology' (Riles 2011: 11). In this focus on concrete details, the social studies of finance have emphasized a certain kind of *materiality*. The form of materiality is not the analysis of material structures. Rather, this is a focus which foregrounds the mundane practices, techniques and mechanisms that enable financial relations and exchange in the first place. Eschewing any easy distinction between 'material' and 'ideal' realms, the social studies of finance have been preoccupied with the lived materiality of markets and the technologies and devices which make those markets a material reality. As Mackenzie has noted, what remains 'most characteristic of a perspective rooted in the social studies of science and technology is its concern with the *materiality* of markets: their physicality, corporeality, technicality … The properties of artefacts, technological systems, conceptual tools, and so on are not 'details' that sociological analyses should set aside' (Mackenzie 2009: 2–3).[3] In this kind of emphasis the mundane techniques of finance are not secondary or marginal but primary to the ways in which markets are shaped and, by extension, key to the kinds of social and political pressures markets exert.

The emphasis that this perspective lays on questions of technical materiality extends also to the very nature of human agency. Agency is figured not as some inherent or specialized force rooted in human actors, but, rather, a capacity that is itself inseparable from the web of practices of which it is a part. Callon, for example, conceives of *agencements* as capacities deeply reliant on the devices and technologies which make action possible in a very concrete and material way. Market *agencements* are the ensemble of 'socio-technical' devices through which 'persons and things are translated into calculative beings … marked typically by circulation, pricing and exchange' (Callon, Millo and Muniesa 2007: 4–5; Callon 1998; see also Aitken 2010a: 227). Agents are not inherently rational or calculative, but, rather, are formatted by 'market devices', and are entangled in agencements which help enable certain forms of calculation. 'Actors should not be seen as having fixed natures or fixed characteristics', notes Mackenzie, 'The equipment that makes an actor what it is, the particular material processes of calculation it engages in … all these shape the nature of actors' (Mackenzie 2009: 22). Agency is itself, in this perspective, a technical device understood in terms of its concrete materiality.[4]

Fringe Finance draws upon this focus on materiality and the devices which constitute and enable markets in the first place. Part 1 of this book pays particular attention to three very different sites of conversion – practices in which the financial edge, and the populations that live there, are converted into sources of financial value. These sites include the disparate practices of payday lending, micro-credit and micro-insurance. Not only do each of these practices emerge out of quite distinct contexts, they are also enabled by different concrete mechanisms. Payday lenders, for example, have constituted a market for a very particular kind of short-term loan through the techniques of financialization – by relying on the architecture of the global financial and payments system, and by assembling several very large global networks of lenders stitched together through complex financial transactions. The rapid growth over the past decade of commercialized micro-credit has been enabled by the mundane practices of securitization. Finally, micro-insurance has resulted in a series of 'little financializations' in the everyday lives of those largely outside of the mainstream financial world. Micro-insurance, like all practices of fringe finance, has become an important space of innovation. Chapter 4 notes in particular agricultural index insurance and remittance insurance products which both reframe populations at the edge as risk-bearing subjects and harness the unique conditions of those edges as risks in the first place. Each of these distinct sites, I argue, cannot be understood outside of their own material and technical conditions of emergence.

A second broad theme this book develops from the social studies of finance relates to performativity. Performativity is rooted in Austin's insight that language can often constitute the object which it purports only to describe

(Austin 1962: 6).[5] For Judith Butler, performativity is an iterative act, statements which, when performed over time, enact the objects they address. A 'performative', Butler has famously argued, 'is that discursive practice that enacts or produces that which it names … [the] reiterative power of discourse to produce the phenomena that it regulates and constrains' (Butler 1993: 12). The social studies of finance have been deeply influenced by approaches to performativity in work that has surveyed the ways in which the financial realities are performed. As Michel Callon has noted in a highly influential formulation, forms of economic knowledge 'do not merely record a reality independent of themselves: they contribute powerfully to shaping, simply by measuring it, the reality they measure' (Callon 1998: 32). This has triggered a range of important work deeply concerned with the role of knowledge in shaping 'economic' objects (Mackenzie and Millo 2003: 137; Mackenzie 2006; Watson 2009; Langley 2010: 73; Brassett and Clarke 2012; Karl 2013). Cast across a wide surface, performativity is now a concept at the core of attempts to reclaim the analysis of finance as a social object.

This work on performativity reframes neoliberalism not as a mode of retrenchment – as a practice oriented only toward 'deregulation' and the removal of the mechanisms of intervention – but as a set of practices with their own deeply inscribed productivity. Neoliberal practices, such as those at the heart of contemporary financial markets, are not simply concerned with negation and the withdrawal of regulation, but are deeply implicated in the proliferation of – the *performance* of – novel modes of governing economic and social life. To accent this particular inflection of performativity, I draw on a series of arguments developed by Timothy Mitchell who argues that performativity entails detailed attention to the boundaries which constitute the economic as a discrete and identifiable category (Mitchell 2006: 1116; see also Mitchell 2002, 2005, 2007; Aitken 2010b). Performing economic categories entails drawing particular lines between the formally 'economic' and the 'non-economic' and moving particular practices from one side of those lines to the other.[6] 'To argue that the power of economics is performative', notes Mitchell, is to recognize its role in processes designed 'to constitute the border between the market and the nonmarket' (Mitchell 2007: 248). Performing these lines, and transferring peoples and assets across that line, are deeply political interventions designed to settle what counts as formalized and legitimate economic categories.

Chapter 5 draws on this performativity literature in order to focus on the diverse range of ways in which micro-lending has been constituted and performed. In reaction to legal and political challenges to its legitimacy, fringe finance operators have often sought to enact regulations designed to settle permanently the legal status of micro-lending. Drawing on the performativity literature I argue that regulatory mechanisms for fringe lending are performative; that regulations bring into being – and *formalize* – the objects they purport only to manage. As Seabrooke notes, however, we need to understand 'legitimacy as contestation between claims by those who seek to govern and the conferral or rejection of such claims in everyday practice by those being governed' (Seabrooke 2007: 3). As I argue throughout Part 2, the performance of micro-lending as a legitimate practice is not secured once-and-for-all. Rather, this is a process that has been characterized by contestation at all levels.

A third major intersection with the social studies of finance, relates to questions of financial subjectivity. This entails what Langley and Leyshon refer to as 'the often complex ways in which multiple financial subjects are summoned up and assembled in the cultural and material production of contemporary financial markets' (Langley and Leyshon 2012: 369). Particular attention has recently been targeted on the assemblage of subjects in ways consistent with neoliberal conceptions of an enterprising or investing self, an actor capable of managing his or her own financial life in a responsibilized manner. This has required attention to 'how individuals are positioned as being responsible for "managing" their own financial subjectivities in ways that conform to wider discourses … of personal responsibility and risk management associated with neoliberal financial markets'[7] (Hall and Appleyard 2012: 460; see also French and Kneale 2009).

As Paul Langley has noted, however, the assembly of financial subjects is uneven and profoundly *uncertain*. Subjects do not fill the positions to which they are summoned in an automatic manner, but relate to subjectivity in a messy and often ambiguous fashion. Subjectivities are forged in complex and uneasy ways which entail misidentifications and contradictions that attend all forms of subjectivity. The 'embodiment of the mass investment culture of financialization', argues Langley, 'is likely to be highly problematic … contradictions interrupt the processes of identification in everyday investment' (Langley 2007: 80). Paying attention to the disturbances and competing identities (worker, consumer) which complicate identification, Langley has charted the ambiguities with which financial subjectivity is lived.

In Chapter 6, I draw on and intersect with this work on financial subjectivity by opening a parallel track relating to questions of *incorporation*. Extending Langley's insight regarding the unease with which subjects relate to financial identities, I emphasize questions about the concrete conditions in which populations are asked to move into certain forms of financial subjectivity. Subjectivity, however, invokes metaphors of *position* – claims about the location occupied within systems of discourse or practice. Incorporation, by contrast, invokes metaphors of *placement*; the action associated with arrangement or the particular methods with which objects are 'set in place'. Placement lays emphasis not on the position occupied by bodies (however ambiguous), but on the processes of movement and arrangement. Incorporation is a particular kind of placement; the processes through which populations outside of the financial economy are set within, fed into or enrolled into its spaces. Incorporation is less focused on the subjectivities to which bodies are summoned, or the positions modelled for them, than it is on the processes through which those bodies are asked to move, the channels and currents they are asked to navigate *en route*, or the methods by which they are drawn in.

Incorporation is complimentary to the concern with subjectivity, and the uneasiness with which subjects assume the positions to which they are summoned. Paying attention to the practices of incorporation allows a certain diagnosis of the terms and conditions with which populations are enrolled into financial spaces. In contrast to any simple map of 'inclusion' and 'exclusion', incorporation inquires into concrete forms of enrolment. This focus, I argue, expands our critical language by making available a vocabulary not of pristine conditions of 'inclusion' but of forms of incorporation that are ambiguous, coercive, immobilizing or limiting. Rendering incorporation as a question of empirical examination allows us to understand greater proximity to formalized financial services not as an unproblematic or benign condition, but as a process riddled with its own risks. As the experiences associated with fringe finance increasingly underscore, economic disenfranchisement is not only the result of *exclusion from* but also of *adverse incorporation within* newly formalized financial arrangements. To make these connections, I bring the debates on questions of financial subjectivity into dialogue with two critical concepts developed in anthropology – 'adverse incorporation' and 'immobility'. These concepts help critically diagnose greater forms of 'inclusion' not as mechanisms of access or enfranchisement but often as practices built around ambiguity, enclosure and displacement. Although this type of focus on enclosure and placement can imply a certain instrumental intent, I do not mean to imply that it is bereft of contestation. Nor do I want to suggest that incorporation is a process that is fully imposed upon subjects that are passive recipients. Rather, as Chapter 7 explicates, alternative forms of incorporation and placement are possible including forms of incorporation oriented not toward the extraction of financial value but toward the mobilization of social being.

The plan of this book

> ... the analysis in question should not concern itself with the regulated and legitimate forms of power in their central locations, with the general mechanisms through which they operate. On the contrary, it should be concerned with power at its extremities, in its ultimate destinations, with those points where it becomes capillary, that is, in its more regional and local forms ... the point where power ... becomes embodied in techniques, and equips itself with instruments and eventually even violent means of material intervention.
>
> (Foucault 1980: 96)

This book is concerned with financial power and practice at its 'extremities' and the borders that are redrawn at those edges. The main claim of this book is that the borders of finance are ambiguous, are contested and are not easily understood in terms of the simple language conventionally used to diagnose the edges of the financial world: a language of 'inclusion/exclusion' or 'inside/outside' (see Langley 2008). I also argue that, at the same time, these borders have become objects of intense and profitable financial intervention over the past twenty years. As a result these borders are not strict lines, but what Edward Casey has referred to as edges. 'Edges', notes Casey, 'supply bounds to the in-between', but there 'is no edge of edging, no ultimate edge in the activity of having or giving an edge to something … there is edging out and out and out, but there is no definitive or final single edge' (Casey 2008: 9–10). Echoing Casey, this book argues that borders in global finance should not be assumed as given or unproblematic, but need to be subjected to forms of empirical, political and conceptual reflection. This book reflects on the borders of finance by making an argument about one set of practices that inhabits those borders. It argues that fringe finance is a diagram which opens a particular way of acting upon the edges of finance and the populations that live at those edges: as a set of sites that could be made accessible to financial capital (*conversion*); as a set of practices that could be afforded legal or regulatory legitimacy (*formalization*); and as a series of vulnerable populations that could be rendered objects of financial knowledge and intervention (*incorporation*). The critical intent of this argument is twofold: both to diagnose this diagram by providing glimpses into some of the particular practices that have been assembled in its shadow; but also to disrupt this diagram by upending some of the easy claims it maps regarding the ease or efficacy of seemingly unproblematic processes of financial 'inclusion'.

To accomplish this kind of argument, this book is divided into two parts. Part 1, *Sites of Conversion*, places in the foreground three particular practices which work to extract financial value from the very edges of mainstream finance. As this part of the book argues, conversion lies at the very heart of financialization. If, as Leyshon and Thrift note, financial capitalism is characterized by the incessant prospecting for new financial asset streams, it is the practices of conversion which render 'inert' bodies into financial objects. The three chapters of Part 1 each examine a distinct practice – payday lending, micro-credit and micro-insurance – which accomplish, in distinctive ways, the rendering of those with only partial or no access to mainstream finance into some form of value which is often then returned to mainstream financial markets. The intention of these chapters is twofold. First, these three chapters each provide a glimpse into fringe finance as a diagram of idealized relations – a diagram that charts clean, geometric lines. A diagram is an abstract machine, a map of particular relations which exist 'without friction'. Each chapter in Part 1 makes visible the diagram of fringe finance in idealized form. Second, the chapters in Part 1 are important because they also underscore the inescapable *diversity* of this diagram; a mapping with multiple variations. Although there is a common connective tissue which permeates all practices of fringe finance – a concerted and organized rendering of the edges of finance as sources of financial value – it can be mapped in diverse kinds of ways. Each chapter in Part 1 examines a fragment of this diversity.

Maps are particularly resonant to the analysis of these practices because fringe finance entails a reordering of spatial relationships – a kind of resettling of the borders of finance and of the relations that link (or separate) the centre and edges of finance. Part of the reason why Deleuze's conception of diagram is instructive is because it places particular emphasis on the spatial relationships key to any set of social practices. Because capital is a set of relations spread across space and entails the movement of objects across or 'at a distance', maps are crucially important metaphors of financial power and agency. Each of the practices examined in Part 1 of the book both reveal a kind of shared commitment to an idealized mapping of the edges of finance as a fertile site but, at the same time, emphasize an astonishing variety of particular ways in which that shared ambition could be pursued. The cases which make up Part 1 were chosen not because they are somehow exhaustive of the practices of fringe finance, but, rather, because, when taken together, they make visible the irreducibly diverse ways in which fringe finance as a diagram is taken up.

It is in this framing that Chapter 2 addresses payday lending and argues that its recent growth and consolidation has been enabled by a series of important connections to some of the largest institutions in mainstream global financial markets: capital recirculated through mainstream equity markets; deep integration into the global financial and payments architecture; and, most importantly, the transformation of the largest payday lenders into financialized networks. As this chapter concludes, payday lending has become an extension of, is interior to, the spaces of global finance. Chapter 3 foregrounds a different practice – financialized micro-credit – which has been enabled by a much different set of financialized mechanisms; not the expansion of lending networks into new territories (as in payday lending) but the opening of channels through which both capital can flow into micro-credit networks and value can be dispersed to a wide body of global investors. Micro-credit has been dramatically transformed over the past decade into a thoroughly commercialized practice, a transformation greatly enabled by a unique approach to securitization. Chapter 4, in turn, features the most recent, but in some ways, most strikingly ambitious of fringe financial practices – micro-insurance. As this chapter suggests, micro-insurance is enabled by the techniques of risk management – actuarial science, probability, risk analysis – and by an important set of innovations which seek to harness forms of value derived from the unique and particular crucibles of experience which characterize the very edges of mainstream finance.

Part 2 of this book, *Fringe Finance as a Social Practice*, focuses on the incoherencies, contestations and interruptions that attend fringe finance in practice. If Part 1 focuses on the pristine and geometric lines charted by fringe finance as a diagram – as an abstract machine – Part 2 places emphasis on the ways in which the practices enabled by that diagram encounter forms of contestation, often result in unintended practices, and are implemented in the face of messiness not always well anticipated by those who imagine clean lines of installation. This is not to place the 'diagram' in sharp contrast with 'actually existing' practices that do not conform to the clean lines imagined in that diagram. Rather this is to insist on the complex relations that mark abstract idealizations and the practices often authorized or inscribed in the name of those idealizations. As Deleuze argues, the diagram is confronted with the 'twisting line of the outside', with inescapable complexities which evade the clean lines diagrams tend to sketch. Diagrams, to put it differently, are simultaneously abstractions imagined 'without friction' *and* designs that become implicated in uneven practices. If finance is a social practice, as the social studies of finance insists, then it is deeply marked by contestation and impossibilities. As each of the chapters in Part 2 emphasize, fringe finance is a practice constituted in and out of incoherence, interruption or contestation. These are the uneven forces that are interior to fringe finance; not somehow 'reactions' to some more fundamental set of relations, but key to the shape and form that fringe financial practices assume over time.

Chapter 5 addresses the practices of *Formalization*, a mapping of fringe financial services as legitimate, and formally settled domains of practice. As this chapter argues, at the very core of these efforts is an attempt to 'make up' micro-lending (historically dubious, politically controversial) as a regularized and formally legitimate form; processes which are deeply contested. Chapter 6 focuses on the question of incorporation, concrete ways in which fringe financial practices *incorporate* the populations which they target. Unlike the diagrams which figure a straight-forward movement from spaces of 'exclusion' to 'inclusion', this chapter argues that fringe-lending enrols populations into formal financial practices, but in ways that exert greater pressure or costs on those populations, erect barriers of various kinds, and deepen forms of immobilization.

Chapter 7 is offered as both an important coda to the issue of incorporation and a set of conclusions to the argument as a whole. This chapter reviews one set of practices – peer-to-peer or 'social' lending – that attempt an alternative mode of incorporation. This alternative focuses not on enrolling those outside of the financial world into circuits of financial value, but, rather, into folds of *social* practice. As this chapter argues, however, these alternative circuits of incorporation have recently themselves become financialized – subject to intense interest from large institutional investors keen to harness them as innovative sources of financial value. In this strange tension between contestation and innovation, social lending networks are condensations of the pressures and contests that make up the present (and futures) of fringe finance.

In making this kind of argument, this book places emphasis on the very edges of finance; the places where finance 'becomes capillary'. Far from unimportant or secondary, the edges are fundamental to how the global political economy is constituted. The edges are also the places where certain processes key to global finance, and to its powerful centre, are most visible.[8] The practices of conversion examined in Part 1, for example, although staged in relative obscurity, are nonetheless critical to the ways in which value is harnessed for, and returned to, the institutions that form the very centre of global finance. The 'making' of finance is rendered visible, in a particular way, at its own edges. Put simply, where might the practices through which finance is made – the practices that shape what finance is, how it expands its grip, how it might be interrupted – be more visible, more crucially and intensively felt, than at its very borders? As Rob Walker suggests, although borders are often imagined as if they occupy 'zero width', they 'nevertheless host the most intense practices'. This book offers a glimpse into one set of intense efforts (most intense, of course, for the vulnerable populations who are their target) hosted at the edges of finance; practices concerned with the *formalization, incorporation* and, perhaps most importantly, the *conversion* of the financial edge.

Notes

1 This un/underbanked population, and the populations reviewed in this book, are immensely diverse ranging from those without any financial access to those with stabilized, but not fully functional relationships with deposit institutions.

2 Geneaology, notes Bevir, is 'suspicious of attempts to portray a thing as unified and its transformation as peaceful … a decentered approach, where to decenter is to show how apparently uniform traditions or practices are in fact social constructs that arise from individuals acting on diverse and changing meanings' (Bevir 2010: 428).

3 As Mackenzie later concludes, '… *which* markets we have matters, and that is a question not simply of their overall characteristics but of the details of their design, the technological infrastructures that support them, and the way economic agents in them are constructed' (Mackenzie 2009: 182).

4 This focus on technical devices and agencements, although material in focus, also pays particular attention to ideas and knowledge. See for example Riles' work on legal devices:

> Global financial governance is … a set of routinized but highly compartmentalized knowledge practices, many of which have a technical legal character … a set of mechanical, legal, institutional and documentary technologies for resolving those problems, such as documents, legal opinions, computer scientists, lawyers, government bureaucrats, and theoretical academic work.
>
> (Riles 2011: 10–11)

5 In Austin's term: to utter a peformative sentence 'is not to *describe* my doing of what I should … or to state that I am doing it: it is to do it' (Austin 1962: 6, emphasis in original).

6 This paragraph draws upon and develops Aitken 2010b: 84.

7 Hall and Appleyard, for example, have examined the work of financial education and training and its 'role in articulating, legitimizing and performing … discourses of idealised investment banking subjects who embody essentialised masculine qualities' (Hall and Appleyard 2012: 458).

8 A similar argument is posed, in a particular way, by Riles who foregrounds issues of 'collateral' knowledge in the legal techniques associated with global financial markets. Here collateral has a double meaning not only as a very specific financial technique but also as a practice on the margins of – collateral to – the more

dramatic dimensions of global finance. For Riles, despite the 'humdrum back office image' associated with collateral knowledge, and perhaps because of it, it offers a revealing glimpse into 'more foundational' aspects of global financial governance. Because 'collateral is paradigmatic of private regulatory solutions in the financial markets', Riles argues,

> I seize on the broad range of concrete legal, institutional, and social practices surrounding the maintenance of collateral relations as a kind of motif, or lens through which to ask more foundational questions about the character of governance in the global markets … a sidelined, technical activity, a point of view that is crucial to and yet always self-consciously on the margins – collateral to, yet sustaining, the market itself.
>
> (Riles 2011: 20)

References

Aitken, R. 2007. *Performing Capital: Toward a Cultural Economy of Popular and Global Finance.* New York: Palgrave.

Aitken, R. 2010a. 'Ambiguous Incorporations: Microfinance and Global Governmentality'. *Global Networks.* Vol. 10, No. 2: 223–243.

Aitken, R. 2010b. 'Regul(ariz)ation of Fringe Credit: Payday Lending and the Borders of Global Financial Practice'. *Competition and Change.* Vol. 14, No. 2: 80–99.

Aitken, R. 2013. 'Finding the Edges of Payday Lending'. *Perspectives on Global Development and Technology.* Vol. 12, No. 3: 377–409.

Austin, J. 1962. *How to Do Things with Words.* Oxford: Clarendon Press.

Baptist, E. 2010. 'Toxic Debt, Liar Loans and Securitized Human Beings: The Panic of 1837 and the Fate of Slavery'. *Common-Place.* Vol. 10, No. 2.

Best, J. and M. Paterson, Eds. 2009. *Cultural Political Economy.* London: Routledge.

Bevir, M. 2010. 'Rethinking Governmentality: Towards Genealogies of Governance.' *European Journal of Social Theory.* Vol. 13, No. 4: 423–441.

Brassett, J. and C. Clarke. 2012. 'Performing the Sub-Prime Crisis: Trauma and the Financial Event'. *International Political Sociology.* Vol. 6: 4–20.

Butler, J. 1993. *Bodies that Matter: On the Discursive Limits of Sex.* London: Routledge.

Callon, M., Ed. 1998. *The Laws of the Markets.* London: Basic Blackwell.

Callon, M., Y. Millo and F. Muniesa. 2007. 'An Introduction to Market Devices'. *Marked Devices.* Eds. M. Callon, Y. Millo and F. Muniesa. London: Wiley-Blackwell: 1–12.

Casey, E. 2008. 'Keeping Art to Its Edge'. *Rethinking Facticity.* Eds. Fr. Raffoul and E.S. Nelson. New York: Suny Press.

Chala, A. *et al.* (2009) 'Half the World is Underbanked'. New York: Financial Access Initiative New York University.

De Goede, M. 2003. 'Beyond Economism in International Political Economy'. *Review of International Studies.* Vol. 29, Issue 1: 79–97.

De Goede, M. 2004. 'Repoliticising Financial Risk'. *Economy and Society.* Vol. 33, No. 2: 197–217.

De Goede, M. 2005. *Virtue, Fortune and Faith: A Genealogy of Finance.* Minneapolis: University of Minnesota Press.

De Geode, M. 2007. 'Underground Money'. *Cultural Critique.* Vol. 65, No. 1: 140–163.

Deleuze, G. 1988. *Michel Foucault Philosopher.* Tr. Timothy J. Armstrong. London: Routledge.

Deleuze, G. 2006. *Nietzsche and Philosophy.* New York: Columbia University Press.

Demirguc-Kunt, A. and L. Klapper. 2012. *Measuring Financial Inclusion: The Global Findex Database.* Washington, DC: World Bank Policy Research Working Paper 6025.

Du Toit, A. 2004. '"Social Exclusion" Discourse and Chronic Poverty: A South African Case Study'. *Development and Change.* Vol. 35, No. 5: 987–1010.

Epstein, G. Ed. 2005. *Financialization and the World Economy.* Cheltenham: Edward Elgar Publishing.

Federal Deposit Insurance Corporation. 2009. *FDIC National Survey of Unbanked and Underbanked Households.* Washington, DC: FDIC.

Froud, J., S. Johal and K. Williams. 2002. 'Financialisation and the Coupon Pool'. *Capital & Class.* Vol. 26, No. 3: 119–151.

Foucault, M. 1977. 'Nietzsche, Genealogy, History'. *Language, Counter-Memory, Practices.* Eds. Donald F. Bouchard, tr. D.F. Bouchard and S. Simon. Ithaca, NY: Cornell University Press: 64–139.

Foucault, M. 1980. *Power/Knowledge.* Ed. Colin Gordon. London: Harvester Wheatsheaf.

Foucault, M. 1984. 'Nietzsche, Genealogy, History'. *The Foucault Reader.* Ed. Paul Rabinow. New York: Pantheon Books: 76–100.

Foucault, M. 1991. 'Questions of Method'. *The Foucault Effect: Studies in Govermentality.* Eds. Graham Burchell, Colin Gordon and Peter Miller. Chicago, IL: University of Chicago Press: 73–86.

French, S. and J. Kneale. 2009. 'Excessive Financialization: Insuring Lifestyles, Enlivening Subjects, and Everyday Spaces of Biosocial Excess'. *Environment and Planning D: Society and Space.* Vol. 27, No. 6: 1030–1053.

French, S. and A. Leyshon and T. Wainwright. 2011. 'Financializing Space, Spacing Financialization'. *Progress in Human Geography.* Vol. 35, No. 6: 798–819.

Gill, S. 1995. 'Globalization, Market Civilization, and Disciplinary Neoliberalism'. *Globalization, Critical Concepts in Sociology.* Vol. 2: 256–281.

Hall, S. and L. Appleyard. 2012. 'Financial Business Education: The Remaking of Gendered Investment Banking Subjects in the (post-Crisis) City of London'. *Journal of Cultural Economy.* Vol. 5, No. 4: 457–472.

Harmes, A. 2001. 'Mass Investment Culture'. *New Left Review.* 9 (May/June): 103–124.

Hook, D. 2005. 'Genealogy, Discourse, 'Effective History': Foucault and the Work of Critique'. *Qualitative Research in Psychology.* Vol. 2, No. 1: 3–31.

Horyn, C. 2012. 'Bonnie the Mannequin's Wild New York Adventure'. *The New York Times Magazine.* 13 December.

Karl, A. 2013. '"Bank Talk": Performativity and Financial Markets'. *Journal of Cultural Economy.* Vol. 6, No. 3: 63–77.

Kunz, R. 2011. *The Political Economy of Global Remittances: Gender, Governmentality and Neoliberalism.* London: Routledge.

Langley, P. 2007. 'Uncertain Subjects of Anglo-American Financialization'. *Cultural Critique.* Vol. 65: 67–91.

Langley, P. 2008. *The Everyday Life of Global Finance.* Oxford: Oxford University Press.

Langley, P. 2010. 'The Performance of Liquidity in the Subprime Mortgage Crisis'. *New Political Economy.* Vol. 15, No. 1: 71–89.

Langley, P. and A. Leyshon. 2012. 'Financial Subjects: Culture and Materiality'. *Journal of Cultural Economy.* Vol. 5, No. 4: 360–373.

Leyshon, A. and N. Thrift. 1997. *Money/Space: Geographies of Monetary Transformation.* London: Routledge.

Leyshon, A. and N. Thrift. 2007. 'The Capitalization of Almost Everything: The Future of Finance and Capitalism'. *Theory, Culture & Society.* Vol. 24, Nos. 7–8: 97–115.

Li, T. 2009. 'To Make Live or Let Die? Rural Dispossession and the Protection of Surplus Populations'. *Antipode.* Vol. 41, No. 1: 66–93.

Mackenzie, D. 2006. *An Engine Not a Camera: How Financial Models Shape Markets.* Cambridge, MA: MIT Press.

Mackenzie, D. 2009. *Material Markets: How Economic Agents are Constructed.* Oxford: Oxford University Press.

Mackenzie, D. and Y. Millo. 2003. 'Constructing a Market, Performing Theory: The Historical Sociology of a Financial Derivatives Exchange'. *American Journal of Sociology.* Vol. 108, No. 1: 107–145.

Marx, K. 1999 [1887] *Capital: A Critique of Political Economy, Vol. 1: Book One: The Process of Production of Capital.* Moscow: Progress Publishers/Marx-Engels Internet Archive.

McDowell, L. 2010. 'Capital Culture Revisited: Sex, Testosterone and the City'. *International Journal of Urban and Regional Research.* Vol. 34, No. 3: 652–658.

Mitchell, T. 2002. *Rule of Experts: Egypt, Techno-Politics, Modernity.* Berkeley: University of California Press.

Mitchell, T. 2005. 'The Work of Economics: How a Discipline Makes its World'. *European Journal of Sociology.* Vol. XLVI, No. 2: 297–320.

Mitchell, T. 2006 'Rethinking Economy'. *Geoforum.* 39: 1116–1121.

Mitchell, T. 2007. 'The Properties of Markets'. *Do Economists Make Markets: On the Performativity of Economics.* Eds. D. Mackenzie, F. Muniesa and L. Sui. Princeton, NJ: Princeton University Press.

O'Brien, R. 1992. *The End of Geography.* New York: Council on Foreign Relations.

Preda, A. 2006. 'Socio-Technical Agency in Financial Markets: The Case of the Stock Ticker'. *Social Studies of Finance.* Vol. 36, No. 5: 753–782.

Preda, A. 2009. *Framing Finance: The Boundaries of Markets and Modern Capitalism.* Chicago, IL: University of Chicago Press.

Riles, A. 2011. *Collateral Knowledge: Legal Reasoning in the Global Financial Markets.* Chicago, IL: University of Chicago Press.

Sassen, S. 2005. 'When National Territory is Home to the Global: Old Borders to Novel Borderings'. *New Political Economy.* Vol. 10, No. 4: 523–541.

Seabrooke, L. 2007. 'Everyday Legitimacy and International Financial Orders: The Social Sources of Imperialism and Hegemony in Global Finance'. *New Political Economy.* Vol. 12, No. 1: 1–18.

Shiner, L. 1982. 'Reading Foucault: Anti-Method and the Genealogy of Power-Knowledge'. *Theory and History.* Vol. 21, No. 3: 382–398.

Smith, G. 2011. 'Selective Hegemony and Beyond Populations with "No Productive Function": A Framework for Enquiry'. *Identities: Global Studies in Culture and Power.* Vol. 18, No. 1: 2038.

Stäheli, U. 2013. *Spectacular Speculation: Thrills, the Economy, and Popular Discourse.* Stanford, CA: Stanford University Press.

Strange, S. 1998. *Mad Money: When Markets Outgrow Governments.* Ann Arbor: University of Michigan Press.

Taylor, M. 2014. 'Financial Inclusion at the Margins of Agrarian Change'. Paper presented to the Annual Meetings of the International Studies Association, Toronto Canada, 29 March.

Tromble, M. 2005. *The Art and Films of Lynn Hershmann Leeson: Secret Agents, Private I.* Berkeley: University of California Press.

Walker, R.B.J. 2010. *After the Globe, Before the World.* New York: Routledge.

Walters, W. 2006. '"The End of the Passing Past": Towards Polytemporal Policy Studies'. *Analysing Social Policy: A Governmental Approach*: 167–186.

Walters, W. 2012. *Governmentality: Critical Encounters.* London: Routledge.

Watson, M. 2009. 'Investigating Potentially Contradictory Microfoundations of Financialization'. *Economy and Society.* Vol. 38, No. 2: 255–277.

Young, A. 1910. 'The Counterfeiters of Coin and the Counterfeiters of Securities'. [Graphic Image] *Puck.* Vol. 68. No. 1752.

Zaloom, C. 2006. *Out of the Pits: Traders and Technology from Chicago to London.* Chicago, IL: University of Chicago Press

Part I

Sites of conversion

2 Mapping the logics of expansion

The globalization of payday lending

> Because the economy is not found as an empirical object among other worldly things, in order for it to be 'seen' by the human perceptual apparatus it has to undergo a process, crucial for science, of representational mapping … the map shifts the point of view so that viewers can see the whole as if from the outside, in a way that allows them, from a specific position inside, to find their bearings. Navigational maps were prototypical; mapping the economy was an outgrowth of this technique.
>
> (Buck-Morss 1995: 440)

As Susan Buck-Morss notes, categories are often constituted in visual form, in processes of representational mapping which not only delineate inside from outside but which also provide a way in which the inside can be 'seen' and navigated. This is especially true of capital, a category that is particularly spatial – a category of practice often constituted in relations across space, as a force with particular capacity to move seamlessly, or as emphasized in this book, as a set of threads which help connect centres and edges. Although finance capital is often conceived as deeply implicated in novel ways of experiencing time, it is also inescapably spatial (Vogl 2012: 82). In the wake of the 2008 financial crisis, two striking maps offered innovative, albeit quite distinctive ways, of 'seeing the whole' of capital. One of these, *Intercontinental Ballistic Microfinance,* was launched by Kiva Microfunds in 2011. Kiva is a unique micro-credit platform that links individual lenders and borrowers by extending relatively small amounts of capital to borrowers around the world. *Intercontinental Ballistic Microfinance* makes visible both the volume of lender–borrower connections Kiva has brokered since 2005 (4,033,920) as well as the global webs those credit practices have traced. What results is a four minute visualization-in-motion that dramatizes each loan as a moving point evoking the stylized trajectories of cold war missile paths; a slowly growing web of flows which gradually come to fill global space. (See Figure 2.1.)

A second map, *Stock Ticker Orbital Comparison* (STOC), offers an even more expansive space filled and shaped by the ambitious reach of capital. (See Figure 2.2.) STOC, developed by James Grant and Todd Spencer, is a map of an expansive universe the planets and orbits of which are

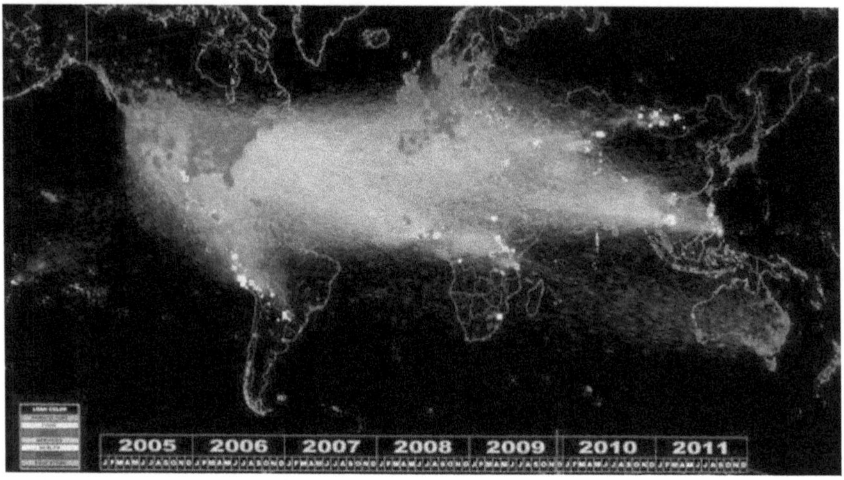

Figure 2.1 Intercontinental Ballistic Microfinance
(Kiva 2011)

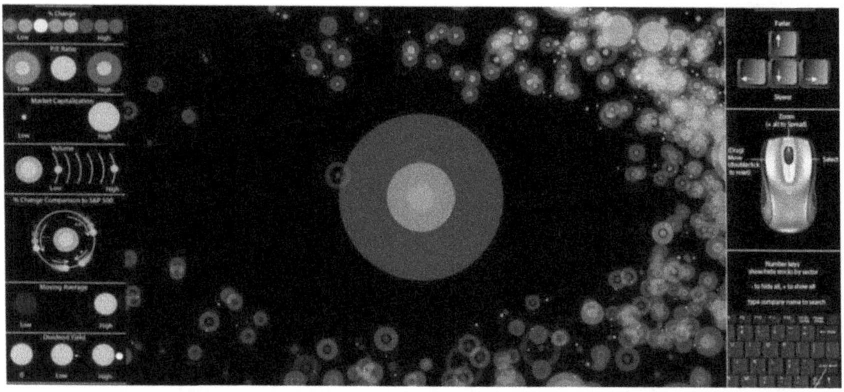

Figure 2.2 Stock Ticker Orbital Comparison
(Uniform Chaos 2008)

representations of real time stock marking trading activity.[1] The universe STOC establishes (or allows users to establish) is populated by planets each of which is a direct representation of a particular stock and its relationship to the benchmark S&P 500 index. Actual volume of trading, for example, is transcribed as the orbital distance the planet travels, while a comparison of performance to the S&P 500 determines the speed with which each planet travels that orbit. The colour of each planet is determined by percentage change in share price from the prior close and the planet size is related to overall market capitalization. Other factors – planet atmosphere width, colour, moon sizes – are transcriptions of price/earnings ratio, dividend yield, and moving average. The 'sun' of this planetary system is a representation of data relating to the overall performance of the S&P 500. STOC not only offers an interactive visualization of financial trading data but is also a metaphor of the financial markets as a kind of all-encompassing space; a body that fills the very bounds of our knowable world.

Taken together, these maps echo Buck-Morss' contention that capital is, in some important ways, a visual body. Part of the reason that I lay particular emphasis on Deleuze's notion of diagram is because it allows us to conceive of capital as a cartography of the 'points which it connects up'. Both *Intercontinental* and *STOC* are particular exercises in mapping. They each offer their own particular versions of a longstanding cartography of capital as an expansive force; finance as an ever-expanding presence, mapped as a force capable of overcoming space. *Intercontinental*, a map progressively criss-crossed by flows which transcend space, and *STOC*, a diagram of capital as a universe unto itself, both draw finance as an all-encompassing and enlarging force; representations of an agent capable of occupying and shaping new territories. 'The financial market', notes Vogl (2012: 75), 'is presented as a frictionless universe'; a space within which capital moves without resistance.

A main argument of this chapter is that the diagram of fringe finance, in some important ways, draws upon, is a *derivative* of, the longstanding 'representational mapping' of finance as an expansive force. Although it is marked by its own specificity, fringe finance is a diagram which imagines finance as a body that can occupy new territories and create its own frictionless universe. This ambition is mapped as a series of efforts to expand the reach of finance in a systematic and organized fashion, to render its own edges an object of financial knowledge and intervention.

In broad terms this argument echoes recent debates regarding financialization, which examines the ways in which the practices, language and arrangements of finance are given new prominence, exert increasing power or are thrown into spaces beyond its own reach. To give this argument some definite shape, this chapter examines one particular site of conversion, one site at which the financial edge is converted into forms of financial value – the practices of payday lending. Payday lending, virtually unknown before 1990, has now become an enormously important method of addressing the global populations which exist at the edges of mainstream finance. Payday lending – and cognate practices like deposit advances and payroll loans – entail very short term credit extended for the period of a single pay period at relatively high costs.

I argue in this chapter that payday lending encodes a particularly important map of the relation between the centre and the edges of global finance. Two developments now characterize payday lending and the unique relation it forges between centre and edge. First, I argue that the distinction between 'fringe' and 'mainstream' finance is dissolving in light of the ways in which payday lending relies on the practices and techniques of mainstream finance. As I have argued elsewhere (Aitken 2006: 493), the fringes of the financial world are not separate from mainstream finance but are 'threaded to its interior'. A second, and related development, is the intensely *global* forms payday lending now takes. I argue in this chapter that what now lies at the heart of payday lending are globalized networks of credit provision made possible by complex financial transactions and arrangements. These globalized networks have transformed payday lending from a distinctively Anglo-American practice into a global form of credit expanding rapidly in Eastern Europe, Mexico, Latin America and beyond. Taken together, these trends imply that fringe finance is now a subset of global finance, an extension of global finance at its very edge. Payday lending now forms global chains, moreover, which are capable of extracting value from the edges of the financial system and drawing that value back into the very core of financial markets. In these emergent global financial chains, financialized global networks of payday lending are constituting a version of the centre of finance at its very edge.

This is not to imply that there are determinant edges to finance which payday lending simply overcomes. Indeed payday lending, unlike sites of conversion examined in Chapters 3 and 4, addresses a population which has at least some form of relation to capital if however fleeting or partial. The 'underbanked' populations addressed by payday lending exist at, but not fully beyond, the edges of capital; populations which often have partial ties to mainstream financial institutions. Neither is this to suggest that there is some stark line beyond which there exist no forms of credit relations. As Marcus Taylor (2012) argues the spaces 'beyond' mainstream finance are often saturated with credit relations extended by moneylenders, informal sources, social networks or coercive underground money, some of which is made possible by broader circuits of capital. Rather, this is to argue that payday lending now addresses the indeterminate fringes of the financial economy in ways that are more thoroughly consolidated, formalized and *globalized* than previous forms of credit relations.

To make this argument, this chapter proceeds in three main steps. A first section situates the argument of the chapter as an extension of recent debates across the social sciences on financialization. Although, as this section notes, there are now many diverse perspectives on financialization, there is a particular importance of Leyshon and Thrift's emphasis (2007) on the 'incessant prospecting' for objects that could be converted into asset streams. A second section begins to build on this formulation by noting some of the particular ways in which the financialization of payday lending has unfolded. This section argues that payday lending is a site which hosts a very particular reworking of the spaces only partially served by the mainstream financial system into more organized sources of financial value. This entails, most importantly, increasingly complex ways in which the 'fringe' practices of payday lending are reliant on the techniques and networks of mainstream finance. A third section builds on this analysis by noting the construction of globalized networks of payday credit provision; a sector increasingly characterized by the global networks of financial exchange and value it has constituted. A conclusion returns to the unique relation between the financial centre and edge that payday lending maps.

Financialization

As Eric Helleiner (1994) has famously noted, one of the most 'spectacular' developments of the past forty years has been the 're-emergence of global finance'. One set of concerted attempts to understand this development clusters around the concept of financialization. Financialization refers in general to the increasing prominence of finance across a variety of economic, political and cultural registers. Van der Zwan (2014: 100) has usefully categorized financialization into three types of analyses which loosely share an interest in the ways in which 'an increasingly autonomous realm of global finance has altered the underlying logics of the industrial economy and the inner workings of democratic society'. (See also Epstein 2005: 3.)[2] A first broad cluster of analysis frames financialization in terms of the processes of accumulation which increasingly have taken financial form. As Krippner (2011: 4) has put it in a well-known formulation, financialization refers to 'the tendency for profit making in the economy to occur increasingly through financial channels rather than through productive activities'. (See also Krippner 2005: 181; for a general introduction see Dembinski 2009.) These discussions emphasize the ways in which even non-financial firms increasingly derive the largest share of profits from financial activities and especially from circuits of credit and investment (Baragar and Chernomas 2012: 337; Blackburn 2006: 43–44; Van der Zwan 2014: 104).[3] As a result the 'ratio of monetary and financial assets of non-financial corporations to their tangible assets was increased' dramatically (Duménil and Lévy 2004: 38–39). Financialization 'signifies a regime of capital accumulation in which value extraction takes place increasingly through financial markets and institutional investors, rather than through the circuits of commodity production' (Pani 2014: 216). In this regime, finance operates not as a mechanism which can facilitate the smooth transfer of capital, risk or credit, but as an end in and of itself oriented toward gains earned through short-term price fluctuations (Aalbers 2008: 149–151). This novel form of accumulation is also marked by steady growth in the actual size and depth of the financial economy. In the USA, for example, the financial sector has grown steadily between 1947 and 2006, a period which witnessed a dramatic growth in the proportion of GDP constituted through financial activities from 2.5% of US GDP to 8% of US GDP (Philippon 2008: 2).[4]

A second cluster of analyses of financialization pay particular attention to 'increased shareholder value orientation' (Van Treeck 2009: 908). The increasing importance of financial markets across all facets of the global political economy has exerted an important set of pressures on firm behaviour. The maximization of shareholder value, and the consolidation of returns to shareholders have become paramount in the ways in which firms are governed (Blackburn 2006: 42–43).[5] 'The growing power of equity markets', notes Montgomerie, 'shifted management practices in publicly listed firms from long-term gains through dividend payments toward short-term profit strategies based on movements in share prices' (Montgomerie 2008: 237). Because shareholder value is key to the ways in which corporate behaviour is governed, many non-financial firms are now predominantly oriented not to their own productive calculations but to the importance of financial criteria. Put succinctly, 'financial markets exert pressures on non-financial corporations, and the managers running them, to adopt business practices promoting shareholder value' (Van der Zwan 2014: 107). The emergence of shareholder value as a basis of firm orientation is also a redistributive process which redirects important financial rewards to managers able to influence share prices or determinants of shareholder value.

A third broad conversation of financialization relates to the cultures of everyday financial practice, financialization as it is experienced in the practice, culture or knowledges of everyday life.[6] This entails a focus on the wider lens of relationships that now connect diverse social groups including working-class and everyday populations to financial markets (Harmes 2001; Langley 2008; Christopherson *et al.* 2013: 352). Enrolling a wider range of populations into the financial markets has resulted in a kind of 'rise of the citizen as investor'; a set of pressures which have contributed to a reformulation of our sense of self (Van der Zwan 2014: 111). What attends financialization is a powerful set of cultural impulses which emphasize the importance of a certain kind of 'ownership' society grounded not in the physical confines of work or production, but in the crucible of financial exchange and entrepreneurial effort. 'The processes associated with financialized accumulation thus subtly alter the conception of citizenship and of the public sphere' (Christopherson, Martin and Pollard 2013: 354; see also Pathak 2014: 91).[7] Echoing a certain variant of neoliberalism, the cultures that result from the financialization of everyday life tend to require a certain kind of regulation of the self. For Martin, finance is not simply a mode of economic practice, but a 'subjectivity and a moral code' which 'promises a way to develop the self' or a form of 'self-mastery that channels doubt over uncertain identity into fruitful activity' (Martin 2002: 8–9). The metaphors most prevalent to finance – especially investment – imply a kind of self capable of managing itself over time and across uncertainty.

The inflection of financialization I want to develop in this chapter, and use as an important touchstone throughout the book, is rooted in the work of Leyshon and Thrift who argue that much of the discussion on financialization 'too frequently continues to breathe the rarefied air of professional financial markets' (Leyshon and Thrift 2007: 102). For Leyshon and Thrift financialization has tended to focus on the 'dramatic' practices of speculation or the 'superstructure' of the financial world. In contrast to this focus, they argue for analytical attention directed to the 'base', to the mundane practices which make certain forms of financial exchange possible. Before financial practices can be consummated, there must first be a prior process which identifies and formats the assets that serve as the basis of financial circulation; 'a source of value from which financial innovation can proceed' (Leyshon and Thrift 2007: 98). This requirement entails the search for new assets and the conversion of those assets into income streams that could be inserted into financial instruments. This implies an incessant search for new asset streams 'which then – and only then – allows speculation to take place' (Leyshon and Thrift 2007: 98). Although financialization can often imply immaterial forms, the process Leyshon and Thrift describe emphasizes the inextricable links between virtual forms of exchange and the actual assets which, in however distant a form, provide some kind of grounding for financial innovation. Financial capitalism, notes Pani (2014: 216–217), is 'entangled with the 'real' economy, deriving essential flows of value from real assets that constitute the bread and butter of its reproduction … a process that allows financial speculation to reach directly into, and extract value from, the mundane geographies' of everyday life (Pani 2014: 216–217). This entails deeply inscribed connections to material objects which are then inserted into larger webs of global financial exchange. For Leyshon and Thrift this requires the discovery of:

> flows of income that allow all manner of things to proceed on their way … . financial companies have to keep a tether to assets, however far removed, even as they are involved in speculation. The financial system, like all capitalist entities, must be able to constantly reproduce itself to survive and that means that it must continuously prospect for new asset seams.
>
> (Leyshon and Thrift 2007: 98)

The language of this analysis is *extractive*; a prospecting for *seams* of (latent) material that could be distilled or converted into objects with financial value.[8] In delineating a process of prospecting and extraction, conversion and instrumentalization, this analysis echoes the maps which depict finance as an expansive body (Montgomerie 2008: 245). Prospecting entails the search for 'entirely new income streams … the identification of a particular geography of revenues which were previously considered off-limits' (Leyshon and Thrift 2007: 101). The kind of extraction which lies at the mundane beginnings of financialization involves incursion into novel spaces, a map of exploration in which global forces penetrate unknown territories. This exploration, moreover, gestures at the possibilities of limitless expansion. As Leyshon and Thrift note, finance is both an expansive and creative force capable of converting a wide array of new financial objects as long they have some capacity as stable sources of income. 'What we can see now', they argue, 'is an impulse to identify almost anything that might provide a stable source of income, on which more speculation might be built' (Leyshon and Thrift 2007: 98).[9] This is an immensely innovative but also mundane practice, foregrounding the actual techniques with which objects, some quite distant from the dramatic spaces of 'high finance', are installed as the stable basis of exchange (see Rolnik 2013).[10]

This approach implies that spatial relations lie at the heart of financialization. The spectre of limitless innovation and expansion implies a kind of financialization that is deeply implicated in the reordering of spatial relationships. In the context of an incessant prospecting for new seams of latent assets or sources of value, the 'mundane geographies' of our everyday lives are increasingly opened and connected to the 'rarefied' spaces of global finance. French, Leyshon and Wainwright (2011) suggest a kind of 'spacing of financialization' which acknowledges the constitutive role of space in the kinds of practices central to contemporary financial markets. Most importantly, for them, financialization is a process which displaces across space some of the contradictions that now characterize forms of financial accumulation in the global political economy.

This suggests, in turn, the deeply inscribed forms of spatial unevenness which attend financialization, inequalities across space in the ways in which various populations access resources or exercise claims on assets. Financialization 'is not a geographically neutral process: it has emanated from, and has been controlled from, particular places, while subjecting other places and spaces to its strictures and implications' (Christopherson et al 2013: 352).[11] This results in distinctive 'financial ecologies', in the plural, marked by forms of geographic difference and widely uneven degrees of connection to (or distance from) forms of financial knowledge or practice.[12]

The attention to the spatial practices of finance – to what Leyshon and Thrift refer to as the changing geography of revenues which make new financial objects possible – raises important questions which have only recently become important to debates in IPE. Johanna Montgomerie, for example, has aptly noted that much of the conversation around financialization has been disproportionately focused on forms of financial practice addressed to privileged savers or investors. 'The financialization literature', she argues, 'tends to address only those individuals participating in long-term investment schemes or able and willing to borrow heavily. These groups are no doubt in a relatively privileged position compared to the many individuals excluded from access to mainstream financial products or without enough extra income to put into savings' (Montgomerie 2008: 247).[13] On one hand, this insight aptly reflects the relatively uneven focus in the financialization literature on the privileged populations able to participate in financial markets with some degree of autonomy. On the other hand, however, Montgomerie's observation implies a stable distinction that might be drawn between the financial markets oriented to privileged actors, and the kinds of spaces which are external to financialization, a distinction that is itself reworked, instrumentalized and ultimately undermined in the practices of payday lending.

Payday lending and the fringes of finance

As Leyshon and Thrift (2007: 109) argue, although 'a great deal of attention is paid to innovation in financial markets of various kinds, what is often overlooked is that asset structures can also be the subject of innovation, both in how they are treated and what can be counted as an asset' (Leyshon and Thrift 2007: 109). The main claim of this chapter is that payday lending has become a particularly intense site of conversion – a place where those on the edges of the financial world are converted into forms that are accessible to mainstream financial agents.

This larger financialization is related to the proliferation of a relatively simple form of credit, 'a small, short term unsecured loan to meet the borrower's expenses until his or her next payday … [guaranteed] with a post-dated cheque or pre-authorized debit' (Marsh, Dildar and Janzen 2010: 6). Because payday lending addresses an increasingly large population of borrowers at the edges of finance, it increasingly serves as a mechanism capable of extracting value at those edges and channelling that value back into the centre of global finance. This characterization of payday lending and its cognates – deposit advances, payroll lending, home credit – as a source of mainstream financial value exists in contrast with a conventional view that payday lending occupies a kind of murky space of 'alternative' finance outside of the mainstream world of large banks.

Despite this characterization, payday borrowers are neither fully separate from nor fully incorporated into mainstream banking institutions but exist in a certain kind of ambiguity. On one hand, payday borrowers are not well or fully served by mainstream financial institutions, often finding, in particular that they lack access to basic credit instruments. On the other hand, payday borrowers are not without links of some form with mainstream financial institutions. Payday borrowers almost always have some form of financial account held with a mainstream deposit institution, an actual requirement for a form of credit secured by a post-dated cheque or payment authorization. Unlike the populations addressed in Chapters 3 (micro-credit) and 4 (micro-insurance), payday borrowers are required to have some, albeit often minimal, relationship with mainstream deposit institutions (Gross, Hogarth and Schmeiser 2012: 3). These borrowers are neither outside of the reach of mainstream finance nor fully absorbed within it, often 'banked in the mainstream but loaned to in the fringe' (Fourcade and Healy 2013: 568).

Neither, however, are fringe and mainstream capital neatly separate from each other. Rather payday lending is deeply implicated in and enabled by the practices of mainstream finance. As Langley (2008: 183) argues, 'high-interest networks of everyday borrowing are not separate from mainstream financial and capital market networks but are interstitial in nature … there is little that is distinctive about booming networks of everyday borrowing, whether they be "mainstream" and "alternative", "formal" and "informal", or "prime" and "sub-prime"' (Langley 2008: 183). This 'interstitial' relationship suggests, I argue, an important complexity to 'fringe' as a metaphor for the kinds of spaces occupied by payday lending. Fringe does not refer to exteriority, but to an indeterminate edging that is neither inside nor outside of the object to which it is attached (see Aitken 2006). Fringe is a metaphor of the kinds of murky border zones where an edge dissolves into its own traces while remaining threaded to the main object it helps contain; a kind of 'blurring of patterns of internality and externality' (Mezzadra and Neilson 2012: 70). Payday lending is a form of fringe finance not because it exists outside of the realm of mainstream finance (or, for that matter, because it is somehow unimportant or of minor significance) but because it is precisely one spot where mainstream finance is threaded by traces to its own edges.

Mainstream/fringe lending

Fringe lending is deeply reliant on the practices and architecture of mainstream finance in a number of important ways. Payday loans can only be extended, for example, through the architecture of mainstream payments and banking networks. This includes access to payment linkages which allow lenders not only to circulate capital widely through their own networks but also, crucially, to access borrowers' accounts through post-dated cheques or other forms of payment authority. Access to the Automated Clearing House (ACH) banking payments network in the USA has allowed payday lenders to access the financial accounts or debit mechanisms of borrowers in order to process payments.[14] The non-amortizing single 'balloon' payment, the most distinctive feature of payday loans, is only made possible by the ways in which loans can be secured via payment or debit obligations which flow through mainstream deposit institutions. Perhaps the most striking of the debit obligations these networks enable are continuous payment authorities (CPA). Many payday lenders, especially online lenders, now enrol borrowers into 'recurring payment' or 'recurring transaction' arrangements which allow lenders to remove funds from borrowers' accounts with deposit institutions or to execute ongoing transactions on borrowers' credit cards. These arrangements are typically authorized by borrowers as continuous access to their accounts via debit or credit cards using banking and payments networks. The use of the continuous payment arrangements are particularly widespread among UK payday lenders. According to the Financial Conduct Authority, 'CPA use is widespread … the main collection instrument of online lenders', noting that 85% of online loans now proceed with the use of CPAs (Financial Conduct Authority 2013: 63).

Because the payments for payday loans rely on the architecture of mainstream financial and banking networks, fringe lenders increasingly resemble the mainstream worlds with which they are said to contrast. This resemblance is so tightly fitted that many banks have sought to instrumentalize the demand for short-term credit by designing their own analogue of payday lending in the form of deposit advance products. Deposit advance is an arrangement between banks and account holders who routinely receive regular electronic deposits, often from salary deposits, social assistance entitlements or other government transfers. Credit is extended for very short periods of time, often until the next scheduled electronic deposit, and repayment is automatically debited from the account upon receipt of the next qualifying electronic deposit. Because banks 'capture repayment of advances from the incoming electronic deposit before the consumer can use this funds for other expenses' (CFPB 2013a: 12), deposit advances are designed, like payday loans, to assert a certain priority in borrowers' repayment scheduling. Deposit advances are also relatively expensive forms of short-term credit (Bourke, Horowitz and Roche 2013: 12). In basic design features, deposit advances resemble payday lending: 'these loans typically have high fees, are repaid in a lump sum in advance of the customer's other bills, and often are not subject to fundamental and prudent banking practices through which a bank can determine the customer's ability to meet other necessary financial obligations' (FDIC 2014: 2). Unlike payday lending, however, deposit advances do not conform to most definitions of payday loans (or 'deferred deposit' loans), and are not typically subject to the web of regulations which now govern payday loans.

Increasingly mirrored in the mainstream financial world from which they are often portrayed as distinct, payday lenders have become deeply reliant on a repertoire of financial services organized through those mainstream financial institutions. Payday lenders are reliant on investment analysis, accounting and auditing services, insurance and reinsurance products, and complex financial instruments such as derivatives to manage risk in the diversity of markets in which they operate.[15] The most important linkage between fringe lending and mainstream finance, however, is forged in the absorption of payday lending into mainstream circuits of capital. Payday lending has become a node in mainstream circuits of global capital as both an attractive object of investment in its own right as well as a significant outlet for mainstream financial capital. Payday lenders of all varieties now routinely harness capital from large mainstream investors – hedge funds, institutional investors, large global banks and investment funds – as the basis for their own working capital which then circulates through their own lending networks. Some of this capital has been generated in a string of Initial Public Offerings (IPOs) through which the largest networks of payday lenders have become public firms fully integrated within mainstream financial markets. Eight of the largest payday lenders now operate as publicly traded firms, the most recent of which is Springleaf Holdings. The most emblematic of these IPOs was Dollar Financial (now DFC Global Corporation) which went public in 2005 when it offered 7.5 million shares at US $16 per share, netting a total offer amount of $120 million.[16] DFC has continued to make important connections to mainstream capital and equity markets. In April 2011, for example, DFC floated a public offering of 6 million shares of common stock, the proceeds of which ($117 million) were used to finance one of its most recent acquisitions, MEM, a short-term internet lending operation in the UK (DFC Global 2012a: 35). DFC has also issued various tranches of convertible notes worth almost $165 million (due in 2028), as well as $600 million worth of unsecured notes due in 2016, (DFC Global 2012b; 2013a: 4) and a new senior secured credit facility, which DFC negotiated with a syndicate of lenders managed by Wells Fargo

Bank in 2011. This global revolving credit facility provides DFC with access to $250 million (DFC Global 2012a: 34). All of these financial manoeuvres were punctuated by a major restructuring of DFC debt in late autumn of 2013 when it announced a major capital raising of $650 million in which it will issue securities for private placement (Marketline 2014a: 38).

DFC is emblematic of the fortunes of payday lending more broadly which has gone through an important process of consolidation over the past five years. This 'maturation' has not charted a straight-forward process of unrelenting growth. Indeed, the actual number of storefront payday lenders in the USA has actually declined over the past number of years dropping from a high of 24,000 outlets in 2007 to just under 18,000 in 2013 (Hecht and Joseph 2014: 7). This decline, however, has been offset by very rapid growth in internet payday lending in all jurisdictions. It has also been offset by consolidated growth by all measures – credit extended, online and storefront presence, borrowers enrolled – among the very largest and most heavily capitalized of lenders (Hecht 2013: 4). When read in combination, these trends suggest a process of intense consolidation in which the sector, squeezed by both increasing regulatory costs (see Chapter 6) and market saturation in its core markets (especially in the USA – see Aitken 2013a) is characterized by a smaller number of increasingly large lenders. This consolidation has been made possible by the increasingly dense linkages between fringe lenders and mainstream circuits of capital, a 'base [which] has continued to meet the increasing capital needs of alternative financial services providers' (Miller and Lee 2013: 17). The expansion of payday lending has been characterized by serious merger and acquisition activity – one investment analysis reports twenty major acquisitions in the sector over the course of 2012 alone (Miller and Lee 2013: 12–14) – as well as by rapid expansion into new geographic and lending territories.

Perhaps the most ambitious example of the kinds of growth and consolidation which have been fuelled by connection to mainstream capital markets is Speedy Cash, a Wichita-based lending network which included a core network of 325 company-owned stores in Canada, the USA and the UK. Initially a regional provider of payday loans and cheque-cashing services, Speedy underwent a pivotal reorganization in 2008 punctuated by the conversion of existing equity into a new corporate structure (Speedy Cash Intermediate Holdings) made possible by a strategic investment by a series of institutional funds affiliated with Friedman, Fleisher and Lowe LLC (Charles 2012: 2). This pivotal investment unleashed a wave of aggressive expansion. Over the course of twelve months beginning in May 2012 Speedy initiated two serious acquisitions and several significant capital injections from the financial markets (Hecht 2013). In 2013, for example, Speedy negotiated the completion of an offering that raised almost US $450 million in a package of senior secured notes followed by two additional 'tack-ons'.[17] This injection, enthusiastically supported by institutional investors, was primarily used to finance the acquisition of an online lender in the UK. This coincided with a separate $125 million offering of senior unsecured notes used as growth capital and as a basis for a dividend provided to shareholders. The growth and consolidation of Speedy into a firm with revenue that 'significantly exceeds typical store level performance for the majority of its principal publicly-traded competitors' (Charles 2012: 4), has been fuelled by successive waves of support from mainstream institutional investors.

In these various ways payday lending, especially in its most consolidated and institutionalized form, is now deeply internal to mainstream capital – firmly constituted *within* and *as* a circuit of mainstream capital, reliant on the conventional financial services that make those circuits function. These circuits of capital undermine any easy distinction between 'fringe' and 'mainstream' capital. The circuits of capital associated with payday lending are also unbounded in a much broader sense; increasingly spread across *global* spaces and organized as *globalized* webs of credit extension.

The globalized edges of payday lending

Maps of expansion often double as maps of occupation, as mechanisms with which claims on a particular space could be made visible. These kinds of maps document the ways in which particular forces both move into and inhabit new territories. They also announce and legitimize their presence in new spaces. Over the past decade, as payday lending has become the object of both regulatory attention and increasing interest from capital markets, it has also increasingly expanded into 'new frontiers' beyond its largest markets in North America. On the one hand, the most significant market for payday lending remains the USA. One estimate suggests that total loan dollar volume by 2010 climbed to US $19.9 billion which resulted in total fees collected of $3.4 billion (Montezemolo 2013: 9). As Hecht and Joseph (2014: 1) report, payday lending volumes in 2013 amounted to $45.9 billion which generated revenues of almost $9 billion. On the other hand, however, global growth has accelerated even more dramatically and now accounts for the most innovative and significant sources of profit for the sector (see also Aitken 2013a).[18] In some important ways, payday lending, a distinctively American invention, is now constituted in and out of its global conditions of existence – a subset not only of mainstream capital but of global finance.

The construction of global webs of payday lending has taken many forms including the extension of large networks of payday lenders across and beyond Anglo-American markets. This expansion, in some important ways, has been enabled by the reorganization of ownership claims – notably share transfers, mergers and acquisitions, and equity transactions – brokered through global financial markets. The Australian market for payday lending, for example, has experienced steady growth over the past fifteen years, and is now populated by six major lending networks (Australia 2011: 22–25), the largest of which, Cash Converters and the Cash Store, have longstanding financial connections to larger North American payday lenders. It is in the

UK, however, where the most significant forms of growth in international payday lending have occurred. Beginning in 2005, many American lenders aggressively expanded into the UK.[19] This infusion of global payday lending has resulted in a significant boom in all forms of fringe credit in the UK. Between 2006 and 2010, a period that coincides with important international investment in payday lending networks, 'the number of people using high cost short term credit in England quadrupled … to 1.2 million people' (Australia 2011: 24). The Office of Fair Trading estimates that there are 240 legally registered lenders operating in the payday lending market. These lenders extended £2.2 billion during the fiscal year 2011/12 which was a significant increase from the £900 million extended in 2008/2009 (Osborne 2013).

For some commentators this dramatic rise of payday lending in the UK is the most emblematic signal of the globalization of fringe finance; the 'only wild west for payday lenders' (quoted in House of Commons 2012: 13), or 'our least penetrated, most underserved and fastest growing market' (O'Connor 2011). Despite these testaments, however, the most dramatically consequential expansions of fringe lending now unfold outside of the Anglo-American world. Mexico has become the most important of the spaces now targeted by fringe lenders as sites of expansion. In part, the intense interest of fringe lenders in Mexico is a function of a broader set of shifts which Soederberg (2012: 562) describes as deepening attachments to 'a debt-driven accumulation strategy'. Despite these shifts, and although Mexico has a significant financial sector, mainstream deposit institutions have shown little interest in poor populations. The penetration of conventional financial services in Mexico, is among the lowest in the hemisphere, registering only 9.6 bank branches per 100,000 inhabitants (Banco Walmart 2009: 14). This is particularly evident in rural areas where only 6% of the population have access to formal financial accounts (Meagher *et al.* 2006: 26–27). Less than 25% of the population nationally enjoy access to basic financial accounts (Obermann 2006: 8). Access to consumer credit is more uneven than the distribution of general financial services. The penetration of consumer credit in 2011 measured only 3.5% of GDP, marking Mexico as one of the thinnest consumer credit markets in the Americas (Credito Real 2013: 6). The 'target market' for fringe lenders is constituted out of the 75% of Mexicans without access to credit or with only scattered connections to financial practices more broadly. Although there are some signs that nascent consumer credit markets may be emerging – outstanding consumer lending balances increased from MX 1623.5 billion in 2008 to MX 2 7771.1 billion in 2013 (Euromonitor International 2014: 3) – private consumer credit is strikingly undeveloped. Mexico's level of private credit as a whole measures 26% of GDP which is notably below the average for Latin American countries (Obermann 2006: 2; Gelpern 2007). When plotted in relation to GDP per capita, Mexico's relative lack of credit marks it as one of the least financially penetrated consumer economies globally, and a market that lenders perceive as seriously 'under-served' (Banco Walmart 2009: 15).[20]

In this context there has recently been serious international investment in Mexico's fringe and consumer lending sectors. Most controversially has been the consolidation of Banco Walmart as a key source of credit for poor and working-poor Mexicans. Walmart launched a Mexican banking division in 2001 after its own American experiment was derailed when it withdrew its application for an American banking licence in the face of stiff domestic opposition. By 2009, Banco Walmart had opened almost 200 locations and began offering a diverse range of products, including consumer, short-term, and instalment loans as well as credit cards and traditional deposit services. (Banco Walmart 2009) Over the past number of years Banco Walmart has focused on extending to their own customers basic credit cards, consumer loans and even micro-credit products (Soederberg 2012: 572). 'The primary aim of Walmart', argues Soederberg, 'is to eventually become a key source of credit for low-income Mexicans, so they can buy Walmart products' (Soederberg 2012: 573).

Banco Walmart, however, is merely the most controversial face of deepening forms of globalized fringe credit extended to poor, working and middle-class Mexicans. World Acceptance, for example, a large American consumer finance firm has methodically assembled a large network of Mexican payday lending operations. By 2011, this network of outlets was extending almost US $875 million in loan value to a wide range of middle- and working-class Mexicans (World Acceptance 2012). American forms of payday lending have been the most quickly growing forms of consumer credit over the past few years in particular. As one analyst has noted, payday loan volumes in Mexico are now 'growing at a greater pace than the number of borrowers' (Euromonitor International 2014: 1), an indicator of rapid expansion. Gross payday lending in 2013 grew by an estimated 21%, a rate that outpaced growth in Mexican levels of employment, average salaries or general growth in consumer credit (Euromonitor International 2014: 2).

Mexico, along with other countries in Latin America, especially Brazil, has also witnessed growth in cognates of payday lending such as payroll lending. Payroll lending extends a non-amortized form of credit to employees who then have the loan amount (plus all applicable fees) removed, often electronically, on the receipt of their next payroll deposit. Credito Real, a firm with important connections to American institutional investors has been one of a number of experiments which have created profitable circuits of fringe lending through payroll mechanisms. Real Credito has now enrolled 500,000 active clients and has issued over 4 million loans to more than 2 million customers over the past number of years (Credito Real 2013). This growth was punctuated by a successful IPO in 2012 which generated US $170 million in proceeds which will be used to further expand payroll lending among larger employers, service sector firms and government agencies.

The global spread of fringe lending, although most emblematic in Mexico, is now active across other global frontiers of expansion. Many fringe lenders have entered Eastern Europe, Latin America, India and China. The Home

Credit group, for example, is a Dutch-based multinational lender explicitly oriented to 'mass retail consumers'. Between 1997 and 2013, Home Credit managed to enrol almost eight million customers in a variety of short-term and instalment loans. More striking is the range of European and Asian markets it has been able to enter: the Czech Republic, Slovakia, the Russian Federation, Kazakstan, Belarus, China, India, Indonesia and the Philippines (Home Credit 2014: 3). Echoing the maps of expansion which underpin the broader globalization of fringe lending, Home Credit invokes an explicit language of discovery and exploration; an attempt to experiment in and assemble a global network of short-term credit provision directly targeted to 'new and under penetrated markets' (Home Credit 2014: 14).

The constitution of global webs of fringe credit have not, however, simply been constituted by the straight-forward extension of payday lending outward from its American origins in some unchanged form. Rather, global expansion has been deeply implicated in various forms of innovation. The most important global webs of payday lending have been constituted by a series of firms who have innovated new delivery methods and financial linkages. One key innovation, for example, has been the intensifying use of online credit platforms by the large global providers of payday loans. The growth in online payday lending now far exceeds growth in conventional storefront payday loans. Moreover, most lenders with an international ambition have adopted online lending as a strategic key to entering foreign markets. Cash America, a large public American lender, has both redeemed the slow growth of its own storefront payday lending and secured a dynamic international presence via its successful online arm, Enova International (O'Connor 2011). Enova now offers payday loans and other forms of credit across multiple jurisdictions including the USA, the United Kingdom, Australia, Mexico, and Canada through a suite of seven online platforms (Cash America 2014: 2). Enova, 'one of the few, if not only, fully licensed non-bank online lenders of scale' (Cash America 2014: 7), has consistently expanded internationally, recently announcing expansion projects in China and Brazil designed to provide 'global financial resources for under-served consumers' (Cash America 2014: 10; see also Gilhooly: 2013).[21] These international markets, according to Enova's own regulatory filings, 'offset the loss of revenue from certain domestic markets in which we no longer offer consumer loans or have reduced our product offerings' (O'Connor 2011). As the American market for payday lending becomes saturated or stabilized, Enova signals a form of globalized growth for payday lending bound up in innovative strategies designed to penetrate untapped global markets.

The most consolidated face of this globalization, however, consists of complex globalized lending networks which integrate constituent parts across space, often stitched together through financial and stock market transactions involving the transfer of ownership claims. These networks are important because of the particular flow of capital they enable, both the volume of capital they transport to the very edges of the financial system *as well as* the ways in which they extract financial value back – in the form of dividends, private equity, share value, financial fees and income streams from loans – to the very centre of the financial system. These networks now sediment circuits of capital which connect the centres and edges of global finance.

In the remainder of this section, I want to note three particular networks of globalized fringe credit which have recently become consolidated in unique ways. This is not to imply that there have not been earlier experiments in the provision of credit at a global level. Indeed, one of the key antecedents for global fringe credit is International Personal Finance (IPF), a firm rooted in the British model of 'home credit'. IPF has established global operations in Poland, Romania, Hungary, the Czech Republic and in Mexico where it now extends credit to almost 750,000 customers and generates net receivables which increased in 2011 by 24% (IPF 2011: 52; IPF 2014: 26). Nonetheless, globalized payday lenders have become consolidated in ways that allow them a presence more widely. A first large global payday lending network – centred around the American payday lender EZCORP – has been constituted across a diverse set of platforms, stitched together through complicated financial transactions. EZCORP now sits atop a sprawling network which consists of 1,400 locations and branches across the USA, Australia, Mexico, Canada and the UK; a network which generates annual revenues of US $1.01 billion and an operating profit of US $139 million (Wright Investors' Service 2014b: 1–3; Marketline 2014b: 7).[22] EZCORP has generated levels of net income which have steadily increased to US $122 million in 2011 from US $68 million in 2009 (EZCORP 2011a: 26). In 2011, EZCORP extended a total of US $750 million in consumer finance products of various forms (EZCORP 2011a: 8) through its US and Mexican stores, its various online platforms, a Canadian payday lender ('Cashmax') and through its various associations with Cash Converters, a dominant Australian payday lender and with Abermarle and Bond, a major international consumer finance firm with over 700 locations worldwide (Marketline 2014b: 15).

The diversity of this network is reflected in the complexity with which it has been assembled. Part of EZCORP's growing global footprint, has been the result of aggressive financial transactions involving acquisitions in Mexico. Revenue from its Mexican operations, for example, grew 56% in 2012 alone, while income from its American payday lending operations accounted for only 19.4% of overall consolidated income, down from 25.4% in 2010 (Scharf and Wong 2012).[23] This stake in the Mexican fringe lending market was deepened in 2012 through a series of stock market transactions which allowed EZCORP to assume a 60% ownership in Prestaciones Finmart, a financial firm which owns Crediamigo, an important Mexican payroll lender. Crediamigo offers non-collateralized loans through payroll deduction agreements with over 150 government agencies and other employers. EZCORP assumed an ownership claim in Crediamigo via a stock transaction valued at US $38.8 million, a transaction it defended to investors as a way to more fully access an 'attractive and under-served market' with 'favourable demographic trends in Mexico' (EZCORP 2012a). EZCORP has built on the existing success of Crediamigo by aligning it even more closely to American financial markets – EZCORP was able to negotiate the first ever public market securitization of Mexican payroll loans in an issue of MXN $420 million (EZCORP 2012a) – and leveraging this transaction in ways which allow it 'to grow in Latin America generally and enter into new lines of business that complement our successful … operations in Mexico' (EZCORP 2012b).

The centrepiece of EZCORP's global strategy, however, is a 'global strategic alliance' it has established with Cash Converters International. Cash Converters, a large multinational lender with operations spanning 21 countries is now the single largest payday lender in Australia. In March 2011 EZCORP signed an agreement with Cash Converters International 'to enter into a global strategic alliance to develop and introduce a suite of financial services products' (Marketline 2014b: 14). Although EZCORP and Cash Converters have been formally entangled in each other for several years, the 'global strategic alliance' announced in 2011 has been made possible by a series of financial transactions ultimately oriented to the 'global roll-out of integrated financial services' (EZCORP 2011b). At the centre of this programme is the formation of several joint ventures designed to facilitate 'faster growth in more geographies', including, in particular, growth opportunities in Mexico and Brazil (EZCORP 2011b: 1–2). The core of this global strategic alliance has been built through a series of stock transfers that have allowed EZCORP to acquire over 124 million Cash Converters shares. This has resulted in a 33% ownership stake in Cash Converters as well as the control of two of the five seats on its Board of Directors, allowing a degree of interpenetration at the level of strategic and financial management.[24] In another share-transaction that was financed by its own share offerings, EZCORP assumed a 30% stake in Albermarle and Bond, one of the UK's largest consumer finance and pawn brokering businesses owned in part by Cash Converters (EZCORP 2012a: 12). As a result, EZCORP now influences a network of payday lenders across four continents and dozens of different lending platforms, stitched together through two large public firms, each of which continue to grow in dynamic ways.

Although global webs of payday and fringe lending have often originated in the USA, the financial arrangements which make these webs possible have also emerged from other locations. A second important globalized network of fringe lending has been constituted by Grupo Elektra, a Mexican credit network with expansive operations across the Americas consisting of 6,000 financial and retail outlets Latin America and the USA (World Market Intelligence 2014: 5). The group as a whole reported revenue of US $5.3 million in 2012 (World Market Intelligence 2014: 8). Elektra now operates the largest, and most controversial, micro-lending network in Mexico. Both a model for and competitor to Banco Walmart, Elektra's financial arm was assembled in 2002 when it launched Banco Azteca by opening branches in each of 815 existing consumer-goods retail locations (Soederberg 2012: 571). The brainchild of Mexican billionaire Ricardo Salinas, Azteca was explicitly designed 'to demonstrate the importance of offering financial services to the under-served segment of the Mexican population' (quoted in Bruhn and Love 2009: 8). By 2006, Azteca was reporting 40% annual rates of growth and 30% growth in net deposits (Gelpern 2007: 1527). Earning high profits fuelled in part by high rates of interest, Azteca began to expand rapidly in Latin America with operations in Guatemala, Brazil, El Salvador, Panama, Argentina, Honduras, Peru, and Colombia. By 2011 Azteca's loan portfolio was growing by over 50% per year, punctuated by a 63% rise in gross loans, which helped secure annual rates of growth in profit of 20% and in revenue of 19% (Suarez 2012; Soederberg 2012: 572).[25]

Grupo Elektra altered its own footprint in the world of fringe credit in February 2012 when it negotiated a financial transaction that consummated its purchase of Advance America, the largest American payday lender. Advance America operates 2409 centres in the USA as well as both storefront and internet lending in Canada and the UK (World Market Intelligence 2014: 6). The staggering deal was executed as a transaction in global capital markets based on Advance America's market capitalization of US $658 million (GlobalData 2014: 1–4). The arrangement, announced by Salinas as an attempt to integrate Elektra's presence at the 'bottom of the pyramid' across North America, consists of a US $780 million transaction in which Banco Azteca paid a 32.7% premium (based on market capitalization) for Advance America shares (Suarez 2012; Burtzlaff and Schmid 2012; Wright Investors' Service 2012). The deal was a logical extension of five years of international expansion in which Advance America launched a new international brand, National Cash Advance, and initiated aggressive expansion plans in Canada and the UK. This programme of international expansion, as its own regulatory filings indicate, sought a certain kind of 'geographic diversification [to] … mitigate the risk and possible financial impact of unfavorable legislative changes' in its domestic markets (Advance America 2011: 5–6). Nonetheless, and despite this longer history of international expansion, the incorporation of Advance America into Grupo Elektra has resulted in a unique network with a much broader scope and penetrating reach into 'middle-income working individuals … in the United States, Mexico and in other Latin American countries' (GlobalData 2014: 1). In announcing the acquisition, Salinas acknowledged a certain eagerness 'to expand our services to the United States and to continue meeting the needs of the financially underserved' (Harrison 2012: 14; Thompson 2012); a kind of globalization directed back to the core of global financial markets.

Although the Elektra development announced a certain phase of global ambition, the most emblematic face of global payday lending remains the dense credit network which has now been assembled around DFC Global. DFC Global aims to provide 'neighbourhood financial services on an international scale' and to become the 'leading international diversified financial services company serving primarily unbanked and under-banked customers' around the world. DFC is among the handful of market leaders in the USA, operates the largest payday lending network in Canada and the UK and has transformed itself over the past decade into a coherently organized global presence squarely focused on constituting a global market for payday lending. The network which DFC has assembled includes 1,400 retail storefront locations and multiple internet platforms which serve diverse markets across Europe and North America: the UK, Canada, the USA, Sweden, Finland, Spain and the Republic of Ireland (Wright Investors' Service 2014c: 1). This network generated sales of US $1.12 billion in 2013, its fourth straight year of growth. Perhaps more importantly, the bulk of these sales have long been generated outside of its American operations. 'Although DFC Global is headquartered in the United States, it derives most of its sales outside of its home market: sales in the United Sates were US $129.7 million which was only 11.6% of 2013 sales' (Wright Investors' Service 2014c: 3; see also Pierce and Soto 2012: 4; Datamonitor 2012: 17–18).

DFC's profitable global network of payday lenders has been enabled through a series of acquisitions made possible through share transactions or other financial manoeuvres. This has allowed DFC to consummate at least 100 acquisitions since 1990 (DFC Global 2012a: 6; DFC Global 2012b; Datamonitor 2012: 25). The centrepiece of this deep reliance on global financial markets is a complex global credit facility denominated across a range of currencies – USD, GBP, CAN, EUR – and broad enough to facilitate DFC's operations across borders (DFC Global 2012a: 34). These arrangements have allowed DFC to assemble a global profile and footprint punctuated most recently by an aggressive foray into Romanian storefront lending and the purchase of two large internet lenders, MEM (Month End Money, a British lender) and Risicum (Finland) in 2013 (Dollar Financial 2013: 4).

DFC has also innovated important ways in which its customers could become objects of knowledge. Although DFC addresses itself to very particular populations – the market segments that exist on the fringes of the global financial system – it does so in ways that frame those populations in unique terms. This has been most importantly accomplished by DFC in its innovative use of credit analytics. Over the past decade, during which it has aggressively expanded globally, DFC has developed a sophisticated technique for global credit analysis. Rooted in its Berlin office, DFC's approach seeks to gather and integrate a wide range of 'big data'. In ways that resemble the financial modelling and projection techniques developed by mainstream deposit and lending institutions, DFC's credit analytics mobilize data from both its own real-time stream of internal credit assessments, as well as from broader consumer behaviour and profile analyses.

Key to this approach is a concerted effort to assemble increasingly sophisticated data about its customers and the profiles they come to occupy. Although all large lenders engage in credit analysis, DFC is often recognized as an important innovator. Investor analysts who assess DFC have consistently noted its innovative credit analytics capacity, and its preoccupation with *knowing* the population it addresses, which, in turn, allows it to take on greater risks. As DFC's Chief Financial Office put it in a series of legal proceedings, 'the more data we collect, the better our credit analytics and the more effective our collections become … we think we can make more by lending somewhat more because we are better able to analyze to whom we're lending and how to get them to repay us' (West Palm Beach Police Pension Fund 2013: 11). This analysis also incorporates broader macro-economic trends in an attempt to project credit and collections performance in relation to a wider range of factors (DFC Global 2012b).

At the core of this credit analytics approach is a language that is both homogenous and flexible. Developed in Berlin, DFC has managed a remarkably consistent application of credit quality standards in all of its diverse markets. The model has also proven flexible, allowing DFC analysts to take into account particular factors or constraints – macro-economic shocks, regulatory developments, longer local consumer credit trends – and to impose versions of its model globally. As one investor analyst recently observed, DFC 'has developed a very sophisticated and flexible operating system that can be readily adapted to country specific monetary, language and regulatory needs' (Furtado, Kemnec and Maltz 2012: 7). The kind of globalization that DFC has pursued has not been animated by any simple extension into 'under-penetrated' markets but also by a concerted effort to know, and by extension, to shape the populations that exist in those markets.

It is in these terms that DFC has become an increasingly important 'centre of calculation' for fringe lending, a site where knowledge of fringe borrowers is generated and assembled in particular kinds of ways. This entails not only the gathering of customer data from local sites but also the aggregation of that data and its insertion into larger profiles. Among all of the large global payday lending networks, DFC has been the most preoccupied with the population it addresses and the ways in which that population might be categorized. In doing so, DFC offers a certain codification of the global underbanked as a recognizable category. Over the past decade DFC has increasingly framed its market as a global 'Alice demographic' – a reference to a global population increasingly characterized as 'asset limited income constrained'. This category, which has provided a pivot for DFC in its recent processes of strategic and corporate planning, targets a flexible and broad set of populations under various forms of economic distress. The Alice category refers not only to those conventionally understood as outside of the mainstream financial system, but also working and even middle-class populations under various, even fleeting, forms of economic difficulty. This is a category with a certain global ambition – a category designed to address a diverse and growing global population under the weight of various degrees of economic unease. As Jeff Weiss, Chairman and CEO of DFC has put it, Alice populations are becoming increasingly characteristic of a global economy marked by uncertainty and instability:

> Stagnant and declining wages in many parts of the world, coupled with significantly higher prices for goods and services, are causing the people in higher income brackets to migrate into our ALICE demographic in increasing numbers … To satisfy their short-term credit needs … it continues to be our mission to be the leading provider of diversified financial services to this ALICE demographic – the asset limited income constrained demographic.
>
> (DFC Global 2012b: 13)[26]

DFC Global is now the most sustained and institutionalized attempt to exert financial leverage at the edges of global finance. It has also, however, become preoccupied with the ('underbanked') populations that live at those edges and how those populations might be constituted as particular objects of knowledge. The expansive strategy it has mapped is linked to a rendering of the population it addresses in similarly expansive terms. Its own investor presentations, for example, are riddled with references to its target population as a 'demographic [which] is large and growing'; signalling a 'significant opportunity in emerging global economies; Asia, Africa, South America' (Dollar Financial 2013: 10). This attaches a double meaning to the kinds of conversion DFC seeks; not only the conversion of the financial edge into a source of

Figure 2.3 Our Customer Base is Large and Growing (Dollar Finance 2014: 9)

financial value but also at the same time, a conversion of those who live at those edges into a population with its own inherent logic, its own 'natural' and 'expanding' properties. Taken together, these renderings underscore DFC as particularly emblematic of the diagram at the heart of fringe finance – a mapping of the edges as a space capital could enter and fill. DFC's version of this diagram draws a population in a particular way, a body that could be constituted and reshaped into a 'significant unmet global demand for financial services'.

The large networks which now facilitate a global market for payday lending are simultaneously dramatic and mundane. They are dramatic because of the expansive mapping they chart. These networks are also mundane because their own expansive reach is made possible by the humble materials of routine financial arrangements. The most expansive of these networks – DFC and its gesture at a 'natural' and 'expanding' market seemingly without limit – is enabled by the commonplace architecture and investment practices of mainstream finance. This underscores the ways in which payday lending occupies the strange distance between centre and edge; a space it manages to both *open* and *overcome*.

Conclusion: a version of global finance at its edge

> Flat as the table
> it's placed on.
> Nothing moves beneath it
> and it seeks no outlet.
> Above – my human breath
> creates no stirring air
> and leaves its total surface
> undisturbed …
> Everything here is small, near, accessible.
> I can press volcanoes with my fingertip,
> stroke the poles without thick mittens,
> I can with a single glance
> encompass every desert
> with the river lying just beside it …
> I like maps, because they lie.
> Because they give no access to the vicious truth.
> Because great-heartedly, good-naturedly
> they spread before me a world
> not of this world.
>
> (Szymborska 2014)

As Deleuze (2006: 36) notes, a diagram maps the 'relations between forces' that are part of any abstract design of practices. In some important ways, maps are deeply associated with diagrams of expansion, often used as instruments which facilitate the exploration and occupation of new territories. The history of cartography, as Brian Harley notes, is 'primarily a handmaiden to the history of geography defined as the history of geographical discovery and exploration' (quoted in Akerman 2009, 3–4). Capital, in particular, has often been intimately linked to maps of expansion and exploration – maps of capital as a force that can overcome boundaries and enter new spaces seamlessly. This chapter has argued that fringe finance is often situated as a subset of these expansive maps; one more site where capital is mapped as a force that might fill new spaces it enters 'without friction'. If financialization is, as Leyshon and Thrift (2007) argue, a process characterized by prospecting for new assets streams, then payday lending is one of its contemporary sites of innovation. The kind of financialization pursued in and through global payday lending maps process of occupation, i.e., an opening of spaces to the immediate presence of payday lenders. This construction of lending networks with a global reach has been made possible via financial transactions involving the exchange of ownership claims – share ownership, merger and acquisitions, equity investments. This process, moreover, effectively undermines any easy claim we might want to make about the distinctions that bound 'mainstream' and 'fringe' finance. The practices of payday lending are not a contrast with, but are now interior to, a subset of global finance. Most importantly, payday lending offers a reorganized map of the relation between the edges and the centres of global finance. This is a map in which institutionalized global payday lending networks constitute a version of the centre of global finance at its very edge. In doing so, this map charts a way in which capital could flow to the edges and return value – via stock prices, return on equity or all variety of financial paper and payments – to the very centre of global finance.

At the heart of all conventional forms of cartography is a fantasy that maps represent the 'real' in a pristine and pure fashion. Borges' famous one-paragraph story, *On Exactitude in Science,* imagines a map as fully large and exacting as the empire it seeks to represent, a kind of cartographic perfection in which the map corresponds to, is a *replica* of, the territory it sketches 'point for point'. 'In that Empire', writes Borges,

> the Art of Cartography attained such Perfection that the map of a single Province occupied the entirety of a City, and the map of the Empire, the entirety of a Province. In time, those Unconscionable Maps no longer satisfied, and the Cartographers Guild struck a Map of the Empire whose size was that of the Empire, and which coincided point for point with it.
> (Borges 1964: 90)

Satirizing the fantasies that lie at the heart of cartography, Borges' map of empire implies an unspoiled form of mastery – the map as a representation that perfectly resembles the object it projects.

As Borges' map attests, however, there is an impossibility associated with maps and the kind of mastery of territory they imply. Spreading before us 'a world not of this world', maps invoke clean, Euclidean lines that cannot correspond to the lived realities or crucibles of experience that comprise the social practices and spaces which they represent. The geometries which maps invoke are not matched with a practical world in some immaculate form. The diagram, as both Deleuze and Foucault remind us, after all, is a mapping 'without friction' – lines that exist in abstract form without messy obstacles. The diagram – the abstract mapping – which gives fringe lending much of its shape is an impossible gesture, a representation of financial 'relations between forces' that does not acknowledge the frictions and obstacles payday lenders often encounter. In practice, the expansive ambitions of payday lending have not been smoothly delivered but have encountered all variety of incoherencies or resistances. Enova, for example, an emblem of both financial innovation and international ambition, has recently been the target of the first formal regulatory action mounted by the Consumer Finance Protection Bureau (CFPB). Among a series of other violations, the CFPB sanctioned Enova and has required it to pay US $19 million in fines or consumer refunds for deceptive collection techniques and for the destruction of records and recorded customer phone calls. In its judgement the CFPB noted a failure 'to maintain and provide records and information relevant to the Bureau Examination', and 'unfair and deceptive practices' (CFPB 2013b). At almost the same time, Cash Store, one of the largest Canadian payday lenders, and a leading exponent of globalization, filed for bankruptcy protection in Canada. Although Cash Store extended C$187.41 million of payday loans in 2013, its overall sales declined by 1.3% in the wake of rapid expansion globally (Wright Investors' Service 2014a: 3).

Although the Cash Store drama is in its early moments, it implies the possibility that the ambitions associated with financialization and global expansion are more fragile than they might seem. Strikingly, shareholder value – the object that lies at the heart of financialized expansion – has not been positively or uniformly enhanced by the construction of globalized payday lending networks. Both DFC and EZCORP, for example, have experienced poor financial valuations over the period that coincides with their most intense global expansion. EZCORP's globalized ventures have failed to achieve any meaningful returns via shareholder value over the past number of years; a form of valuation key to the very capital markets in which it has increasingly subsumed its own ambitions. 'During each of the previous three calendar years', one key investor analyst has put it, 'this stock has fallen in value … EZCORP is trading at 0.64 times book value. This means that theoretically, the net value of the assets is greater than the value of a company as a going concern' (Wright Investors' Service 2014b: 4).[27] The diagram that animates globalized payday lending sketches a relation in which capital extended to the fringes of finance will return value to its centre via financial paper, income streams and, most importantly, enhanced shareholder value.

The immediate experience of some of the largest globalized lending networks, however, has been far more ambivalent.

This is not to imply that the diagram is an important concept only as a kind of 'ideal type' against which we might open lines of comparison with actually existing practices that never quite measure up. Neither is this to suggest that a diagram is an unimportant distraction; an analysis pitched at an abstract level against the grain of those actual lived practices. Although the unevenness, contestations and incoherencies which accompany any diagram and its complex relation to lived practices are important – indeed this is the focus of Part 2 of this book – there is also importance in placing analytical emphasis on the abstract lines that lie at the heart of any diagram. Diagrams are significant, in part, precisely in their abstraction, as revealing glimpses into the ambitions that animate particular clusters of practices and the idealized lines that mark those ambitions as relations across space. A diagram, however, is a map not only of abstract lines, but also of multiple variations. The diagram that animates fringe finance maps the edges as a space that could be more fully occupied by mainstream financial practices. Despite the common element of this diagram – the conversion of the edges of finance into sources of value – the specific lines charted can vary. Payday lending and the story of financialization it marks is only one particular variant of this diagram. There is a diversity of particular forms invoking quite distinctive registers of innovation and unique framings of the populations addressed; a diversity particularly visible in the lines mapped by the specific practices of micro-credit (Chapter 3) and micro-insurance (Chapter 4).

Notes

1 The representation of finance as an all-encompassing universe in its own right is not unique to *Stock Ticker Orbital Comparison*. Rather, it is common to a genre of artistic interventions that characterize the post-crisis moment (see Aitken 2013b).
2 As Epstein (2005: 3) has famously put it, financialization 'means the increasing role of financial motives, financial markets, financial actors and financial institutions in the operation of the domestic and international economies'. (See also Orhangazi 2008: 4; Davies 2012: 318.)
3 For Baragar and Chernomas (2012: 337), this financialization of accumulation is built on ever increasing forms of (exploitative) debt: 'Increased household indebtedness … is a means through which the rate of exploitation of labor by capital can be enhanced … However, it is the financial sector that benefits.'
4 It is important to note that for some observers, financialization is less a material process than one focused squarely on finance as knowledge of information (see Knorr Cetina and Preda 2007: 116–117).
5 As Blackburn (2006: 42–43) argues, 'making a good profit is no longer enough; a triple A rating is also needed'.
6 For a useful assessment of the importance of knowledge/power in relation to financialization see Montgomerie (2008: 243).
7 For Pathak (2014: 91) this has resulted in a 'normalization of indebtedness and the stigmatization of over indebtedness as a corollary of "delinquent" dispositions and

dependencies … an overemphasis on individual agency – financial behaviour and choices – and a neglect of ever-worsening structural constraints'.

8 I am grateful to Randall Germain for his observation regarding the ways in which financialization addresses itself to hitherto *inert* objects or practices.

9 Leyshon and Thrift (2007: 99) go on to affirm that 'it is now possible to use just about anything as a platform for more speculative financial activity … just so long as it represents a stable and continuing income stream'.

10 Although much of this mundane work is accomplished by technical experts well beyond the political power of the state, it has also been consummated by state agents and through forms of state policy (Rolnik 2013: 1066).

11 As Hall (2011: 406) echoes, 'very little attention has been paid to how space and place intersect with processes … of financialization more generally'.

12 French et al. conclude, processes of financialization 'unfold across space and evolve in relation to geographic difference so that distinctive ecologies of financial knowledge, practices and subjectivities emerge in different places … some places are better connected to networks than others' (French *et al.* 2011: 812)

13 As Hall (2011: 406) notes, 'the majority of work has focused on financial consumers, with elite financial subjects and the spatiality of the international financial system remaining black boxed'.

14 New York State has recently acknowledged as much with an investigation into illegal payday lending that makes use of ACH networks. 'Access to the ACH system is the foot in the door that online payday lenders need to prey on vulnerable New Yorkers. And banks have proven to be – even if unintentionally – an essential cog in the vicious machinery that these purveyors of predatory loans use to do an end-run around New York law' (Lawsky 2013: 2).

15 This financialization of payday lending will likely intensify over the coming number of years. While securitizing a portfolio of loans may be unusual – for now – the idea of bundling up personal loans is gaining ground. Earlier this year, Springleaf, a speciality finance company, sold two securitizations of unsecured personal loans (see Hecht 2013).

16 Although DFC Global continues to operate as a publicly traded firm there is a proposed attempt to make it private that could, if successful, remove DFC from the public stock markets in 2015.

17 One important sign of the increasingly positive attention Speedy has secured is the declining amount of effort that has been required to place these offerings. The initial offering required a 'fully marketed roadshow' to mobilize support among investors while the May 2012 'tack-on' required only a three-day roadshow and the February 2013 'tack-on' issue consisting of US $100 million required only a one-day marketing effort (Jeffries 2013: 33).

18 Parts of this section are reworked and updated variations of an argument first published in Aitken 2013a.

19 As Gibbons, Malhotra and Bulmore (2010: 4) note although five of the largest lenders in the British market are owned or controlled by American lenders, the most dominant lender in the market – Wonga – is an outgrowth of domestic credit networks.

20 It should be noted that another very important part of the landscape for the rapid expansion of consumer credit in Mexico is the relative lack of regulation. Although there have been some nascent regulatory discussions occurring in the recent wave of payday lending (Euromonitor International 2014: 2), the sector operates without any substantive regulations (See Gelpern 2007: 1523; Racanello and Garcia 2009: 7).

21 Its success has also made Enova a tempting candidate for an IPO as Cash America has long been rumoured to be interested in spinning it off as a separate public firm. In September 2011, for example, Cash America competed regulatory filings for an Enova IPO but withdrew those filings in July 2012.

22 These figures represent a growth in revenue of 3.6% but a decline in operating profits of 32.6% over the previous year (Marketline 2014b: 7).

23 As one financial analyst has put it, 'Mexico remains a strong growth vehicle for the company and should drive future results' (Scharf and Wong 2012).

24 It should be noted that this partnership was dealt a setback when EZCORP cancelled a stock transaction in the wake of the recent announcement of a new Australian interest rate cap. Nonetheless the global strategic alliance remains, punctuated by the ongoing interpenetration of EZCORP and Cash Converters at the highest levels of management and financial organization.

25 Soederberg (2012: 572) notes defaults rates of just 1% compared with an average of 5.3% for affluent clients. Much of these impressive financial results are implicated, however, in burdensome costs imposed on borrowers.

26 Although DFC claims only to tap into, to *serve*, this large, pre-existing market, its own practices have been deeply implicated in the processes, and the conditions which constitute the vulnerable populations which constitute its markets.

27 DFC Global has received an almost identical record of shareholder valuation. DFC is only trading at 0.79 times book value. Although its intangible assists (866 million) were higher than its common equity (430 million) which means that price to book ratio may not be of much use for valuation analysis in this case (Wright Investors' Service 2014c: 4).

References

Aalbers, M. 2008. 'The Financialization of Home and the Mortgage Market Crisis'. *Competition & Change.* Vol. 12, No. 2: 148–166.

Advance America. 2011. *Annual Report 2010.* Spatenburg, SC: Advance America Cash Advance Centers Inc.

Aitken, R. 2006. 'Capital at Its Fringes'. *New Political Economy.* Vol. 11, No. 4: 479–498.

Aitken, R. 2013a. 'Finding the Edges of Payday Lending'. *Perspectives on Global Development and Technology.* Vol. 12, No. 3: 377–409.

Aitken, R. 2013b. 'Performing the Limits of Finance'. *Journal for Cultural Research.* Vol. 18, No. 1: 78–97.

Akerman, J. 2009. 'Introduction'. *The Imperial Map: Cartography and the Mastery of Empire.* Ed. J. Akerman. Chicago, IL: University of Chicago Press: 1–9.

Australia. 2011. *The Regulation of Short Term, Small Amount Finance: Regulation Impact Statement.* Canberra: Government of Australia.

Banco Walmart. 2009. *Banco Walmart: Investor Presentation.* Mexico City: Banco Walmart.

Baragar, F. and R. Chernomas. 2012. 'Profits from Production and Profits from Exchange: Financialization, Household Debt and Profitability in 21st-Century Capitalism'. *Science & Society.* Vol. 76, No. 3: 319–339.

Blackburn, R. 2006. 'Finance and the Fourth Dimension'. *New Left Review.* Vol. 39, No.39: 39–70

Bourke, N., A. Horowtiz and T. Roche. 2013. *Payday Lending in America: How Borrowers Choose and Repay Payday Loans.* Washington, DC: Pew Charitable Trusts.

Bruhn, M. and I. Love. 2009. *Expanding Access to Finance and Entrepreneurial Activity: Evidence from Mexico.* Washington, DC: World Bank.

Buck-Morss, S. 1995. 'Envisioning Capital: Political Economy on Display'. *Critical Inquiry.* Vol. 21, No. 2: 434–467

Burtzlaff, D. and M. Schmid. 2012. *Advance America, Cash Advance: Research Brief.* Birmingham: Stephens Inc.

Cash America. 2011. *Alternative Financial Services: Cash America Investor Presentation.* Fort Worth, TX: Cash American International Inc.

Cash America. 2014. *Form 10-K: Cash America International, Inc. 2013 Annual Report.* Forth Worth, TX: Cash America International, Inc.

Center for Financial Services Innovation. 2013. *2012 Financially Underserved Market Size Study.* Chicago, IL: Center for Financial Services Innovation.

CFPB. 2013a. *Payday Loans and Deposit Advance Products: A White Paper of Initial Data Findings.* Washington: Consumer Financial Protection Bureau.

CFPB. 2013b. *Administrative Proceeding, 2013-CFPB-0008, Consent Order.* Washington: Consumer Financial Protection Bureau.

Charles, B. 2012. *Speedy Cash Holdings Corporation: Profile.* New York: R.W. Pressprich & Co.

Christopherson, S., R. Martin and J. Pollard. 2013. 'Financialisation: Roots and Repercussions'. *Cambridge Journal of Regions, Economy and Society.* Vol. 6: 351–357.

Credito Real. 2013. *Credito Real: Investor Presentation.* Mexico: Sociedad Financiera de Objeto Multiple.

CS Financial. 2012. *DFC Annual Report 2011.* Edmonton: CS Financial.

Datamonitor. 2012. *DFC Global Corp, Company Profile.* London: Datamonitor, 2012.

Davies, A. 2012. 'The Rise of Speculative Value in the Era of Financialization and Ponzi-Scheme Capitalism'. Paper given at annual meeting of the Centre for Research on Socio-Cultural Change. Manchester.

Deleuze, G. 2006. *Nietzsche and Philosophy.* New York: Columbia University Press

Dembinski, P. 2009. 'Finance: Servant or Deceiver'. *Financialization at the Crossroad.* New York: Observatoire de la Finance/Palgrave Macmillan.

DFC Global. 2012a. *Annual Report 2011.* Berwyn, PA: DFC Global Corp.

DFC Global. 2012b. *Investor Presentation.* Berwyn, PA: DFC Global Corp.

Dollar Financial. 2013a. *Investor Presentation – November 2013.* Berwyn PA: DFC Global Corporation.

Duménil, G. and Lévy, D. 2004. *Capital Resurgent: Roots of the Neoliberal Revolution.* Cambridge, MA: Harvard University Press.

Epstein, G. Ed. 2005. *Financialization and the World Economy.* Cheltenham: Edward Elgar Publishing.

Enova International. 2012. *Form S-1.* Chicago, IL: Enova International Inc.

Euromonitor International. 2014. *Consumer Lending in Mexico.* New York: Euromonitor International.

EZCORP. 2011a. *Form 10-K: Annual Report for Year Ended 30 September 2011.* Austin, TX: EZCORP Incorporated.

EZCORP. 2011b. *EZCORP to Form Global Strategic Alliance with Cash Converters.* Austin TX: EZCORP Incorporated.

EZCORP. 2012a. *Profile and Investment Thesis of Crediamigo.* Austin, TX: EZCORP Incorporated.

EZCORP. 2012b. *EZCORP to Acquire Controlling Interest in Crediamigo.* Austin, TX: EZCORP Incorporated.

FDIC. 2014. *Guidance on Supervisory Concerns and Expectations Regarding Deposit Advance Products.* Washington, DC: Federal Deposit Insurance Corporation 6714–6701-P.

Financial Conduct Authority. 2013. *Detailed Proposals for the FCA Regime for Consumer Credit*. London: Financial Conduct Authority.

Fourcade, M. and K. Healy. 2013. 'Classification Situations: Life-Chances in the Neoliberal Era'. *Accounting, Organizations and Society.* Vol. 38, No. 8: 559–572.

French, S., A. Leyshon and T. Wainwright. 2011. 'Financializing Space, Spacing Financialization'. *Progress in Human Geography.* Vol. 35, No. 6: 798–819.

Furtato, D., M. Kemnec and S. Maltz. 2012. *DFC Global Corp.: Company Note.* New York: Jeffries Group Inc.

Gelpern, A. 2007. 'Wal-Mart Bank in Mexico: Money to the Masses and the Hoe-Host Hole'. *Connecticut Law Review.* Vol. 39, No. 4: 1513–1538.

Gibbons, D., N. Malhotra and R. Bulmore. 2010. *Payday Lending in the UK: A Review of the Debate and Policy Options.* London: Centre for Responsible Credit.

Gilhooly, M. 2013. *Enova Media Fact Sheet*. Chicago: Enova International.

GlobalData. 2014. *Advance America, Cash Advance Centers, Inc. (AEA) – Financial Analysis Review.* New York: Global Company Intelligence.

Gross, M., J. Hogarth and M. Schmeiser. 2012. 'Use of Financial Services by the Unbanked and Underbanked and the Potential for Mobile Financial Services Adotpion'. *Federal Reserve Bulletin*. Vol. 98, No.4: 1–20.

Hall, S. 2011. 'Geographies of Money and Finance II: Financialization and Financial Subjects'. *Progress in Human Geography.* Vol. 36, No. 3: 403–411.

Harrison, C. 2012. 'Elektra Agrees to Buy Advance America to Provide U.S. Loans'. *Bloomberg BusinessWeek*. 15 February.

Hecht, J. 2013. *Forging Ahead: Growth, Opportunity and the Direction of the Alternative Financial Services Sector.* San Francisco, CA: Stephens Inc.

Hecht, J. and K. Joseph. 2014. *Industry Note: Operating and Regulatory Trends in the Alternative Finance Space.* San Francisco, CA: Stephens Inc.

Helleiner, E. 1994. *States and Re-Emergence of Global Finance.* Ithaca, NY: Cornell University Press.

Home Credit. 2014. *Consolidated Annual Accounts for the Year Ended 31 December 2013*. Amsterdam: Home Credit B.V.

House of Commons (UK). 2012. *Debt Management: Responses to the Committee's 14th Report of Session 20110–12*. London: Business, Innovation and Skills Committee.

IPF. 2011. *International Personal Finance: Annual Report*. London: International Personal Finance PLC.

IPF. 2014. *International Personal Finance: Fixed Income Roadshow.* London: International Personal Finance PLC.

Jeffries. 2013. *Current Themes in the Debt and Equity Capital Markets for the Consumer Finance Industry.* New York: Jeffries and Company Inc.

Kiva. 2011. *Intercontinental Ballistic Microfinance.* San Francisco, CA: Kiva Microfinance.

Knorr Cetina, K. and A. Preda. 2007. 'The Temporalization of Financial Markets: From Network to Flow'. *Theory, Culture and Society.* Vol. 27, Nos. 7/8: 116–138.

Krippner, G. 2005. 'The Financialization of the American Economy'. *Socio-Economic Review.* Vol. 3, No. 2: 173–208.

Krippner, G. 2011. *Capitalizing on Crisis: The Political Origins of the Rise of Finance.* Cambridge, MA: Harvard University Press.

Langley, P. 2008. *The Everyday Life of Global Finance.* Oxford: Oxford University Press.

Lawsky, B. 2013. *Illegal Online Payday Loans Offered and Sold To New York Customers.* Albany, NY: Department of Financial Services.

Leyshon, A. and N. Thrift. 2007. 'The Capitalization of Almost Everything: The Future of Finance and Capitalism'. *Theory, Culture & Society.* Vol. 24, Nos. 7–7: 97–115.

Marketline. 2014a. *DFC Global – Mergers and Acquisitions, Partnerships and Alliances and Investments.* London: Marketline Analysts.

Marketline. 2014b. *Company Report: Ezcorp, Inc.* London: Marketline Analysts.

Marsh, S., Y. Dildar, R. Janzen. 2010. *Payday Lending: In Search of a Local Alternative.* Toronto: Wellesley Institute/Centre for Community Based Research.

Martin, R. 2002. *Financialization of Daily Life.* Philadelphia, PA: Temple University Press.

Meagher, P.P. Compos, R. Christen, K. Druschel, J. Gallardo and S. Martowijoyo. 2006. *Microfinance Regulation in Seven Countries: A Comparative Study.* Baltimore, MD: IRIS Center.

Mezzadra, S. and B. Neilson. 2012. 'Between Inclusion and Exclusion: On the Topology of Global Space and Borders'. *Theory, Culture and Society.* Vol. 29, Nos. 4/4: 58–75.

Miller, B. and A. Lee. 2013. *Doing Diligence: M&A and Capital Raising Transactions Today, Tomorrow and Into 2014.* Dana Point, CA: Community Financial Services Association.

Montezemolo, S. 2013. *The State of Lending in America and Its Impact on U.S. Households.* Washington, DC: Center for Responsible Lending.

Montgomerie, J. 2008. 'Bridging the Critical Divide: Global Finance, Financialisation, and Contemporary Capitalism'. *Contemporary Politics.* Vol. 14, No. 3: 233–252.

O'Connor, S. 2011. 'Payday Sector in Search of New Frontier'. *Financial Times.* 6 December.

Obermann, T. 2006. *A Revolution in Consumer Banking: Developments in Consumer Banking in Latin America.* Atlanta: Federal Reserve Bank of Atlanta.

Osborne, H. 2013. 'Wonga Increases its Typical APR by 1,600%'. *The Guardian.* 21 June 2013.

Orhangazi, Ö. 2008. *Financialization and the US Economy.* Cheltenham: Edward Elgar Publishing.

Pani, R. 2014. 'A Fetish and Fiction of Finance: Unraveling the Subprime Crisis'. *Economic Geography.* Vol. 90, No. 2: 213–235.

Pathak, P. 2014. 'Ethnopolitics and the Financial Citizen'. *The Sociological Review.* Vol. 62: 90–116.

Pierce, E. and I. Soto. 2012. *DFC Global Corp: Company Note.* New York: Roth Capital Partners.

Philippon, T. 2008. *The Evolution of the US Financial Industry from 1860 to 2007: Theory and Evidence.* New York: mimeograph, New York University.

Raccanello, K. and D. Garcia. 2009. *Predatory Credit and Credit Law in Mexico.* Unpublished paper.

Rolnik, R. 2013. 'Late Neoliberalism: The Financialization of Homeownership and Housing Rights'. *International Journal of Urban and Regional Research.* Vol. 37, No. 3: 1058–1066.

Ross, A. 2014. 'More Banks Discontinue Deposit Advances'. Bankrate.Com. 17 January. Accessed 1 May 2014.

Scharf, D. and F. Wong. 2012. *EZCORP: Investment Analysis.* New York: JMP Securities.

Soederberg, S. 2012. 'The Mexican Debtfare State: Dispossession, Micro-Lending and the Surplus Population'. *Globalizations.* Vol. 9, No. 4: 561–575.

Suarez, M. 2012. *Grupo Elektra, Market Analysis.* Mexico City: BBVA Research.

Szymborska, W. 2014. 'Map'. *The New Yorker.* 14 April 2014: 46–47.

Taylor, M. 2012. 'The Antinomies of 'Financial Inclusion': Debt, Distress and the Workings of Indian Microfinance'. *Journal of Agrarian Change.* Vol. 12, No. 4: 601–610.

Thompson, A. 2012. 'Grupo Elektra: Selling to the Poor Pays'. *Financial Times.* 17 February.

Thompson, M. 2009. Interview with Author. April 10.

Uniform Chaos. 2008. *Stock Market Orbital Comparison.* Norristown, PA: Uniform Chaos.

Van der Zwan, N. 2014. 'Making Sense of Financialization'. *Socio-Economic Review.* Vol. 12: 99–129

Van Treeck, T. 2009. 'A Synthetic, Stock–Flow Consistent Macroeconomic Model of "Financialisation"'. *Cambridge Journal of Economics.* Vol. 33, No. 3: 467–493.

Vogl, J. 2012. 'Taming Time: Media of Financialization'. *Grey Room.* Vol. 46: 77–83.

West Palm Beach Police Pension Fund. 2013. *W. Palm Beach Police Pension Fund v. DFC Global Corp.* Berwyn, PA: United States District Court Easter District of Pennsylvania.

World Acceptance. 2012. *World Acceptance: Investor Presentation.* Greenville, SC: World Acceptance Corporation.

World Market Intelligence. 2014. *Grupo Elektra, S.A de C.V.: Swot Profile.* New York: World Market Intelligence.

Wright Investors' Service. 2012. *Advance America, Cash Advance Centers Inc.: Research report.* Milford, CT: Wright Investors' Service.

Wright Investors' Service. 2014a. *Company Profile: Cash Store Financial Services Inc.* Milford CT: Wright Investors' Service.

Wright Investors' Service. 2014b. *Company Profile: EZCORP Incorporated.* Milford, CT: Wright Investors' Service.

Wright Investors' Service. 2014c. *Company Profile: DFC Global Corporation.* Milford, CT: Wright Investors' Service.

3 The financialization of micro-credit

Chapter 2 orbits around a contention that maps of expansion are particularly relevant to the ways in which fringe finance operates as a diagram. These maps often frame finance capital as a particularly expansive force capable of entering and filling spaces from which it was previously distant. Maps that foreground expansion are also, of course, deeply linked to empire. The very language associated with expansion – exploration, occupation, extension – is riddled with metaphors of empire. As historians of cartography have routinely argued, maps and empire are deeply implicated in each other. Not only do maps provide a kind of visual legitimation of empire – as Bassett (1994: 320) argues, 'maps ... promoted empire ... sanctioned and even celebrated its progress' – they also, at a more practical level, constitute an instrument of imperial governance in their own right. Before it can be governed, any territory needs first to be mapped, surveyed and rendered knowable in ways often enabled by maps and the sciences (cartography, topography, surveying) with which maps are associated. This is particularly apt for empires which are spread across space, lack territorial contiguity and have no real coherence until they are rendered knowable in the graphic but two dimensional forms made possible by maps. As Edney argues 'maps came to define the empire itself, to give it territorial integrity ... The empire exists because it can be mapped; the meaning of empire is inscribed into each map' (Edney 1997: 2). Maps are also key to the expansions of empire in a more technical sense; tools with which territorial claims could be settled, devices with which borders could be demarcated, and, perhaps most importantly, mechanisms with which imperial intervention could be planned.

Maps of empire, however, are not limited to themes of expansion. The cartography of imperial space is also often preoccupied with certain kinds of *mobilities*. This entails all varieties of maps which stress pathways, routes, relations, flows and, most importantly, *channels of access*. Although not separate from motifs of expansion, these maps offer an inflection of empire in terms of the settled routes and points of access empires allow. The oldest of these are simply maps of exploratory routes, paths of discovery that allowed European explorers to codify certain ways of passage over time. As Bassett notes, 'the practice of indicating explorers' itineraries on maps suggested possible routes of expansion … subsequent expeditions benefited from knowledge of the terrain traversed by previous explorers' (Bassett 1994: 318). As European empires became more established, maps began to feature more settled routes, drawing regularized networks of flows and mobilities of all kinds. Although the imperial maps which stress relational pathways come in an astonishing diversity of forms – mapping networks of commercial, military or cultural diffusion – one particular variant of this genre which became important in the late nineteenth and early twentieth century emphasized the routes of trade which stitched empires together. The Empire Marketing Board (EMB), for example, came to operate as a particular exemplar of this genre. Established in 1926 the EMB was a short-lived but innovative British experiment designed to mobilize support for 'imperial preference' within Britain and its colonies. The EMB, under the guidance of Stephen Tallents, assembled a range of avant-garde filmmakers, visual artists and cultural bureaucrats in an attempt to create unique posters, films and publicity material that would dramatize a reworked sense of empire as a deeply integrated economic space. The EMB circulated 'messages of a common humanity … a visual language of interdependence between Britain and its colonies … new moral communities across distance' (Kothari 2014: 44; see also Aitken 2007: 104–106).[1] Key to this imaginary are the flows of commodities and the thickened channels of access which constitute empire as an integrated space. *Highways of Empire* (Figure 3.1), one of the EMB's signature pieces, makes empire visible as a map of flows stretched across space.

Figure 3.1 Highways of Empire
(MacDonald 1926) Library and Archives Canada/Bibliothèque et Archives Canada www.collectioncanada.gc.ca

This chapter transposes this concern with routes and points of access as a metaphor for one of the key preoccupations of fringe finance. Although maps of the global routes of empire place particular emphasis on the trade in commodities and productive capital, I nonetheless suggest that they offer an apt analogue of one of the forces which lie at the heart of fringe finance. What *Highways of Empire* makes visible is a space marked by routinized pathways which facilitate the flow of a certain kind of capital both to and away from the edges. I argue in this chapter that at the core of fringe finance is a concern with the construction of points of access and channels of movement. The mapping examined in Chapter 2 that animates payday and fringe lending is essentially a diagram of occupation. That diagram maps the edges as a space that capital could enter and inhabit; establishing a presence – physical or virtual – in new territories.[2] The map of fringe finance, in that particular case, is focused on the new territories settled by capital and the large networks that now have a presence with a global reach. This chapter, by contrast, emphasizes a deeply related but slightly different inflection of the ways in which fringe finance is diagrammed. As this chapter argues, at the heart of fringe finance is a preoccupation not only with the occupation of new territories, but also with the construction of new channels that could facilitate flows of capital into and around the edges of the global economy. This is not to suggest that maps of expansion and mobility are somehow distinct. The kinds of expansion of fringe lending emphasized in Chapter 2 presuppose the importance of flows. The expansion of payday lending is, at the same time, a mapping of the flows of capital into new territories and back to the centre as shareholder value or return on equity. This chapter argues that alongside maps which emphasize the new spaces that fringe finance enters are maps which pay particular attention to the construction of channels of access and flows.[3]

To make this kind of broad argument, this chapter examines one particular site – financialized micro-credit – which has been increasingly drawn closer into mainstream circuits of capital. Micro-credit, although initially formulated as a kind of anti-poverty practice often supported by philanthropic funding or state subsidies, has, over the past decade, become deeply commercialized and more closely integrated into private markets. I argue in this chapter that this privatization has been enabled by and through the construction of particular sets of financial pathways. These particular techniques of financial movement facilitate the flow of capital both to the edges of the financial system as well as from those edges into mainstream financial webs. These techniques have both opened channels of access for global investors (intermediation) and allowed capital to be dispersed from the edges to diverse global investors (securitization). Financialized micro-credit offers a novel way of conducting capital to and from the edges of the financial system; through both techniques of *access* and intermediation and techniques of *dispersal* accomplished through securitization. It is in these terms that I argue that micro-credit is an important site of financialized experimentation; not merely a place where mainstream financial techniques are 'applied' but a space in which those techniques are innovated.

In order to develop this kind of argument, this chapter is divided into three sections. A first section sets some of the context for the chapter by emphasizing the commercialization of micro-credit. As this section notes, although this privatization of micro-credit has been subjected to a wide range of critiques, less attention has been paid to the specific financial mechanisms that have converted micro-credit borrowers and receivables into investable assets. A second section begins drawing some of the specific dimensions of this kind of conversion by focusing on the channels of access opened via microfinance investment vehicles (MIVs). As this section argues, MIVs are a key form of intermediation which has pried open vital channels which allow global financial investors to access micro-credit assets in various forms. A third section extends this analysis by foregrounding the most significant routing associated with financialized micro-credit, the practices of securitization. This section suggests that the securitization of micro-credit receivables both parallels but innovates beyond the asset-backed securities so associated with the subprime crisis. In doing so, securities not only direct capital to the very edges, but also help *disperse* capital from the edge back into a web of diffused investors. A conclusion emphasizes a kind of riskiness associated with the diagram that lies at the heart of financialized micro-credit. The injection of capital to its very edges and its dispersal back outward signals a kind of risky persistence with the types of financialization that were associated with the 2008 financial crisis. The most important of these risks, however, are not transferred onto dispersed global investors, as mapped in diagrams of securitization, but are, in one way or another, often placed directly onto the vulnerable borrowers who are the very source of value those investors seek to instrumentalize.

Commercialized micro-credit

Vail (2010) has made an eloquent case for a political economy organized around the possibilities of decommodification. Decommodified practices 'challenge and limit the scope of commodification by fencing off non-market spheres from market encroachments … [and] by creating non-commodified economic circuits' (Vail 2010: 313). For Vail, micro-credit programmes constitute one vector in the web of decommodified practices, a 'non-commodified economic circuit' apart from and outside of the profit logic which governs mainstream financial spaces. Micro-credit networks, notes Vail, 'have helped to alleviate poverty and to create alternative pathways for development' (Vail 2010: 312). Although initially conceived in Vail's terms as a practice designed to unleash alternative development possibilities, micro-credit no longer occupies that kind of political-economic territory, but has been repositioned into a space that is internal to mainstream global markets.

In this shift toward markets, micro-credit has travelled some distance from its origins dating from the work of Mohamed Yunus in the mid-1970s. Mohamed Yunus's work among women in Bangladeshi villages led to the Grameen Bank which was initially focused on the extension of small amounts of credit to the very poor to support micro-enterprises. In lieu of tangible collateral, micro-credit loans are 'secured' through a process of group solidarity rooted in the social capital that poor women generate amongst themselves. In this initial formulation, micro-credit was envisioned as an alternative to local loan-sharks, to burdensome collection techniques and to deepening levels of indebtedness. By extension, micro-credit was also conceived as a source of job-creation and income generation (see Bateman: 2010). Although it emerged from non-profit organizations as an anti-poverty device, micro-credit is now increasingly recast in terms of the language of the market and private competition (Bisen 2009).[4] This has resulted in a steadily consolidating layer of micro-credit institutions (MFIs) organized as private and profitable operations (Kasala 2010: 2). Commercial modes of operation have been driven by both the widely reported reliability of micro-borrowers and the rapid growth of micro-credit over the past decade. By 2008, for example, there were 1,395 recognized MFIs, with 86 million borrowers and a gross loan portfolio of US $45,000 million. These amounts were the result of a 21% annual growth rate in 2008 in the number of micro-borrowers and a 34% growth in loan portfolios (Gonzalez 2009). This commercial turn is deeply related to a broader set of market-oriented shifts in the management of micro-credit at all levels. Micro-credit has become increasingly organized in relation to long-term goals of financial self-sustenance, resulting in the gradual but systematic removal of subsidy programmes alongside the introduction of competitive markets (Economist Intelligence Unit 2009; Mendoza and Vick 2010: 564). Pivotal in this move to the market and the 'discovery' of micro-borrowers by private capital was the World Bank's intense promotion of micro-credit in the 1990s, a move which set micro-credit in relation to the World Bank's complicated enthusiasm for liberalized capital markets (Roy 2010).

The introduction of forms of market governance has been intensely contested by many micro-credit activists concerned about 'profit empowerment' and 'mission drift'.[5] Critics have also often placed commercialized micro-credit in the larger context of neoliberalism, as one more development practice which has enabled market governance and the individualization of risk. Because micro-credit embraces privatized schemes of self-improvement, it is consistent with a political economy which has emphasized the retrenchment of welfare programmes, processes of market restructuring and the erosion of state transfers to individuals. This can lead to a form of micro-credit which 'empowers' not by expanding opportunities for poor women but by shifting risk onto individuals directly. The "empowerment' in microfinance', notes Fernando (2006: 5), 'may be viewed as a governmental strategy consistent with cuts in welfare spending and a market-led approach to development more generally'. This privatization of risk seems increasingly at odds with the forms of solidarity which were foundational to the earliest conceptions of micro-credit. As commercialized micro-credit practices took hold throughout the 1990s, many critics began to note the fragmentation of forms of solidarity. Rankin, for example, has detailed the ways in which commercialized MFIs have tended to mobilize solidarity not as the basis of collective struggle, but as a practice which could be instrumentalized as a source of market value. In practice, Rankin notes, 'solidarity' in commercialized 'microfinance models advocated by mainstream donors … respond[s] more to lenders' concerns with financial sustainability and profit than to established traditions of … collective action' (Rankin 2002: 11). This emasculated notion of solidarity echoes the broader reformulation of risk and security envisioned by neoliberals away from forms of social security which emphasize the socialization of risk (Brodie 2009). In contrast, neoliberals have espoused practices which seek an individualization of risk and a conception of self and citizen as 'entrepreneurs of the self' (Rose 1999).

Micro-credit is often implicated in neoliberal reforms in other kinds of ways. Critics like Weber have noted the ways in which micro-credit coincides with financial sector deregulation. Over the past decades, key advocates of commercialization became preoccupied with the kinds of 'regulatory reforms' that would allow MFIs to flourish as profitable enterprises, often stressing the need for a competitive financial services market. In these arguments, micro-credit has become a kind of 'local' variant of a much broader process of neoliberalism. Micro-credit, argues Weber, can be 'conducive to efforts to advance financial sector liberalization … a "micro-level" strategy … [that] mirrors at the "local" level the wider trend of neoliberal restructuring' (Weber 2006: 360). In this context, commercialized micro-credit is increasingly sketched by its critics as a practice which benefits not the very poor, but elite financial agents. This entails a kind of 'perversion' of micro-credit in ways that situate financial calculations, and not issues of poverty reduction, at its core. As Sinclair (2012: 12) observes, 'poverty reduction has been marginal … Most investment funds, acting as the principal intermediaries between those with capital and the MFIs pumping out the loans to the poor, have little idea about microfinance in practice, and are motivated by a perverse set of incentives'.

Bateman echoes this analysis by noting that much of the credit extended in the 'new wave' of commercialized micro-credit was used not to support income-generating micro-enterprises, but to fund consumption (Bateman 2010: 136). This displacement of income generation has been fuelled, according to Bateman, by a network of interests (financial analysts, investors, fund managers and consultants) who have benefited from incentive-driven contracts with staggering incomes. Moreover, micro-credit orbits around a practice – entrepreneurialism – which is central to the symbolic language of neoliberalism. In this emphasis on individual self-reliance, micro-credit substitutes individual security for state sanctioned (social) security and, by extension, helps create conditions for the continued removal of public services. Bateman (2010: 164–65), argues that commercialization 'actually represents a quite fundamental schism with the various … community driven movements that supported microfinance in the past … the microfinance model [lies] within the most fundamentalist and anti-poor variant of capitalism: neoliberalism. Microfinance is 'local neoliberalism'. In these various ways commercialized micro-credit operates to legitimize and instil neoliberal economic practices as a particular form of capitalist accumulation.

Taken together, these critiques sketch commercial micro-credit as a device which enables a certain kind of accumulation for elite and powerful financial agents.[6] Despite the important connections these critiques chart between neoliberal reforms and micro-credit, they nonetheless paint a somewhat general picture which places micro-credit within the broader structural reorganization of the global economy. Consequently, they place less attention on the specific techniques and mechanisms which have made commercialized micro-credit possible in the first place, and the ways in which those mechanisms draw particular relations between mainstream global finance and the populations that occupy its very edges. Unlike payday lending which addresses a population with some, albeit often fleeting and partial, relation to mainstream deposit institutions, micro-credit focuses mainly on those populations without any sustained connection to financial institutions or those who do not hold accounts of any kind.

This should not imply, however, that there is no connection between micro-credit and mainstream finance. Indeed, the commercialization of micro-credit has been enabled by increasingly dense connections between the extension of small forms of credit and broader webs of global finance. Commercialization, to put it differently, has pivoted upon a particular kind of financialization in which global investment is a key to the expansion of micro-credit. This often entails a shorthand in which MFIs are encouraged to 'earn ample profits and expand as rapidly as profits allow. Commercialize. Attract private investors' (Cull *et al.* 2009a: 171; United Nations Capital Development Fund 2006: 88). One particular way in which this connection to global investors has been forged, for example, is through techniques of financial valuation. In order for objects to exist as financial assets, they must first be rendered legible within particular regimes of valuation. The financial value of assets must be calculated, verified and circulated in recognizable ways (Sinclair 2003). A working group organized by global credit rating agency Standard & Poor's has designed a nascent rating methodology in order to translate micro-credit investments into metrics of value recognized and used by standard financial institutions. Developing ratings for micro-credit investments, advocates argue, will allow investors to evaluate credit and investment quality, assess investment risk and make useful comparisons with alternative investment choices. The working group noted that 'globally recognized metrics can enhance transparency within the micro-credit industry … across borders' (Standard & Poor's 2009: 7). Ratings are also framed as a mechanism that will allow MFIs to 'benchmark' themselves against each other and develop appropriate management and investment strategies (Eddy and Kochubka 2008: 3). These efforts at establishing ratings have culminated in the emergence of three major rating agencies (Microrate, Planet Rating and Micro Credit Rating International) committed to the systematic evaluation of micro-credit investment products.

The most striking technique of valuation, however, relates to a series of initial public offerings (IPOs). The most notable of these episodes is Compartamos, a Mexican micro-finance institution that sold a 30% stake of its equity in the Spring of 2007. Banco Compartamos was founded as a not-for-profit MFI enabled by initial investments from a group that included private 'social investors', the International Finance Corporation and Accion, an American NGO that had, in turn, secured its initial funding from USAID. By the early 2000s Compartamos began to transform itself into a private micro-credit bank open to forms of private investment. The IPO in 2007 was underpinned by an aggressive growth strategy (and escalating set of interest costs) that saw Compartamos expand rapidly among poor and working poor Mexicans. The offering, which attracted staggering interest among global investors, was 13 times over-subscribed and netted the 'owners' of Compartamos, including Accion, a rate of return that has been estimated as the equivalent of roughly 100% a year compounded over eight years (Aitken 2010: 224; Danel and Lebarthe 2008). This audacious attempt to enter global capital markets fully fledged has not been an isolated incident. The most prominent micro-credit operation in India, SKS Micro-credit, consummated an IPO in August 2010. Similar to Compartamos, SKS financed rapid growth by entering into sophisticated arrangements with key players in American and European financial markets. The offering attracted enormous attention from institutional investors and was 13 times over-subscribed which resulted in a company valuation of US $1.5 billion. This valuation was more than seven times the company's post-issue book value and 40 times the company's earnings for 2010 (Reille 2010; Schlein and Chu 2010: 3).

IPOs offer a very particular and dramatic technique of valuation. As a method concerned with directly transferring ownership to private financial agents, IPOs facilitate collective judgement and immediate valuation. The reliability of these judgements can, however, corrode over time. The SKS IPO, for example, was greeted with both a great deal of interest as well as concern about over-valuation. SKS experienced a decline in net profit of 38% between October and November of 2010. The timing of the SKS IPO, on the eve of a much broader Indian micro-credit crisis (see also Chapter 6), punctuated a sense of unease regarding market valuations.

Nonetheless, and despite the timing which placed the SKS IPO alongside a crisis in Indian micro-credit, it remains a very dramatic, and relatively successful point of contact between micro-credit and the global capital markets. Over the course of 2013 and 2014, SKS has managed to achieve financial results that continue to attract the interest of global investors of various kinds. After seven consecutive quarters registering losses, for example, SKS returned to profitability in the third quarter of 2013 (ASBL 2013: 2). This profitability has allowed it, once again, to mobilize capital from European and American investors. Moreover, SKS has distinguished itself in the wake of the broader micro-credit crisis in India as the only remaining MFI with a national reach which managed successfully to meet all of its debt obligations (ASBL 2013: 5).[7] Partly because it is able to access financing from global capital markets, SKS is now 'the only pan-Indian player with a presence in over 15 states' (ASBL 2013: 1). The SKS experience, initiated by its dramatic IPO, over the longer-term, has cemented a certain link between Indian micro-credit and the practices of mainstream global finance.

These dramatic IPO episodes underscore the degree to which commercialized micro-credit has become implicated in mainstream financial practices. As Mackenzie has emphasized, however, the most significant dimensions of our contemporary financial world are often the mundane and material practices that enable financial exchanges, prices and knowledge in the first place (Mackenzie 2009: 2–3). This is particularly apt in the case of financialized micro-credit which has been enabled not only by dramatic points of collision with global financial markets, but by the channels and routes which allow routine flows of capital in the first place.

Channels of access: intermediating micro-credit

In order to constitute micro-credit an investable asset, there need to be formalized and regularized routes opened through which it can be accessed by global capital. One important channel has been opened by micro-credit investment vehicles. MIVs are specialized financial vehicles that link investors with investment opportunities in micro-credit in a variety of ways. 'MIVs channel private capital to MFIs primarily through loans, but also through equity and guarantees, enabling MFIs to lend to more micro-entrepreneurs' (Luminis 2013: 2). MIVs essentially direct capital from investors into MFIs providing a stabilized point of access to the latent value inherent in micro-credit. This is latent value extracted from the 'high growth, low delinquency rates, strong margins, and scalability of micro finance' (Luminis 2013: 2). To harness this value MIVs have channelled investments through a relatively confined set of practices: fixed income mutual funds, commercial fixed income investment funds, blended value funds, holding companies and private equity funds (Unitus Capital 2009: 7). Although there are over 100 recognized MIVs of various sizes, the bulk of assets are managed by a handful of large institutions: BlueOrchard, Oikocredit, Omidyar Network, Profund and FinnFund (Symbiotics 2013: 5).[8] Beginning in 2008 both the volume of assets under management as well as the performance of the funds MIVs managed experienced rapid growth. It was estimated that assets under management by MIVs grew from US $1.8 billion in 2005 to US $6.5 billion by 2008 (Unitus Capital 2009: 19; Luminis 2013: 2). By 2012 total assets under the financial management of MIVs exceeded US $8.1 billion (MicroRate 2013: 4). In 2009 the annual growth in the volume of capital managed by MIVs slowed only marginally to 22% from 28% in 2008 but it dropped to 12% growth in 2010 in the ongoing fallout from the financial crisis (CGAP 2009; Microrate 2010: 3; 2011: 5). Because they constitute the most significant set of micro-credit intermediaries, MIVs have opened the single largest set of channels for global financial investment; over 40% of global investment in MFIs is now channelled through MIVs (Luminis 2013: 2).

The role of MIVs as a particularly important technique of intermediation is evident in the complexity of channels they have opened. Oikocredit, for example, the largest MIV in terms of total micro-credit assets under management, has developed increasingly dense forms of intermediation among a range of disparate actors (MicroRate 2011: 9). In 2011, Oikocredit was able to disburse 90% (US $196.1 million) of lendable development funds available to it (Oikocredit 2012: 4). It accomplished this by assembling a unique network of investors and stakeholders. This network includes individual investors, social investment organizations, non-governmental development organizations (especially those connected to churches) as well as large private sector financial firms. Invoking a quasi-cooperative style of organization, Oikocredit channels investment from 45,000 investors and 595 'members'. The funds raised from both investors and members have been channelled into a range of loan capital instruments and investments which, in turn, have helped fund loans to 26 million micro-borrowers via 896 project partners (Oikocredit 2012: 20). In linking these diverse actors, MIVs are consolidating a unique channel which allows investors to access micro-borrowers as an increasingly mainstream financial asset.

Although access to credit tightened in the period since the 2008 financial crisis, MIVs have continued to register important results. The average yield on direct debt portfolios held through MIVs has returned to pre-crisis levels of 7.7% per annum (Symbiotics 2013: 5). Similarly, the growth in investment in MIVs remains consistent with the overall growth in micro-credit loan portfolios. In 2012, for example, the total assets under MIV management grew by 17%, a figure relatively in pace with the 18% growth rate in the global micro-credit portfolio (MicroRate 2013: 7).[9] Moreover, the geographical distribution of the investments placed by MIVs continues to diversify in important ways. Although Eastern Europe and Central Asia continue to be the most solicited region for MIVs (receiving 41% of all investment capital from MIVs in 2012) there were significant placements in Latin America and the Caribbean (31% of placements) and a rapid growth of investments placed in the Middle East and North Africa (Symbiotics 2013: 13). Across all formats and geographical portfolios, it is estimated that the aggregated assets of the top 100 MIVs now exceed US $13 billion assembled via 83 private placement funds, 11 public placement funds, and 11 structured fixed income products, all of which now constitute a total offshore market for micro-credit investment which exceeds US $20 billion (CFAS 2013: 11).

MIVs were initially established in order to open pathways between a relatively unique investor class (often initially led by key 'social' investors uniquely committed to micro-finance) and a largely untested set of outlets for their capital clustered around the credit extended to poor micro-borrowers.[10] As micro-credit became increasingly institutionalized, and more importantly, as conventional institutional investors became attracted to the sector, mainstream financial institutions of all kinds began to experiment in their own mechanisms of intermediation. Over the past decade some of the largest players in global financial markets have begun to develop their own profitable channels for private capital flows into micro-credit markets. The earliest MIVs were organized around specialist micro-credit organizations – such as BlueOrchard or Oikocredit – and were often anchored, at least initially, by key investments from public agencies. This significance of public sector participants in MIVs has decreased over the past five years in particular. Over the same period of time, private financial institutions 'remained the prominent source of finding for all reporting MIVs' (Symbiotics 2013: 24). Some 61% of total assets managed by MIVs originate from private sector sources while public sector funders now inject only 21% of capital investments in MIVs (Symbiotics 2013: 24). Of particular importance is the role of large private institutional investors which now dominate MIVs, comprising 56% of total annual investment (MicroRate 2013: 7).

Punctuating these trends are recent waves of private intermediation. This wave of intermediation orbits around firms capable of developing micro-credit investment vehicles with a global reach and of assembling large players – often institutional investors – from global financial networks. The most significant of this recent wave of intermediation is ResponsAbility Investments AG. Launched in 2003 by a group of financial institutions led by Credit Suisse, ResponsAbility now manages a suite of 'impact investing' products designed to maximize both financial return and a prescribed set of quantifiable social performance indicators. At the heart of this initiative is the Global Microfinance Fund, an investment vehicle with a pronounced global reach. Directed by Credit Suisse and denominated in US dollars (but with classes hedged against the Swiss Franc and the Euro), the fund currently manages investments valued at US $1.4 billion in 400 companies across 80 countries assembled by management teams based in Zurich, Lima, Mumbai and Nairobi (ResponsAbility 2013a: 2). The Global Microfinance Fund is routinely pointed to by investor analysts as a kind of model for investment vehicles more fully tied into key global financial institutions. The Fund channels investment capital into a wide range of MFIs, although places particular weight on the largest and most dynamic micro-credit providers. The largest single stake the fund has, for example, is a large investment in Mexican MFI Compartamos which comprises 2.4% of the fund (MicroRate 2013: 8). Guided by mainstream financial criterion, the Fund also acknowledges the importance of key social performance indicators, reporting that it has achieved a kind of 'global impact investing' by channelling investments that have ultimately helped extend credit to 23.5 million MFI clients, 78% of whom are female (ResponsAbility 2013b: 1; see also MicroRate 2013: 8).

The integration of micro-credit into global circuits of capital via instruments like the Global Microfinance Fund has its own particularity. The fund, like other MIV instruments, is often conceived by investors in portfolio management terms as an important source of diversification. The fund, according to its management team, 'offers broad possibilities for diversification and addresses the needs of private and institutional investors with medium- to long-term horizons' (ResponsAbility 2013a: 1). The possibilities of diversification are linked most importantly to the ways in which micro-credit operates in a space detached from global macro-economic trends. As its own investment profile notes, 'correlation between the ResponsAbility Global Microfinance Fund and other asset classes is slight, as borrowers from MFIs move in circles remote from developments on the global market' (ResponsAbility 2013a: 1). Because borrowers circulate in a sector somewhat removed from formal economic activity, financial analysts have speculated that micro-credit is partially insulated from global economic shocks or trends. As a 'separated' credit practice, micro-credit can effectively constitute an important source of value as a source of investor portfolio diversity. Micro-credit provides 'attractive opportunities for portfolio diversification since the risk adjusted returns exhibit low correlations with other assets … due to the fact that many clients of microfinance institutions are part of the informal economy, which is less sensitive to macroeconomic cycles' (Galema, Lensink and Spierdijk 2009: 6; see also Deiana 2009: 1; Fernandes 2012: 58[11]; Luminis 2013: 4).[12] In this formulation the very location of micro-borrowers at or beyond the edges of the global economy is itself converted into an investable asset; a source of value in its own isolation from and 'low correlation' with privileged circuits in the global economy.

The diverse investment vehicles which MIVs constitute in practice are intermediaries which establish routes for investors into the complicated but valuable spaces of micro-credit. MIVs create points of access which channel capital into MFIs and, by extension, constitute micro-credit and the borrowers they serve as an investable asset; an attractive investment opportunity with a growing place in asset allocation formulas for increasingly large institutional investors. Channels of access, however, are only one form of financial pathway associated with financialized micro-credit. The financialization of micro-credit has been enabled by flows of capital that trace multiple directions, including practices organized not only around the attraction of capital to its very edges but also its dispersal.

Securitization and the techniques of dispersal

One technique that has been at the heart of financialization is securitization, a method with which an underlying set of assets is used as collateral for securities issued against those assets which are then distributed to a wide range of investors. Although derived from the value of the underlying assets, securitization is ultimately a process with which the risk of those assets is severed and distributed widely. In these terms securitization is a technique of dispersal, a mechanism which disaggregates risk and distributes it widely. When used in relation to credit practices, securitization entails the bundling of credit receivables into a pool of assets by the originating firm and the 'delinking of the credit risk of the collateral asset pool from the credit risk of the originator' (Fernandes 2012: 57). This delinking is typically done through a transfer of the underlying assets to a separate special purpose vehicle which removes those risks from the balance sheets of the originator (Bystrom 2008: 2111). Put simply by Soederberg (2013: 600), securitization 'separates the loans from the lender'. This securitized credit model involves a certain kind of conversion – the pooling of credit receivables into financial securities which can then be exchanged by investors in financial markets. Because it converts credit receivables into a financial asset stream, securitization separates the risk of credit and places that risk onto investors; a kind of pathway which disperses risk widely.

Because the immediate forces which led to the 2008 financial turmoil were deeply related to the significant growth in securitized subprime credit, securitization erupted into the political debates which crested in the wake of the subprime crisis (Dymski 2009a; Gowan 2009: 15; Helleiner 2009: 17; Jain 2009; Juliusz and Machaj 2009: 303; Turner 2009: 43). Although mortgage credit grew significantly throughout the entire postwar period, this growth was unevenly distributed by class and race (Dymski 2009b). This financial exclusion was partially reversed by a suite of government policies which encouraged banks to expand their reach into under-serviced communities. By the 1990s lenders began to expand mortgage credit to excluded groups, albeit at rates of interest much higher than those offered to mainstream clients. As subprime lending became profitable, and real estate values continued to escalate, these mortgages were increasingly bundled as securities that were sold to a dispersed field of end investors. As the Turner report outlines, the logic of securitization 'allowed loans to be packaged up and sold to a diversified set of end investors ... [and] reduce risks for the whole banking system' (Turner 2009: 15). In practice, however, large financial institutions began to use securitized credit not to disperse but to move risk off of their balance sheets while often retaining some degree of control over the assets.[13] Most commonly banks were able to move these assets into 'off balance sheet entities', including SIVs, which were unconstrained by capital minima' (Jabłecki and Machaj 2009: 303; Helleiner 2009: 17). SIVs became constitutive of an elaborate 'shadow banking' system established by large American banks consisting of investment mechanisms that exist outside of normal banking regulations. On the one hand, banks and other financial institutions used securitization strategically as a method with which they could detach themselves, or at least cleanse the formal stance of their balance sheets from risky assets. Through securitization 'banks got rid of their portfolio of assets ... transferring them to entities created for that purpose called "conduits"' (Giron and Chapoy 2013: 175). These 'conduits' allowed financial institutions to retain some degree of connection to assets from which they were simultaneously distant.

On the other hand, although securitization was promoted as a technique for the dispersal of risk, it actually inserted opaque forms of distance between investors and the assets they held. This was further compounded by the large volume of complex mortgages that formed the base of asset-backed securities and distorted credit ratings issued by agencies under pressure from banks for favourable credit assessments. The products from which securitized products derived, notes Gowan (2009: 15) 'came from ... unidentifiable sources, whose credit-worthiness and cash-flow capacity was not known ... they were, at best extremely risky because more or less totally opaque to those who bought them'. (See also Turner 2009: 28; Jain 2009.) Although liberalized financial markets are deeply associated with discourses of transparency (see Best 2005), the securitization of subprime mortgages often constituted a dense web of financial arrangements in which risk was often rendered enigmatic and inaccessible.

Despite its controversial association with the 2008 financial crisis, securitization nonetheless remains a vital link between global finance capital and micro-credit networks. Over the past decade, micro-credit providers have deepened their reliance on securitization as a way of 'enabling risk transfer over a larger gamut of financial institutions' (Fernandes 2012: 56). Like the securitized credit model it emulates, securitized micro-credit entails the separation of loan receivables from the originating MFI. The receivables are transferred to a special purpose vehicle and securities are issued which are linked to future revenue associated with the receivables. These arrangements allow MFIs to channel the risk associated with micro-loans into global capital markets (Bystrom 2008: 2111). These kinds of securitization have facilitated, over the past decade, the conversion of micro-loans into a form which is immediately accessible to global investors (Chen 2008).

Securitization has been of particular importance to Indian micro-credit networks. In 2003, for example, ICICI Bank (India's largest private bank) structured an ambitious securitization for SHARE Microfin Limited, India's largest MFI. Established in 1989 as a non-profit organization, SHARE transformed itself into a commercial entity in 1999. Five years after this transformation SHARE had extended almost US $20 million to over 400,000 recipients, the vast majority of whom were women. The 2003 securitization was facilitated when ICIC bought 25% of its loan portfolio for US $4.3 million (Meehan 2004: 13–14).

MFIs have been attracted to securitization by the prospect that it might expand pools of available micro-credit capital. The proceeds from securities allow MFIs to immediately re-invest funds into further micro-loans, allowing a kind of 'churning of loans' that would not be available if they simply waited to re-extend loan capital once it was repaid by borrowers. In this process, existing loan receivables serve as collateral against which ever-larger flows of private investment into micro-credit could be mobilized. Securitization is also often framed as a larger technique of market discipline. For its advocates, securitized credit offers MFIs a device with which they can be disciplined by the modes of comparison which predominate in mainstream financial spaces. By injecting micro-credit networks into the spaces of global finance governed by a common scientific language, securitization regulates MFIs as bodies that are legible in terms of the 'objectivity' and 'rigour' enforced by financial accounting, auditing and investment analysis. As Trivedi puts it:

> Microfinance securitization is an important alternative for financing that … permits MFIs to … access the capital markets and avail of transparent, market-linked financing … These transactions compel the MFI to adhere to the rigour of financial markets … to meet capital market standards. Securitization offers not only a link to global capital markets but also exposure to 'capital market standards' generative of a particular kind of financial governance.
>
> (Trivedi 2011: 69)

Most of the offerings which have circulated within domestic Indian financial institutions involve 'direct' securitization techniques in which the 'buyers of these securities [directly] own a portfolio of micro loans' (Fernandes 2012: 57). There has also been, however, a wave of securitization specifically targeted to global capital markets built around more complicated sets of derivative instruments. BlueOrchard, for example, one of the largest MIVs, has experimented in a programme of securitization often centred around collateralized debt obligations (CDOs), a mechanism which organizes claims on the streams of income generated by an underlying debt obligation. In this kind of securitization, investors do not usually directly own loans but rather have certain (sometimes tiered) claims on payments which flow from credit receivables. In 2004 BlueOrchard organized an initial CDO which was structured for a duration of nine years and a capital allocation of US $40 million spread over five tranches of various risk levels. The CDO was made possible by both key public agencies (the Overseas Private Investment Corporation) and private financial agents including J.P. Morgan as well as a series of foundations, institutional investors and asset funds/managers (Meehan 2004: 15–16). These kinds of securities, oriented toward global capital markets, have become increasingly commonplace in Indian micro-credit markets. SKS, for example, has continued to have recent success in 'large securitization transactions … [including] a INR 3.2 million securitization' negotiated in September 2013 (ASBL 2013: 5).

These kinds of securitization, which now criss-cross Indian micro-credit networks, have become crucial sites of financial innovation. This is to suggest that micro-credit has become an important site of innovation in its own right; a site of experimentation and intervention at which (global) financial practices are reworked and shaped in particular kinds of ways. In the post-2008 context in which securitized credit is often greeted with political and regulatory hesitation, micro-credit has hosted increasingly important experiments in financialization – one of the sites now most closely associated with innovation in the use of securities. Even in the immediate aftermath of financial turmoil, new efforts in securitization continue to be mounted. In 2009, for example, Indian micro-credit networks were energized by a series of securitized offerings managed by a large Indian investment firm, IFMR Capital. IFMR Capital has become the leading exponent of financialized micro-credit in India and a leading innovator in financial mechanisms designed to manage the 'orderly transfer of risk' (IFMR 2012). Since its inception IFMR Capital has facilitated INR 11 billion of financing through loans and structured finance arrangements with 21 key Indian MFIs, mounting the first ever single-originator, multi-originator and revolving securitizations in the Indian micro-credit sector (IFMR 2012: 4). IFMR has structured securitized credit arrangements for MFIs which 'may not have the risk appetite, … [and] the capital required for holding all such assets on their balance sheets … [or] may not have an understanding/knowledge of sophisticated risk management practices to manage their balance sheet exposures' (IFMR 2013: 4–7). This entails sustained effort designed to inject mainstream financial knowledge and practices into Indian micro-credit networks. 'Large numbers of relatively small and well-run MFIs', notes IFMR, 'do not have the knowledge or competence to access capital markets on their own' (IFMR 2013: 8). Framing itself as a source of mainstream financial acumen, IFMR has placed its most important emphasis on the securitization of micro-credit receivables.

This ambition was recently punctuated when IFMR organized the first ever formally rated securitization of micro-credit in India. This arrangement involved the packaging of micro-credit loans issued by a large private Indian MFI, Equitas. The underlying assets for the Equitas offering was a bundle of 55,993 joint liability group loans, worth a principal amount of US $10.4 million (Ananth 2010). Unlike earlier securitizations, the Equitas offering was partially collateralized by obligations extended by Equitas amounting to 11.4% of the principal amount (Ananth 2010). This offering, moreover, now serves as a model of an increasing number of both single and multi-originator securitizations which have been accomplished over the past five years. In 2010, for example, IFMR organized a securitization that bundled receivables from 42,000 micro-borrowers issued by several MFIs. In contrast to the Equitas offering, which securitized risk issued by one institution rooted in one particular location, the 2010 securitization attempted a more sophisticated offering by aggregating (and then dispersing) risk from diverse geographical and institutional contexts. More recently, IFMR has executed two transactions which underscore the breadth of its work as a financial intermediary. Its most important single-originator securitization, IFMR Trust Pioneer II, was assembled from 55,993 micro-loans (Fernandes 2012: 59–61). A second multi-originator transaction was also recently consummated by assembling an asset stream linked to the income generated by 37,627 micro-loans, a pool which was itself aggregated from four Indian MFIs and then sold as securities to a body of diverse investors from global capital markets. This offering, known as IFMR Capital Mosec-1, is the largest multi-originator securitization in Indian micro-credit markets (Fernandes 2012: 59–61).

Key to these securitizations have been significant innovations, such as the partial collateralization mechanism, specifically crafted to address some of the concerns arising from the role of securitized credit in the subprime debacle. Because securitization severs loan originators from the risk of those loans, many subprime mortgage lenders began to originate risky loans, or to neglect the quality of loans that were issued. 'Since the originator immediately sells off the loans in securitization, the originator has fewer incentives to take the time and money to screen borrowers' (Chen 2008: 787). Because the risk of the underlying credit receivables is transferred to distant investors, neither loan originators nor the financial institutions which structure securitized credit offerings have a direct or long-term interest in ensuring the quality of those underlying assets or managing them over a long time-horizon. As one official notes, 'where all risks are passed on to the end investor, asset originators and financial intermediaries have little incentive to perform the required due diligence at the time of origination and purchase, or to monitor the underlying assets on a continuous basis to ensure consistent performance' (Fernandes 2012: 59). What can entail in securitized credit mechanisms is a dispersal not only of risk but also of accountable oversight for the quality or integrity of the assets against which securities are issued.

IFMR, and the network of financial institutions it has helped stitch together, has developed a repertoire of mechanisms designed to address the kinds of concerns that attend securitization in the post 2008 context. The requirement that Equitas and other MFIs retain some degree of risk associated with the original loans is part of a strategy designed to exert pressure on originators to manage loan portfolios in a responsible and efficient manner. 'The first-loss risk that Equitas bears is to ensure that the originating MFI maintains high quality of origination and servicing' (IFMR 2009: 4). This distribution of risk also faces inward as IFMR, operating as the financial intermediary most closely associated with the structuring of securities, has also often explicitly taken on some degree of risk associated with the underlying asset or income streams. For example, in 2010 IFMR took on some of the risk of its key multi-originator securitization by directly purchasing some of the offering itself. In this arrangement, the originators of the underlying micro-loans, were required to continue servicing the loans over the life of the transaction and in doing so, retain first loss exposure risk. As arranger of the securitization, IFMR invested in the second loss or subordinated tranches of its securitization and in doing so took on risk associated with its own offering, leaving senior tranches exclusively for global capital market investors (Fernandes 2012: 59). In its most recent multi-originator securitization, IFMR similarly 'retains part of the second loss to ensure that incentives are well aligned' (IFMR 2013: 19). These efforts at ensuring exposure to risk – at having 'skin in the game' – are rapidly becoming a consolidated practice in Indian micro-credit networks.

At a different level, IFMR has extended these innovations by bundling together loans from multiple MFIs and from diverse geographical settings. By doing so, by shifting its profile more fully to multi-originator deals, the securitized offerings it assembles increasingly consist of underlying loans aggregated from diverse settings with quite distinct default-risk profiles. This approach – complex multi-originator securitizations organized around explicit risk management strategies accessible to relatively small MFIs – is beginning to constitute the most recent frontier in the financialization of micro-credit and has led to renewed interest in the financialized model in India. IFMR has issued 13 major multi-originator micro-credit securitizations since 2010 alongside a handful of relatively minor offerings, which cumulatively have extended INR 400 core to 13 MFIs across various geographical settings. These securitizations have, in turn, facilitated loans to 1.2 million micro-borrowers (Gada and Agarwal 2011: 5; Ramnath 2012). The construction of securitized micro-credit pools framed in terms of greater geographic diversity is designed to reduce the risk of localized credit deterioration, an outcome tragically central to the 2010 Andhra Pradesh crisis. IFMR's Mosec 1, for example, is assembled from micro-loans originating from 15 districts across three states (IFMR 2013: 19).

The securitized micro-credit model not only survived but has thrived in the wake of both the financial crisis in 2008 and the more particular crisis in micro-credit centred in Andhra Pradesh in 2010. The kinds of securitizations accomplished in and through these innovations are often framed as the ultimate form of a strategy designed to locate micro-borrowers more directly into the space of global finance. Enthusiasm among global investors for micro-credit securities is generated, at least in part, by micro-borrowers themselves as a body of reliable and disciplined borrowers. Securitized credit models are premised on the possibilities associated with direct and unmediated access to micro-borrowers as objects directly accessible to investors in global capital markets. It is, Bystrom (2008: 2114) notes, 'the (historically impressive) credit health of the pool of microloans that is important for the capital market. By bringing the actual borrower closer to the global capital market, there … [are] gains to make'. These securitizations not only provide global investors access to the edges of the financial system, but also operate as a mode of dispersion through which the capital generated at those edges is scattered widely. This emphasis on dispersal is most importantly framed as a method for managing and disassembling risk – for spreading the risk of micro-credit loans across a wide, often global, field of end investors. Although framed in this way, as a unique method of dispersing risk, securitization, in some important ways, actually facilitates a complex movement of risk; not only moving risk away from the edges of the financial system but, in some important ways, amplifying the kinds of risks experienced by those who live at those edges.

Conclusion: channels of persistent risk

Financialized micro-credit animates maps not of occupation but of access and dispersal. Converting micro-credit into a source of global financial value has entailed a particular preoccupation; the charting of pathways through which global capital could access micro-credit receivables or micro-borrowers as well as mechanisms that could disperse the capital generated from micro-credit, often as streams of or claims on income, to a wide body of global investors.[14] This map, both of capital injected to the edges and its dispersal outward, facilitates the construction of investable assets, which are attractive to global investors. These assets presuppose particular flows of capital – ways of channelling finance capital into, around and away from the edges of the global financial system.

In these ways, financialized micro-credit has become not only a site internal to the space of global finance, but also an important site of intervention where the practices of global finance are experimented and reworked in an important kind of way; one of the innovative edges of securitization. Financialized micro-credit has now become, even more intensely in the post-crisis context, a space not, conceptually at least, at some isolated edge of global finance, but a practice now resonant of its very centre, reflective of the kinds of innovations, practices and language that characterize finance 'writ large'.

In doing so, however, in establishing points of access for some of the largest institutions in global financial markets, practices of securitization may also be exposing the micro-borrowers who constitute the base of securities to a broad set of risks. Securitized credit rests on a fragile foundation in which end-investors are severed from underlying assets (Sinclair 2003: 452). The securitization of subprime mortgages, for example, dramatically, and negatively, altered the ways in which investors were able to understand and manage the risk associated with the assets that ultimately underpinned securities (Turner 2009: 83). Securitized micro-credit risks exposure to these same kinds of instabilities that became associated with subprime mortgage assets.[15] Although some of the recent securitizations innovated by IFMR have attempted to address these problems by ensuring that loan originators are entangled in the risk they generate, it remains unclear if these measures can reverse the instability that can often accompany credit securitization.

There is also the risk associated with the widening distance that securitization opens between micro-borrowers and the credit that is extended on their behalf. 'A securitized loan', notes Chen (2008: 788), 'is no longer held as a single asset … but is split into interests held by multiple investors … This poses difficulties for poor borrowers who face unpredictable events'. Although micro-credit has always been deeply riddled with power relations, securitized micro-credit involves a novel reorganization of the 'cramped spaces' of everyday practice. Most experiments in securitization result in a dramatic shift in the ways in which micro-loans are held – extended and managed not by an institution with some presence in the communities in which they operate, but by distant foreign investors. Although micro-credit is premised on the maximization of social capital, securitization can erode these social bonds, or what remains of those bonds, in the face of the anonymous global relationships it often enacts.

Financialized micro-credit also risks the prospect of higher rates of interest imposed on those least able to afford it. Proponents claim that incorporation into global markets will generate greater levels of competition and will facilitate lower prices for credit. In practice, however, there has been a mixed set of experiences with interest rates. Investors keen to extend capital are almost always focused on MFIs with high rates of interest and profitability which compare favourably with other investment opportunities. In order to offer attractive terms to investors, MFIs have had to pass on high interest charges to their customers (Gonzalez 2010a: 1–6).[16] As the discussion of IPOs above indicates, there is evidence accumulating that high interest rates are often pursued as an *explicit* strategy designed to attract global capital (Aitken 2010: 232).[17]

Although financialized micro-credit is promoted as a process that will lead to greater availability of credit in widely standardized ways, it may actually lead to new forms of stratification in global credit markets. This is evident in the way in which only a small tier of relatively developed MFIs have been financialized. Less than 10% of MFIs make up the 'top tier' of institutions capable of the kind of reach, profitability and managerial practices that financial markets require.[18] IFMR, for example, notes that it has recruited only 'first or second tier' MFIs as participants in its innovative investment mechanisms (IFMR 2013: 4). What could result is a reclassification of micro-credit into one category capable of integration within global financial spaces, and a series of other institutions lacking the profitability or the 'culture' required of those spaces.

The weight of these risks became crystallized in 2010 in a crisis which crested in Andhra Pradesh (AP) closely associated with a pattern of suicides among borrowers plagued by escalating costs. By October, micro-credit practices were directly implicated in the suicides of 54 micro-borrowers in AP (Rai 2010). Although Chapter 6 will address the crisis in AP in some detail, it is worth noting at this point that at the core of the crisis in AP was a boom in micro-credit fuelled in part by financialized expansion, including important experiments in securitization. Like most states in India, AP has experienced a dramatic shift away from a state-sanctioned model of 'self-help groups' (SHGs) which function in a vein roughly similar to the traditional Grameen approach.[19] Over the past decade SHGs have been displaced by rapid growth in commercialized micro-credit which orbits around private capital investment. The most significant growth has come in the form of Non-Banking Finance Companies (NBFCs) which dominate the sector (Sane and Thomas 2011: 7). New MFI ventures expanded at a rate of 80% per year reaching 27 million borrowers by 2010 (CGAP 2010: 2). This boom, fuelled by private investment led, however, to serious instability in micro-credit markets. The earliest signs of mounting pressure came in 2005 when the AP government closed 50 branches of two large MFIs accused of coercive lending and collection techniques (Sane and Thomas 2011: 11). In October 2010 a much broader crisis erupted fuelled by costly loans, coercive collection and widening cycles of debt among borrowers. In the wake of this crisis, the AP government issued a controversial ordinance which enacted constraints on the micro-credit sector in several key ways (Arunachalam 2011; see also Bateman 2012). Explicitly framed as an attempt to address the 'usurious interest rates and coercive means of recovery resulting in … impoverishment and in some cases leading to suicides', the ordinance prohibited unregistered MFIs – essentially the bulk of private MFIs – from issuing loans or recovering outstanding balances (CGAP 2010). By November 2010 the vast majority (over 90%) of outstanding loans were no longer being recovered. In the first month alone, almost US $2 billion in repayments virtually ceased (Chakraborty 2012).[20]

As the AP episode indicates, securitization, although inscribed as a mechanism that could diffuse risk, can actually become acutely, even tragically, implicated in the intensification of risks at certain moments. Evident in 2008, and punctuated again in 2010 in AP, are the complex ways in which securitized credit can expose borrowers to forms of cascading risk. Even as a certain kind of scepticism to financialization and commercialization began to mount in the aftershocks of 2010, the entanglements of micro-credit within financialized relationships, and in the risks those relationships entail, have continued to deepen enormously. Viewed within the crucible of these deepening entanglements (and the cruel costs associated with them) the futures of micro-credit seem to chart a kind of risky persistence with the kinds of practices that have animated the financial turmoil and upheaval of finance 'writ large' over the past decade. Not only has the genre of risks and financial manoeuvres associated with 2008 not disappeared, it has, in particular ways, resurfaced at the very edges of global finance. This implies the importance that the distribution, calculation and commodification of risk occupies in the broader processes of financialization – a set of concerns related not only to the mechanisms of securitization but also to the technologies of insurance.

Notes

1 The classic historical work on the Empire Marketing Board is Constantine 1986.

2 This is not to make too fine a distinction between equity and debt financing as many payday lenders have also been deeply enabled by debt financing arrangements.

3 I do not mean to imply that these two mappings are in some way distinct from each other or in contrast to each other. Indeed, as Chapter 2 notes, the maps which diagram the expansion of fringe lending into new territories imply or even presuppose maps of flow. In that chapter I note that at the heart of maps of fringe lending is a set of relationships in which capital flows into the edges of the financial system and is 'returned' via shareholder value to the centre.

4 This has been accompanied by an important shift in the official discourses of micro-credit, especially those promoted by the World Bank. At the core of this

shift has been a systematic emphasis not on income generation or gender equity but on a language of 'financial inclusion'. (See also Chapter 6.)

5 For advocates, only the market can mobilize the capital required to provide meaningful access to credit. In this regard, see Chu (2007: 139: 143); Cull *et al.* (2009a: 2009b); Hechler-Fayd'herbe (2009: 2); Rhyne and Christen (1999: 4); Schlein and Chu (2010: 2). For objections to the commercialization of micro-credit, see Augsburg and Fouillet (2010: 350); Lascelles (2008); Rosenberg *et al.* (2009); Schmidt (2010); Yunus (2006); Yunus and Chu (2008: 5).

6 Taken together, these critiques imply that micro-credit constitutes a form of what Harvey (2004: 76) has referred to as 'accumulation by dispossession'. For Harvey, this concept is an attempt to upend Marx's analysis which places 'primitive' and 'capitalist' accumulation on either side of a stark divide. 'Accumulation by dispossession can occur in a variety of ways … Yet it is omnipresent in no matter what historical period' (Harvey 2004: 76).

7 'SKS is the only AP-based MFI to have honoured all its debt obligations besides raising equity capital' (ASBL 2013: 5).

8 Symbiotics (2013: 5) identifies 111 recognized MIVs in 2012.

9 There has also been some broadening of MIV intermediation beyond the purview of the 'big five' firms. In 2012, the total share of MIV investment held in the top five firms dropped from 46 to 42%. The median size of all 111 recognized MIVs is now US $35 million (MicroRate 2013: 9).

10 IFMR (2012: 5) argues that micro-credit is not only untested but has 'little access to capital markets due to lack of visibility, transparency, common data platforms and little under soot business dynamics'.

11 As Fernandes (2012: 58) argues the 'low correlation observed between returns on this asset class and other mainstream assets classes such as equities, bonds, commodities and bullion is because in the short run, the small-scale activists and occupations engaged by borrowers continue irrespective of the happenings in mainstream markets'.

12 As Luminis (2013: 4) argues: 'Microfinance investments provide investors with a unique opportunity to diversity their portfolio. These investment show low correlation and stable returns.'

13 Although securitization was designed to prevent concentration of risky assets, 'in this case it did the opposite … roughly 75 percent of the losses experienced during the crisis were concentrated in the leveraged financial system' (Jabłecki and Machaj 2009: 302).

14 Of course maps of occupation and of flows are not distinct but often require and presuppose each other.

15 This exposure to risk has been evident over the course of the subprime crisis. On one hand, there is some research which suggests that there continues to be relatively low correlation between the performance of MIVs and the broader financial economy during the crisis (CGAP 2009: 1; Deiana 2009; Galema et al. 2009). On the other hand, although the global financial crisis did not displace processes of micro/financialization, it has exerted pressure in several ways (Gonzalez 2010a: 1; Lascelles and Mendelson 2009: 7; Microrate 2010: 5; O'Donohoe and Rozeria de Mariz 2010: 3).

16 75% of MFIs charge rates focused on profit-maximization rather than poverty reduction.

17 Proponents suggest that high rates are necessary not only as a way to attract private capital but also to cover high operating costs (Gonzalez 2010a: 1–6; Polgreen and Bajaj 2010).

18 As one group of analysts notes, 'investors seeking pure profits would have little interest in most of the institutions that are now serving poor customers' (Cull et al. 2009b: 69).

19 It is important to note that SHGs have a long and important history in AP (CGAP 2010: 2). See also Sane and Thomas (2011).

20 These defaults have had a dramatic impact on the broader Indian financial sector which has taken an increasing stake in micro-credit over the past decade (Polgreen and Bajaj 2010).

References

Aitken, R. 2007. *Performing Capital: Toward a Cultural Economy of Popular and Global Finance.* New York: Palgrave.

Aitken, R. 2010. 'Ambiguous Incorporations: Microfinance and Global Governmentality'. *Global Networks.* Vol. 10, No. 2: 223–243.

Ananth, B. 2010. *New Financial Instruments for Social Enterprises.* Delhi: IFMR Capital.

Arunachalam, R. 2011. *The Journey of Indian Micro-Finance: Lessons for the Future.* Chennai: Aapti Publications.

ASBL. 2013. *SKS Microfinance: Company Analysis.* Mumbai: Antique Stock Broking Limited.

Augsburg, B. and C. Fouillet. 2010. 'Profit Empowerment: The Micro-Credit Institution's Mission Drift'. *Perspectives on Global Development and Technology.* Vol. 9, No. (3/4): 327–355.

Bassett, T. 1994. 'Cartography and Empire Building in Nineteenth-Century West Africa'. *Geographical Review.* Vol. 84, No. 3: 316–324.

Bateman, M. 2010. *Why Doesn't Microfinance Work? The Destructive Rise of Local Neoliberalism.* London: Zed Books.

Bateman, M. 2012. 'How Lending to the Poor Began, Grew and Almost Destroyed a Generation in India'. *Development and Change.* Vol. 43, No. 6: 1385–1402.

Best, J. 2005. *The Limits of Transparency: Ambiguity and the History of International Finance.* Ithaca, NY: Cornell University Press.

Best, J. 2009. 'How to Make a Bubble: Towards a Cultural Political Economy of the Financial Crisis'. *International Political Sociology.* Vol. 3, No. 4: 461–465.

Bisen, A. 2009. *The Contemporary Social Construction of Micro-Credit Industry: From Mission to Market.* Sydney: B. Bus thesis, University of Technology.

Brodie, J. 2009. 'From Social Security to Public Safety: Security Discourses and Canadian Citizenship'. *University of Toronto Quarterly.* Vol. 78, No. 3: 687–708.

Bystrom, H. 2008. 'The Microfinance Collateralized Debt Obligation: A Modern Robin Hood?' *World Development.* Vol. 36, No. 11: 2109–2126.

CFAS. 2013. *Risk Management in Microfinance: A Practitioner's Perspective.* Zurich: CFA Society Switzerland.

CGAP. 2009. *MIV Performance and Prospects: Highlights from the CGAP 2009 MIV Benchmark Survey.* Washington DC: Consultative Group to Assist the Poor.

CGAP. 2010. *CGAP Mix 2010 Sub-Saharan Africa Microfinance Analysis and Benchmarking Report.* Washington DC: Consultative Group to Assist the Poor.

Chakraborty, S. 2012. 'MFI Sector Will Take Years to Recover: Philip Vassiliou'. *Business Standard.* 27 March. http://www.business-standard.com/article/finance/mfi-sector-will-takeyears-to-recover-philip-vassiliou-112032700042_1.html.

Chen, Z. 2008. 'Securitizing Microcredit: The Implications of Securitization for Microcredit Institutions' Human Rights Missions'. *Columbia Human Rights Law Review.* Vol. 39: 757–794.

Chu, M. 2007. 'Commercial Returns at the Base of the Pyramid'. *Innovations* (Winter/Spring): 115–146.

Constantine, S. 1986. 'Bringing the Empire Alive: The Empire Marketing Board and Imperial Propaganda'. *Imperialism and Popular Culture.* Ed. J. Mackenzie. Manchester: Manchester University Press, 192–231.

Crotty, J.C. 2009. 'Structural Causes of the Global Financial Crisis: a Critical Assessment of the 'New Financial Architecture'', *Cambridge Journal of Economics.* Vol. 33: 564.

Crotty, J.C. and G. Epstein. 2009. 'Avoiding Another Meltdown'. *Challenge.* Vol. 52, No. 1: 5–26.

Cull, R., A. Demigruc-Kunt and J. Morduch. 2009a. 'Micro-Credit Meets the Market'. *Journal of Economic Perspectives.* Vol. 23, No. 1: 167–192.

Cull, R., A. Demigruch-Kunt and J. Morduch. 2009b. 'Micro-Credit Tradeoffs: Regulation, Competition, and Financing'. *World Bank Policy Research Working Paper* 5086. Washington, DC: World Bank.

Danel, C. and C. Lebarthe. 2008. *A Letter to Our Peers.* Mexico: Banco Compartamos.

Deiana, M. 2009. *Ethical Investments and Microfinance Mutual Funds: An Empirical Analysis.* Luxembourg: Luxembourg School of Finance, Unpublished Master of Science thesis.

Dymski, G. 2009a. 'Racial Exclusion and the Political Economy of the Subprime Crisis'. *Historical Materialism.* Vol. 17, No. 2: 149–179.

Dymski, G. 2009b. 'Afterword: Mortgage Markets and the Urban Problematic in the Global Transition'. *International Journal of Urban and Regional Research.* Vol. 33, No. 2: 427–442.

Economist Intelligence Unit. 2009. *Global Microscope on the Micro-Credit Business Environment.* London: Economist Intelligence Unit.

Eddy, J. and G. Kochubka. 2008. *Developing a Global Ratings Framework for Micro-Credit Institutions.* New York: Standard & Poor's.

Edney, M. 1997. *Mapping an Empire: The Geographical Construction of British India, 1765–1843.* Chicago, IL: University of Chicago Press.

Fernandes, K. 2012. 'A Structured Finance Approach to Microfinance'. *Securitization and Structured Finance Handbook 2011/12.* Colchester: Euromoney Yearbooks: 56–65

Fernando, J.L. ed. 2006. *Microfinance: Perils and Prospects.* London: Sage.

Gada, K. and R. Agarwal. 2011. *Update on Indian Securitisation Market.* Delhi: IRCA.

Galema, R., R. Lensink and L. Spierdijk. 2009. *International Diversification and Microfinance.* Tilburg Netherlands: Network for Studies on Pension, Aging and Retirement, Discussion Paper 05/2009–023.

Giron, A. and A. Chapoy. 2013. 'Securitization and Financialization'. *Journal of Post Keynesian Economics.* Vol. 35, No. 2: 171–186.

Gonzalez, A. 2009. 'Innovations in Insuring the Poor: Index Insurance Applied to Agriculture, the Mexican Case'. *International Food Policy Research Focus Brief.* Vol. 17, No. 15: 1–2.

Gonzalez, A. 2010a. 'Analyzing Microcredit Interest Rates'. *Mix Data Brief.* No. 4. Washington, DC: Micro-Credit Information Exchange.

Gonzalez, A. 2010b. 'Is Micro-Credit Growing Too Fast?' *Mix Data Brief.* No. 5. Washington, DC: Micro-Credit Information Exchange.

Gowan, P. 2009. 'Crisis in the Heartland: Consequences of the New Wall Street System'. *New Left Review.* Vol. 55: 5–29.

Harvey, D. 2004. 'The "New" Imperialism: Accumulation by Dispossession'. *Socialist Register*. Vol. 40: 63–87.

Hechler-Fayd'herbe, N. 2009. 'Micro Finance: Three Perspectives on the Achievements, Challenges and Future of Microfinance'. *Credit Suisse Research Quarterly* (June).

Helleiner, E. 2009a. 'Crisis and Response: Five Regulatory Agendas in Search of an Outcome'. *International Politics and Society*. Vol. 1: 11–16.

IFMR. 2009. *Introduction to Securitisation for MFIs*. Delhi: IMFR Capital.

IFMR. 2012. *Data Quality and Analysis in the Context of Capital Markets*. Chennai: IFMR Capital.

IFMR. 2013. *Multi-Originator Securitization as a Risk Transfer Mechanism in Microfinance*. Chennai: IFMR Capital.

Jabłecki, J. and M. Machaj. 2009. 'The Regulated Meltdown of 2008'. *Critical Review*. Vol. 21, No. 2–3: 301–328.

Jain, A. 2009. 'Regulation and Subprime Turmoil'. *Critical Perspectives on International Business*. Vol. 5, No. 1/2: 98–106.

Juliusz, J. and M. Machaj. 2009. 'The Regulated Meltdown of 2009'. *Critical Review*. Vol. 21, No. 2/3: 301–328.

Kasala, M. 2010. 'Labeling Micro-Credit as Socially Responsible Investing: What's the Risk?' *Working Paper*. Minneapolis, MN: Capella University.

Kothari, U. 2014. 'Trade, Consumption and Development Alliances: the Historical Legacy of the Empire Marketing Board Poster Campaign'. *Third World Quarterly*. Vol. 35, No. 1: 43–64.

Lascelles, D. 2008. *Micro-Credit Banana Skins 2008: Risk in a Booming Industry*. New York: Center for the Study of Financial Innovation.

Lascelles, D. and S. Mendelson. 2009. *Micro-Credit Banana Skins 2009: Confronting Crisis and Change*. New York: Centre for the Study of Financial Innovation.

Luminis. 2013. *Microfinance Investment: A Primer*. Luxemburg: Luminis/MicroRate.

Mackenzie, D. 2009. *Material Markets: How Economic Agents are Constructed*. Oxford: Oxford University Press.

Meehan, J. 2004. 'Tapping the Financial Markets for Micro-Credit: Grameen Foundation USA's Promotion of this Emerging Trend'. *Working Paper*. Washington, DC: Grameen Foundation USA.

Mendoza, R.U. and B.C. Vick. 2010. 'From Revolution to Evolution: Charting the main Features of Microfinance 2.0'. *Perspectives on Global Development and Technology*. Vol. 9, No. 3: 545–580.

MicroRate. 2010. *State of Micro-Credit Investment: The MicroRate 2010 MIV Survey*. Arlington, VA: MicroRate Incorporated.

MicroRate. 2011. *The State of Microfinance Investment 2011: MicroRate's 6th Annual Survey and Analysis of MIVs*. Arlington, VA: MicroRate Incorporated

MicroRate. 2013. *The State of Microfinance Investment 2013*. New York: MicroRate.

O'Donohoe, N. and F. Rozeria de Mariz. 2010. *All Eyes on Micro-Credit Asset Quality: Micro-Credit Global Valuation Survey 2010*. New York: J.P. Morgan Global Research.

Oikocredit. 2012. *Annual Report 2012: Investing With Cooperative Values*. Amersfoort: Oikocredit.

Polgreen, L. and V. Bajaj. 2010. 'India Microcredit Faces Collapse from Defaults'. *New York Times*. 17 November. www.nytimes.com/2010/11/18/world/asia/18micro.html (accessed 17 November 2010).

Rai, V. 2010. 'India's Microfinance Crisis is a Battle to Monopolize the Poor'. *Harvard Business Review*. Blog2 November.

Ramnath, N.S. 2012. 'Bridging the Gap in Microfinance'. *Forbes India*. 20 April.

Rankin, K. 2002. 'Social Capital, Microfinance and the Politics of Development'. *Feminist Economics*. Vol. 8, No. 1: 1–24.

Reille, X. 2010. *SKS IPO Success and Excess*. Washington, DC: CGAP.

ResponsAbility. 2013a. *ResponsAbility Global Microfinance Fund: Fund Profile*. Zurich: ResponsAbility Investments AG.

ResponsAbility. 2013b. *ResponsAbility Global Microfinance Fund: Monthly Report September 2013*. Zurich: ResponsAbility Investments AG.

Rhyne, E. and R.P. Christen. 1999. *Micro-Credit Enters the Marketplace*. Washington, DC: United States Agency for International Development.

Rose, N. 1999. *Powers of Freedom: Reframing Political Thought*. Cambridge: Cambridge University Press.

Rosenberg, R., A. Gonzales and S. Narain. 2009. *The New Moneylenders: Are the Poor Being Exploited by High Microcredit Interest Rates?* Washington, DC: Consultative Group to Assist the Poor.

Roy, A. 2010. *Poverty Capital: Microfinance and the Making of Development*. London: Routledge.

Sane, R. and S. Thomas. 2011. 'A Policy Response to the Indian Micro-Finance Crisis'. *Social Science Research Network*. http://ssrn.com/abstract=1842926

Schlein, M. and M. Chu. 2010. 'Micro-Credit Goes Public: How Capital Markets Can Help Fight Poverty'. *Forbes* 30 April.

Schmidt, R.H. 2010. 'Micro-Credit, Commercialization and Ethics'. *Poverty & Public Policy*. Vol. 2, No. 1: 99–137.

Sinclair, H. 2012. *Confessions of a Microfinance Heretic: How Microlending Lost Its Way and Betrayed the Poor*. New York: Berrett-Koehler Publsihers.

Sinclair, T.J. 2003. 'Global Monitor: Bond Rating Agencies'. *New Political Economy*. Vol. 8, No. 1: 147–161.

Soederberg, S. 2013. 'Universalising Financial Inclusion and the Securitisation of Development'. *Third World Quarterly*. Vol. 34, No. 4: 593–612.

Standard & Poor's. 2009. *Micro-Credit: Taking Root in the Global Capital Markets, Part 2*. New York: Standard & Poor's.

Symbiotics. 2013. *2013 Symbiotics MIV Survey*. Geneva: Symbiotics.

Trivedi, R. 2011. 'An Emerging Asset Class'. *Microcapital Brief* (25 September).

Turner, A. 2009. *The Turner Review: A Regulatory Response to the Global Banking Crisis*. London: FSA.

United Nations Capital Development Fund. 2006. *Building Inclusive Financial Sectors for Development*. New York: United Nations Capital Development Fund/United Nations Department of Economic and Social Affairs.

Unitus Capital. 2009. *MIV Overview*. Bangalore: Unitus Capital.

Vail, J. 2010. 'Decommodification and Egalitarian Political Economy'. *Politics and Society*. Vol. 38, No. 3: 310–346.

Weber, H. 2006. 'The 'New Economy' and Social Risk: Banking on the Poor?' *Review of International Political Economy*. Vol. 11, No. 2: 356–386.

Yunus, M. 2006. *Poverty is a Threat to Peace*. Nobel Lecture, Oslo (10 December).

Yunus, M. and M. Chu. 2008. 'Is it Fair to do Business with the Poor? Report on a Debate between Muhammad Yunus and Michael Chu'. *Geneva Papers on Inclusiveness*. Geneva: World Microfinance Forum Geneva.

4 Bodies at/of risk

Micro-insurance and the vulnerable life course

> … mutuality and life assurance are excellent things for those who enjoy a certain comfort and wish to safeguard it, but they remain quite fruitless, not to say inaccessible, for the poorer classes. Security is a commodity bought like any other: and as its rate of tariff falls in proportion not with the misery of the buyer but with the magnitude of the amount he insures, insurance proves itself a new privilege for the rich and a cruel irony for the poor.
>
> (Proudhon quoted in Ewald 1991: 206)

In June of 1900, James Chatham, an employee of the Scottish Life Assurance Company (and a fellow of the Institute of Actuaries), commissioned a map from Bartholomew, a prominent Edinburgh engraving and publishing firm. The map that resulted, *Life Insurance Map Showing Extra Premiums for Residence in Various Countries* (Figure 4.1), makes visible differential pricing for life insurance based on the 'dangers' associated with different places of residence. Striking in the way it encodes a certain orientalist logic, *Life Insurance Map* is, in part, a representation of danger. Although couched within the objective language of cartography, *Life Insurance Map* is actually a deeply productive gesture which brings into being, and makes visible the kinds of dangers it purports merely to represent. In doing so, *Life Insurance Map* exists as part of what Edward Said has described as the 'imaginative geography' which maps the non-Western world as sites of particular danger, threat or untamed chaos. This imaginative geography maps the 'aspects of the Orient that set it off from the West' including, most importantly, the 'dangerous spaces beyond familiar boundaries' (Said 1977: 170; see also Campbell 1998). The invocation of danger plays a particularly important role in representations that imagined the non-Western world as 'uncivilized' cultures with populations unfit to govern themselves. Unlike the fantasies that frame cartography as an objective science, a kind of immaculate reflection of some pre-existing reality, Said's 'imaginative geography' places particular emphasis on the creative and productive work accomplished in geographical representations. These representations do not reflect, but produce space, and invoke the dangers that help define those spaces in particular kinds of ways. This 'imaginative geography' of orientalist danger is most striking in the ways in which

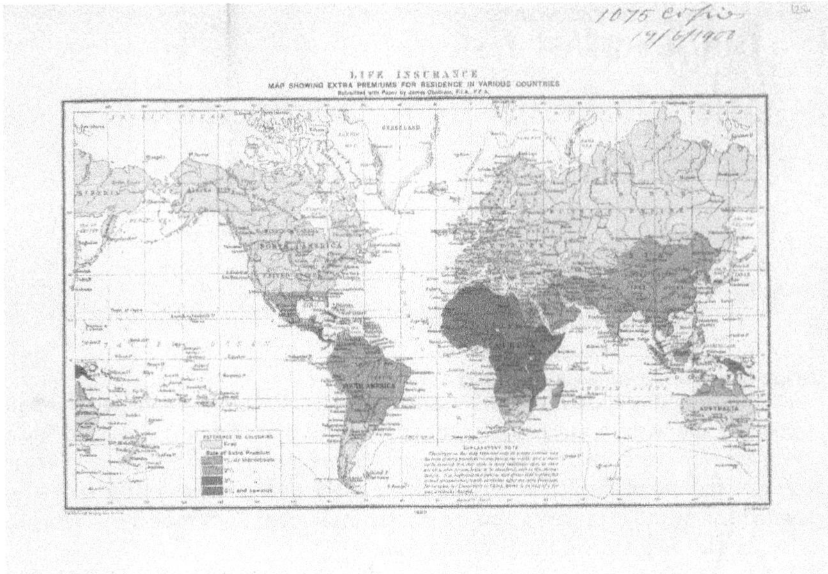

Figure 4.1 Life Insurance Map Showing Extra Premiums for Residence in Various Countries
(Bartholomew 1900, Courtesy National Library of Scotland)

Life Insurance Map represents Africa as a darkened space marked by exceptional danger.

Life Insurance Map is also, however, a pricing mechanism. The map translates the dangers it diagrams into a particular formula for the pricing of life insurance products. In doing so it not only constitutes danger but also converts that danger into a kind of commodity. In this move there is a kind of double constitution of danger, first as spaces that might be characterized by differentiated levels of uncertainty and second, as 'risks' that could be known with calculative precision and rendered as objective prices. It is in this context that *Life Insurance Map* exists at an uneasy intersection between orientalist preoccupations with the inherent dangers located in 'other' spaces and the commercial impulses which seek to transform those dangers into commodified objects governed as particular prices; an intersection of calculation and danger, the knowable and the uncertain.

In these intersections *Life Insurance Map* is, I argue, a prescient distillation of themes that are key to the particular site of conversion examined in this chapter, the practices of micro-insurance. Micro-insurance – the systematic attempt to extend basic insurance to the large global population without access – is a practice that constitutes the edges of the global economy as particularly dangerous places. Insurance providers and underwriters have often mapped the edges as places so mired in uncertainty that they were largely avoided. In reversing this neglect, in explicitly addressing the edges of the global economy, micro-insurance remakes those uncertainties into risks.

'Nothing', Ewald famously argues, 'is a risk in itself; there is not risk in reality. But on the other hand, anything *can* be a risk … insurance is first and foremost a schema of rationality, a way of breaking down, rearranging, ordering certain elements of reality' (Ewald 1991: 199). Micro-insurance is a particular kind of financial contract in which the edges of the global economy are constituted as risks, as objects with a probabilistic and objective regularity; a conversion into objects that could be secured by financial guarantees offered against certain kinds of 'dangers'. Micro-insurance offers a unique form of conversion, different in scope and intent from the practices reviewed in Chapters 2 and 3. Micro-credit, for example, is enabled most importantly by the processes of securitization which require a bundling of loan receivables and which ultimately form a technology of *dispersal.* At the heart of securitization is dispersion, the distribution of risky investments widely across a broad field of investors. Micro-insurance is animated not by the dispersal of risks mined from the edges of the financial system, but by their combination and aggregation. Insurance operates by constituting particular populations of risks, the aggregation of which allows both calculable certainty and profitable indemnification. As Ewald has noted, 'the technology of insurance is an art of "combinations" … an art of combining various elements of economic and social reality according to a set of specific rules' (Ewald 1991: 197). At the same time, and as *Life Insurance Map* implies, insurance is also a dividing practice, a method for categorizing bodies into insurable and uninsurable lives, those with manageable and knowable risks, and those without.

In the antinomies of combination/exclusion and known/unknown it charts, micro-insurance is, I suggest in this chapter, deeply relevant to the genealogies of finance. As historians of insurance have long noted, the 'insurantial imagination' required a novel way of conceiving time, obligation and the ethics of prudential conduct. As Geoffrey Clarke argues, the introduction of insurance in England 'registered a new attitude towards time. Increasingly, the past and present, and future were thought of as functionally integrated by means of a stable statistical order that underlay, and therefore unified human and natural phenomena' (Clarke 1999: 3). As the practices of micro-insurance attest, insurance continues to require that individuals remake themselves as agents responsible not only for their own accumulated debts, but also for the risks they might encounter across some future horizon. In invoking this dense language, insurance is not easily or seamlessly introduced in any context, but encounters contestation from those who experience it as unfamiliar, unethical or outside of prevailing cultural norms and practices. It is in this sense that insurance is key to the genealogies of finance, one site where finance is revealed not as a rational or already existing form but as an assemblage with its own incoherences and interruptions.

The main argument of this chapter is that micro-insurance is a form of prospecting; a practice in search of novel kinds of value. This is of particular importance for the large global populations who are without any access to basic formalized risk management or insurance schemes. Insurance remains the most dramatically uneven of all financial practices – more concentrated and less accessible than credit or basic accounts globally. The most striking significance, however, relates to the complex innovation now accomplished in micro-insurance settings. I argue in this chapter that micro-insurance hosts important forms of innovation designed to extract value from the unique, and often distressing conditions which predominate at the very edges of the global economy. Micro-insurance also manages to insert that value into chains of formal insurance which connect to some of the largest risk carriers in global financial markets. This kind of innovation, I argue, entails the identification and harnessing of value from the vulnerable conditions that characterize those populations who live beyond the full reach of mainstream global finance. To emphasize this innovation I pay particular attention to two key recent experiments designed to extract value from vulnerable contexts: the emergence of index based agricultural insurance products and remittance insurance practices for migrants and their families. Both of these are cases which convert vulnerability into risks which can then be transferred as fungible assets into global risk markets.

To develop this kind of argument, this chapter proceeds in three steps. A first step briefly establishes the historical context for the chapter. As this section notes, insurance is a practice which historically has occupied a unique cultural economy – a practice that entailed a new culture emphasizing the future not as something governed by chance or fortune but as a field of risks that could be instrumentalized in calculative form. A second section moves to the intimate scale of everyday practices by emphasizing the preoccupation of micro-insurers with a certain kind of 'cultural' or 'behavioural' or 'psychological' change. This sections draws on Foucault's conception of neoliberalism and risk to argue that micro-insurance is a practice deeply resonant with neoliberal conceptions of an enterprising self. A third section turns to micro-insurance as a recent set of experiments in converting those who live on the very edges of the financial system into insurable – and fungible – assets. In ways that parallel the historical introduction of insurance, micro-insurers have had to innovate unique practices of risk transfer in order to instrumentalize risk and value in the particular conditions of the financial edge. These novel innovations are most visible in several practices – weather index and remittance insurance – designed as adaptations to the unique conditions which prevail at the very edges of the global economy.

Insurance and genealogies of finance

As Chapter 1 notes, although finance is often framed in our political present as a rational and scientifically legitimate practice, this depiction is both a recent and historically significant achievement. Genealogies of finance have recently trained attention onto the complex and diverse ways in which finance was assembled as a scientific pursuit purged of its association with practices that would taint those claims (De Goede 2005; Mackenzie 2006; Preda 2009;

Stäheli 2013). This assemblage of finance involved diverse practices: the separation of finance and gaming, legal struggles to codify finance as a legitimate pursuit, the cultural processes through which finance was depicted as a desirable social force and, above all else, the association of financial exchanges with all variety of scientific expertise (risk management, financial analysis, financial economics). 'From radically unknowable and aleatory, financial markets are transformed', notes Preda, 'into an object of systematic investigation … the rhetoric of finance as a branch of scientific knowledge, paired with mathematical tools … public admission into the pantheon of science' (Preda 2009: 111–112).

The starting premise of this chapter is that insurance is key to these genealogies, as a site of intense contestation over the cultural, legal and political status of finance. At the same time, however, insurance has also been a key source of experimentation in the languages of instrumental and calculative rationality so important to the scientific framing finance would come to assume (see Aitken 2014; de Goede 2005; French and Kneale 2009). Insurance has been a site key to *both* the construction of finance as a rigorous form of scientific rationality as well as the contestations which attended those constructions. If genealogy is a method uniquely committed to 'the dispersion of forgotten things', then insurance is central to the dispersed genealogy of finance.

The most important element which situates insurance within the genealogies of finance is the foundational link between insurance and risk. One of the key ways in which the financial exchanges began to distance themselves from the dubious worlds of crime and gambling, was to associate themselves with the category of risk, expressed as a calculative and mathematical category. The movements and spasms of financial markets were no longer depicted as random or uncontrollable, but as shifts with their own scientific predictability and logic. By the beginning of the twentieth century financial exchanges and institutions were increasingly emphasizing a new scientific knowledge of financial risk – the work of analysts, economists and modellers who could depict the financial markets as spaces governed by scientific laws. 'Increasing mathematical abstraction', notes Marieke de Goede, 'places the way in which finance calculates and classifies risk beyond public comprehension and debate' (de Goede 2004: 200). The codification of risk, and the sciences that could know and measure it, were key to the long process through which financial markets would slowly become the domain of experts.

Although 'risk' as a category is central to our political present, it is actually a relatively recent, and somewhat uncertain invention inseparable from the histories of insurance. 'Risk', Ewald argues, 'has no precise meaning other than … as an essential element of insurance; the fundamental element, even' (Ewald 1991: 199). Key to the identity insurance would claim as it became consolidated as a legitimate practice, risk was an attempt at quantifying uncertainty in ways that echoed an emergent faith in the possibility of complete and certain scientific knowledge. In contrast to notions of fortune, risk is a way of understanding, and intervening into, uncertainty not as an uncontrollable given, but as a force that could be known, regularized and managed.

This codification of risk as a scientific practice contrasting with fortune or chance – a 'drastic change in the ways in which uncertainty was rendered fungible as risk' (Lobo-Guerrero 2011: 355) – was also deeply confronted by forms of contestation that conceived it as a dangerous episode of cultural change. For Alborn, insurance was nothing less than a 'creator of culture: of new ways of telling stories, counting people, and examining bodies' (Alborn 2009: 13). Widespread contestation of insurance was, on the one hand related to early associations with fraud, speculation and even murder. Early life insurance in both Italy and England often entailed little more than bets on the lives of strangers including financial instruments which paid out on the death of famous figures (Clark 1999). Moreover, early life insurance contacts were often associated with dubious criminal activity, including murder. Reports circulated in eighteenth-century London, for example, that life insurance contracts were mechanisms devised to extract profit from murder or petty conflict, incentivizing deadly crime. By the beginning of the nineteenth century, as life insurance spread from England to Europe and beyond, it was nonetheless still seriously encumbered by its association not with scientific but criminal pursuit. 'Life insurance', notes Murphy, 'was neither popular among Europeans nor high in demand among Americans. The few Americans familiar with the idea of insuring a persons' life often associated it with gambling, murder or fraud' (Murphy 2010: 2).

The category of risk, and its attempt at a mathematical formulation of uncertainty, was a direct challenge to conventional conceptions of time and fate. 'The creation of risk where none was previously perceived to exist had major economic and social consequences' (Alborn 2009: 304). Although a number of explicitly 'moral' issues tainted the claims of insurance – including its often explicit association with gambling – it was the way in which it mounted a formal valuation of human life that cast the longest shadow over nineteenth-century sensibilities. 'Resistance to life insurance', notes Zelizer, 'was largely the result of a value system that condemned the materialistic assessment of death' (Zelizer 2011: 21). In particular, the quantitative focus of insurance, its inclination to establish actuarial value on human uncertainty, made visible a will to commodify in its barest form. As Alborn notes simply, 'more directly than any other enterprise apart from slavery, life insurance set a price on human life' (Alborn 2009: 11). This calculative mechanism at the heart of insurance, crudely a 'price' affixed on human life, would become both its most unique innovation as well as its most profound source of public contention.

The rationalization of finance was neither a seamlessly nor quickly realized achievement. Over the full course of the nineteenth century there were various iterations of a protracted contest between insurance interests and the social and cultural forces it antagonized. The 'shift from a plural and largely varied set of practices in the eighteenth century to a relatively uniform system grounded in claims to actuarial knowledge by the mid nineteenth century was still one of enormous magnitude' (McFall 2007: 592). Insurance was marketed and framed in a diverse often incongruent range of ways throughout the nineteenth century: as a prudent form of self-responsibility; as a morally sound provision for women and children left in need; as a scientific mechanism linking collective risks; as well as thinly disguised forms of speculation or gambling (Zelizer 1979). Although insurance by the twentieth century came to occupy a more uniform, and more fully scientific status, it was characterized by unstable and contradictory meanings throughout the nineteenth century. By the middle of the nineteenth century the identity of insurance is made more complex by the introduction of insurance dividends which injects into many insurance schemes a basic or conventional investment mechanism (Alborn 2009). This mechanism of explicit individual self-interest is laid alongside other meanings of insurance as an altruistic form as well as lingering associations with gambling. The 'prudent, collective and altruistic aspirations', notes McFall, 'coexisted alongside some of the worst excesses of gambling and speculation' (McFall 2007: 593).[1] Although key to the emerging preoccupations with science and modernization, insurance remained throughout the nineteenth century a kind of hybrid form caught between diverse meanings, old and new.

The eventual codification of insurance as an accepted and normal science was punctuated in three particularly important moments. The first of these entailed the invention of 'insurable interest' as a mechanism designed explicitly to purge life insurance of its association with morally dubious contracts. Insurable interest was constituted in 1774 in reaction to widespread concern that insurance was not primarily a mechanism for managing risk but a vehicle for speculation and gambling. *The Act for Regulating Insurances on Lives* (most commonly known as the *Gambling Act*) prohibited life insurance 'except in cases where the persons insuring shall have an interest in the life of the persons insured' (Zelizer 1979: 71; Merkin 1980). In practical terms, the law required that policyholders demonstrate a sound 'material' interest in the life insured. This included not only those with a direct personal relationship to the body insured but also creditors who used life insurance as collateral for credit. The notion of insurable interest carves out a narrow legal space for insurance arrangements as contracts explicitly distanced from gaming or speculation. In the words of the legislation,

> no insurance shall be made by any person … on the life or lives of any person … wherein the person or persons for whose use, benefit, or on whose account such policy or policies shall be made, shall have no interest, or by way of gambling or wagering: and the every assurance made contrary to true intent … shall be null and void.
>
> (Quoted in Lobo-Guerrero 2011: 38; see also Alborn 2009: 308; Alborn 2008).

A critical moment in its rationalization, the conception of insurable interest sought to establish a rational intention at the heart of life insurance.[2]

A second, if much longer point of codification, relates to the official adoption of actuarial science. Although fire and marine insurance have a long medieval history, and life insurance became common by the eighteenth century, it is really only in the nineteenth century that programmes of actuarial science became stabilized. The development of reliable actuarial procedures, and tables for mortality in the case of life insurance, was an arduous process involving refinement over time. The shift from reliance on samples derived from 'representative' cities or communities (the famous Northampton tables in the UK) to more generalized tables of probabilities was only accomplished in the nineteenth century (Clark 1999). Actuarial science provided 'a way to render the economic interests of life assurance companies as secondary and incidental to the discovery of a grand mathematical secret that could be manipulated to the benefit of all' (McFall 2007: 602). This science, however, was neither quickly nor completely consolidated. The Northampton tables proved difficult to generalize beyond a certain period of applicability. Moreover, the exportation of life insurance beyond the British context confronted insurer's with obstacles as they refined actuarial technique across different settings. The attempt to create an American mortality table, for example, – one that would reflect the unique mortality probabilities in nineteenth-century American society and not simply import English assumptions – proved particularly difficult. 'Statistical knowledge', Murphy notes, 'was never complete ... throughout the nineteenth century the American life insurance industry privately struggled to understand what the average rate of mortality for Americans really was; a newfound respect for statistics did not alter the inherent difficulty in obtaining such information' (Murphy 2010: 45–46; see also McFall 2011).[3] Nonetheless, and despite the difficulties it generated, by the middle of the nineteenth century all insurance disciplines were committed to actuarial science as catalysts for profitability, stability and ongoing legitimacy, however long and imperfect that scientific commitment would take in practice.

A third and final major point of codification for life insurance was its eventual self-image as a technical and business operation. Although insurance firms self-consciously marketed themselves in a variety of ways throughout the eighteenth and early nineteenth centuries (often as an altruistic mechanism deeply linked to the security of care for women and children), by the middle of the nineteenth century they gradually adopted what Zelizer has referred to as an 'entrepreneurial' approach. This entailed the adoption of a language of managerialism, the presentation of insurance practices as a sound business practice and the reframing of insurance from a 'moral' obligation to a form of 'investment'. By the late nineteenth century insurers were increasingly revising products to enhance investment and savings features, appealing to themes of rational self-interest (Murphy 2010: 7).[4] In adopting more rational types of product lines and marketing strategies, insurers were both a reflection of and a major contributor to broader changes in American and European economies which were increasingly comfortable with financial categories of risk and speculative self-interest. 'After the 1870s', notes Zelizer, 'as the notions of economic risk and rational speculation grew progressively more acceptable … life insurance gained prominence and moral respectability' (Zelizer 2011: 24).[5]

In these ways – in the move from dubious fringe to financial science, in the contestations it provoked, in the unevenness with which it was purged of 'irrational' or non-scientific traces, and in its very implication in the invention and placement of actuarial risk at the heart of finance – insurance is a kind of distillation of the broader genealogies of finance. Insurance achieved a certain kind of rational status only through a process as uneven as it was dramatic. This rationalization of insurance, however, was not a once-and-for-all achievement, but is an ongoing and unfolding process key to the practices of micro-insurance.

Liberalism and the micro-insurantial imagination

Insurance, although a distinctively European invention, has always been subject to various attempts at internationalization. As two historians have noted, simply, 'one of the cultural "assets" the British and Europeans took with them wherever they went was insurance' (Borscheid and Haueter 2013: 9). Apart from and alongside life insurance issued on the lives of slaves (see Murphy 2010), the first waves of European insurance expansion involved the globalization of marine and fire insurance designed to manage risk associated with both intensified marine trade and large plantation production deeply tied into the industrial revolution. Despite this intense international interest, insurance has been adopted globally in very uneven and haphazard ways. It is only since 1970, in the wake of neoliberal reforms, that a global insurance market has re-emerged. Market oriented reforms opened new markets for international insurers in ways that reinforced this growth. The 'past decades', Borscheid and Haueter (2013: 28) argue, have witnessed 'inordinate growth of insurance groups operating on an international scale'.

This global expansion of insurance, however, has been both incomplete and geographically uneven. It has been estimated, for example, that less than 5% of those in need globally have access to basic insurance (Lloyd's 2009: 6). Moreover, many countries from Africa, Asia and Latin America suffer insurance penetration rates (often expressed as a ratio premium value to Gross Domestic Product) of less than 1% including Vietnam, India, Indonesia, Nigeria, Philippines, Egypt and Bangladesh which is at 0.2% (EYGM Limited 2013: 7; Lloyd's 2013: 5). This is particularly true of sub-Saharan Africa where 'insurance was completely unknown as recently as the turn of the twentieth century' (Borscheid 2013: 312). All of Africa, with the notable exception of South Africa, has an insurance penetration of approximately 1% (KPMG 2013: 10; Swiss Re 2013: 13). It is in this context that micro-insurance has emerged as a concerted effort to provide forms of insurance to those without coverage.[6] Allianz, one of the largest players in global insurance markets, now estimates a latent global micro-insurance market of 2.6 billion people capable of generating annual premiums of US $40 billion (Allianz 2013: 5).[7] Over the past decade alone, more than 500 million uninsured have been successfully enrolled in micro-insurance schemes, a number that could double by 2020 (Churchill 2013).[8]

Although initially formulated by a diverse assemblage of public agencies, non-governmental organizations, private insurers, underwriters and international organizations, there has recently been notable enthusiasm among private insurers increasingly keen to develop more fully commercialized modes of delivery. 'Micro-insurance', notes Swiss Re, 'is increasingly being viewed as a vast untapped growth segment for the insurance sector' (Swiss Re 2013: 1). In the wake of this enthusiasm, micro-insurance, now constituted as an emerging 'asset class', has attracted enormous attention from private investors in global financial markets. Leapfrog Investments, for example, has established the first two significant global micro-insurance investment funds. In doing so, Leapfrog assembled a unique set of investors including 'social' investors such as the Soros Economic Development Fund and Accion, key players associated with the international financial institutions including the European Investment Bank and the International Finance Corporation as well as more traditional financial agents such as JP Morgan (World Market Intelligence 2013).

These forms of micro-insurance, like all insurance, stage a unique encounter between individual and collective identity. On one hand, insurance facilitates a kind of private market for individual security in the face of uncertainty. On the other hand, however, insurance is made possible only by the collectivization of risk. At the heart of insurance as a technique, and what makes profitable guarantees against uncertainty possible, is the construction of pools of individual risks each with regularized probabilities. By constructing pools with calculative probabilities, risks are both spread across a larger group and rendered manageable. Even though insurance often enables the transfer of risk to others – via local or global risk markets or reinsurers – it requires a kind of individualization of risk in which we are rendered responsible for managing our own uncertainty and for managing the 'investments' that would fold us into these spaces of risk transfer and dispersal.

This location at the intersection of collective and individualized responses to risk locates insurance at the very core of liberalism, albeit in complex kinds of ways. In the nineteenth century, and as part of the general contests over the meaning and status of their product, insurers struggled to define life assurance as a practice that could readily link self-interest with more traditional conceptions of religiously or morally sound conduct. In McFall's terms, these approaches invoked life assurance by emphasizing 'not the rational maximization of self-interest as such, but rather of a specific variant of self-interest as a route to the fulfilment of social and familial duty' (McFall 2007: 594).

Perhaps most importantly, however, the reconciliation between insurance and classical liberalism pivoted on conceptions of thrift. The regularity of long-term small-amount payments and the overall constraints it imposed on thin incomes helped constitute insurance 'in terms of providing a necessary discipline of thrift … the need to insure for the future, ensuring payments, generating security for the family, and providing moral support when other temptations were more alluring' (O'Malley 2002: 101).[9] A site of intense contestation, insurance became central to liberal modes of self and citizen (Ewald 1991).

The kinds of individual conduct insurance has enabled has taken on a particular set of inflections in the context of neoliberalism. In ways similar to commercialized micro-credit (see Chapter 3), micro-insurance is associated with the decline or retrenchment of the welfare state. In the diagram offered by private insurance, security is achieved not through a mechanism of social solidarity or by spreading risk across the entirety of the social body, but by establishing selective risk pools available as commodities – a conversion of risk from social to individualized form. As Ericson, Doyle and Barry (2003: 6) note, the '"moral economy" of the "private insurance model" is to minimize welfare social transfers and maximize liberal risk transfers to the level of organizations and individuals'. Micro-insurance emphasizes individual responsibility and, by extension, operates in a space consonant with the erosion of social insurance.

Most importantly, micro-insurance enfolds neoliberal preoccupations with a kind of enterprising subject of risk. Neoliberalism, in contrast to classical liberalism, is not concerned with restoring some sphere of natural liberty, or the removal of constraints on naturally free economic actors. Rather, neoliberalism is focused on the construction of practices and contexts in which competitive conduct could be mobilized. Neoliberalism, argues Burchell, is concerned with 'artificially arranged or contrived forms of the free, entrepreneurial … conduct of economic-rational individuals … not so much a given of human nature as a consciously contrived style of conduct'[10] (Burchell 1991: 271). Neoliberal 'styles of conduct' contrast, in particular, with conceptions of social citizenship. This entails a concern with the ways in which the welfare state sheltered its citizens from the risks of market competition. Social security, the rational distribution of risk across the social body, rested on an assumption that risk was wholly negative in ways that undermined individual life chances. For neoliberals, however, this formulation dangerously protected individuals from the productive elements of risk. To open some distance with social security, neoliberals have sought a kind of 'enterprising' self; a way of responsibilizing the self as a form of capital that can be calculated, worked on and maximized over the long-term. For this 'enterprising self', risk is not something to be avoided, but rather a key to a form of citizenship deeply attuned to personal 'investment' and responsibility. 'The enterprising self', summarizes Rose, 'will make an enterprise of its life, seek to maximize its own human capital … both an active and a calculating self, a self that calculates *about* itself and acts *upon* itself in order to better itself' (Rose 1999: 154; see also Binkley 2011; Lemke 2011). As Foucault has argued in his assessment of neoliberalism, enterprise is most fundamentally concerned with the construction of spaces where risk could be encountered in direct ways. In neoliberal conceptions of enterprise, Foucault suggests,

> society as a whole will not be asked to guarantee individuals against risks … Society … will merely be asked to see to it that every individual has sufficient income … to insure himself against existing risks … it does not entail providing individuals with a social cover for risks, but according everyone a sort of economic space within which they can take on and confront risks.
>
> (Foucault 2008: 14)

Most importantly this offers a diagram of individuals as bodies capable of bearing risk in relatively unmediated ways.

Insurance is increasingly conceived as a technology of enterprise which allows us to confront risk directly and maximize the kinds of investments we make in our own lives. Insurance is commonly framed as a site where we can both manage but also take on risk; a site not only of long-term security but also of investment. 'Insurance', summarizes O'Malley, 'no longer is imagined to be about preventing poverty through regular little acts of sacrifice. Rather, it is envisioned as the creation of wealth through the active ("voluntary") investment of disposable ("surplus") income – a vision of life insurance as fully commodified' (O'Malley 2002: 109). Private insurance becomes, in this formulation, a fully marketized form, and a way of governing ourselves as little forms of capital, capable of bearing risk and generating returns over time.

This is a framing that is also key to the spaces of micro-insurance; a language of risk-management and, above all else, enterprise. 'Through credit, savings and insurance products', Swiss Re has put it, 'low-income households are able to mitigate their risks, gain access to credit that can be used to establish new business ventures, and expand their income-generating options … which enables people to manage their assets in a way that generate income and options' (Swiss Re 2013: 6). In this language, insurance is not a form of solidarity or even a gesture at thrifty self-management, but a key device with which individuals can begin to govern themselves as 'entrepreneurs of the self'.

Framed in this manner, micro-insurance encodes an ambition directed at what it might mean to be human. As Timothy Alborn puts it, insurance reconstitutes human bodies 'as "risks" bearing calculable economic values … [as] *commodified* lives, simultaneously acting as inalienable subjects and being acted upon as financial instruments' (Alborn 2009: 4). Insurance situates the risk-bearing subjects it constitutes into pools of risk which, in turn, circulate as financial assets. In doing so, the kind of financial conversion insurance achieves is directed, first and foremost, at the intimate space of individual lives. These everyday lives, however, are both rendered calculable and mobilized into broader fields of scope, ultimately enrolled into the denser webs which connect them to the spaces of global financial markets. Although ultimately focused on these larger spaces of global finance, this framing is related most immediately to the insertions of insurance within and across everyday sensibilities; a body of practice increasingly preoccupied with implanting the 'insurantial imagination' at the very edges of uncertainty.

Imagining the insurable body

For insurance to be adopted widely, insurers have had to intervene deeply into the everyday cultures they have targeted. This has involved reconstituting populations, often everyday populations, as certain kinds of subjects – as bodies with insurable risks, as agents with considered knowledge of insurance practices and as subjects capable of managing their own uncertainties. This requires, most importantly, the dissemination of what O'Malley has referred to as the 'insurantial imagination' – the widespread acceptance of insurance as a concept and as a practice.

These efforts designed at enrolling everyday populations into an 'insurantial imagination' continue to preoccupy micro-insurers and the populations they target at the every edges of the global economy. Of particular concern for micro-insurers have been relatively low levels of participation in micro-insurance offerings. Although micro-insurance, in general, has grown markedly over the past few years, insurance adoption has been less than projected by programme planners (Matul *et al.* 2013). For most commentators, this slower uptake has been explained as a question of cultural or even psychological narrowness – the function of either individual psychologies or broader cultures unfamiliar with (or hostile to) insurance. 'Attitudes towards insurance may be influenced by a wide range of fears and beliefs that do not necessarily have a rational explanation' (De Bock and Gelade 2012: 21–22). Partly this is a function of the complexity of insurance, practices fraught with greater conceptional confusion than debt or credit. 'The logic of insurance', write two commentators, simply, 'does not seem easy to internalize!' (De Bock and Gelade 2012: 7). Framed in an orientalist language, these views locate opposition to insurance as a part of a broader culture committed not to rational calculation but to misplaced fear or superstition. Uninsured populations, claims one set of writers 'are alarmingly uninformed about the concept of insurance … some even reported misconceptions and superstitions, such as the superstition that buying insurance is "calling death to you"' (Dror, Dalal and Matul 2010: 7).[11]

To address these 'irrationalities', micro-insurers have mounted educational efforts targeted directly at uninsured populations. In these programmes the financial selves of the uninsured (and the broader cultures they populate) have become important sites of intervention. Training and educational modules are now routinely framed as instances of 'cultural' intervention, concerted efforts to delineate a 'deeper understanding of the logic and concept of insurance' (De Bock and Gelade 2012: 25). Training and educational programmes are often precisely organized as attempts to undo opposition to insurance by emphasizing the basic concepts associated with insurance – premium, exclusions, and contract design (Dror *et al.* 2010: 9).

Most micro-insurance schemes now mount some form of training, educational or financial literacy programming which focus on 'how insurance works' 'understanding risks' and 'why insurance is of value to families with low income' (Dror *et al.* 2010: 6). Often informed by behavioural economics, training programmes target the behavioural barriers to widespread adoption of insurance products. Programmes seek to combine familiarity with insurance alongside broader financial skills which might help uninsured individuals evaluate options and 'identify financial needs and match their needs to the best policy' (Matul *et al.* 2013: vi–3). Best practices around micro-insurance education now emphasize training as an active practice designed to provide uninsured populations with tools to manage their own longer-term risks.

In doing so, however, education efforts have often taken on a broader neoliberal hue; a construction of insurance not as mere protection against uncertainty but as a broader project aimed at a certain kind of entrepreneurial or investment practice in everyday life.[12] Micro-insurance education, according to Dror *et al.* (2010: 1), should orbit around the 'systematic effort to teach risk management strategies and the role of insurance in order to promote better risk management practices amongst low-income households' (see also Dalal 2011). Moreover, micro-insurance training also tends to emphasize the requirement for longer time horizons in the calculation of individual financial practice. Drawing on 'investment' as a metaphor central to neoliberal modes of self and citizen, micro-insurance training often implores uninsured populations to adopt a novel orientation to time – a conception of time both as something that might be rationally managed (via insurance), and a self that could be governed and addressed over a long period of time beyond the immediacy of the present. Investment, notes Nikolas Rose, requires the self 'to project itself a future, and seek to shape itself in order to become that which it wishes to be' (Rose 1999: 154). Micro-insurance training refigures the self as an object of long-term intervention, imploring us to 'think about losses and gains, weigh present and future tradeoffs, struggle with self-control' (Dalal and Morduch 2010: 1). Micro-insurance requires a sensibility which not only establishes a long-term frame of calculation but renders the future itself 'salient'. 'One of the main reasons poor households struggle to invest in the future – through either savings or insurance', Dalal and Morduch (2010: 6) argue, 'is that future needs are not "salient"'. Rendering the future salient – translating it into calculable terms – is key to the subject of micro-insurance, a self attuned to its own projected desires over time.

Many micro-insurance training programmes now emphasize insurance as a technique that could help households begin to calculate the fabric of their lives. Training programmes encourage the uninsured to use insurance as a kind of introduction of calculative rationality into the little economic practices that compose everyday lives. 'For many risks in lower income countries', Collier notes, 'insurance provides a first-time estimate of the monetary costs of the risk being insured. Many households may be unaware of the monetary cost of their production risk – many households have likely never been exposed to this way of thinking' (Collier, Skees and Barnett 2009: 413). Micro-insurance training programmes are a point of entry for the 'way of thinking' associated with long-term calculation, investment and risk management.

Increasingly trainers have adopted active learning techniques which provide participants with some form of direct experience of insurance. Games and other interactive media are frequently used in micro-insurance education as devices capable of providing participants with experiential learning contexts. *Treasure Pot*, for example, is a game developed by the Indian Micro Insurance Academy designed to allow uninsured participants an experience of insurance and its benefits. The game consists of two rounds, the first of which involves assigning participants random health-related outcomes, many of which exceed the financial resources they are allotted at the beginning of the game. A second round replicates the health events of the first round, but this time with outcomes indemnified by insurance. The 'treasure pot' which lends the game its name is a reference to the pooling of risks required in the second round of the game by a simple insurance scheme all players join. *Treasure Pot*, according to its designers, 'enables illiterate community members to understand the notion of insurance and how pooling risks offers better financial outcomes … Thanks to risk pooling, in the second round all the participants can deal with the health events they encounter' (Dror et al. 2010: 37; http://www.microinsuranceacademy.org/treasurepot).

Treasure Pot is emblematic of a broad range of efforts designed to showcase 'risk pooling' and other concepts central to insurance. To accomplish this, it invokes an imaginative training technique designed to allow its participants, in a quite direct way, to dramatize insurance practices to themselves. This imaginative vocabulary evokes both the technical details of insurance as a practice as well as a broad range of abstract concepts with which it is inextricably associated – time, uncertainty, calculation. Most important among the abstract concepts is risk which audiences are required both to understand and to bear in direct kinds of ways. In both this imaginative effort and the ambition to reach wider audiences, these programmes are analogues of micro-insurance more broadly, and its commitment to innovation at the uncertain edges of the global economy.

'Insuring the uninsurable': transferring risk from the edge

As Lobo-Guerrero argues, insurance is inextricably linked to the danger of the unknown spaces beyond its own grasp. Describing it as a kind of 'entrepreneurial' practice (and using a language resonant of imperial adventure), he depicts insurance as a practice constructed to 'extract revenue' from places, and uncertainties, deemed dangerous or unruly. To accomplish this, insurance has often adopted modes of exploration which move across the lines that separate known from unknown dangers, manageable from unmanageable uncertainties:

> Inventors and developers of novel insurance products and practices have historically characterized themselves by operating at, and beyond, the margins of tolerated normality. Seeking to secure against the uncertain, they venture into areas for which knowledge is patchy, at best, chart the spaces that were until then considered uninsurable or catastrophic. By means of exploring and adopting novel forms of knowledge, speculating about possible and imagined futures, engineering financial manoeuvres ... insurers always seek to insure the uninsurable and generate profit from doing so.
>
> (Lobo-Guerrero 2011: 10)

This preoccupation with the 'margins of tolerated normality' has often entailed mechanisms capable of transferring unique uncertainties to large risk carriers, private investors or the capital markets more broadly. In this section I argue that micro-insurance has been at the very forefront of insurance innovation; a setting where private insurers and international risk carriers have increasingly staged innovative risk transfer mechanisms. Micro-insurance schemes, for example, have often developed the most significant experiments in insurance design and new delivery channels. This has involved the delivery of insurance through existing retailers, utilities companies, financial firms, as well as, most importantly, the use of mobile technologies to reach a much wider audience (see Smith, Smit and Chamberlain 2011; Beiner 2012).[13]

The most important innovations associated with micro-insurance, however, are concerned with the ways in which uncertainties might be instrumentalized in the particular crucible of socio-economic pressures and dislocations that characterize the frontiers of the global economy. In order to convert vulnerability, there must first be objects of financial value, and calculable risks, that can be inserted into financial chains – a problem that continually confounds micro-insurers seeking ways to price, underwrite and deliver insurance among the working and very poor. In response to this set of dilemmas, micro-insurers have had to develop innovative risk transfer mechanisms; what Lobo-Guerrero refers to as engineered 'financial manoeuvres' designed to address the uninsured in ways that instrumentalize the unique lives and spaces they inhabit.

Household derivatives: weather index insurance

Micro-insurance, I argue in this chapter, has required both unique ways to know risks among those at the financial edge and novel sources of value to help convert those risks. I want to point, in particular, to two key examples, the first of which involves weather index insurance. Because many low-income populations are tied to agricultural settings, crop insurance has long been important to development policy and practice. Multiple Peril Crop Insurance (MPCI), a standard crop insurance mechanism used in many wealthy agricultural markets, requires the collection of data relating to actual yield at the farm level and the direct assessment of actual individual losses, all of which can be costly in contexts where farms are small and variable (Collier, Skees and Barnett 2009: 405). Because these high costs are often passed on to farmers, traditional products have often been either too costly or otherwise unattractive to farmers.

Because MPCI does not export well to 'emerging markets', many micro-insurers have been recently experimenting with forms of index weather insurance. Index weather insurance provides guarantees not against actual losses, but on some observable and objective index which serves as a proxy for risks smallholder farms face. Weather index insurance issues payments triggered by an independent index which is often closely associated, in actuarial terms, with the occurrence of agricultural losses. In index insurance, 'indemnity payments are based on values obtained form an index … rather than upon the assessed losses of each individual policyholder' (World Bank 2011: 15; see also Stein 2011: 11). This almost always entails some use of objective (and independent) weather related data or some other quantifiable measure as an index for agricultural risk. Although most indices are related to meteorological data objectively gathered at recognized weather stations, other index sets are sometimes used such as satellite imagery data as a threshold for grassland insurance (Leblois and Quirion 2010: 8). Regardless of the actual index used, insurance contracts are organized around payouts triggered by particular thresholds in the index data set, such as low or high rainfall levels in relation to specified geographical or seasonal parameters.

Because it is attached to – derived from – data as a proxy for uncertainty, index weather insurance is an adaptation of a larger suite of financial products known as index-based risk transfer products, many of which are essentially derivatives instruments which allow investors to buy, commodify or hedge risk,[14] what James Vickery refers to as a kind of *household derivative* (Vickery 2010). 'The origins of weather index insurance come from the international weather derivative market, where major corporations hedge weather risks' (World Bank 2011: 15). The earliest advocates explicitly framed index insurance as 'financial weather contracts' or, more explicitly as a process involving the 'issuing [of] derivatives on weather elements' in ways that model and adapt practices developed in the financial 'weather market' (see Stoppa and Hess 2003). Index insurance is a kind of derivative instrument repackaged to address the unique vulnerabilities of smallholder farms on the very edges of the financial economy (Skees 2010: 2).

Index insurance has become central to micro-insurance innovation across the developing world, particularly in India. Adoption of micro-insurance in

India has been fuelled by both the key importance of agriculture to the broader Indian economy and the particular sensitivity of this sector to rainfall variations, especially pronounced in the context of Monsoon rains (Gine *et al.* 2010: 4). This occurs in a context in which almost 70% of India's cultivable land is rain-fed and not well-served by accessible or reliable irrigation (Matsuda, Kurosaki and Sawada 2013: 2). In the shadow of these factors, India was the first site of experimentation in weather index insurance and hosted the first index product, a rainfall index insurance policy underwritten by LCICI-Lombard General Insurance Company in 2003 (Clarke *et al.* 2012: 2–3). This initial offering was sold to 200 groundnut and castor farmers to help protect against the possibility of drought (Skees 2010: 11). Designed specifically for Mehboobnagar, a region of Andhra Pradesh which had experienced three consecutive drought seasons, the offering issued payments to smallholder farms (of less than 0.8 hectares) for official rainfall levels below 400 mm (and below 200 mm within specific sub-periods during the contract duration). The offering specified maximum claims of 14,000 rupees for small farms (Kelkar, James and Kumar 2006: 23). The offering resulted from a project developed by Basix, an organization committed to the promotion of 'sustainable livelihoods' among India's poor and working-poor, ICICI Bank in India, and Lombard, a Canadian general insurance company (Gine *et al.* 2010: 11). The 2003 pilot grew substantially with additional experimental offerings over the following two years[15] (Manuamorn 2007: 2). By 2005, a larger network was beginning to cohere around the possibility of a 'scaled up' version of index insurance available to a much wider uninsured population. These efforts attracted new private entrants into the index insurance sector, including IFCCO-Tokio (a partnership which includes the largest listed insurance group in Japan) as well as AIC, the government-sponsored agricultural insurance agency, which began to offer and market versions of index insurance built around Indian meteorological data provided by the state (Manuamorn 2007: 9).

Despite the modesty of early results, (Binswanger-Mkhize 2012) 'India has [now] the largest, most vibrant weather-index insurance market among developing countries' (Ruchismita and Churchill 2012: 437). The most important step in this ascendancy occurred in 2007 when the Indian government spurred serious growth in the sector by launching the Weather Based Crop Insurance Scheme (WBCIS). An attempt to 'weather proof the income streams of millions of agricultural households', WBCIS is a broad based index insurance scheme provided by a web of public and private insurance companies. The scheme is compulsory for all smallholder cultivators who have received credit from government-sponsored lending programmes delivered through a network of financial institutions (Agriculture Finance Corporation 2011: 77). AIC launched the new scheme in its own pilots over the 2007 growing seasons. Its offerings were products which paid indemnities based on rainfall gauge measures. The scheme is now delivered by both AIC as well as private companies, ICICI Lombard and IFFCO-Tokio, all of which charge actuarial rates, the cost of which is subsidized to some degree by the state (Gine *et al.* 2010: 13; Agricultural Finance Corporation 2011: 75). By 2011, this new scheme resulted in 9.2 million Indian farmers enrolled in various forms of index insurance, generating a premium value to almost US $260 million (Clarke *et al.* 2012: 3). The subsidies, which both national and state governments offer to farmers, effectively cap premium rates and have vastly expanded the market for index insurance products (Ruchismita and Churchill 2012: 441). The programme has now offered several hundred diverse insurance contracts, most of which are based on weather indices relating to 'weighted rainfall', excess rainfall, low/high temperatures and various forms of consecutive 'dry day' measurements.

Although index insurance schemes, at their most fundamental, target individual smallholder farmers, they have sometimes been combined in larger chains of index based risk transfer mechanisms. Most important have been successful attempts to link index insurance contracts, and the smallholder uncertainties they commodify, into larger international risk transfer markets – in effect to transfer these risks, at least in part, to international reinsurance markets. By 2010, over half of the largest index insurance experiments were reinsured, accounting for over 2.5 million cumulative policies (Hazell *et al.* 2010: 44). In the case of India, for example, even though the Basix pilots were too small to attract attention from reinsurers, AIC's index insurance offerings since 2004 have been placed with large international reinsurance companies including Paris RE, Endurance Re and Swiss Re (Hazell *et al.* 2010: 112).[16]

The most ambitious broader financial web involving index insurance, however, is the Global Index Insurance Facility (GIIF), a large global fund anchored by public investments (notably by the European Commission) but administered in conjunction with private insurance expertise. Launched in 2009 by the International Finance Corporation and the World Bank, GIIF has become the largest consolidated fund explicitly designed to develop international markets for index insurance. In order to enhance local capacities and to manage index insurance offerings, the Facility develops partnerships with financial institutions, supports premiums in specific instances and helps develop regulatory approaches consistent with index approaches. The Facility has also developed a strategic partnership with Swiss Re in order to ensure that the projects it supports are fully amenable to reinsurance in secondary risk transfer markets (World Bank 2011: 21). The Facility underwrites index insurance contracts in an attempt to 'achieve returns on equity and build a diverse portfolio of risk from developing countries not previously transferred to the capital and insurance markets' (World Bank 2005: 51). To accomplish this, GIIF has been constructed as a kind of investment itself – a set of pilot and demonstration projects which can help establish index insurance more widely.[17] Although grants from the Facility have included premium subsidies, these are often tied to longer-term commitments for products that can be borne directly by private market solutions. This is predicated, at least in part, on the assumption that 'risk-based pricing motivates consumers to take risk reduction and management measures' (IFC 2013: 5; IFC 2011).

Index insurance innovation has been driven by a number of factors including the ways in which index mechanisms allow an efficient transfer of risk from farmers to private investors. 'Weather derivatives', two observers note, 'allow for a … transfer of systemic risk between different economic subjects … and into global weather risk pools' (Stoppa and Hess 2003: 15). In the language common to insurance planning, index approaches reduce moral hazard, ease transaction costs and reduce adverse selection problems. Because index approaches do not require direct assessment of farm level risks or damages, and because payments are detached from farm-level intervention, costs associated with enrolment and assessment of farmers is greatly minimized. (See International Fund for Agricultural Development 2011: 21.) Moreover, because data sources used for indices exist in longer webs of standardized historical records (contracts routinely require 30 years of reporting records from specific weather stations), index products allow the tabulation of actuarial calculations that can be verified over long and reliable periods of time.[18]

The adoption of index insurance has also been fuelled by a recognition that it can help establish contexts that alter individual behaviour. Architects of micro-insurance schemes have often conceived index insurance as a practice that could militate against 'self-insurance' mechanisms that often distort long-term forms of rational practice. Typical forms of informal 'self-insurance' involve the delay of long-term capital investments and the avoidance of costly inputs over the short-term (such as fertilizers), both of which allow for some degree of flexible liquid reserves to help farmers cope in adverse conditions (Nieto et al. 2010: 234). The short-term calculations that lead to these practices can often, over the long-term reduce efficiencies and undermine outputs. The adoption of efficient index insurance, advocates suggest, can alter these behaviours by opening space for the consideration of longer-term calculations. 'The hope of proponents of agricultural insurance is to alter farmer behaviour in the face of risk in a variety of ways: towards … increasing adoption of new technology, higher input use and greater farm investment, all tending to improve their welfare and national food security' (Binswanger-Mkhize 2012: 188; see also Hess 2010). These hopes often rest on the possibility that formal risk mitigation programmes could allow smallholders 'to make riskier, more profitable investment decisions' in the face of self-insurance approaches which tend to undermine agricultural productivity[19] (Cole *et al.* 2012: vi).

These index products also come, however, with unique forms of uncertainty rooted precisely in the kinds of detachments they enact between the risk they insure and the actual categories they claim to indemnify. Index insurance basically severs indemnity from 'real' uncertainties by linking smallholder farms to abstract financial constructions which act as substitutes for real sources of uncertainty. What makes index products precisely so financially viable – their ultimate separation from specific farm-level fluctuations – is also a potential source of harm. There are real possibilities that insurance payouts could become delinked from actual losses suffered. Payments do not necessarily correspond to losses suffered in local settings. This 'basis risk' means 'that payments are based on realizations of the exogenous index rather than actual losses experienced by' the insured (Barnett, Barnett and Skees 2008: 1773; Skees 2010; Elabed *et al.* 2013: 422). Although indices and uncertainties are correlated, they are not *identical* to each other (Sarris 2013: 382).[20]

There is also uncertainty about the legal and regulatory status of index based insurance products. In ways that directly parallel the long efforts to distinguish insurance from gambling, index insurance is often confronted with considerable legal ambiguity in certain jurisdictions. Put simply by the World Bank 'index products do not align with the traditional definition of insurance, as they do not indemnify actual loss and a policy holder does not actually have to have an insurable interest ... [some suggest that these products amount] to little more than gaming or lottery type activities' (World Bank 2011: xi). At the heart of these concerns is the status of 'insurable interest' in index products. Insurable interest, the cornerstone in common law distinctions between insurance and gambling, prohibits insurance contracts in all cases except where the purchasing party can prove a direct interest in the object insured. How does this concept relate to index products where the object insured is not identical to the direct losses which farmers face? (Barnett 2010: 8). Insurable interest implies the 'need for the insured to possess the interest being covered. [But] defining an insurable interest is not as straightforward in an index insurance contract as it is in a traditional indemnity insurance contract' (World Bank 2011: 52). The possibility that index insurance might not meet the legal threshold for insurable interest or the effective standards that separate insurance and gambling, remain unresolved issues which confront index insurance in many jurisdictions.

Instrumentalizing value from migrant remittances

Insurance has often been innovative and dextrous in the ways in which seemingly inert objects are transformed into new asset streams. Conventionally, this entails harnessing value from the objects that insurance guarantees, such as the earliest forms of marine insurance which extracted value directly linked to the cargoes insured. Frequently however, this has also entailed a wider diversity of techniques including combining insurance with savings or investment mechanisms. This diversity is ultimately underpinned by a wider search for value in places and in forms often ignored by or left inert within mainstream financial circuits. Insurance, to use the language of Leyshon and Thrift (2007), is a key site where asset streams have been prospected from previously inert objects.

One set of places recently prospected by micro-insurers are the circuits of both formal and irregular migration which increasingly criss-cross the global economy. The global population of migrants now constitutes a quickly growing and intensely vulnerable segment of the global economy. It is estimated that in 2013, for example, fully 232 million people (over 3% of the world's population) were international migrants, a number that has increased from

175 million in 2000 and 154 million in 1990 (Wilmoth and Hovy 2013). An immensely diverse population, migrants are also often confronted with uncertainties in extensive and protracted ways. This is particularly true of undocumented migrants who routinely face all variety of risks: abuse, the threat of deportation/removal, the vulnerabilities amplified by lack of access to regular social protection or social services, dangerous working conditions, and the myriad of threats (some deadly) encountered directly while crossing borders. In a particularly intense way, migrants are often confronted with what Aoul refers to as a 'protection gap' of serious proportions; a gap that places migrants between the formal and informal economy, beyond the reach of formal social protection measures, or outside of the entitlements accessible to those with regular citizenship or residency status (Aoul 2012).

Despite the risks which migrants face, they often constitute themselves as a kind of informal insurance for their own families. As they cross borders, and as their own incomes are elevated, they often become a source of support for families which stretch across borders (see Crayen, Hainz and de Martinez 2012, 2013). It is in this context that micro-insurers have recently turned attention to the possibility of transferring the risks migrants bear to private risk markets via insurance schemes. As Churchill succinctly puts it, 'the potential rewards for both insurers and transnational families, of formalizing the informal risk management created by migration can be substantial' (Churchill 2012: 1).

Central to these possibilities are the complex streams of remittances which now flow through the transnational circuits migrants establish. Remittances from migrants to home countries now constitute some of the largest (and most stable) of global financial flows in particular countries, especially India, China, Mexico, the Philippines, Nigeria and Egypt. Recorded remittance flows will reach US $414 billion in 2013, up 6.3% from the year before, and are projected to reach $700 billion by 2016[21] (Ratha et al. 2013; see also Brown, Carmignani and Fayad 2013). Remittances are now almost three times the size of official development assistance and dwarf private portfolio and equity flows into developing countries. In fully 14 countries remittance flows exceed official foreign exchange reserves (Ratha *et al.* 2013: 2). At a smaller scale, remittances often constitute the most material face of what Castaneda has referred to as a 'transnational household economy', a 'family and economic unit divided between two nations' (Castaneda 2012: 14). Although remittances are constituted out of small and irregular amounts which flow through both formal and informal channels, they nonetheless constitute an important stream of value that insurers have begun to instrumentalize via novel insurance offerings. Several micro-insurance experiments now tap into remittances as a way to convert the risk migrants face and the informal insurance they provide into a financial object legible to global financial agents.

Although some micro-insurance policies are designed for internal migrants, the most innovative and complex approaches have focused on transnational migration.[22] This entails a growing inventory of approaches which address either side of the transnational household economy; seeking to insure migrants in their host country or to provide insurance for family members in countries of origin. Pioneer life, for example, one of the oldest and largest life and general insurance companies in the Philippines, has innovated micro-insurance targeted directly to the large global population of Overseas Filipino Workers (OFWs). Its first attempt to address migrant workers was launched in May 2009 when it helped constitute the Overseas Filipino Savers and Wellness Club in conjunction with the micro-insurance Innovation Facility (Rimando 2010). Governed by an agreement with the Catholic Bishops Conference of the Philippines which provides a key distribution channel through savings and wellness clubs established in schools and churches, the programme targets the families of OFWs and enrols them in both a life insurance scheme as well as a small-scale savings regime. In addition, Pioneer Life mounts financial literacy sessions. An attempt to tap into the remittances which return to family members (and to encourage recipients to set aside some of remittances they received), the programme targets, in particular, families who are vulnerable to the irregularity of remittance flows (Pioneer Life 2012).

This initial experiment in insurance to OFWs has led to a much broader collaboration between Pioneer Life and the bureaucracies which manage registered migrants in the Philippines. In November 2012, Pioneer Life signed a Memorandum of Understanding with the Overseas Placement Association of the Philippines, the largest organization of licensed overseas employment and placement services. The agreement, which provides insurance to all registered migrants during overseas placements, is the result of an amendment to Filipino law (Republic Act 10022) which requires the provision of free but compulsory insurance for OFWs, paid directly by the placement agencies (FPV 2012). The 500 placement agencies that make up the association offer an insurance package to all migrants they represent which includes accidental and natural death benefits, disability benefits and repatriation costs in the case of death as well as medical evacuation/repatriation provisions and compassionate care benefits which cover the costs of one family member to visit in the case of critical illness or injury. Perhaps the most innovative dimension of the Pioneer plan allows for 'subsistence allowances' (for up to 6 months) for 'any migrant worker who is involved in a case of litigation for the protection of his/her rights in the receiving country' (Anonymous 2012).

The Filipino experiment is only one of several emerging attempts to provide insurance for migrants who flow through regularized channels. The Indonesian government has long been interested in insurance products for its approximately 2.5 million migrants who work legally abroad. A programme developed between 2006 and 2010 provides indemnity against 'cases of loss, damage, violence of financial loss' (International Organization for Migration 2010: 26). The Indonesian Migrant Worker Insurance Program (IMWIP) is, like the Pioneer offering, compulsory for registered migrants. Unlike the Filipino programme, however, migrants themselves are required to contribute, bearing the cost of their own coverage directly.[23] The standard policy adopted for migrants covers both the entire period of work abroad as well as a five month period in advance and one month upon returning from that work period. The standard policy offers coverage for death, illness, failure to depart, unemployment during contracted period, legal problems, early removal, physical or sexual assault, mental illness, placement failure or losses due to actions of third parties during return to Indonesia (Farbenblum, Taylor-Nicholson and Paoletti 2013: 90–91).

A more widely popular form of micro-insurance, directed to both formal *and* irregular migrants has been mounted by Spain's SegurCaixa, the insurance component of La Caixa, a large savings and loan cooperative with over 4,500 branches serving working and middle class populations. Because La Caixa operates as a cooperative structure, and because it makes use of a wide branch footprint across the country, it can offer insurance products to migrant workers at costs that are relatively low but which do not require premium subsidies. To date, SegurCaixa's reaches 80,000 migrants with policies designed for both their own losses as well as the losses felt by family members in countries of origin; offering 'coverage on both sides of the border' (Magnoni et al. 2010: 6). The core of its coverage for migrants involves death and repatriation insurance as well as an offering that extends regular monthly income to bereaved families in countries of origin in the case of death (Churchill 2012). Its two most explicit products designed for migrants include *SegurCaixa Repatriación*, which offers protections designed to cover the cost of repatriation, companion flights for bereaved relatives and a Eu 3,000 payout in the case of death, and *Seguringreso,* a form of accident coverage for accidental and critical disabilities (see Magnoni *et al.* 2010: 7–8).

Among the most ambitious schemes, however, are those which both harness remittances explicitly and simultaneously redirect remittance flows into and through insurance mechanisms. These experiments both tie into remittances and offer indemnities against the uncertainty remittance disruption can often create; leveraging remittances as the basis of premiums and constructing distribution networks on top of existing remittance transfer networks. Country of origin schemes are particularly attractive to irregular migrants because the 'undocumented status of many immigrants can pose serious challenges when purchasing insurance products in their host countries' (Powers, Magnoni and Zimmerman 2012: 355). Because undocumented workers can often find it difficult to access insurance in host countries, the only meaningful options they can access are those rooted in country of origin. Not only, however, do these schemes harness remittances in country of origin as a basis for premiums, but also often sublimate remittances into insured assets. These schemes effectively convert or translate remittances into other forms of financial asset for remittance recipients.

The most important innovator in these kinds of remittance insurance offerings is Seguros Futuro, El Salvador's only cooperative insurance firm, which has successfully mounted repatriation and remittance-life products to migrants and their families (Churchill 2012). Explicitly designed to 'foster a risk management culture in families receiving remittances', the Seguros experiment began as an attempt to address the immense financial hardships associated with the death of migrants for transnational families (Seguros Futuro 2011: 2; ICMIF 2011). Although many families attempt to self-insure against these risks (by, for example, sending multiple members of their families into the USA), Seguros has tried to develop formalized risk management mechanisms and more 'rational' and long-term responses to the uncertainties that govern their lives. As commentators have noted, 'mechanisms that allow transnational families to use a portion of their remittances to purchase formal insurance could help reduce their vulnerability' (Powers, Magnoni and Zimmerman 2011: vi). After years of experimentation, Seguros now offers a combined repatriation/remittance insurance package for the families of migrants. One configuration of the programme offers both comprehensive repatriation insurance (collection of remains in the USA or Canada, formal repatriation of body, consular arrangements and air transport to El Salvador) and 12 continued remittance payments in the event of death. The remittance component 'provides the family with an ongoing monthly remittance for one year' up to a limit of US $850 per month (Powers, Magnoni and Zimmerman 2011: 18). In the words of project coordinators, the repatriation/remittance offering, 'complemented by financial education, will reduce the vulnerability of clients and encourage conscientious investment of remittances' (Seguros Futuro 2011: 3). In emphasizing 'long-term investment', and in constructing a mechanism that channels remittance flows into a longer term horizon, the Seguros scheme both absorbs remittances and converts them into a certain kind of financial asset – in an immediate sense, it redirects and supplants the flow of remittances. Remittances are no longer irregular flows of short term liquidity, but are reconstituted as a *financial* asset with longer durability.

The kind of conversion enacted in these schemes instrumentalize a certain kind of financial value in remittance flows, irregular or informal flows which are reconstituted into insurance assets. In doing so, remittances are converted into and displaced by a stream of insurance guarantees. Ultimately, formalized remittances are converted into risk assets that can, themselves, be transferred to international risk markets as investable assets. These are experiments which extract value from the unique conditions that prevail among the most vulnerable populations in the global economy, a novel method of converting the (inert) chains that thread transnational families together into formalized and longer-term financial value both for migrants and for the financial agents which accomplish it.

Converting remittances into formal risk management mechanisms also constitutes migrants and their families as certain kinds of financial subjects (Langley 2007). By emphasizing remittances as a key to longer-term practices of 'investment', these kinds of insurance schemes enact a neoliberal form of economic self and citizenship. Increasingly, as Kunz has demonstrated, the global remittance regime 'is based upon, and contributes to, the spreading and deepening of neoliberal forms of governing' (Kunz 2011:171).[24] Experiments like the Seguros offering mobilize migrant families as actors that might take responsibility for their own economic security by adopting longer-term conceptions of enterprise:

> a narrowly-defined market-promoting model of financial citizenship that exults self-sufficiency, entrepreneurship and empowerment as its key elements and an idealized transnational financial subject who is responsible for guaranteeing not only their own economic and social security but also contributing to the economic and social development of their community of origin through their … productive investments and enterprise.
>
> (Zapata 2013: 97)

Both index and remittance insurance evoke the sense of experiment that Lobo-Guerrero situates at the heart of insurance; an 'entrepreneurial' approach to insurance and its own frontiers. In this context, enterprise has a double meaning. On one hand, it signals the enterprising work required to prospect for and construct new asset streams among those places and bodies not well acquainted with insurance. Both index and remittance insurance embody this kind of entrepreneurial approach; creative and novel experiments in adapting financial techniques for and harnessing value form the unique conditions (the unique fragilities, displacements and human vulnerabilities) that exist at the very edges of the financial economy. Both sets of experiments have improvised unique ways to instrumentalize unique forms of (latent) value. On the other hand, these experiments imply a second inflection of enterprise noted in the second section of this chapter – a mode of self and citizen uniquely committed to individual responsibility and self-investment. Index and remittance insurance offer mechanisms built around a contention that individuals, even those most vulnerable to (yet often invisible within) global economic pressures, could become subjects capable of bearing responsibility for their own risks, and for the commodification and transfer of those risks to others. In doing so, these experiments mark out the striking but complex relationship between insurance and liberalism. Micro-insurance is an ambitious mapping of risk, and of the ways in which those risks could be managed at the edges of the global economy. It is the depth of this ambition – an attempt to extract value from the dramatic fragility which predominates at those edges – which invokes important questions not only about the implantation of insurance across new contexts, and in new and innovative forms, but also, at the same time, about the possible limits of the formalized risk management logic insurance so keenly seeks to achieve.

Conclusion: risk management/social protection

Insurance, as I have argued in this chapter, occupies a unique location in the genealogies of finance. It is central to both the historical processes by which finance became recast as a rational pursuit as well as the ongoing processes through which the shape, reach and status of finance continue to change. This chapter locates micro-insurance within the larger context of these genealogies as a case where the complexities that mark finance at its own edges are made particularly visible. Most intimately, micro-insurance seeks to convert the everyday populations it targets as subjects capable of some degree of capacity to bear risks on their own. This is accomplished by encouraging subjects both to take responsibility for the management of their own risks and to access private insurance as a way to aggregate and transfer those risks. This is often framed as a long-term act of investment, of projecting for the self a future. At a broader level, micro-insurance enacts innovative practices at its own frontiers. Confronted with the unique vulnerabilities and economic disenfranchisement which typifies the very edges of the global economy, micro-insurers have had to find innovative mechanisms to extract financial value.

In these various ways, micro-insurance is now established alongside micro-credit as a prominent financial practice explicitly targeted at the global poor, and key to the ways in which those populations might be converted into financialized assets. Insurance, however, first in Europe and then in North America, was introduced alongside struggles for various forms of social protection, not as its perfect substitute. By contrast, micro-insurance is often introduced in contexts either devoid of meaningful social protection measures or ravaged by welfare state retrenchment, economic collapse or austerity of one kind or another. Although advocates, especially those associated with NGOs, consistently note that micro-insurance cannot be implemented in abstracted form or as a singular response to larger issues of poverty or inequality, micro-insurance schemes are often implemented in stark isolation from other kinds of social or political interventions. In this kind of isolation, micro-insurance offers a form of risk mitigation which is, limited by the premiums that insured populations are able to afford. Insurance, in this basic sense, remains a form of 'investment', the returns of which are prescribed, or at least constrained in some general way, by initial allocations. This arrangement contrasts with notions of social security or social insurance in which levels of security are guaranteed in advance; a way of securing risk not by amortizing it against premiums but by spreading it across society. 'As a risk-pooling tool', Deblon and Loewe note, 'financed mainly by premiums, micro-insurance involves a horizontal redistribution of income between peers with comparable risk profiles, rather than on a vertical redistribution from the rich to the poor' (Deblon and Loewe 2012: 49). As a technique of risk aggregation, micro-insurance contrasts with the commitments of social security by facilitating returns that are directly related to an initial investment.

The growth of micro-insurance is, moreover, consistent with broader trends in global insurance networks of which it has become a subset. Insurance networks, now among the most significant players in global financial markets, have been dramatically reshaped since the early 1970s when most insurance operators remained confined to national or local markets. Since the collapse of the Bretton Woods regime insurance networks have become more complex, more fully globalized and more deeply integrated into global financial markets. A number of trends have created favourable conditions for the rapid global growth of insurance since the early 1970s: the decline in welfare state transfers has helped constitute a larger market for private insurers; capital account liberalization has allowed for greater penetration of large global insurance firms into formerly protected markets; and the gradual dissolution of regulatory distinctions between insurers, banks and investment houses has allowed greater opportunities for insurance firms to establish important and increasingly sophisticated linkages between insurance offerings and global capital markets (Borscheid and Haueter 2013: 28–29). Micro-insurance is a subset of these globalizing insurance networks; a set of practices interior to these global networks. It is also a connective tissue which enfolds the rituals of insurance (its languages, practices and ways of ordering value) into the everyday lives of populations at the very edges of the financial economy.

One of the languages micro-insurance most readily inserts into the fabric of everyday lives is the discourse of risk management. As Michael Power has noted, 'risk management is becoming an administrative paradigm for all forms of organization' (Power 2004: 55). For Power, this ubiquitous language of risk management brings with it, despite its benefits, its own overstated claims. It signals, most importantly, a fantasy that uncertainty could be both perfectly knowable and expertly managed. In its wake, Power calls for a new political discourse of uncertainty which would acknowledge limits to our capacities (or even inclinations) to know and manage future uncertainty. This new discourse of uncertainty would foreground 'a public politics in which myths of perfect manageability are laid to rest but necessarily imperfect, humanly designed and operated, risk management systems continue to support an engagement with unknowable futures' (Power 2004: 58). For Power there is both a practical and political intention in proposing a new politics of uncertainty. Pragmatically, this political discourse acknowledges a certain inescapable uncertainty that attends any rendering of the future. More politically, however, this discourse embraces uncertainty as the prerequisite for the construction of possible alternative futures. Before any future can be realized, it must first be both uncertain and, by extension, possible. 'It would depend essentially on human capacities to imagine *alternative futures* to the present, rather than quantitative ambitions to predict *the future*' (Power 2004: 61, emphasis in original). The spaces of fringe finance, as Chapter 7 will attest, are not immune to calls for more 'humanly designed and operated' financial practices. The main lines of force transversed by fringe finance, however, are converging not on alternatives to, but practices which exist precisely *within* the logic of mainstream financial or risk management. This entails not only an attempt to incorporate the very edges of the global economy into the ambit of mainstream financial practices, but also an ambition to consecrate those practices as *formalized* (and legitimate) forms.

Notes

1 As Alborn affirms: 'the prudential and speculative sides of life insurance combined in the nineteenth century to create new ways of thinking about life and death … [when] confronted with these many associations between life insurance and gambling, most Victorians were quite content to have it both ways' (Alborn 2009: 305–311).

2 I do not want to overstate the importance of this moment, however, as many historians have noted the ambiguity of the Gambling Act and the longer process required to draw a more discrete line between life insurance and gambling (Alborn 2008: 4).

3 McFall has argued that life insurance companies were generally and consistently quite cautious about adopting statistical and mathematical certainty – doing so only on a 'glacial pace' (McFall 2011).

4 As early as the 1850s, for example, insurers were consistently offering 'life insurance bonuses' which began to split earnings between shareholders and policyholders (Alborn 2009: 166–167).

5 As Zelizer notes, by the 1870s American insurers generally moved away from moral themes in advertising to themes more consistent with rational business explanations (Zelizer 1979: 94).

6 Over the course of 2012, for example, the volume of gross weighted micro-insurance premiums Allianz issued rose 37% from 57.4 Euro to 78.6 Euro. This translates into an increase of 340% in the number of insured persons in its portfolio up to 17. 1 million, making it the largest single global provider of micro-insurance (Allianz 2013: 18; Allianz 2013: 14; Bajaj Allianz 2012).

7 Note that Swiss Re estimate the total potential market for micro-insurance based on two groupings – the 'commercially viable' micro-insurance market consisting of the 2.6 billion people who earn between US $1.25 and $4 a day, and a further 1.4 billion (the 'extreme poor') who subsist on less than $1.25 per day (Swiss Re 2010: 9).

8 Some of this growth in micro-insurance has come from the formalization or extension of informal risk mitigation schemes such as mutual aid associations which pool their resources, burial societies which defray funeral costs in exchange for regular contributions and rotating savings and credit associations (Midgley 2012: 157). As Timothy Besley notes, these mechanisms are generally considered 'informal' because they are rarely organized as formal contractual arrangements, even though they are often governed by clear norms or expectations (Besley 1995).

9 This enunciation of insurance as thrift, however, was confronted with serious obstacles. Life Insurance would not only 'paralyze man's efforts' but jeopardize the very principle of self-help. 'It is calculated to encourage reliance upon something beside economy and industry' (quoted in Zelizer 1979: 82).

10 This footnote draws upon and is elaborated in Aitken 2014.

11 De Bock and Gelade also report on a widely circulated case of research among African communities in which insurers have often been confronted with a cultural norm of 'balanced reciprocity' which ostensibly conflicts with insurance practices. Of particular concern was a cultural claim that premiums should be refunded if no payout occurs (De Bock and Gelade 2012: 6).

12 With respect to investment Dalal and Morduch note that insurance training programmes should emphasize the ways in which 'insurance, like savings, can be seen as an investment that yields future cash flows' (Dalal and Morduch 2010: 5).

13 This innovation has been partly facilitated by the micro-insurance Innovation Facility, an initiative managed by the International Labor Organization's Social Finance Programme committed to 'pushing the frontiers of micro-insurance around the world'. (See Micro-insurance Innovation Facility 2013; UK Actuarial Profession Micro-insurance Working Party 2012.)

14 It is important to note that perhaps the earliest reference to index based insurance occurs in 1949 in a Ph.D. dissertation written at the University of Chicago by Harold Halcrow whose dissertation committee included Milton Friedman, a figure who would become singularly associated with the proliferation and widespread adoption of derivatives products (see Halcrow 1949; Smith and Watts 2012: 6).

15 Moreover, by 2005, Basix also began to offer generic index products 'suitable for all principle grass-fed crops within the same agroclimatic region' (Manuamorn 2007: 10)

16 The Mexican government has offered its own unique experiment in the broader use of index insurance. The government has developed several index products, held with international insurance companies, as a hedge for public payouts by the state in the case of catastrophic weather-related agricultural damage. The index products essentially allow the state to offer payouts without placing an onerous burden on public finances (Gonzalez 2009; see also Fuchs and Wolff 2011: 508; Skees 2006: 38).

17 In the words of key managers, GIIF 'is particularly interested in risk transfer projects that address the entire product development cycle leading to actualization of tangible results' (Maina and Buehler 2012: 12)

18 But for a sceptical view see Binswanger-Mkhize (2012) who notes that index insurance may still not be as effective or rational as self-insurance mechanisms.

19 Cole et al. do report that there is some preliminary evidence that 'access to index-based insurance increases the use of agricultural inputs, such as fertilizer' (Cole *et al.* 2012: viii).

20 In 'the presence of basis risk it is possible that households end up without payouts … and yet still may pay premiums' (Sarris 2013: 382).

21 Note that this is an inherently conservative figure because it captures only recorded remittance flows. Unrecorded flows could substantially increase these figures.

22 One prominent programme focused on internal migrants entails a suite of workers' personal accident and health insurance developed for internal migrant workers in China. Since March 2009, the project has insured over 500,000 workers. See People's Insurance Company of China 2012.

23 Most often the compulsory insurance is arranged by placement agencies which are allowed to recover costs directly from migrants. Despite its comprehensiveness, the programme has lost serious credibility and been haunted by widespread complaints since its inception, including the suggestion that claims are simply not processed in a timely or effective manner (Farbenblum, Taylor-Nicholson and Paoletti 2013: 88; International Organization for Migration 2010: 27).

24 Kunz (2011: 173) usefully argues that the neoliberal subjectivities that have become associated with the global remittance trend (GRT) are deeply gendered. As imagined in the GRT, 'the individual is composed of, and responsible for her/his human capital; the individual is responsible for managing her/his own needs and well being … Yet … this creation of neoliberal subjectivities … is a deeply gendered process.'

References

Agricultural Finance Corporation. 2011. *Report on Impact Evaluation of Pilot Weather Based Crop Insurance (WBCIS)*. Mumbai: Department of Agriculture and Cooperation, Ministry of Agriculture, Government of India.

Aitken, R. 2014. 'A Genealogy of Financial Conduct'. Unpublished manuscript.

Alborn, T. 2008. 'A License to Bet: Life Insurance and the Gambling Act in the British Courts'. *Connecticut Insurance Law Journal*. Vol. 14, No.1: 1–20.

Alborn, T. 2009. *Regulated Lives: Life Insurance and British Society, 1800–1914*. Toronto: University of Toronto Press.

Allianz. 2013. *Micro-insurance at Allianz Group: 2012 Full Year Report*. Munich: Allianz SE.

Anonymous. 2012. 'Pioneer Inks MOA for OFW Insurance Needs'. *The Philippine Star*. 21 November 2012.

Aoul, S. 2012. 'Migration and Social Protection'. Talk given at the launch of the *Micro-insurance Compendium*, Geneva.

Bajaj Allianz. 2012. *Annual Report 2012*. Delhi: Bajaj Allianz Life Insurance Co. Ltd.

Barnett, B. 2008. 'Poverty Traps and Index-Based Risk Transfer Products'. *World Development*. Vol. 36, No. 10: 1766–1785.

Barnett, B. 2010. *Challenges with Developing Weather Index Insurance for Rural Areas of Lower Income Countries*. Humboldt: GlobalAgRisk Inc.

Barnett, B., C. Barnett and J. Skees. 2008. 'Poverty Traps and Index-Based Risk Transfer Products'. *World Development*. Vol. 36, No. 10: 1765–1785.

Beiner, C. 2012. 'Pricing in Micro-insurance Markets'. *World Development*. Vol. 41: 132–144.

Besley, T. 1995. 'Nonmarket Institutions for Credit and Risk Sharing in Low-Income Countries'. *Journal of Economic Perspectives*. Vol. 9, No. 3: 115–127.

Binkley, S. 2011. 'Psychological Life as Enterprise: Social Practice and the Government of Neo-liberal Interiority'. *History of the Human Sciences*. Vol. 14, No. 3: 83–102.

Binswanger-Mkhize, H. 2012. 'Is There too Much Hype about Index-Based Agricultural Insurance?' *The Journal of Development Studies*. Vol. 48, No. 2: 187–200.

Borscheid, P. 2013. 'Sub-Saharan Africa: Overview'. Eds. P. Borscheid and N. Haueter. *World Insurance: The Evolution of a Global Risk Network*. Oxford: Oxford University Press.

Borscheid, P. and N. Haueter. 2013. *World Insurance: The Evolution of a Global Risk Network*. Oxford: Oxford University Press.

Brown, R., F. Carmignani and G. Fayad. 2013. 'Migrants' Remittances and Financial Development: Macro- and Micro-Level Evidence of a Perverse Relationship'. *The World Economy*. Vol. 36, No. 5: 636–660.

Burchell, G. 1991. 'Peculiar Interests: Civil Society and Governing "The System of Natural Liberty"'. *The Foucault Effect: Studies in Governmentality*. Eds. G. Burchell, C. Gordon and P. Miller. Chicago, IL: University of Chicago Press: 119–150.

Campbell, D. 1998. *Writing Security*. Minneapolis: University of Minnesota Press.

Castaneda, E. 2012. 'Living in Limbo: Transnational Households, Remittances and Development'. *International Migration*. Vol. 51, No. 1: 13–35.

CEREMS. 2012. *Feasibility of Resource Mobilization Among Migrant Communities for Developing Health Micro-insurance in the Country of Origin*. Geneva: International Labour Organization/Micro-insurance Innovation Facility.

Churchill, C. 2012. *The Win-Win Potential of Micro-insurance for Migrants*. Geneva: International Labour Organization.

Churchill, C. 2013. *Micro-insurance: 1 Billion Covered by 2020*. Luxembourg: Micro-insurance Network.

Clarke, G. 1999. *Betting on Lives: The Culture of Life Insurance in England, 1695–1775*. Manchester: Manchester University Press.

Clarke, D., O. Mahul, K. Rao and N. Verma. 2012. *Weather Based Crop Insurance in India*. Washington: International Bank for Reconstruction and Development.

Cole, S., G. Basitan, S. Vyas, C. Wendel and D. Stein. 2012. *The Effectiveness of Index-Based Micro-Insurance in Helping Smallholders Manage Weather-Related Risks.* London: EPPI-Centre, Social Science Research Unit, Institute of Education, University of London.

Collier, B., J. Skees and B. Barnett. 2009. 'Weather Index Insurance and Climate Change: Opportunities and Challenges in Lower Income Countries'. *The Geneva Papers.* 34: 401–424.

Crayen, D., C. Hainz and C. De Martinez. 2012. *Remittances, Banking Status and the Usage of Insurance Schemes.* Munich: IFO Institute.

Crayen, D., C. Hainz and C. De Martinez.2013. 'Remittances, Banking Status and the Usage of Insurance Schemes'. *The Journal of Development Studies.* Vol. 49, No. 6: 861–875.

Dalal, A. 2011. *Emerging Practices in Consumer Education: Briefing Note.* Luxembourg: Micro-insurance Network.

Dalal, A. and J. Morduch. 2010. *The Psychology of Micro-insurance: Small Chances Can Make a Surprising Difference.* Geneva: Micro-Insurance Innovation Facility.

De Bock, O. and W. Gelade. 2012. *The Demand for Micro-insurance: A Literature Review.* Geneva: Micro-insurance Innovation Facility.

De Goede, M. 2004. 'Repoliticising Financial Risk'. *Economy and Society.* Vol. 33, No. 2: 197–217.

De Goede, M. 2005. *Virtue, Fortune and Faith: A Genealogy of Finance.* Minneapolis: University of Minnesota Press.

Deblon, Y. and M. Loewe. 2012. 'The Potential of Micro-insurance for Social Protection'. *Protecting the Poor: A micro-insurance Compendium, Vol. 11.* Eds. C. Churchill and M. Matul. Geneva: International Labour Organization.

Dror, I., A. Dalal and M. Matul. 2010. *Emerging Practices in Consumer Education on Risk Management and Insurance.* Geneva: Micro-insurance Innovation Facility, Briefing Note 3.

Dror, I., K. Jenkins, K. Motegi. and J. Siltanen. 2011. *A Landscape Study of Micro Insurance Education.* New Delhi: Micro Insurance Academy.

Elabed, G., M. Bellemare, M. Carter and C. Guirkinger. 2013. 'Managing Basis Risk with Multiscale Index Insurance'. *Agricultural Economics.* Vol. 44: 419–431.

Ericson, R., A. Doyle and D. Barry. 2003. *Insurance as Governance.* Toronto: University of Toronto Press.

Ewald, F. 1991. 'Insurance Risk'. *The Foucault Effect: Studies in Governmentality.* Eds. G. Burchill, C. Gordon and P. Miller. Chicago: University of Chicago Press, 197–210.

EYGM Limited. 2013. *Global Insurance Outlook.* London: EYGM Limited.

Farbenblum, B., E. Taylor-Nicholson and S. Paoletti. 2013. *Migrant Workers' Access to Justice at Home: Indonesia.* New York: Open Society Foundations.

Foucault, M. 2008. *The Birth of Biopolitics: Lectures at the College De France, 1978–79.* Ed. Michel Senellart. London: Palgrave Macmillan.

FPV. 2012. 'Largest Recruitment Group Signs up with Pioneer Insurance for OFW's Insurance Needs'. *Balita.* 8 November 2012.

French, S. and J. Kneale. 2009. 'Excessive Financialisation: Insuring Lifestyles, Enlivening Subjects, and Everyday Spaces of Biosocial Excess'. *Environment and Planning: Society and Space.* Vol. 27, No. 6: 1030–1053

Fuchs, A. and H. Wolff. 2011. 'Concept and Unintended Consequences of Weather Insurance: The Case of Mexico'. *American Journal of Agricultural Economics.* Vol. 93, No. 2: 505–511.

Gine, X., L. Mendard, R. Townsend and J. Vickery. 2010. *Micro-insurance: A Case Study of the Indian Rainfall Index Insurance Market*. New York: Federal Reserve Bank of New York.

Gonzalez, A. 2009. 'Innovations in Insuring the Poor: Index Insurance Applied to Agriculture, the Mexican Case'. *International Food Policy Research Focus Brief.* Vol. 17, No. 15.

Halcrow, H. 1949. 'Actuarial Structures for Crop Insurance'. *Journal of Farm Economics.* Vol. 31, No. 3: 418–443.

Hazell, P., J. Anderson, N. Balzer, A. Hastrup Clemenson, U. Hess and F. Rispoli. 2010. *Potential for Scale and Sustainability in Weather Index Insurance for Agricultural and Rural Livelihoods.* Rome: International Fund for Agricultural Development/World Food Programme.

Hess, U. 2010. *Index Insurance.* Presentation prepared for the *Innovative Finance Marketplace* workshop, 4 March 2010, Paris, France.

ICMIF. 2011. *Solidarity and Protection Beyond Borders.* Washington, DC: ICMIF Micro-insurance.

IFC. 2011. *Global Index Insurance Facility.* Washington, DC: International Finance Corporation.

IFC. 2013. *IFC-Global Index Insurance Facility: Response to the EU Green Paper on the Insurance of Natural and Man-Made Disasters.* Washington, DC: International Finance Corporation.

International Fund for Agricultural Development. 2011. *Weather Index-Based Insurance for Agricultural Development: A Technical Guide.* Rome: International Fund for Agricultural Development/World Food Programme.

International Organization for Migration. 2010. *Labour Migration from Indonesia.* Jakarta: IOM Indonesia.

Kelkar, U., C. James and R. Kumar. 2006. *The Indian Insurance Industry and Climate Change.* New Delhi: Teri Press.

KPMG. 2013a. *Financial Services in Africa*. Cape Town: KPMG Africa.

KPMG. 2013b. *Regulatory Practice Letter RPL 13–11: Payday Loans and Deposit Advance Products – CFPB Report; FDIC, OCC and Federal Reserve Guidance.* Wilmington DE: KPMG LLP.

Kunz, R. 2011. *The Political Economy of Global Remittances: Gender, Governmentality and Neoliberalism.* London: Routledge.

Langley, P. 2007. 'Uncertain Subjects of Anglo-American Financialization'. *Cultural Critique.* Vol. 65: 67–91.

Leblois, A. and P. Quirion. 2010. *Agricultural Insurances Based on Meteorological Indices: Realizations, Methods and Research Agenda.* Note Di Lavoro Della Fondazione Eni Enrico Mattei, 71.

Lemke, T. 2011. 'Critique and Experience in Foucault'. *Theory, Culture and Society.* Vol. 28, No. 4: 26–48.

Leyshon, A. and N. Thrift. 2007. 'The Capitalization of Almost Everything: The Future of Finance and Capitalism'. *Theory, Culture & Society.* Vol. 24, Nos. 7–7: 97–115.

Lloyd's. 2009. *Insurance in Developing Countries: Exploring Opportunities in Micro-insurance.* London: Lloyd's of London.

Lloyd's. 2013. *Lloyd's Global Underinsurance Report*. London: Lloyd's of London.

Lobo-Guerrero, L. 2011. *Insuring Security: Biopolitics, Security and Risk.* London: Routledge.

Mackenzie, D. 2006. *An Engine Not a Camera: How Financial Models Shape Markets.* Cambridge MA: MIT Press.

Magnoni, B., A. Lovoi, J. Brown and R. Thornton. 2010. *Risk Across Borders: A Study of the Potential of Micro-insurance Products to Help Migrants Cope with Cross Border Risks.* New York: Inter-American Development Bank.

Maina, P. and M. Buehler. 2012. *Global Index Insurance Facility.* Washington, DC: International Finance Corporation.

Manuamorn, O. 2007. *Scaling Up Micro-insurance: The Case of Weather Insurance for Smallholders in India*. Washington, DC: International Bank for Reconstruction and Development.

Matsuda, A., T. Kurosaki and Y. Sawada. 2013. *Rainfall and Temperature Index Insurance in India: Project Documentation.* Tokyo: Institute of Economic Research, Hitotsubashi University.

Matul, M., A. Dalal, O. De Bock and W. Gelade. 2013. *Why People Do Not Buy Micro-insurance and What Can We Do About it*, Geneva: Micro-insurance Innovation Facility.

McFall, L. 2007. 'The Disinterested Self: The Idealized Subject of Life Assurance'. *Cultural Studies* Vol. 21, Nos. 4–5: 591–609.

McFall, L. 2011. 'A "Good, Average Man": Calculation and the Limits of Statistics in Enrolling Insurance Customers'. *The Sociological Review.* Vol. 59, No. 4: 662–684.

Merkin, R. 1980. 'Gambling by Insurance: A Study of the Life Assurance Act 1774'. *Anglo-American Law Review*: 331.

Micro-insurance Innovation Facility. 2013. *Annual Report 2012*. Geneva: International Labour Office.

Midgley, J. 2012. 'Social Protection and the Elderly in the Developing World: Mutual Aid, Micro-Insurance and the State'. *Journal of Comparative Social Welfare.* Vol. 28, No. 2: 153–163.

Murphy, S. 2010. *Investing in Life: Insurance in Antebellum America*. Baltimore: The Johns Hopkins University Press.

Nieto, J., S. Cook, P. Laderarch, M. Fisher and P. Jones. 2010. 'Rainfall Index Insurance to Help Smallholder Farmers Manage Drought Risk'. *Climate and Development*. Vol. 2, No. 3: 233–247.

O'Malley, P. 2002. 'Imagining Insurance: Risk, Thrift, and Life Insurance in Britain'. *Embracing Risk: The Changing Culture of Insurance and Responsibility.* Chicago, IL: University of Chicago Press: 97–114.

People's Insurance Company of China. 2012. *Learning Journey: Migrant Worker's Personal Accident Health Insurance.* Geneva: Micro-insurance Innovation Facility.

Pioneer Life. 2012. *Overseas Filipino Workers' Family Savers and Wellness Club: Learning Journey.* Geneva: Micro-insurance Innovation Facility.

Power, M. 2004. *The Risk Management of Everything: Rethinking the Politics of Uncertainty.* London: Demos.

Powers, J., B. Magnoni and E. Zimmerman. 2011. *Formalizing the Informal Insurance Inherent in Migration: Exploring the Potential Links Between Migration and Micro-insurance.* Geneva: International Labour Organization, Micro-insurance Paper No. 7.

Powers, J., B. Magnoni and E. Zimmerman. 2012. 'Formalizing the Informal Insurance Inherent in Migration: Exploring the Potential Links Between Migration, Remittances and micro-insurance'. *Protecting the Poor: A Micro-insurance*

Compendium, Vol II. Eds. C. Churchill and M. Matul. Geneva: International Labour Office: 349–365

Preda, A. 2009. *Framing Finance: The Boundaries of Markets and Modern Capitalism.* Chicago, IL: University of Chicago Press.

Ratha, D., C. Eigen-Zucchi, S. Plaza, H. Wyss and S. Yi. 2013. *Migration and Remittance Flows: Recent Trends and Outlook, 2013–2016, Migration Development Brief 21.* Washington, DC: World Bank, Migration Remittances Team, Development Prospects Group.

Rimando, M. 2010. *Saving for the Future, Protecting Migrant Workers and their Families.* Manilla: International Labour Organization.

Rose, N. 1999. *Powers of Freedom: Reframing Political Thought.* Cambridge: Cambridge University Press.

Ruchismita, R. and C. Churchill. 2012. 'State and Market Synergies: Insights from India's Micro-insurance Success'. *Protecting the Poor: A Micro-insurance Compendium, Volume II.* Eds. C. Churchill and M. Matul. Geneva: International Labour Organization.

Said, E. 1977. 'Orientalism'. *The Georgia Review.* Vol. 31, No. 1: 162–206.

Sarris, A. 2013. 'Weather Index Insurance for Agricultural Development'. *Agricultural Economics.* Vol. 44: 381–384.

Skees, J. 2006. *Index Insurance for Weather Risk in Lower-Income Countries.* Washington DC: USAID.

Skees, J. 2010. *Challenges for Use of Index-Based Weather Insurance in Lower-Income Countries.* Lexington, KY: GlobalAgeRisk.

Smith, A., H. Smit and D. Chamberlain. 2011. *Beyond Sales: New Frontiers in Micro-insurance Distribution.* Geneva: International Labor Organization.

Smith, V. and M. Watts. 2012. *Index Based Agricultural Insurance in Developing Countries: Feasibility, Scalability and Sustainability.* Seattle, WA: Bill and Melinda Gates Foundation.

Stäheli, U. 2013. *Spectacular Speculation: Thrills, the Economy, and Popular Discourse.* Stanford, CA: Stanford University Press.

Stein, D. 2011. *Rainfall Index Insurance in India: Dissertation Submitted to the Department of Economics.* London: London School of Economics and Political Science.

Stoppa, A. and U. Hess. 2003. 'Design and Use of Weather Derivatives in Agricultural Policies: The Case of Rainfall Index Insurance in Morocco'. Paper prepared for *Agricultural Policy Reform and the WTO: Where Are We Heading?* 23–26 June, Capri Italy.

Swiss Re. 2010. *Sigma Report: Micro-insurance – Risk Protection for 4 Billion People.* Zurich: Swiss Re Ltd.

MidSwiss Re. 2013. *Sigma Report: World Insurance in 2012.* Zurich: Swiss Re Ltd.

UK Actuarial Profession Micro-insurance Working Party. 2013. *Life Micro-insurance Pricing Module.* London: UK Actuarial Profession's Working Party on Micro-insurance.

Vickery, J. 2010. *Micro-insurance: A Case Study of Rainfall Index Insurance in Semi-Arid India.* New York: Federal Reserve Bank of New York.

Wilmoth, J. and B. Hovy. 2013. *232 Million International Migrants living Abroad Worldwide.* New York: United Nations Department of Economic and Social Affairs.

World Bank. 2005. *Managing Agricultural Production Risk: Innovations in Developing Countries.* Washington, DC: International Bank for Reconstruction and Development.

World Bank. 2011. *Weather Index Insurance for Agriculture: Guidance for Development Practitioners.* Washington, DC: International Bank for Reconstruction and Development.

World Market Intelligence. 2013. *Leapfrog Investments Market Analysis.* New York: World Market Intelligence.

Zapata, G. 2013. 'The Migration-Development Nexus: Rendering Migrants as Transnational Financial Subjects Through Housing'. *Geoforum.* Vol. 47: 93–102.

Zelizer, V. 1979. *Morals and Markets: The Development of Life Insurance in the United States.* New York: Columbia University Press.

Zelizer, V. 2011. *Economic Lives: How Culture Shapes the Economy.* Princeton, NJ: Princeton University Press.

Part II

Fringe finance as a social practice

5 Making regular

Fringe-lending as a formal practice

In 1898, Hoyle, a savage critic of New York's financial interests, wrote a striking critique of the ways in which 'Wall Street operators' were increasingly able to disguise what he perceived as their essentially immoral practices within a cleverly constituted set of 'dignified headings'. 'We know', Hoyle pointed out, 'that the men who live in uptown mansions and belong to uptown churches think themselves to be, and want the world to consider them as "financiers"' (Hoyle 1899: 11). Despite this attempt to conceal themselves in the symbolic gestures of dignified life, Hoyle was still able to name Wall Street operators for what he thought they were. 'These men and their silent partners', he concluded, 'are the managers of the most stupendous gambling game the world has ever seen … a game that has its daily doings reported free of charge and at great length in every prominent newspaper in the country under the heading of "Financial Markets" or "Wall Street Doings" or some other dignified heading' (Hoyle 1898: 11). For Hoyle, even though Wall Street was clearly associated with dubious political and social pursuits, it was able nonetheless to cleanse itself by cultivating the endorsement of legitimate adornment. Key to the power of finance, for Hoyle, is its sanctioned claim to formal legitimacy; a claim made real in its cultivated associations with a culture of legitimate social life. Hoyle's assessment, I want to suggest in this chapter, offers an important signal of the kinds of cultural crucibles that the practices of fringe finance occupy. As Chapter 4 has argued, although finance appears in our political present as a scientific, rational and, by extension, legitimate practice, genealogies of finance reveal it to be a category long subject to contestations regarding its association with (and disentanglement from) dubious political, ethical or social practices: whimsy, irrationality, emotion, chance and, perhaps most importantly, gaming.

As Hoyle suggests, the settling of finance as a rational category is bound up in the ways in which it claims a certain kind of projected legitimacy. This chapter expands on Hoyle's assessment by noting the ways in which the legal and regulatory debates around fringe lending place particular emphasis on issues of formal legitimacy. Over the past decade there have been serious regulatory discussions about fringe lending: in the USA, Canada, the United Kingdom, Australia, South Africa and at the European Union. One of the reasons that these various discussions have been important is because they have featured prominent debates about the very borders of finance: questions about where the borders of legitimate and permissible finance should lie. These questions have most importantly been taken up in relation to issues regarding the formalization of fringe lending – the legal settling of a category of credit practices often categorized as predatory, usurious, harmful, illegal or, in some cases, criminal. The central claim of this chapter is that the regulatory and political debates around micro-lending have become an emblematic contemporary site where the legitimate and legal borders of finance are contested, shaped and reworked.

The most important outcome of many of these global debates over the past decade has been a wave of regulations governing fringe lending in new and diverse ways. Although they have taken a wide diversity of forms, I argue in this chapter that this body of regulation is performative, that these regulations bring into being, *perform*, the objects they purport only to manage. Across diverse settings, many lending and consumer finance regulations not only seek to manage but also formalize fringe lending as a legally legitimate and settled practice. This formalization, this regularization, has been enormously productive for lenders because it insulates them from legal and regulatory claims regarding their legitimacy. This regulatory performativity has been, at least in part, an outcome shaped by lenders themselves. Over the past decade many lenders and lobby groups have become preoccupied globally with the formalization of fringe lending and its reformulation as a legally settled and permissible form. This entails particular work aimed at a resettling of the boundaries of finance; a reworked diagram which maps the murky practices of high-cost credit as formalized objects. To accomplish this, fringe lenders have often sought to carve out new mechanisms of formal legitimacy which redraw the boundaries of finance and the borders that delineate legitimate from illegitimate, permissible from prohibited financial practices. In doing so, in redrawing these boundaries, fringe finance is a site where the borders of global finance are visibly negotiated and reworked. As this chapter suggests, three mechanisms of formal legitimacy have been particularly important to the regularization of fringe lending over the past decade: mechanisms of authorization, pricing formulae, and consumer protection devices.

Formalization, although key to the diagram and ambitions of fringe finance, is both a contested and unfinished project. As this chapter suggests, contestation is not simply a reaction to some prior or more fundamental move, but a practice internal to the processes of formalization. A growing web of activists, anti-poverty advocates, consumer protection specialists and 'social finance' organizers have been active in both disputing the claims to legitimacy of fringe lenders but also in shaping the kinds of regulation that have precisely sought to secure that legitimacy. In doing so, activists have been influential in the formulation of micro-lending regulation. The regulatory regimes that have emerged as a result are highly uneven; practices that alternately authorize and constrain, open and close, limit and deepen the possibilities of fringe finance. As I argue in this chapter, formalization has proven to be a malleable and sometimes unpredictable practice. Taken together, these various tensions imply a certain kind of unevenness in the ways in which formalization has been diagrammed and pursued. Although the diagram of fringe finance maps a straightforward process of formalization – a kind of clean reworking of the borders of legitimate financial practices – this chapter notes a kind of essential diversity to what formalization might mean and the political ends to which it might contribute.

Unevenness, however, is not only a description of the ways in which projects of formalization have unfolded. It is also an apt description of the kinds of activism and practice mounted by those opposed to formalization. The chapter concludes with a reflection on the inconsistencies of this kind of activism by emphasizing the geographical limits of its reach. Although, as Chapter 2 notes, forms of micro-lending have begun to reach into globalized spaces of practice, they have not been matched by equally expansive forms of activism. This activism has been oriented to a kind of 'regulatory localism', specifying local, national or subnational policy prescriptions for a space of practice that now exceeds that localism. Although many forms of globalized political action criss-cross the global political economy, micro-lending activism is definitively local in nature and seemingly ill-equipped to confront the web of globalized connections and practices that now animate the payday lending sector. The future possibilities *and* limitations of fringe lending will be shaped by the outcomes of these contests and by the capacities of a nascent fair credit movement to address itself in a meaningful manner to a global space of practice it mostly evades.

In this focus on unevenness this chapter is the first of three that constitute Part 2 of this book which aim, when taken together, to emphasize fringe finance not only as a diagram of clean lines (the theme that animates Part 1), but also as mappings that entail serious contestation, multiplicity or incoherences. Each of the chapters of Part 2 lay emphasis on a particular process that is central to the diagrams of fringe finance – in the case of this chapter, the ambition of formalization. Each of the chapters, however, emphasizes these practices as ambitions which are contested or uneven. Contestation, complexity and incoherences are not external to regulation of financial life, but help constitute the shape those practices take. The chapters of Part 2 emphasize the 'twisting lines' that attend all diagrams regardless of the clean lines they mark.

To develop this kind of argument, this chapter is divided into three broad sections. The first section grounds the paper in the concept of performativity. This section both reviews performativity as a concept that now occupies a key spot in the social studies of finance, and suggests that regulation can often be performative; practices that bring into being the objects they seek merely to manage. A second section builds on this conceptual frame by developing an argument that examines an international wave of regulatory practices over the past decade, much of which orbits around the possibilities that payday and micro-lending might be formalized as a legally settled and permissible object. This section argues that this regulation consists of mechanisms of formal legitimacy which redraw the borders of legitimate financial practice. A third section notes, however, that formalization is an essentially uneven project. At one level, formalization occupies the very centre of a diagram concerned with the extraction of value from the very edges of the financial system. At another level, however, the processes which codify actual terms of formalization are malleable in ways that can be twisted in unexpected or contested directions. This section emphasizes these twisting directions by documenting the work of the increasingly complicated networks of activists and advocates who have tried to shape regulatory initiatives in ways which not only regularize but which also limit fringe lending. To complicate the picture further, a conclusion documents some of the tensions and limitations of this activism. The futures of payday lending, this section concludes, will be shaped by the ways in which these activist networks will continue both to confront the expansive claims of lenders and come to terms with the globalized reach of those claims.

Performativity

As earlier chapters argued, separating finance from its 'others' has entailed sketching borders which mark finance (rational and technocratic) from those practices (gaming, emotion, panic, deceit, chance) which might taint its claims to legitimacy (Aitken 2007; de Goede 2005; Preda 2009; Stäheli 2013). In this chapter I want to situate the intense legal and regulatory debates around fringe lending, and the strategies developed by lenders to resolve those debates, as one fragment in these larger genealogies of finance and its borders. The main claim advanced in this chapter is that fringe and micro-lending is now one particularly important site where the contemporary borders of finance are negotiated and reworked. To suggest that the devices designed to regulate fringe lending are implicated in the ways in which the borders of finance are constituted, is to suggest that they bring into being the objects they purport only to manage, that it is, in some important ways, they are performative.

The origins of performativity lie in the work of J.L. Austin and his contention that words are utterances which not only describe but also perform actions. Performative utterances are those forms of language that create what they purport only to describe. These kinds of utterances, argues Austin, 'do not "describe" or "report" … The utterance is the performing of an action' (Austin 1962: 5–6). Performativity, understood broadly, refers to a broad range of practices which 'do not merely record a reality independent of themselves: they contribute powerfully to shaping, simply by measuring it, the reality they measure' (Callon 1998: 32). In Judith Butler's influential formulation, performativity is achieved not through single utterances but in iterative processes through which particular objects or identities are cited. It is only through this iteration – this repeated but fragile citation – that identities are performed. Identities, for Butler, are the ongoing effects of a system of discourse in which bodies become knowable. 'Reiteration', summarizes Butler, 'is the means through which that effect is established anew, time and again … processes of reiteration, re-establishment, and sedimentation' (Butler 2010: 149). As Sherlock (2014: 10) suggests, 'social identity categories … must be re-cited in order to remain normative' (Sherlock 2014: 10). Performative gestures are also 'conventional' in that they are reiterated through time in ways that work to 'compose' the bodies that are their effect (Loxey 2006: 120).

Performativity, especially as formulated by Butler, however, is not only a reference to the ways in which identities and objects are constituted but also the fragility of those very processes. Because bodies are identified in processes of iteration, they are vulnerable to corrosion and 'misfires' over time. Performativity, in Butler's terms, invokes a 'deconstructive' gesture 'which assumes that the process of making something introduces failure and undoing as a necessary part of that operation' (Butler 2010: 152).

Debates around performativity in relation to 'economic' categories now emphasize the ways in which economics, in Donald Mackenzie's terms, 'is not just about "knowing" the world, accurately or not. It is about producing it' (quoted in Esposito 2013: 103).[1] Although economics has often been resistant to the types of critical or cultural theory that now pervade the social sciences and humanities, performativity has begun to reframe economics as a body of knowledge deeply implicated in the object it claims to measure or describe. In Mackenzie and Millo's influential formulation, 'economics does not describe an existing external "economy", but brings that economy into being: economics *performs* the economy, creating the phenomena it describes' (Mackenzie and Millo 2003: 108; Brassett and Clarke 2012: 4). Put a bit differently by Breslau, the 'correspondences between economic theory and economic reality are not discovered but built' (Breslau 2013: 829–830). Performativity recasts economics not as an explanatory but productive form of knowledge – generating the very categories it reports by making the economy knowable in a very particular kind of way.

Eschewing the linguistic emphasis in Austin's work, much of the work on performativity in relation to finance has emphasized the calculative technologies and mechanisms which constitute and shape objects not in some abstract manner but in imminently tangible and material ways. This has entailed detailed attention to the actual devices which make calculation and pricing possible and which allow financial capital to form, circulate and be recorded.[2] This work emphasizes devices which make possible 'the seemingly rational calculations of valuation which, folding the uncertain future into the present as risks/returns, are crucial to the performance of contemporary financial markets' (Langley 2010: 76). Mackenzie and Millo, for example, argue that the models and formulae designed to assess derivatives pricing shaped those prices in ways that eventually conformed to the expectations the models generated. The 'model', they argue, 'did not describe an already existing world: when first formulated, its assumptions were quite unrealistic ... Gradually, though, the financial markets changed in a way that fitted the model' (Mackenzie and Millo 2003: 137). This type of analysis echoes Callon's influential contention that markets are performed not in language but in the kinds of devices, formula and 'equipment' which make calculation possible. Before financial exchange can occur, devices need to be constituted which allow calculations to be made, which generate or display prices and which allow accounts to be taken or settled. In Henriksen's (2013: 409) assessment this emphasizes 'the power of economics ... in formatting devices and frames for the equipment of calculative agents ... the frames of market action underpinning the operation of global capitalism at the capillary level are defined and produced'. Although these devices are often conceived as neutral conduits, they actually make calculation possible and, in doing so, perform the financial movements they claim merely to record.

Although it has been the impetus for creative forms of analysis, performativity has also generated important points of controversy. On one hand, the emphasis in the performativity literature on the techniques of finance – on what Langley (2010: 73) describes as the 'calculative devices, models, formulas and so on which do not simply record financial movements and machinations, but actually make possible pricing, exchange and circulation' – has been criticized as a form of analysis which submits to the technical rationality so central to the legitimizing claims of finance as a scientific pursuit. This approach, suggests Breslau, risks reproducing 'a technocratic narrative in which markets are materializations of economic theory' (Breslau 2013: 830). In more explicitly political terms, this is a risk that broader political or social questions are evacuated in an approach fixated narrowly on the technical infrastructure which makes particular financial or economic realities possible. As Christophers (2014: 83) puts it, 'the performativity of economics can end up being a rather empty truism unless the wider social and political materiality of such performativity is explored and conceptualized'. This echoes a larger debate regarding the explicitly political or normative dimension of an approach aimed at disrupting the claims of economic arrangements as natural or simply given objects. Triggered in part by Callon's own admonition to 'abandon the critical position', this is a controversy concerned with clarifying both the broader political context in which particular performative practices emerge and the kinds of political interventions performativity might enable.

Perhaps most vexing, however, is a distinction which Butler herself has registered between two different versions of performativity. This distinction rests on differences of inflection between illocutionary utterances which entail the authorizing capacity of a single speaking sovereign, and perlocutionary speech which depends on external conditions and which 'does not immediately or necessarily yield to the efficacy of sovereign authority' (Butler 2010: 151). For Brassett and Clark (2012), this entails a distinction between 'self actualizing statements' (performative utterances) and the 'overlapping' discourses that produce subjects capable of 'hearing' such utterances. Although illocution tends to emphasize the capacities of specific subjects to bring into being particular realities, perlocution implies that 'the social context in which an utterance is performed is crucial in determining the success of any given performance' (Brassett and Clarke 2012: 7). For Butler, illocutions are associated with sovereign power because they can authorize what they speak while perlocutions operate across more decentered planes involving the conditions in which particular realities are shaped:

> If illocutions produce realities, perlocutions depend upon them … Whereas illocutionary performatives produce ontological effects (bringing something into 'being'), perlocutionary performatives alter an ongoing situation. In this sense, the illocution appears more clearly to rely on a certain sovereign power of speech to bring into being what it declares, but a perlocution depends on an external reality and, hence, operates on the condition of non-sovereign power.
>
> (Butler 2010: 151)

Although these disputes are significant, there is also a way in which they often draw overly strict lines between inflections of performativity that might usefully be placed in tension with each other. The capacity of an authoritative speaker, for example, can only derive from broader discourses and practices which make that utterance possible and which establish points of receptivity for audiences. 'Illocution and perlocution are not as distinct as they might seem since the former implies the citation of a conventional language by which the speaker's authority is instated, much like the effect of the perlocution is never separate from the conditions that make it possible' (Karl 2013: 67). This implies the importance of what Brassett and Clarke refer to as a pragmatic approach sensitive to the complex ways in which different inflections of performativity relate in particular contexts. This suggests that performativity is not 'a question of isolating *either* particular speech acts/knowledge claims *or* developing detailed histories of the cultural production of [financial practices] … Rather the question is how to retain a pragmatic sensitivity to the contingency … of each' (Brassett and Clarke 2012: 5).[3] This view implies the importance of analyses which foreground the complex authorization of financial practices, the broader political context in which these performances are shaped, and the irregularities that escape those forms of regulation.

Regularizing a formalized field

Fringe finance is a diagram of the places where the reach of mainstream financial institutions is frayed. Although the populations that occupy these edges have always been exposed to a wide variety of credit relations, these practices have often been informal, self-organized, or legally dubious. In the USA, for example, poor populations continued to access high-cost credit throughout the postwar period even though usury laws were increasingly enforced against them. 'Notwithstanding courts' harsh penalties for such transactions', notes Spector, 'high-interest lending never disappeared; rather, it simply operated outside the bounds of the law' (Spector 2008b: 972). The fringe lending I examine in this chapter, by contrast, is definitively characterized by the ways in which it aims at reworking the borders that separate legally permissible from illegitimate finance in unique ways. This is not to dispute the claim made by Marcus Taylor (2012) that these edges are places long saturated in complex credit relations. I am suggesting, rather, that what is unique about fringe finance as a diagram is its mapping of these edges as spaces that could be addressed by formalized and regular practices. Many of the major fringe lending associations have made repeated public calls for forms of regulation that would formalize fringe lending as a legally permissible practice. 'Legislation', argues the Canadian pay day lenders association, 'should provide for a viable market that fosters competition so that consumers have needed access to credit' (CPLA 2009; MPUB 2013: 27).[4]

This ambition is animated by two interrelated objectives. First, the preoccupation with formalization is partly driven by a requirement to insulate lenders from the legal risk associated with their ambiguous status. Beginning in the 1990s, payday lenders in particular were exposed to increasingly complex legal struggles. At the core of these proceedings are issues relating to high rates of interest. Class action suits were launched across North America which began to exert pressure in rulings that awarded damages for usurious rates of interest. 'The rate of interest here is so incredibly high', notes one judgement, 'that it falls within the type of contract which is so objectionable that its illegality taints the entire contract' (quoted in MPUB 2009: 29). Another infamous ruling, issued by the Manitoba Court of Queen's Bench, asserted, simply, that 'courts will not assist lenders in the business of loaning short-term money at criminal interest rates' (quoted in Irving 2010: 163). Given the size of the largest networks of fringe lenders, and the volume of loans these networks extend, the mounting costs associated with these rulings quickly became an important long-term risk.[5]

A second objective bound up in the ambition of formalization is the possibility of widespread expansion. Many fringe lenders are increasingly keen to grow larger – a shape made possible by forms of legal formalization. 'Since the industry emerged', argues one lender, 'it has been plagued by legal uncertainty … The legal questions surrounding the industry have served as a major barrier to entry and a regulated market will produce far more lenders than are in the market today' (310 Loan 2007: 15; see also Aitken 2012).[6] In the face of serious legal risk and uncertainty, fringe lenders have turned to strategies designed not to cope in underground spaces but to forge a novel space for themselves as formally and legally settled practices.

As Timothy Mitchell has argued, this kind of formalization involves a very particular kind of line-drawing. Mitchell pays particular attention to the performative power involved in drawing and adjusting the lines that separate the practices that exist within the formally and legally defined space of economic relations and those outside of that space. 'To argue that the power of economics is performative', notes Mitchell, is to recognize its role in processes designed 'to constitute the apparent border between the market and the non-market … mechanisms that reorganize how people live, the political claims they can make, and the assets they can control' (Mitchell 2007: 248; see also Aitken 2010). Over the past 15 years in particular, fringe lenders have become particularly preoccupied with this kind of performativity, with moving itself across the lines that separate mainstream and illegitimate finance; with new mechanisms of formal legitimacy which both *authorize* but also *prefigure* payday lending as permissible and legitimate.[7]

Authorizing fringe lending

> Payday lending as we know it originated … when … legislatures were persuaded to create a special exemption to their state usury laws … for small dollar-lending. Under the protective umbrella of that new exemption, payday lending has spread and grown rapidly over the past two decades.
>
> (Richard Cordray, Director, Consumer Financial Protection Bureau, quoted in Cordray 2014)

For Brassett and Clarke (2012: 10), a pragmatic approach to performativity requires sensitivity to 'the chance exposures of political dilemmas and contests'. The pursuit of formalization by micro-lenders has been part of a much broader set of global political manoeuvres which have reshaped consumer credit regulation over the past decade. The most common approaches 'promotes access to consumer credit … consumer choice and the … individual management and responsibility for one's finances' (Ramsay and Williams 2009: 8).[8] Perhaps the most ambitious of these initiatives has unfolded in Australia in a process designed to establish a uniform national financial and credit environment in and around a newly consolidated regime governed by the national Australian Securities and Investment Commission (ASIC) (Australia 2009).[9]

Alongside and as part of these broader episodes of regulatory reform has been the authorization of fringe lending as a legally permissible form. One of the most important sets of regulatory mechanisms associated with fringe lending are illocutionary gestures of sovereign authorization. These mechanisms either authorize payday/micro lending by explicit legislative recognition or offer formal exemption from existing usury laws or regulatory restrictions. Many American states, for example, have crafted explicit legal authorizations of payday lending in forms of legislation designed to clarify its legal status.[10] Michigan explicitly authorizes payday lending and in doing so allows fees well beyond those allowed by the *Credit Reform Act* which generally caps lending rates at 25% APR. The Michigan law essentially legalizes payday lending, establishing a licensing process which authorizes lenders to operate without legal or regulatory uncertainty (Statute MCL 487.2121; see also Smith 2006). These rules are echoed in other permissive states which have used legal or regulatory mechanisms to authorize payday lending; regulations which have 'afforded payday lenders with avenues to displace and escape state usury limits' (Bellam and Talai 2012: 6). Some 27 states have now passed legislation which offers permissive authority for payday lending as a legally immune practice (see National Conference of State Legislatures 2013).

A similar, if protracted version of authorization has been managed in South Africa. Over the past 20 years there have been successive attempts to address both the widespread growth of micro-lending as well as entrenched (racialized) inequalities in access to credit stemming from the apartheid regime. In 1992 the government exempted small loans (under R 10,000) from the interest rate limitations of the *Usury Act* (originally passed in 1968), a move which facilitated growth in both existing small-loan credit as well as in microfinance initiatives.[11] Successive waves of regulatory changes have continued to authorize high-cost credit.

At the heart of each of these waves of reforms are carefully crafted legal exemptions from existing interest rate caps or usury laws. The 1999 reforms, for example, were enabled by a formal exemption order which allows registered moneylenders to lend at costs which exceed the 20% per annum rates which apply under the Usury Act.[12] An Exemption Notice issued in 2006 similarly provides for a regulatory exemption from caps on the cost of credit for transactions by lenders who are authorized by the National Credit Regulator.[13] The Exemption Notice invests ultimate authority of both exemption and withdrawal in mechanisms of executive power. As Kirsten (2006: 4) notes the 'exemption essentially licensed micro-lenders to create a separate, largely unregulated, tier of credit provision to people on the fringes of the banking system'. Innovated over three waves of regulatory reform, techniques of formal exemption in South Africa have constituted large markets for financialized credit.

The most important instances of this formal exemption, however, are the regulatory mechanisms recently established for payday lending in Canada. Section 347 of Canada's *Criminal Code* renders any loan which imposes interest above 60% APR subject to criminal prosecution. As Irving notes, the 'emergence of a widespread payday loan industry in Canada is surprising … because … until recently, the vast majority of these highly visible and profitable outfits committed a criminal offence each and every time they provided a loan' (Irving 2010: 160). To address the legal uncertainty of a practice which is both widespread in use but legally vulnerable, industry lobbyists began to push for forms of regulatory certification (Kozbar 2012: 39). In 2006 the Federal government passed legislation which allowed payday lenders to be exempted from the criminal prohibition – that is to allow much higher rates of interest – in provinces which establish licensing and regulatory regimes. At the core of this legislation is an illocutionary utterance, a sovereign gesture which formalizes payday lending even as it charges prohibited rates of interest. Balancing this exemption is a requirement that lenders operate with provincial licences and follow consumer-protection regimes. The exemption is effective only 'in a province that has legislative measures that protect recipients of payday loans and that provide for limits on the total cost of borrowing' (Statute RS c. C-46, 2:3; see also Consumer Measures Committee 2004).[14] Several provinces have enacted enabling legislation that effectively legitimizes the practice with few constraints (Nova Scotia Bill No. 87; see also Saskatchewan Bill No. 43, 2006–07; and Ben-Ishai 2008: 335–336).

The first experiments in this new regulatory space entailed contending political impulses in the first province – Manitoba – to adopt regulations under the Federal exemption. Manitoba empowered an existing agency, the Manitoba Public Utilities Board (MPUB), to establish an overall limit to the cost of credit for payday loans. After extensive hearings the MPUB established a maximum price for credit that was lower than recommendations from the main industry lobbyist – the Canadian Payday Loan Association (CPLA) – at CAN $17 per $100 loaned. Moreover, Board Findings were couched in a language that seemed hesitant to embrace payday lending as an 'acceptable' form. The MPUB expressed explicit concern about the legitimacy of payday lending and the ways in which it extracted profit from forms of economic distress. The initial Manitoba order, for example, noted that 'payday borrowers should realize that payday loans are so expensive that they should be avoided, to be considered only in the absence of access to credit from mainstream lenders, family or "doing without"' (MPUB 2008: 4).[15] The Board's initial regulatory formulation explicitly questioned the business model of lenders who imposed high costs or used coercive collection techniques (See Kodar 2011: 464–465).

This assertive approach taken by the MPUB, however, would prove to be an exception in a much wider regulatory programme that would come to extend legitimacy to payday lending without ambiguity. The initial MPUB order, for example, was challenged by lenders in the Manitoba Court of Appeal on the grounds that the Board exceeded its jurisdiction. The court essentially agreed with the position of lenders by noting that the Board had enunciated its order as a 'moral judgement' it was not empowered to make. The court noted that by passing legislation authorizing exemption from the interest prohibition in the *Criminal Code*, both the Federal and Provincial governments had intended a kind of legitimacy for the sector that placed it beyond 'moral' reproach. The appeal court ruling noted that 'both Canada and Manitoba, in creating the legislative scheme in question, have recognized that there is a societal need for the payday lending industry' (quoted in Kozbar 2012: 46). The court eventually affirmed payday lending as 'regulated but viable industry':

> Parliament ... and Manitoba ... have determined for policy reasons a legitimate need for the existence and operation of a payday loan industry ... [The board] expressed its view against the morality of payday loans. It expressed an intention to make loans less available and less attractive to consumers ... the Public Utility Board has exceeded its jurisdiction.
>
> (Court Judgment by the Manitoba Court of Appeal 2009 MBCA 1:17)

The Manitoba order has become an important touchstone for other provincial regulatory bodies; a recognition that the appeal court decision 'secures for high-cost providers a guarantee of market entry' (Kozbar 2012: 48). Nova Scotia, for example, became the second jurisdiction to enact payday regulations by establishing much higher permissible costs of credit – initially fixed at CAN $31 per $100 loaned (later reduced to $25 per $100 loaned) (Kodar 2011: 476). In crafting its findings, the Nova Scotia body explicitly and formally distanced itself from the logic of the Manitoba order:

> The Manitoba Board ... lost sight of the fact that the payday lending industry has emerged as a credible and legitimate part of the marketplace ... [It] took the view that the payday loan industry is not an ethical one, and that rates should be set so low as to drive lenders out of business. Implicit in the Federal Government's Bill C-26, and the Manitoba Government's response, is governmental acknowledgement that there is, indeed, space in the marketplace for payday lenders.
>
> (Nova Scotia Utility and Review Board 2008: 89–90; see also Aitken 2012: 216)

This kind of logic has now been echoed in several other provincial jurisdictions where payday lending regimes have been established. What has resulted is a kind of settling of payday lending not only by legislative exemption but by regulatory practice. As Kozbar notes (2012: 4) this approach to regulation helps to 'legitimize the object of regulation by simultaneously conceiving it as socially necessary'. This is also now echoed in Manitoba which acknowledges the legitimacy of payday lending. The most recent regulatory order, for example, explicitly, if somewhat uneasily, reaffirms the legitimate role for payday lending in the province. According to the Board's own Findings, 'the Province has chosen to allow payday vendors to offer this product ... the Board recognizes that licensed payday lenders are offering a loan product that is desired by its customer group and fills a need not met by mainstream banking institutions' (MPUB 2013: 64). Rebuked by the courts and by other provincial regulators, Manitoba has cemented something of a (lukewarm) legitimacy for a 'regulatory object [which] possesses an equivocal moral-political status' (Kozbar 2012: 51). Nonetheless, the Manitoba government continues to impose a pricing regime that is, in some ways, even more punitive to the industry than the initial 2008 order. The most recent order maintains the cap on the cost of credit at CAN $17 per $100 borrowed but also restricts lenders from issuing loans which exceed 30% of borrower's net pay (Kodar 2011: 467).

The jurisdictions which have pursued exemption are characterized by unique local conditions. The unique conditions that have ushered in concerns for credit in post-Apartheid South Africa, for example, are quite distant from those that propelled moves toward formalization in the North American payday lending sector. Nonetheless what connects these various gestures is their performative clarity; the ways in which they authorize the object they claim only to manage. Because it relies on the sovereignty of a single speaking subject, authorization is a particularly crucial mechanism capable of extending an unimpeachable legal status. As a technique of formalization, sovereign authorization 'confers legitimacy to what some consider abusive lending practices' (Bellam and Talai 2012: 8). Performing fringe lending, however has entailed broader sets of mechanisms which assemble knowledge and practice form diverse locations, and which allow fringe capital to be invoked not only as an authorized practice, but as a practice that is calculated and priced in a particular kind of way.

Price mechanisms

A second set of mechanisms of formal legitimacy, and one related to the techniques of authorization, are the pricing mechanisms which regulatory regimes have constituted. Because the cost of credit has been so important to the legal and political disputes which have called into question its legitimacy, price mechanisms have been particularly crucial to regulatory regimes for micro-lending. These pricing mechanisms are important to the formalization of fringe lending because they both work to make prices possible – that is establish methods of calculation with which prices are constituted – and to certify those formulae as fair and legitimate. The legitimacy of micro-lending is *prefigured* in the pricing mechanisms, formulae and calculative devices which make the actual prices of fringe lending (its most politically contentious element) possible and visible.

The prices for fringe lending are not the product of unimpeded market forces. Rather, there is an astonishing variety of mechanisms which actually format and calculate prices. This entails a series of complex rules which govern the ways in which prices for fringe lending are actually made visible. Consumer price requirements across much of the Anglo-American world were definitively shaped by American truth-in-lending regulations initially developed in the 1960s and 1970s. Truth-in-lending requirements inscribe 'a standardized annual percentage rate … to facilitate comparison shopping for credit so that borrowers could choose rationally between competing creditors … [and] to inform prospective borrowers about the true cost of credit' (Duggan 2010: 688). These requirements, including the benchmark American Regulation Z, presuppose standardized price formulae as a kind of foundation for the exercise of calculative agency in consumer markets. As the official guidance manual for Regulation Z notes, 'APR, which must be disclosed in nearly all consumer credit transactions, is designed to take into account all relevant factors and to provide a uniform measure for comparing the cost of various credit transactions' (Federal Reserve 2013: 8; American regulation is Section 1026.22 15 U.S.C. 16–1 *et seq.*). Now established as a standard component of all consumer credit contracts, APR operates as a basic foundation for markets in which prices can be compared and assessed in relative ease.

These pricing calculations are, nonetheless, increasingly under strain by micro-lenders keen to divert attention from the high costs with which they are associated. Lenders have consistently argued that micro-loans entail relatively high costs of delivery that render them incomparable to other kinds of credit products. Moreover, lenders note that because they are issued for very short durations, calculations based on an annual frame of time are not appropriate. In some jurisdictions, these arguments have convinced regulators to abandon APR as a pricing standard. All of the provincial level regulatory regimes in Canada, for example, establish pricing practices based not on APR but on a new norm which expresses the price of payday loans in terms of dollar amount in fees per CAN $100 borrowed (Duggan 2010: 703).

The regulatory regimes that govern fringe lending not only clarify the rules with which prices can be displayed or made visible. They also often establish the actual mechanisms with which those prices can be calculated and established in the first place. The most common way this occurs is through restrictions or caps on rates of interest. For example, 22 American states now invoke some form of interest rate restriction on payday lending, in ways that establish a wide range of maximum prices ranging from effective rates of 28% to 780% APR (McKernan, Ratcliffe and Kuehn 2013: 213).[16] These 'caps' however do not effectively operate as a simple ceiling on the price of credit. Rather, there is evidence accumulating that interest rate restrictions are actually price-setting mechanisms. Because the price of credit tends to converge onto the prices established through caps or interest-rate restrictions, these regulations often operate as a *de facto* pricing formula (Personal Finance Research Centre 2013: 97).

As pricing mechanisms, however, interest rate restrictions are neither simple nor straightforward. Some measures invoked in payday lending regimes, for example, relate price to income. These often prevent an extension of loans at costs which exceed a certain ratio of loan principal to borrower income. In some instances, loans are extended at lower prices to those who receive social assistance (Gibbons, Malhotra and Bulmore 2010: 25). In addition, pricing mechanisms often invoke multiple forms of pricing on various components of loan costs. Loan costs are often divided into both interest and finance or origination fees, recognizing arguments by lenders that short-term credit can be costly to originate. The price of payday loans in Florida, for example, facilitate a maximum of 10% interest and a maximum US $5 origination fee roughly translating into an APR of 390% for a 14 day $100 loan (Personal Finance Research Centre 2013: 103). Similarly, in Oregon payday lenders can charge up to 36% APR, a one time loan origination fee of 10% of the amount borrowed up to a maximum of $30, allowing an maximum of 154% APR (Oregon Consumer and Business Services 2012). Some American jurisdictions cap prices by dividing fees into those charged on original loans and those charged on outstanding balances. Ohio, for example, allows maximum interest charges of 5% per month on unpaid balances allowing an APR of 390% on $100 (Personal Finance Research Centre 2013: 103).

Beyond North America, however, 'interest rate restrictions' are established in complex pricing formula often involving benchmark indices. In Germany a maximum interest rate restriction has been established by a series of court rulings which effectively cap credit prices at 200% of average APR computed by the Central Bank. German caps on interest rate restrictions are also shaped by a second condition which prohibits costs which exceed average APR rates by 12 percentage points (Reifner, Clerc-Renaud and Knobloch 2010: 63). Similarly, maximum APR rates for micro-lending in Italy are restricted to 150% of average APR computed by the Ministry of Economy and Finance on a regular basis. Italian rates are differentially calculated according to complex classifications of credit type resulting in the calculation of 23 different rate ceilings[17] (Reifner, Clerc-Renaud and Knobloch 2010: 63).

By establishing parameters for the price of credit, or by operating as effective pricing mechanisms, the recent wave of micro and payday lending regulation is performative; mechanisms which establish the ways in which the actual prices of credit can be circulated, calculated and made visible. In doing so, by extension, these mechanisms also contribute to the formalization of fringe lending. They do so by establishing an effective price for micro-lending sanctioned by public authority. Regulatory regimes have become preoccupied with the configuration of pricing mainly because prices have been so central to the political and ethical debates surrounding forms of predatory lending. Because they transcribe formalized prices for payday and micro-lending in a legally mandated fashion, regulatory regimes address a central question key to the debates regarding the legitimacy of fringe lending. This formalization of payday lending prices, moreover, can sometimes authorize prices – such as Nova Scotia's CAN $31/$25 per $100 loaned – which lie above normal price ranges in jurisdictions without effective price guidelines or restrictions (King 2012). This implies that regulatory regimes can often formalize existing prices in a quite immediate way – that is they convert into formalized utterances the very prices they purport to manage and regulate.

Equipping consumers

As Michel Callon has noted, any form of organized or formatted market 'implies a peculiar anthropology, one which assumes … what we might call calculative agencies' (Callon 1998: 3; but for a slightly different line of analysis see Langley 2013). This entails 'equipping' human bodies and situating those bodies within *agencements*, assemblages of human and non human forms, which enable certain forms of calculation and market behaviour. Formalized markets for fringe credit have also been constituted in regulatory attempts to intervene into the lives of borrowers themselves. Regulatory regimes for fringe lending increasingly attempt to shape and format borrowers as legitimate agents in credit markets, not as victims haunted by predatory relationships but as choosing subjects capable of calculative deliberation.

The mobilization of risk bearing subjects in credit markets has been the particular purview of behavioural economics. Behavioural economics is constituted out of a longstanding critique of neoclassical economics and the assumption it makes regarding the instrumental rationality which founds market behaviour. In contrast to assumptions regarding inherent rationality, behavioural economics treats the rational deliberation of choice not as an already existing capacity, but as an ideal often undermined by cognitive or behavioural limitations. In general, behavioural economics offers a focus 'on ultimate causes of choice behaviour and on how people's cognitive limitations mitigate against optimal choices' (Boeckler and Berndt 2012: 428). Behavioural economics does not, in ultimate form, resist rationality, but seeks to uncover the ways in which it can be shaped in the face of irrational kinds of human conduct. Behavioural economics is concerned to shape conduct and 'to enrol and assemble particular market agents who think and act in rational and calculative ways' (Langley 2010: 74). In a post-crisis context, behavioural economies both acknowledges irrational behaviour and holds out the promise that market forces might be 'perfected' again via the regulation or modification of human behaviour (Boeckler and Berndt 2012: 429).[18]

For behavioural economists, rationality is a capacity that can be cultivated through structured interventions designed to alter or reverse pervasive behavioural tendencies. For Boeckler and Berndt (2012: 430), this is a set of interventions which 'renders the self an effect of sociotechnically distributed rational action'. Regulatory authorities have increasingly sought to constitute these types of distributed market agency in fringe lending markets. These efforts, emerging most fully after 2008, have been concerned with a number of 'persistent' behavioural biases prevalent in credit relations. 'Behavioural biases', notes the British regulator, 'may be why some consumers borrow more than they can afford' (Financial Conduct Authority 2013: 68). Of particular concern for fringe lending markets are a cluster of biases which result in underestimation – systematic 'miscalculations' with which borrowers ignore or minimize the risk they face in high-cost credit (Duggan 2010: 703). This tendency to underestimation often means that borrowers do not apprehend risk or are not able to assess risk as a tangible possibility. For some regulators influenced by behavioural economics, underestimation bias is not only a concern for borrowers, but also a potential source of value and profit for lenders who construct lending models based on biases that prevent fully rational calculation:

> Consumers underestimate the risk or simply do not believe that they will not be able to repay the loan on time, so they do not consider the risks and costs of that happening. This makes it easier for a lender to structure its business model in a way that relies on loans being rolled over, or default charges being added, and not on the borrower's ability to repay on time.
>
> (Financial Conduct Authority 2013: 59)

To address these biases, regulators increasingly experiment with 'the gentle power of nudges' or with devices designed to address these biases in various ways. Perhaps the most common behavioural nudges designed to equip borrowers are more precise disclosure requirements or 'cooling off' periods. Combined, these two requirements are designed to equip borrowers with the capacity to make useful decisions in the face of complicated or stressful borrowing conditions. A cooling off period is emphasized, by behavioural economists, as an envelope of time in which borrowers can more fully assess loan conditions and make decisions with calculative integrity. As two analysts connected to the one British regulatory agency note, 'regulation of the sales and sign-up process to include mandatory cooling-off periods and prevent pressure-selling help reduce the number of people making poor financial decisions on impulse' (Woodcock and Cheung 2010: 38; see also Duggan 2010: 705).

The most recent set of tools experimented by British and American regulators involve risk warnings. Although most regulators require open disclosure of credit terms (this was at the core of 1960s truth-in-lending requirements) risk warnings more explicitly 'nudge' borrowers by delineating the risks they face in stark terms. Many American states, for example, have begun to require warnings which explicate risk and which require lenders to inform prospective borrowers about this risk in explicit terms (Duggan 2010: 706). British regulators have also begun to experiment with risk warnings designed to redress underestimation biases in fringe lending networks. New British payday lending regulations require 'that all financial promotions for high-cost short-term loans will need to carry a "risk warning"' (Financial Conduct Authority 2013: 68). These regulations require risk warnings attached to loan documentation in ways that resemble medical or health warnings appended to unhealthy products:

> Think! Is this loan for you?
>
> Over 2 million short-term loans were not paid off on time in 2011/12. This can lead to serious money problems.
>
> Not paying back your loan on time will significantly add to the cost and may continue to grow, here is some important information to help you.
>
> (Financial Conduct Authority 2013: 69)

These mechanisms – disclosures, cooling off periods, risk warnings – rework the bodies of borrowers as a kind of field of intervention. Behavioural devices attempt to mobilize fringe borrowers as agents capable of some form of regulated agency in credit markets. Regulatory regimes increasingly emphasize devices that can intervene into the behaviour of borrowers and constitute the kind of capacity to bear or calculate risk that market forms assume.

In doing so, by recasting or reformatting borrowers as agents, they contribute, in important ways, to the formalization of fringe lending. Because some of the legal and regulatory risk faced by lenders – especially associated with civil litigation – relates to borrowers who may not be aware of loan provisions or capable of assuming risk in credit contracts, these measures have particular importance. Mechanisms which constitute agents in fringe credit markets stabilize credit contracts vulnerable to legal fairness and truth-in-lending tests. Taken together these various mechanisms of formal legitimacy assemble a 'suitable normative language … [out of] the complimentary discourses of competition and consumer protection' (Kozbar 2012: 49). Despite the ways in which these three sets of practices – techniques of exemption, pricing and borrower behaviour – are all distinctive, they each nonetheless render fringe lending legible as a codified and legally permissible set of practices. Although designed in ways that enmesh fringe lending into codes of legal recognition, these modes of regulation are not, themselves, settled practices, but tools that continue to have a certain degree of political malleability.

'Brokering failure': contesting the regulation of fringe lending

> We may be confused about the difference between cultural construction (which always makes an ontological claim) and performative effects. Our theory would be altogether too happy if we thought that theories always make and build what they prefigure or explain. They do sometimes fail, and they are always brokering failure, whether or not they do actually fail. And this means that fallibility is built into the account of performativity.
>
> (Butler 2010: 152)

The diagram at the heart of fringe finance is preoccupied with formalization.[19] Although a recent wave of regulation prefigures those preoccupations, it has not seamlessly constituted the object it mapped. To borrow the language of Butler, recent waves of regulation are incessantly 'brokering failure'. As Paul Langley notes, in 'enacting and bringing about the risks that they name and price, calculative devices have certainly remained historically contingent and sensitive to habits, customs, circumstances and controversies about their empirical validity' (Langley 2010: 75). I want to suggest in this section of the chapter that contestation is internal to the process of regulation. 'Resistance', Foucault famously noted, 'is never in a position of exteriority in relation to power' (Foucault 1984: 95). The body of regulation that now governs, and stabilizes payday lending, is not the immaculate reflection of the diagram that animates it, but the complex outcome of practices and failures.

I want to highlight three particular sites where the contestation of payday lending has unfolded with a particular resonance. A first setting involves recent changes to state regulations for payday lending in Colorado. Colorado was an 'early adopter' of payday lending in 1992 (see Chessin 2005). In 2000 the *Colorado Deferred Deposit Loan Act* authorized a formal exemption from interest rate restrictions and allowed loans which carried APRs well over 300% (Lake *et al.* 2013: 13).[20] By 2008, however, there was serious agitation from both consumer rights advocates and key voices in the state legislature in favour of reform. These discussions eventually led to a series of amendments to the initial bill and a broader set of reforms to the *Colorado Uniform Consumer Credit Code* which adjusted the fees that lenders could charge and, most importantly, extended to borrowers the right to participate in a voluntary payment plan (with no additional fees) in which the initial loan can be repaid in at least six equal instalments rather than in single payment due on a borrower's payday (Colorado 2011: 136).

The most significant accomplishment in the Colorado plan is a mechanism of amortization. By providing borrowers with the option of paying their loans in instalments, the new regulations essentially allow the loan to be amortized and, in doing so, release some of the pressure that can lead to loan rollovers. A newly established pricing mechanism compliments this attempted amortization. The new rules allow an interest rate of 45% annually, plus an 'origination' fee and a monthly maintenance fee that begins at the end of the second month of duration. Most importantly, the origination fee is refundable on a pro-rata basis for loans that are retired early during the instalment phase, so that the total origination fee is only secured by the lender if the entire instalment period of six months is exercised by the borrower. This pro-rated fee mechanism is designed to ensure 'that lenders could not fully earn the origination fee immediately at the outset of the loan, so they had no incentive to encourage borrowers to refinance and generate new origination fees' (Lake *et al.* 2013: 15). This arrangement establishes an incentive for borrowers to respect a six-month repayment window. Although the Colorado reforms still sanction relatively high fees (fees for the new law average 129% APR compared to 317% for the 2000 law), they have nonetheless lowered average fees (the cost of borrowing US $500 for 12 months drops in the new bill from $1,950 to $580) and expanded the options available to borrowers.

A second space of contestation has been formed in and around debates in Australia regarding the regulation of short-term lending. Reforms to short-term lending have occurred as part of a longer process over the past five years which has resulted in the harmonization of consumer credit laws by the ASIC (Ali, McRae and Ramsay 2013: 412). In launching the new payday loan regulations, the government announced its concern 'that the most financially vulnerable consumers are paying high costs relative to their income when using short term, non-productive forms of finance, resulting in financial harm' (Australia 2011: 7). To address these concerns the government initiated a number of reforms, the core of which was 'a tiered cap [which] balances the interests of consumers with the viability of the industry'[21] (quoted in Personal Finance Research Centre 2013: 101). This entailed, most importantly, a special set of rules for short-term lending below a threshold of AU $2,000.

From the outset of this process, however, the imposition of a tiered set of interest rate restrictions for payday lending was deeply contested. On one hand, lenders mounted a campaign opposed to the adoption of existing 'hard caps' at the state-level as a model for national regulations. New South Wales, Queensland and Victoria all have effective caps on payday loans which prohibit costs above 48% per annum. Because these caps applied generally to consumer credit contracts, lenders argued that they did not take into account the specific costs encountered by payday lenders. In the various consultations that preceded the regulations 'many lenders argued that a 48% cap inclusive of fees and interest … was unsustainable for the short-term, small amount lending industry' (Australia 2011: 40–41). On the other hand, however, many consumer advocates and some government members argued for a meaningful cap on costs as a way to prevent deepening indebtedness among vulnerable borrowers.

The outcome of these contending conceptions of regulatory intervention is somewhat ambivalent. As initially codified, the new regulations were an important rebuke to the ambitions of lenders. In contrast to the kind of diagram authored by lenders – ambitions similar to permissive Canadian regimes – the initial Australian proposals prefigured important constraints on the extension of fringe credit. In a way that parallels the emergent work of the Consumer Financial Protection Bureau (CFPB) in the USA, the Australian regime is characterized by a newly empowered regulatory authority still seeking to define its authority within a somewhat flexible regulatory space. Key to this emerging purview is the imposition of a formal limit on costs of credit specifically designed for payday loans. Unlike caps designed to authorize existing levels of profitability and return, Australian proposals for interest rate restrictions were bitterly contested by industry lobbyists as significant constraints on lenders and the scope of profitability they could claim. The original regulations proposed prohibiting fees beyond an establishment fee equivalent to no more than 10% of the 'adjusted credit amount' alongside maximum allowable monthly fees capped at 2% of adjusted credit amount (essentially imposing a cap of 24% per annum) (Ali, McRae and Ramsay 2013: 434).

A concerted campaign pursued by industry lobbyists, however, did manage to weaken the proposal significantly between the moment of its introduction and its eventual passage in the Australian legislature. An initial prohibition on multiple lending, for example, was replaced with a mechanism which allows lenders more scope in determining loan extensions: 'rebuttable presumptions of suitability' which 'rely on lenders to always act in the best interests of vulnerable borrowers' (Ali, McRae and Ramsay 2013: 428). Moreover, the final version of the regulations creates maximum establishment fees capped at 20% of adjusted credit amount and maximum monthly fees capped at 4% – an effective increase in allowable costs to 48% per annum (Personal Finance Research Centre 2013: 100). Although these fees are more generous to lenders than the initial version, they are nonetheless a departure from the initial formulation championed by the industry. What has resulted in these Australian regulations is a regime which does not correspond seamlessly with the diagrams drawn by lenders but which is, rather, a function of the contending pressures from which it emerged. By extension, the Australian reforms imply the ambivalence or malleability of much of the recent wave of regulatory reform for fringe credit. Unlike many of the permissive regimes constituted elsewhere, especially in North America, the Australian rules were initiated and shaped, at least early on, not by lenders but by groups explicitly concerned about borrowers and the debt that encumbers them. Nonetheless, and despite this policy momentum achieved by critics, the 'reduced protections for payday loan borrowers indicate that the campaign undertaken by the payday loan industry was influential in shaping the final version' (Ali, McRae and Ramsay 2013: 413). Regulatory mechanisms – rules governing disclosures, loan renewals and, most importantly, the cost of credit – are not singular objects but malleable technologies shaped by diverse, often contending, pressures.

A third and final site of contestation – the reformulation of payday lending in the UK – reveals regulation not as a settled or settling practice but as a cycle which oscillates between permissive and restrictive tendencies. The British context for payday lending has, until recently, been characterized by lenders as a 'mature' domain hospitable, like Canada, to the ongoing viability of lenders. Dollar Financial, the largest British lender, has favourably described the British regulatory context as 'settled' while CS Financial (2012), another large international lender active in the UK, has, in its own regulatory filings, noted the 'favourable regulatory framework' as the key factor in its aggressive expansion in the British market (see also Aitken 2013: 386). This is underpinned by a regulatory consensus against the imposition of interest rate restrictions and the adoption of a regulatory model focused mainly on behavioural supports for consumers. A review of high cost credit initiated in 2010 by the Office of Fair Trading (OFT), culminated a long policy development process by explicitly eschewing the possibility of price caps:

> We do not consider that price controls for … payday loans … would be an appropriate solution … The imposition of price controls in high-cost credit markets creates a risk for suppliers that they would generate lower profit levels. It would be reasonable to expect these suppliers to respond to the imposition of a price control by seeking to regain such lost profit by restricting the type and risk of consumers they are willing to supply …

> This potential for reduced access to high-cost credit would be of concern.[22]
>
> (Office of Fair Trading 2010a: 55–56; Personal Finance Research Centre 2013: 98; for technical details see Office of Fair Trading 2010b)

The OFT report was widely understood as a kind of punctuation to a settled regulatory approach that was both formalizing and permissive. As recently as March 2013, for example, the official government response to a commissioned report on interest rate restrictions signalled a continuing commitment to the existing script on regulation. Restrictions 'on the total cost of credit', the government noted, 'could reduce access to credit, reduce the supply of credit' (Business Innovation and Skills 2013b: 7). The position was also explicitly linked to a reaffirmation of the continuing legitimacy, even necessity of payday lending. 'There is', the government argued, 'a role for short term credit in the UK's credit market … this type of credit provides consumers with quick and straightforward access to funds at a time when they can be most in need' (Business Innovation and Skills 2013b: 7).[23] British regulations echoed the broader diagram which grounds claims to formal legitimacy in an argument about the social utility and necessity of payday lending as vital form.

Nonetheless, and despite the definitive tone of these regulatory utterances, the last number of years have been characterized by some important unsettling in the British regulatory approach. The OFT, for example, launched a high profile 'compliance review' of key lenders which noted widespread non-compliance with disclosure requirements, an over-reliance of lenders on loan rollovers and a general conclusion that 'irresponsible lending is not a problem confined to a few rogue traders, but has its roots in the way competition works in this market' (Office of Fair Trading 2013: 30).[24] Although the OFT referred the payday lending file to the Competition Commission, the government initiated a much broader set of regulatory changes by transferring authority for the regulation of all high-cost short-term credit to the Financial Conduct Authority (FCA) formed in 2012.[25] The FCA immediately began working on a series of new regulations designed to respond to intensifying criticism. The regulations invoked new measures which restrict the use of continuous payment authorities, cap the number of loan rollovers at two, require 'risk' or 'health' warnings which 'will contribute towards de-biasing consumers' and impose new 'affordability standards' designed to encourage lenders to more thoroughly ensure that loans do not undermine the financial health of borrowers (Europe Economics 2013: 28). The measures also require that lenders provide borrowers with information on free debt counselling services before any loan can be rolled over (Financial Conduct Authority 2013: 53–54; see also Moore 2013; for actual regulations see Financial Conduct Authority 2014).

Most importantly, these new regulatory developments are punctuated with a new commitment to cap the cost of credit in payday lending markets. In November 2013, several months after reaffirming its commitment to existing regulatory approaches, (and in opposition to advice from the FCA itself[26]) the government introduced regulatory amendments which will require the FCA to publish a consultation paper in July 2014 and establish final rules in November 2014 for a cap on credit prices for payday lending which much be effective by 2 January 2015 (Financial Conduct Authority 2014: 59). As the government has argued, 'with growing evidence in support of a cap and emerging lessons from other countries – especially the cap on costs introduced in Australia this year – the government believes' that the timing is now appropriate to impose a cap (HM Treasury (UK) 2013). The final shape the cap takes, and the pricing mechanism it ultimately establishes for payday lending, are unknown. The discourses which attend the price cap, however, seem to indicate an important setback for payday lenders. The FCA has consistently noted that the mechanism they will establish will likely result in the contraction of lenders in the sector, implying a cap that is not as permissive as arrangements authored by lenders in Canada or some American jurisdictions.[27] The price cap, and the changing debate around payday regulation in the UK underscore the kind of unsettledness and contestation which now appears to mark the regulation of payday lending.

The regulation of fringe lending consists of a malleable set of political and economic technologies. On one hand, regulation has consistently been at the very core of the diagram which maps the financial edge as spaces that could be subjected to formalized interventions. At the heart of this diagram is an impulse which equates formalization with a settling of fringe lending and the political and legal controversies around it. On the other hand, however, the mechanisms of formal legitimacy regulatory regimes inscribe in practice are contested, can be redeployed in unintended critical purposes and can be used as much to confine as to enable fringe lending. Although the diagrams which map fringe finance are often drawn in precise and clean lines, the processes of regulation can often be unsettling, characterized as much by reversals and slippages as by pristine lines of practice. Regulatory contests in Australia and the UK, in particular, are still unresolved processes – sites where regulatory regimes are leveraged not only as mechanisms of formalization but also as limits that might constrain the reach or profitability of fringe credit. These ongoing disputes in Australia and, perhaps most crucially, in the UK will eventually determine whether the mechanisms designed to formalize payday lending might come to inscribe limits in some meaningful manner. The possibilities associated with these limits, however, are themselves complex, subject to their own important political constraints and dilemmas.

Conclusion: regulatory localism and the global futures of fringe finance

> [We need] to point in many ways to the proliferation or multiplication of walls and borders of various kinds, not merely to mark the distinction between internal and external spaces, but also within the space and time of global capital.
>
> (Mezzadra and Neilson 2012: 71)

This chapter places particular emphasis on the borders that proliferate 'within the space and time of global capital' and, crucially, the ways in which those borders are relocated over time. Contemporary legal, political and regulatory debates around fringe lending are one key site at which the very borders of finance are reworked in revealing ways. These debates have resulted in regulation that is performative, that brings into being that which it claims merely to manage. This performativity has hinged on questions of formalization and on what Soederberg (2012: 562) refers to as the strategies which 'expose and integrate spaces of informality into different facets of the capitalist market'.

At one level, formalization lends itself neatly to illocutionary utterances – to the work of a singular or sovereign speaker. The techniques associated with the formal exemption from usury laws or other restrictions are utterances which quite deliberately transport a certain set of lending practices across the line that separates illegal from legal, permissible from illicit. As this chapter has also noted, however, there are broader performative practices associated with formalization involving pricing and behavioural nudges. There is also a broader politics at stake in this performativity as well; a contested field in which regulation consists less of a straightforward delineation of rules as it does a set of tools which can be used for a diversity of often deeply contested purposes.

Regulation and the publics in which it is entangled are constituted within larger political questions. Although Callon has infamously encouraged us to 'abandon the critical position' (Barry and Slater 2002: 301), I want to conclude by noting the particularly critical questions that performativity allows us to take up. Callon's inclination is a useful rebuke, in particular, to styles of critique which have often framed the market as a kind of implacable or overbearing force. This should not obscure, however, the importance of performativity as a mode of analysis designed to disrupt market practices, in all of their irreducible diversity, and the kinds of social dislocations in which those practices are implicated. 'I agree wholeheartedly', affirms Butler,

> that it will not do to say that one opposes 'capitalism' as such … I am less clear that this means abandoning any effort to evaluate and oppose those multivalent operations of capitalism that augment income disparities, presume the functional necessity of poverty and thwart efforts to establish just forms for the redistribution of wealth.
>
> (Butler 2010: 153)

This is particularly crucial for forms of market rationality which are often framed as either 'necessary' or 'technical' in ways that place them beyond critical scrutiny. Performativity, notes Karl (2013: 74–75) affirms that the 'political dominance of market logic may be contested by an analysis that calls its necessity into question … To examine how such notions take hold is to necessarily limit their impact and, if we wish, our complicity in reproducing them' (Karl 2013: 74–75). Although the 'political dominance' of payday and fringe lending is far from secured, performativity nonetheless allows an analysis which undermines the necessity with which it is often framed and regulated.

According to its critics, performativity has sometimes come to reify the technical conditions with which objects are constituted in ways that evade broader political questions. This is particularly relevant to work on the performativity of finance which can sometimes become preoccupied with the practices and techniques of calculation so central to contemporary financial spaces. The insight that performativity makes possible often 'comes at a price of depoliticizing, or even blackboxing, the question of calculation, and bypassing its normative aspects' (Henriksen 2013: 408).

By way of conclusion, I want to emphasize one explicitly political dilemma raised out of the broader processes examined in this chapter – questions related to the very scope and reach of fringe finance and the regulation shaped by those opposed to it. The regulation that now uneasily governs fringe lending has largely operated at the level of *national* (sometimes subnational) policy development. As I noted in Chapter 2, however, this localized scale of operation, although successful in some respects, is inadequate to address the increasingly globalized edges of payday capital (see also Aitken 2013). Put in the language that Casey (2008) uses, there is no clear national edge to the practices of payday or fringe lending, but rather, porous edges that seem consistently expansive and geographically unbounded. These globalized edges, however, are not well matched by the main forms of political activism that have confronted payday lending and the indebtedness it helps constitute. The overwhelming majority of this activism has been rooted in the specificities of particular geographic contexts. As a result, the regulatory and policy mechanisms designed to address fringe lending have been local in scope, with no capacity to engage any of the cross-border or global dimensions of payday lending.

Because creation and contestation are inseparable, activism has been key to the ways in which these local regulatory mechanism, have been constituted. Because this activism is invested in local regulatory practices, however, there exists the possibility it might become, perhaps unintentionally, a parochial gesture, concerned not with social justice in any broad sense but with the protection of local bodies in ways that are abstracted from a larger context. This has often been a narrow agenda focused not on what it might mean to pursue fairness for all, but rather, orbited around legal protections implemented within existing regulatory spaces. To address the increasingly global dimensions of the problems they confront, activists need to develop a conception of financial practice or regulation that is as globalized as the practices they seek to confront: some systematic and explicit formulation of the minimal requirements for fair financial and credit practices and the conditions that might make those applicable across wider spaces of operation.

As this chapter attests, the regulation of payday and fringe lending is performative. The activism which challenges those modes of credit practice is also performative. Because they contest payday lending and the dominant diagram of regulation lenders have sketched, activists are deeply implicated in those diagrams and the shape they ultimately take; their own complex relationships and entanglements with the object they purport to target. The activists opposed to fringe lending have contributed to the forms of (regulated) lending they have sought to oppose. By extension they have also contributed to the limitations of those forms of regulation and to political dilemmas this regulation poses. Addressing these dilemmas requires, over the long term, forms of political action that are, themselves, capable of a certain self-consciousness regarding their own edges and limitations, and a certain awareness of the changing nature of the object they target. The *global* futures of payday and fringe lending will be worked out in the crucible of these dilemmas and the ways in which they are resolved or placed in motion. To address these dilemmas also implies a recognition of the irregularity of fringe finance, a field characterized less by straight lines than by changing and irregular fields, a theme taken up in a different manner in Chapter 6.

Notes

1 As Brassett and Clarke suggest, 'Markets are enacted, and financial subjects are produced through discursive repetition' (Brassett and Clarke 2012: 4).
2 In Langely's terms this type of analysis 'includes all manner of professions, techniques, procedures, formulas and objects' that contribute to 'enacting particular version of what it is to be "economic"' (Langley 2010: 74).
3 Brassett and Clark suggest the importance of a 'pragmatic inclination to embrace the contingent individuated agency of contemporary financial subjects … [and] to engage the chance exposures of political dilemmas and contests (within their historicity) as a productive route forward' (Brassett and Clarke 2012: 10).
4 As Kaufman argues, there is now a widely deployed set of regulatory mechanisms for fringe lending: price caps, size caps, loan term limits, limits on simultaneous borrowing, rollovers, cooling off periods, extended repayment options (Kaufman 2013: 7–8).
5 As Kodar notes, in the Canadian context, 'the fact that lenders were charging criminal interest rates became central to class action lawsuits brought by consumers against lenders for unjust enrichment' (Kodar 2011: 450).
6 CS Financial (2010: 12) affirms this view: 'Working with provincial governments', CS argued, 'we secured balanced consumer protection rules that will facilitate long-term growth. New regulations will be fully implemented in 2010. As a result, we anticipate significant industry consolidation and we have an aggressive organic growth strategy in place.'
7 I should note a longer historical context – in the early part of the twentieth century, a group spearheaded by the Russell Sage Foundation attempted to regularize various forms of credit for those outside of the mainstream.
8 As Ramsay and Williams (2009: 9) note, the score of this neoliberal approach emphasizes credit bureaux and positive credit reporting, truth in lending, financier literacy and financial ombudsmen.
9 This process culminated in a Commonwealth-wide Uniform Consumer Credit Code which requires all lenders, including micro-lenders, to participate in a mandatory licensing scheme and a formal dispute settlement process (Australia 2009).

10 One recent survey suggests a diversity of approaches across American states: 13 states now prohibit the practice in some way while 33 cap the price in either permissive or restrictive ways (McKernan, Ratcliffe and Kuehn 2013: 213).

11 The Micro Finance Regulatory Council of South Africa (MFRC) was given the authority to regulate all micro-lenders operated under the auspices of a new exemption order which required new registration and consumer protection measures. The Supreme Court confirmed the status of MFRC as the regulatory agent in the South African market.

12 Usury Act Exemption Notice of 1 June 1999.

13 Usury Act Exemption Notice 2006.

14 As one Member of Parliament put it, an impulse to 'give their industry both legitimacy and long term viability' (quoted in Kodar 2011: 453).

15 The MPUB noted boldly, that 'payday lenders should not be allowed to profit from the desperation of borrowers who have nowhere else to turn' (quoted in Centre for Responsible Credit 2011: 8).

16 As I outline in the third part of this chapter, Australia has now imposed the most visible, and controversial of the price/interest rate caps on payday lending at the national level.

17 Not all price ceilings or interest rate restrictions apply to payday lending. In the Netherlands, for example, an effective cap of 15% applies for consumer credit arrangements, but payday loans are not regulated (Reifner, Clerc-Renaud and Knobloch 2010: 73).

18 As Boeckler and Berndt 29) argue, 'the belief in forces of free markets is re-stabilized by a shift … Emphasis is no longer on regulation or deregulating the market; rather the market is in the process of becoming perfect, again, by regulating human behaviour.'

19 An analogous perspective to the one developed in this chapter, albeit from a slightly different theoretical perspective is aptly given in Soederberg (2012).

20 Lake et al. (2013: 13) note that the 'legislature authorized their exemption from the state's usury interest laws under the Colorado Deferred Deposit Loan Act in 2000'.

21 A 'tiered interest rate cap or ceiling would place a maximum limit on the cost of credit, with the cap adjusted to meet different segments of the market' (Australia 2011: 47).

22 Put succinctly: the 'OFT concluded that the introduction of any price cap would be complex, expensive, and difficult to administer'.

23 It should be noted, however, that the government always reserve regulatory capacity and authority to impose a cap. A cap, the government noted in the Spring of 2013, 'is not the way to address consumer detriment in the short term credit markets … However … the government does not want to close it off as a potential solution in the future' (Business Innovation and Skills 2013b: 11).

24 The OFT also began to codify a regulatory principle that would become important over the successive wave of reforms – the question of affordability assessment, the requirement to assess 'each borrower's ability to repay a specific loan in a sustainable manner and without experiencing financial difficulties' (Office of Fair Trading 2013: 11).

25 In language that echoes the emergence of the CFPB, the government argued that the new agency 'will have the full suite of powers and resources to take action against non-compliance and to impose stronger regulatory solutions to tackle early signs of consumer detriment' (Business Innovation and Skill 2013b: 13).

26 'The FCA had initially resisted moves to cap interest rates, saying it could drive customers into the arms of loan sharks but the watchdog was overruled by the government' (Jones 2014).

27 Some estimates suggest that as many as 25% of all lenders in the sector may be required to exit the sector (Jones 2014). The OFT's early analysis of price caps also

confirms that serious price caps would contract the overall market for payday lending (see Office of Fair Trading 2010b).

References

310 Loan. 2007. *Evidence Pertaining to Public Hearings Before the Manitoba Public Utility Board to Determine Maximum Allowable Charges and Fees for Payday Loans.* Winnipeg: Public Utility Board.

Aitken, R. 2007. *Performing Capital: Toward a Cultural Economy of Popular and Global Finance.* New York: Palgrave.

Aitken, R. 2010. 'Regul(ariz)ation of Fringe Credit: Payday Lending and the Borders of Global Financial Practice'. *Competition and Change.* Vol. 14, No. 2: 80–99.

Aitken, R. 2012. 'Assembling the Immobile Subject of Fringe Finance'. *Mobilities, Knowledge and Social Justice.* Ed. Suzan Ilcan. Montreal and Kingston: McGill-Queen's University Press: 207–226.

Aitken, R. 2013. 'Finding the Edges of Payday Lending'. *Perspectives on Global Development and Technology.* Vol. 12: 377–409.

Ali, P., C. McRae and I. Ramsay. 2013. 'The Politics of Payday Lending Regulation in Australia'. *Monash University Law Review.* Vol. 39, No. 2: 411–552.

Austin, J. 1962. *How to do Things with Words.* Oxford: Clarendon Press.

Australia. 2009. *ASIC Implementation of the Credit Legislation: Responsible Lending Conduct.* Canberra: Australian Securities and Investments Commission.

Australia. 2011. *The Regulation of Short Term, Small Amount Finance: Regulation Impact Statement.* Canberra: Government of Australia.

Barry, A. and D. Slater. 2002. 'Technology, Politics and the Market: An Interview with Michel Callon'. *Economy and Society.* Vol. 31, No. 2: 285–306.

Bellam, J. and A. Talai. 2012. 'Short-Term Emergency Lending: Examining Usury and Consumer Credit Protection Law in the United States and Canada'. *Western Journal of Legal Studies.* Vol. 2, No. 1: 1–19.

Ben-Ishal, S. 2008. 'Regulating Payday Lenders in Canada'. *Banking and Finance Law Review.* Vol. 23, No. 3: 323–372.

Boeckler, M. and C. Berndt. 2012. 'Geographies of Circulation and Exchange III: The Great Crisis and Marketization "After Markets"'. *Progress in Human Geography.* Vol. 37, No. 3: 424–432.

Brassett, J. and C. Clarke. 2012. 'Performing the Sub-Prime Crisis: Trauma and the Financial Event'. *International Political Sociology.* Vol. 6: 4–20.

Breslau, D. 2013. 'Designing a Market-Like Entity: Economics in the Politics of Market Formation'. *Social Studies of Science.* Vol. 43, No. 6: 829–851.

Business Innovation and Skills. 2013a. *Making Consumer Credit Markets Fairer.* London: Department for Business Innovation and Skills.

Business Innovation and Skills. 2013b. *Government Response to the Bristol University Report on High Cost Credit.* London: Department for Business Innovation and Skills.

Butler, J. 2010. 'Performative Agency'. *Journal of Cultural Economy.* Vol. 3, No. 2: 147–161.

Callon, M. Ed. 1998. *The Laws of the Markets.* London: Basic Blackwell.

Casey, E. 2008. 'Keeping Art to Its Edge'. *Rethinking Facticity.* Eds. Fr. Raffoul and E.S. Nelson. New York: Suny Press.

Centre for Responsible Credit. 2011. *How to Regulate Payday Lending: Learning from International Best Practice*. London: Centre for Responsible Credit.

Chessin, P. 2005. 'Borrowing from Peter to Pay Paul: A Statistical Analysis of Colorado's Deferred Deposit Loan Act'. *Denver University Law Review*. Vol. 83: 392–400.

Christophers, B. 2014. 'Wild Dragons in the City: Urban Political Economy, Affordable Housing Development and the Performative World-Making of Economic Models'. *International Journal of Urban and Regional Research*. Vol. 38, No. 1: 79–97.

Colorado. 2011. *Colorado Uniform Consumer Credit Code*. Denver: Attorney General of State of Colorado.

Cordray, R. 2014. *Prepared Remarks of Richard Cordray, Director of Consumer Financial Protection Bureau*. Nashville, Payday Field Hearing, 25 March 2014.

CPLA. 2009. *Response to Consultation Paper Issued by Manitoba Consumers Bureau*. Hamilton: Canadian Payday Loan Association.

CS Financial. 2010. *DFC Annual Report 2009*. Edmonton: CS Financial.

CS Financial. 2012. *DFC Annual Report 2011*. Edmonton: CS Financial.

De Goede, M. 2005. *Virtue, Fortune and Faith: A Genealogy of Finance*. Minneapolis: University of Minnesota Press.

Duggan, A. 2010. 'Consumer Credit Redux'. *University of Toronto Law Journal*. Vol. 60, No. 2: 687–705.

Esposito, E. 2013. 'The Structures of Uncertainty: Performativity and Unpredictability in Economic Operations'. *Economy and Society*. Vol. 42, No. 1: 102–129.

Europe Economics. 2003. *A New Consumer Credit Regime: Benefits, Compliance Costs and Firm Behaviour*. London: Europe Economics.

Federal Reserve. 2013. *Regulation Z Truth in Lending Act: Consumer Compliance Handbook*. Washington: Board of Governors of the Federal Reserve System.

Financial Conduct Authority. 2013. *Detailed Proposals for the FCA Regime for Consumer Credit*. London: Financial Conduct Authority.

Financial Conduct Authority. 2014. *Detailed Rules for the FCA Regime for Consumer Credit*. London: Financial Conduct Authority.

Foucault, M. 1984. *The Foucault Reader*. New York: Random House LLC.

Gibbons, D., N. Malhotra and R. Bulmore. 2010. *Payday Lending in the UK: A Review of the Debate and Policy Options*. London: Centre for Responsible Credit.

Henriksen, L. 2013. 'Performativity and the Politics of Equipping for Calculation: Constructing a Global Market for Microfinance'. *International Political Sociology*. Vol. 7: 406–425.

HM Treasury (UK). 2013. *Government to Cap Payday Loan Costs*. London: HM Treasury.

Hoyle. 1898. *The Game in Wall Street, and How to Play it Successfully*. New York: J.S. Ogilvie Publishing Co.

Irving, N. 2010. 'Bill 12: The Consumer Protection Amendment Act (Payday Loans)'. *Manitoba Law Journal*. Vol. 34, No. 3: 159–182.

Jones, H. 2014 'Watchdog to Review and Cap Payday Loan Rates'. *Reuters*. 12 March.

Karl, A. 2013. "Bank Talk': Performativity and Financial Markets'. *Journal of Cultural Economy*. Vol. 6, No. 3: 63–77.

Kaufman, A. 2013. *Payday Lending Regulation*. Washington, DC: Federal Reserve Board Division of Research and Statistics and Monetary Affairs – Finance and Economics Discussion Series: 2013–2062.

Kirsten, M. 2006. *Policy Initiatives to Expand Financial Outreach in South Africa*. Washington, DC: World Bank, Access to Finance/Building Inclusive Financial Systems.

Kodar, F. 2011. 'Conceptions of Borrowers and Lenders in the Canadian Payday Loan Regulatory Process: The Evidence from Manitoba and Nova Scotia'. *Dalhousie Law Journal*. Vol. 34, No.2: 443–481.

Kozbar, O. 2012. 'Perils of Governance through Networks: The Case of Regulating Payday Lending in Canada'. *Law and Policy*. Vol. 34, No. 1: 32–54.

Lake, T., N. Bourke, A. Horowitz and T. Roche. 2013. *Payday Lending in American: Policy Solutions*. Washington, DC: The Pew Charitable Trusts.

Langley, P. 2010. 'The Performance of Liquidity in the Subprime Mortgage Crisis'. *New Political Economy*. Vol. 15, No. 1: 71–89.

Langley, P. 2013. 'Equipping Entrepreneurs: Consuming Credit and Credit Scores'. *Consumption, Markets and Culture*. Vol. 17, No. 5: 448–467.

Langley, P. and A. Leaver. 2012. 'Remaking Retirement Investors: Behavioural Economics and Defined-Contribution Occupational Pensions'. *Journal of Cultural Economy*. Vol. 5, No. 4: 473–488.

Loxey, J. 2006. *Performativity*. London: Routledge.

Mackenzie, D. and Y. Millo. 2003. 'Constructing a Market, Performing Theory: The Historical Sociology of a Financial Derivatives Exchange'. *American Journal of Sociology*. Vol. 108, No. 1: 107–145.

McKernan, S., C. Ratcliffe and D. Kuehn. 2013. 'Prohibitions, Price Caps and Disclosures: A Look at State Policies and Alternative Financial Product Use'. *Journal of Economic Behaviour and Organization*. Vol. 95: 207–223.

Mezzadra, S. and B. Neilson. 2012. 'Between Inclusion and Exclusion: On the Topology of Global Space and Borders'. *Theory, Culture and Society*. Vol. 29, Nos. 4/4: 58–75.

Mitchell, T. 2007. 'The Properties of Markets'. *Do Economists Make Markets: On the Performativity of Economics*. Eds. D. Mackenzie, F. Muniesa and L. Sui. Princeton, NJ: Princeton University Press.

Moore, J. 2013. 'Payday Lenders who Prey on the Young Should Face the Law, not the FCA'. *The Independent*. 6 November.

MPUB. 2008. *Order No. 38/08*. Winnipeg: Manitoba Public Utilities Board.

MPUB. 2013. *Report of the Public Utilities Board of Manitoba in Respect of the 2013 Payday Loans Review*. Winnipeg: Public Utilities Board of Manitoba.

National Conference of State Legislatures. 2013. *Payday Lending Statutes*. Washington, DC: National Conference of State Legislatures.

Nova Scotia Utility and Review Board. 2008. *Decision 2008 NSUARB 87*. Halifax: Nova Scotia Utility and Review Board.

Office of Fair Trading. 2010a. *Review of High-Cost Credit: Final Report*. London: Office of Fair Trading.

Office of Fair Trading. 2010b. *Price Controls: Evidence and Arguments Surrounding Price Control and Interest Rate Caps for High Cost Credit*. London: Office of Fair Trading.

Office of Fair Trading. 2013. *Payday Lending Compliance Review Final Report*. London: Office of Fair Trading.

Oregon Consumer and Business Services. 2012. Salem, OR: State of Oregon, Department of Consumer and Business Services.

Personal Finance Research Centre. 2013. *The Impact of Business and Consumers of a Cap on the Total Cost of Credit*. London: Department for Business Innovation and Skills.
Preda, A. 2009. *Framing Finance: The Boundaries of Markets and Modern Capitalism*. Chicago, IL: University of Chicago Press.
Ramsay, I. and T. Williams. 2009. *The Crash that Launched a Thousand Fixes – Regulation of Consumer Credit after the Lending Revolution and the Credit Crunch*. London: W.G. Hart Legal Workshop: Law Reform and Financial Markets.
Reifner, U., S. Clerc-Renaud and M. Knobloch. 2010. *Study on Interest Rate Restrictions in the EU*. Brussels: Iff/Zew/European Commission.
Sherlock, S. 2014. *The Performativity of Value: On the Citability of Cultural Commodities*. New York: Lexington Books.
Smith, L. 2006. 'Has Michigan Legalized Usury?' *Michigan Bar Journal*. October 2006: 24–26.
Soederberg, S. 2012. 'The Mexican Debtfare State: Dispossession, Micro-Lending and the Surplus Population'. *Globalizations*. Vol. 9, No. 4: 561–575.
Spector, M. 2008b. 'Taming the Beast: Payday Loans, Regulatory Efforts, and Unintended Consequences'. *DePaul Law Review*. Vol. 57: 961–996.
Stäheli, U. 2013. *Spectacular Speculation: Thrills, the Economy, and Popular Discourse*. Stanford, CA: Stanford University Press.
Taylor, M. 2012. 'The Antinomies of 'Financial Inclusion': Debt, Distress and the Workings of Indian Microfinance'. *Journal of Agrarian Change*. Vol. 12, No. 4: 601–610.
Woodcock, S. and D. Cheung. 2010. *Consumer Decisions, Information and Understanding – A Behavioural Economics Perspective*. London: Office of Fair Trading.

6 From 'inclusion' to adverse incorporations

As Chapter 5 has argued, practices of fringe finance are now often accompanied by serious attempts to resettle the lines that separate legitimate from illegitimate finance, a redrawing of the very borders of what counts as permissible financial practice. The edges of finance, however, are not defined only in relation to the practices they contain. They are also constituted in relation to the bodies that they enfold. I argue in this chapter that the practices of fringe finance increasingly designate themselves, precisely, as attempts to move 'people across a line from outside to inside' (Mitchell 2007: 248). Although they invoke it in quite distinct ways, fringe financial practices are imagined as mechanisms that could effectively pull 'excluded' bodies across a line that separates the formal financial economy from conditions of financial exclusion. This is most evident in discourses of financial inclusion which mark micro-credit and micro-insurance. Moreover, even those practices not framed in the formal discourse of financial inclusion – fringe lending – are also often imagined as practices capable of moving bodies across the line from outside to inside. In whatever diverse form they appear, these discourses map fringe finance as an absorptive technology, as a mechanism capable of moving excluded bodies into conditions of inclusion and interiority.

The purpose of this chapter is to address, and place in critical context, fringe finance as a diagram of financial *incorporation*; a diagram not only of capital but of the bodies it addresses. This intention, in some important ways, impinges on debates relating to 'surplus populations'. As Marx notes, surplus populations are 'superfluous to capital's average requirements' (quoted in Tyner 2013: 704); a population with 'very limited relevance to capital at any scale' (Li 2009: 67). This population of intense human misery is constituted out of 'disposable' human material kept on the edges of capital as both a source of labour discipline and (latent) labour power. Capitalism, writes Marx, entails a 'disposable industrial army that belongs to capital quite as absolutely as if the latter had bred it at its own cost … an inexhaustible reservoir of disposable labour power … This is the absolute general law of capitalist accumulation' (Marx 1999 [1887]: Ch. 25). In its most 'stagnant' form, surplus populations comprise the *lumpenproletariat*, a group consisting of those – social outcasts, victims of long-term physical or mental illness, prostitutes, 'rag pickers' – which Marx categorized as beyond any possible scope of capitalist value (Denning 2010: 87; see also Fanon 1963; Collins 2011: 39–40; Gidwani and Reddy 2011: 1625)[1].

Although it has sometimes been depicted in functional terms as a mechanism determined by the objective requirements of capital, Li persuasively argues that surplus populations need to be understood in terms of the historical and geographical specificities which shape specific forms of accumulation and dispossession in particular settings (Li 2009, 70).[2] One set of conditions not well assessed in the conventional rendering of surplus populations, but which are key to our present, are the pressures associated with finance. For Marx, surplus populations are constituted in relation to productive capital, a map of their relation to (or removal from) capital only as a source of labour power or 'disposable human material' as workers. It is in this context that Gavin Smith has developed the most notable attempt to trace the relationship between finance and the populations surplus to the needs of capital. Smith's point of departure is a depiction of structural changes which have untied hegemony from social forces connected primarily to productive capital. In its stead is a 'selective hegemony' which enrols only those social forces which can participate in finance: privileged workers with pension assets, private savers attached to financial markets, those with connections to institutional investments. Social forces without connection to finance (precarious workers of all kinds, those without savings or retirement assets) are not an object of hegemonic rule, abandoned as bodies without value to circuits of financial capital. This entails:

> a shift in the relationship … between capital (dominated by finance) and ordinary people … these latter kinds of capitalist socialization found expression in hegemonic projects directed toward selected people rather than the population at large, leaving a residue of people surplus to these projects.
>
> (Smith 2011: 22)

In Smith's formulation, but in ways that echo its longer history as a concept, surplus populations are framed in relation to residue and negation; displacement from economic life or the latent (but mostly deferred) absorption into the spaces of capital. Moreover, the conceptual language associated with surplus populations renders inequality and vulnerability a function of expulsion not enrolment. The point of departure for this chapter, in contrast, is that contemporary financial markets, and the relation of those markets to their own edges, cannot be diagnosed with any simple language of removal.

In this chapter I want to train analytical attention not on the dislocating practices that expel populations from the reaches of capital but on the often disenfranchising processes associated *with* proximity. I want to highlight, as well, the ambiguity of that proximity which is often not well captured as dichotomous forms of either 'inclusion' or 'exclusion'. The questions that animate this chapter relate not to the ways in which vulnerable populations are removed (or held at distance in any singular sense) but how they are *incorporated* and how the terms of those incorporations can often work to deepen economic fragilities, inequalities or exposure to risk.

To do so, I invoke the notion of incorporation to pay attention to the actual terms and conditions of enrolment. Incorporation emphasizes metaphors of *placement* which foreground the active processes with which actors are set in place. Placement is both a site and an action, a location as well as the action required to arrive at that location. In these terms, incorporation asks questions not only about the locations – however contradictory – subjects are asked to occupy, but also the arrangements that make those placements possible: How are subjects channelled into various positions? What are the concrete mechanisms with which subjects are 'put into place'? What kinds of conditions do those arrangements actually constitute in practice?

In practice, methods of incorporation often channel bodies in ways that are not consistent with the positions they are asked to occupy. The main objective of this chapter is to disrupt the clean and unambiguous conception of inclusion mapped in diagrams of fringe finance. This chapter argues that practices of fringe finance are often characterized by a more complex topology than any simple 'inclusion/exclusion' formulation allows. The kinds of incorporation that circuits of fringe finance enact do, in some generic sense, 'include' in the sense that they bring bodies across a line that separates outside from inside, but they do so in ways that are ambiguous. What results is not some simple form of financial inclusion but of *adverse incorporation.*

In making this case, this chapter highlights several key technologies of (adverse) incorporation that practices of fringe finance constitute. At one level, fringe finance often constitutes various forms of 'technology of the self' which encourage individuals to enrol themselves into financial spaces in the name of their own security, freedom or choice. Micro-insurance, as Chapter 4 has argued, accomplishes a kind of financial incorporation by providing the 'under-insured' with mechanisms that allow them to govern themselves as agents capable of managing and bearing risk. Alongside technologies of the self, are mechanisms of incorporation that are more coercive or which are designed in ways that convey individuals not as financially capable agents but as immobilized bodies. Especially prevalent in forms of micro-lending are mechanisms of incorporation which immobilize the individuals they simultaneously include, which enrol individuals in differentiated financial spaces or which establish long-term commitments to high-cost forms of credit. Drawing on conceptions of immobility from anthropology, this chapter argues that fringe finance increasingly relies on techniques of *differentiation, immobilization* and *serialization* which enmesh vulnerable populations in expensive, variegated and long-term circuits.

To develop this type of analysis, this chapter is divided into two broad sections. A first section casts fringe finance as a map of absorption, a diagram which marks an unambiguous shift from spaces of exclusion to conditions of financial inclusion. This section also notes recent IPE literature on subjectivity as a kind of foundation for fuller analysis of the ways in which inclusion discourses position everyday populations within the spaces of capital. A second section sketches the core of the argument of this chapter by developing an inventory of the key techniques of adverse incorporation often constituted in practices of fringe finance. As this section notes, fringe financial practices often implicate the bodies they address in forms of adverse incorporation. This includes forms of incorporation which immobilize populations, which enmesh them in differentiated circuits of financial capital and which establish serialized forms of high-cost lending.

Diagrams of inclusion

Over the past two decades, notions of 'inclusion' have come to circulate in a wide range of settings with increasing policy clout.[3] At its most basic level, social inclusion/exclusion has emerged as an attempt to move beyond strictly material or economistic conceptions of poverty. Peter Townsend, a British writer often credited with introducing the term to the Anglo-American world in 1979, described social exclusion not only as a condition of poverty but a broader condition of marginalization from 'ordinary' customs and social practices (Levitas 2004: 44; Todman *et al.* 2009: 330). Most definitively, social exclusion has come to signal a lack of *participation*; a complex marginalization which prevents full access to the habits, norms, institutions and resources afforded 'normal' populations.[4]

In inclusion discourse, non-belonging is constituted as a combination of linked problems including economic disadvantage, cultural marginality, social stigma, and barriers of all kind to 'normal' levels of health-care, education and social services. As Silver and Miller note, 'poverty is a distributional outcome, whereas exclusion is a relational process of declining participation, solidarity and access' (quoted in Seckinelgin 2009: 207). Social exclusion, as it has emerged in various circles, has an important debt to institutional analysis. Unlike classical liberalism which assesses poverty as the result of individual pathology or irresponsibility, the notion of social inclusion/exclusion situates deprivation as the result of institutional failures or deficiencies.[5]

A particular variant of this kind of inclusion talk has recently become incorporated into the world of finance. Over the last number of years, in particular, financial inclusion has been constituted as an important policy goal which frames a norm of participation in which access to formal financial practices becomes key to social and economic enfranchisement (Manji 2010: 986). Although financial inclusion began circulating as early as 2003, the most important signal of this emergent global policy priority was codified in the G20 Principles of Innovative Financial Inclusion established in 2010. The Principles were accompanied by the formation of the Alliance for Financial Inclusion (AFI), a network of policy makers from financial authorities and central banks in developing and 'emerging' economies. The AFI initiated negotiations that led to the Maya Declaration signed in 2011 which establishes 'measurable commitments' to financial inclusion outcomes. Designed as a protocol signed by national financial authorities, the Maya Declaration commits G20 countries to expand the use of new technologies in order to reach financially excluded populations (Alliance for Financial Inclusion 2012). The global financial inclusion agenda has also been animated by a growing institutional shell which includes the Center for Financial Inclusion (CFI), the Consultative Group to Assist the Poor and the International Finance Corporation, the private financing arm of the World Bank (Soederberg 2013: 598). The Advisory Council for CFI includes representatives from key global financial firms (Morgan Stanley and Citi Financial) as well as academics and advocates associated with commercialized micro-credit. The network which CFI has mobilized has been successful in centring financial inclusion around the importance of private financial markets and commercialized financial practices in the reversal of financial exclusion; 'a state in which everyone who can use them has access to a full suite of quality financial services, provided … in a stable, competitive market to financially capable clients'[6] (www.centerforfinancialinclusion.org/about; see also Center for Financial Inclusion 2013).

CFI's signature policy initiative – an attempt to foster meaningful forms of global financial inclusion by 2020, conceives inclusion as a way of instrumentalizing a certain kind of financial value. This entails, most importantly, harnessing projected rapid income growth in low-income populations that will move large groups out of abject poverty (defined as less than US $1.25/day) and into an income bracket ($4 to $10/day), which although severely constrained, nonetheless will allow some disposable income. As a result of this 'income opportunity', the ability of those in poor segments 'to use formal financial services is set to increase, forming an enormous new market' (Kelly and Rhyne 2013: 8). This increase in pools of income at the lowest end of the economic spectrum, inclusion advocates argue, will make available new capital which could be profitably enfolded into the formal financial system. 'The rise of the $4–$10 class', creates an opportunity for financial inclusion because people at that level have at their disposal 'useful' sums of money that they may increasingly wish to manage in the formal financial sector' (Center for Financial Inclusion 2013: 13). Financial inclusion discourse sediments new lines of visibility in which the financial lives of those at or beyond the borders of capital are suddenly visible as useful forms of financial value.

Financial inclusion discourse is also central, either explicitly or implicitly, to diagrams of fringe finance. Micro-credit, for example, often orbits around a claim about the broadening of financial access and the extension of credit to those without regular access. The rapid expansion of micro-credit over the past 15 years, and the enormous attention it has attracted from development agencies, has been animated by a claim that 'MFIs do break down many barriers to financial inclusion' (Shankar 2013: 72). This has been particularly evident over the past decade during which micro-credit has become enmeshed in an enlarged policy matrix which stresses not only the extension of credit but a broader financial system built on a wide inclusivity across a range of basic financial services. 'Over time, the notion of micro-credit broadened … into the concept of building entire financial systems that serve their poor and low-income populations – financial systems that are "inclusive"' (Littlefield, Helms and Porteous 2006: 1). A kind of point of entry, micro-credit is now often conceived not as an end but as a strategic opening for a reformulation of financial systems that could secure widespread participation.

Similarly, micro-insurance is also often framed explicitly as a form of financial inclusion. Micro-insurance has become key to financial inclusion discourse as a practice that is increasingly concerned with the mobilization of individual financial capacity. 'Micro-insurance safeguards low-income households from using inefficient coping mechanisms in response to shocks' (Radermacher, McGowan and Dercon 2012: 67). This entails recasting individual subjects not simply as recipients of credit but as bodies capable of a broad form of participation in formal financial systems:

> access means more than the ability to obtain loans – financial services are needed to smooth consumption across time, diversify risks and secure livelihoods … Exposure to risk results in households' consumption being highly volatile over time, perpetuating the cycle of poverty … financial inclusion must include access to payments, credit, savings and insurance to achieve effective and sustainable results. Adopting an integrated approach is critical to accelerating the delivery of financial services to marginalized and low-income groups through a variety of strong and dynamic institutions.
>
> (Chatterjee 2012: 549–550)

Financial inclusion, albeit in a more implicit sense, has also been appropriated by other fringe financial practices, including commercialized micro-lending. Payday lending, for example, although not delineated within formal financial inclusion discourse, is often framed by its advocates as a form of inclusion, a way of absorbing populations not well served by formal financial institutions. The particular version of inclusion talk mounted by payday lenders orbits around the categories of 'unbanked' and 'underbanked'. Payday lenders consistently locate themselves in 'unbanked' space, depicting themselves as a practice targeted toward those not well served by mainstream finance. 'Unbanked' is mobilized in this discourse in order to mark a kind of fundamental distance that separates deposit institutions from the vulnerable populations served by fringe lenders. Home Credit, an emerging global chain of fringe and consumer lending products, makes explicit the link to formal inclusion. 'Our business philosophy', Home Credit notes in its public filings, 'promotes financial inclusion: we often work with clients who have little to no credit history, and who are underserved by traditional banks. We enable them to take advantage of all the benefits that financial services can bring them' (Home Credit 2014: 4).[7] In a fairly immediate sense, this discourse is used to depict payday lending as a necessary form, a fragile foothold for borrowers unconnected to or abandoned by mainstream financial institutions.

In regulatory proceedings, investor relations material and in public discourse, fringe lenders frame themselves as a kind of point of inclusion for the un/underbanked. This discourse is relational, establishing a contrast to banks and their retreat from fragile populations increasingly pushed away from mainstream deposit arrangements. As Daniel Feehan, CEO of Cash America, puts it:

> The supply and demand of consumer credit for the underbanked segment of society remains seriously out-of-balance today … Cash America and other non-bank financial services companies have grown dramatically over the past few decades by filling the gaps wherever possible. However, the retreat of traditional lenders, primarily the banks, has greatly outpaced all efforts … The gap continues to widen as more and more people find themselves in the ranks of the underbanked.
>
> (Cash America 2014: 7)

This unbanked discourse, conveniently mobilized by fringe lenders, closely resembles narratives of financial inclusion by depicting payday lending as a mechanism of absorption, an explicit technique with which financially excluded populations can access formalized credit. This is most clearly specified by DFC Global which, as Chapter 5 notes, has rebranded itself as 'a leading international financial services company serving unbanked and under-banked customers'. In this rebranding, unbanked has a kind of double-meaning, both a reference to itself as a formal but non-bank source of credit as well as a depiction of a form of financial inclusion deeply conditioned by banks and their exclusionary practices. 'Traditional banks', DFC suggests, 'cannot efficiently meet the needs of this population … [who] do not use formal financial services to save or borrow' (Dollar Financial 2013: 9). In this language, payday lending is articulated in the wider vocabulary of financial inclusion as a set of novel financial practices themselves crafted as points of access to formalized credit.

Inclusion and financial subjectivity

Because it implies that those beyond finance could become financial agents in one way or another, financial inclusion talk relates to recent discussions in IPE on questions of subjectivity. The 'essence of wealth', claims Maurizio Lazzarato, is 'the production of subjectivity … the injunction to become an economic "subject"' (Lazzarato 2012: 49–50). Subjects are not already existing or automatic components of financial markets, but are the products of complex processes of 'fabrication' and assemblage. In a neoliberal context, this entails attention to the kinds of positions that everyday actors are asked to assume – as investors, savers, pension-holders – in ways that 'hail' them as subjects capable, to some degree, of managing their own financial lives. As Hall and Appleyard suggest, this focus requires attention to the 'performative work involved in the (re)production of financial subjects … how individuals are positioned as being responsible for 'managing' their own financial subjectivities' (Hall and Appleyard 2012: 460). As financial markets have grown in size and scope over the past 40 years, everyday actors are increasingly asked to situate themselves as bodies capable of financial calculation and self-governance (Goggin 2012: 451).

The constitution of neoliberal financial subjectivities has occurred across a diverse range of practices. For French and Kneale, for example, one variant of financial subjectivity (the 'insurantial' subject) has been constituted in enhanced annuity investment products framed for 'careless lives': smokers, investors with health conditions or lifestyle 'impairments'. Enhanced annuities constitute certain kinds of financial subjectivities, reconciling these careless lives with the kinds of responsibilized subjects so important to the neoliberal imaginary (French and Kneale 2012: 402). Neoliberal financial subjectivities are constituted, however, not only among relatively prosperous middle class retirement savers (careless or otherwise), but also among those with much more precarious financial lives. Micro-credit, targeted at those mired in extreme poverty (see Chapter 3), is also increasingly implicated in the installation of neoliberal subjectivities. At the core of most micro-credit programmes is an intent to remake the poor as subjects responsible for their own economic welfare. Micro-credit is now a particularly important place where bodies are remade as agents with the capacity to bear a certain kind of financial autonomy. 'The neoliberal subject', argues Maclean, 'represents a particular configuration of the ideas of risk, responsibility and autonomy that is associated with advanced modernity … [micro-credit is a practice which] encourages subjects to take on responsibility for social risks and their own welfare in the market' (Maclean 2012: 458).

In some important ways, the subjectivities which inhabit financial markets are neoliberal positions, a kind of '"entrepreneur of oneself", who optimizes the use of its human capital in competition with all other economic agents' (Magnani 2013: 136). In other ways, however, subjectivities are both more complex and more uneven than any singular conception might imply. Paul Langley has written both about the diversity of positions associated with financial subjectivity as well as the unevenness of the ways in which actual bodies occupy those positions. For Langley, the financial subject is neither automatic nor fully consistent with simplistic conceptions of a neoliberal subject. Recent iterations of defined contribution pension schemes are, for Langley and Leaver, connected not to any abstracted sense of a rational investor subject, but a 'retirement investor' deeply reliant on 'nudges' informed by behavioural economics. The formatting of pension schemes in relation to behavioural economics has helped assemble 'retirement investors' not as rational actors but as bodies that could be formatted in ways that overcome their own hesitations and irrationalities (Langley and Leaver 2012: 478).

Although summoned to particular positions as investors, everyday subjects often come to occupy those positions in contradictory types of ways. 'Caught amid these contradictions', reminds Langley, 'individuals cannot identify with the subject position of the investor to which they are summoned in an unambiguous manner, and therefore negotiate and contest disciplinary power relations in important ways' (Langley 2007: 80). Many everyday subjects are confronted, in particular, with the contradictions rooted in contending positions they occupy as 'consumers', 'workers' or economic citizens of various kinds. In many instances these various forms of economic identity run up against each other, sometimes in tension, sometimes in affinity with each other.

Because they often emphasize private financial markets, financial inclusion discourses invoke the 'financially excluded' as subjects capable of bearing and governing themselves in those markets. 'Financial inclusion', notes Schwittay, 'is a global assemblage that constitutes materially poor people as fiscal subjects, financial consumers and monetary innovators' (Schwittay 2011: 382). Financial inclusion seeks novel forms of self-governing behaviour in which everyday subjects are capable of managing their day-to-day resources, protecting themselves against vulnerability, making investments, and leveraging assets of all kinds. 'Financial services', argues the CFI, 'foster independence, giving people greater ability to manage their resources … a bank account or enrolment in an electronic payment mechanism is essential for connecting with society's mainstream institutions … [exercising] economic citizenship' (Center for Financial Inclusion 2013: 6).[8] In this formulation, financial inclusion becomes a vehicle of participation in the broadest form and a way of mobilizing an active financial citizen capable of engagement with broader social institutions (Stein, Randhawa and Bilandzic 2011: 11).[9]

Discussions around subjectivity place important emphasis not on the ways in which everyday populations are rendered external to capital, but how they are absorbed as subjects *within* the spaces of capital. At another level, however, subjectivity does not fully capture the complexities with which everyday actors are channelled into financial spaces. The lines of analysis opened in discussions of subjectivity do offer critical perspectives on the ways in which everyday subjects are asked to take up positions – in Langley's terms ambiguous positions – in the interior spaces of financial capital. This analysis is accomplished by invoking metaphors of *position;* the ways in which new subject positions are constituted and how everyday populations are summoned into those positions which, however ambiguously, they come to occupy. Thus focus is on the sites that subjects are 'summoned' into in systems of discourse or practice.

In extending this focus on position, I will argue in the remainder of this chapter for the analytical importance of metaphors of *placement*. Placement has a double meaning as both the location where an object is placed as well as the action associated with arrangement, the particular pathways through which objects are 'set in place'. Placement is less focused on the locations to which bodies are hailed, or the positions modelled for them, than it is on the methods by which those bodies are asked to move or the currents they are asked to navigate en route. Placement implies the analytical importance of the concrete mechanisms that move subjects into place, the plural (often messy) techniques that shape direction and movement. Placement provokes important questions: What kinds of technologies help shape the ways in which everyday subjects are moved into financial practices? What kinds of movement are opened or closed to everyday populations as they are summoned into private financial markets?

Posing these questions is also important because they help mark a contrast with the kinds of clean and unambiguous lines charted by both financial inclusion discourse and by diagrams of fringe finance. As a diagram, financial inclusion offers a straightforward conception of bodies moving across clear and unambiguous lines separating 'exclusion' from 'inclusion'. 'Defined by an absence that is translated into a need', notes Schwittay, 'financial inclusion calls for scalable models of poor-appropriate financial technologies … which can only be achieved by tapping into mainstream financial markets' (Schwittay 2011: 383). This implies both a straightforward border that separates conditions of inclusion and exclusion as well as unambiguous forms of movement which transport bodies across that line in clear and often irreversible ways.

In contrast, and echoing Langley's work regarding the unevenness and ambiguity of everyday financial lives, I argue that the forms of actual financial practice unleashed by dreams of financial inclusion do not correspond to the unambiguous maps with which they are enunciated. Practices of fringe finance actually constitute deeply ambiguous, often adverse, channels through which subjects are absorbed into financial practices. As Deleuze reiterates, borders do not consist of straight or clear lines but trace out lines that pass 'through all points of resistance' (Deleuze 2006: 35–44). This image of twisting lines is particularly relevant to the very edges of the financial system. The financial edges are less a line that separates those who are interior from those exterior to capital as they are a zone in which flows of capital are organized, enabled and restricted in complex ways. The borders of finance are not 'devices that obstruct or block … [but] parameters that enable the channelling of flows and provide coordinates within which flows can be joined or segmented, connected or disconnected' (Mezzadra and Neilson 2012: 59).

Practices of fringe finance simultaneously include and exclude, incorporate and differentiate. Discourses of 'inclusion/exclusion' enact simplistic dichotomies which do not conform with the complex ways in which financial practices in particular, historically situated, contexts are organized. As Langley argues, dichotomies of inclusion/exclusion reduce issues of financial distress or vulnerability into simplistic questions relating to absorption within mainstream financial practices:

> Policy makers, activists, and social scientists tend to draw a clear dichotomy between 'inclusion' and 'exclusion' in addressing issues of contemporary financial inequality. However … this binary reduces a concern with inequalities to a largely singular question: are borrowers excluded from 'mainstream' or 'formal' market finance? … the dichotomous representation of an abnormal and informal space of financial exclusion, and the associated designation of the borrowers that occupy that space as 'alternative', 'high risk', 'sub prime' and so on.
>
> (Langley 2008: 163; see also Chapter 2)

This dichotomous rendering of 'inclusion' and 'exclusion' suggests that absorption within mainstream finance does not, simultaneously, enact new barriers or forms of displacement. There is now, however, a range of work from diverse currents of social and cultural theory which disputes any easy claim to inclusion as a pristine condition. This includes, most importantly, research related to the increasing population of bodies caught in the contradictions of migrant lives – bodies often incorporated into formal or political structures but in ways that, to varying degrees, are denied full citizenship rights or public entitlements. These bodies undermine the conventional premise of sovereignty and citizenship which rests on a firm distinction between 'inside' and 'outside'. As Andrijasevic argues,

> a documented entry into a country through official channels does not guarantee the stability and permanence of a legal status as one can fall 'in' and 'out' of legality … immigration regulations do not operate as mechanisms of straightforward inclusion or exclusion, but rather produce differentiation and stratification.
>
> (Andrijasevic 2009: 397–398)

In a useful turn of phrase these contradictions imply what Alain Badiou refers to as 'an excess of inclusion over belonging'; a kind of condition in which formal inclusion in political or social spaces is not matched with the fuller requirements afforded forms of belonging.

The 'excess of inclusion over belonging', however, now characterizes many social spaces beyond those occupied by the lives of migrants. Attending these spaces carefully requires more complex conceptual frameworks that can capture 'different kinds of folding and filtering that challenge the rigidity of the distinction between inclusion and exclusion' (Mezzadra and Neilson 2012: 60). Acknowledging this complexity requires a critical stance which refuses to take 'inclusion' at face value. This complexity is particularly relevant to practices of fringe finance which are preoccupied with the construction of channels for 'excluded' populations into formal financial practices. The channels erected in and through practices of fringe finance, however, are diverse and ambiguous, pathways that are as likely to chart conditions of *adverse incorporation* as they are any unblemished form of 'inclusion'.

Techniques of adverse incorporation

> To 'belong to someone' is the tragic lot of a bonded debtor, a person who has no autonomy at all.
>
> (Li 2013: 252)

A term with particular resonance in anthropology, adverse incorporation challenges the conceptual claims of inclusion by noting that the insertion of populations into economic or social practices can itself be an important source of vulnerability[10] (Dyer 2012: 262–263). Adverse incorporation suggests, as a point of departure, that 'poverty results not (only) from conditions of "exclusion" … as the orthodoxy maintains, but rather from the adverse terms' of absorption (Philips 2013: 172). This entails a relational perspective on the conditions of poverty, an approach that figures poverty or inequality not as a 'residue' of poor populations themselves, but as an outcome of wider political, economic and social relations. Locating poverty in this wider relational way implicates mainstream or formalized economic practices in the poverty for which they are often framed as a remedy. For Philips, this is a

> focus not on a condition of socioeconomic exclusion as the principle determinant of poverty and marginalization, but rather on the terms on which different social groups are included and incorporated into global economic activity … it is often the case that poor people are not in fact excluded from markets … but rather are included on adverse terms in ways that either perpetuate conditions of chronic poverty or heighten their vulnerability.
>
> (Philips 2011: 390)

Adverse incorporation has particular relevance to discussions of financial inclusion. It avoids locating economic or financial vulnerability as a kind of exception or anomaly, an aberration located somehow outside of capital. Adverse incorporation is used in ways that avoid 'exteriorizing or exceptionalizing poverty, which makes it the product of abnormal or pathological, rather than everyday, social processes' (Mosse 2010: 1158–1159). Adverse incorporation does not foreground 'the role of physical isolation … in constraining access to states, markets and civil society … [but the adverse impact of] specific forms of inclusion' (Howson 2012: 199). To develop this kind of analysis requires attention to the concrete ways in which incorporation actually unfolds.[11] This entails analysis of 'the ways in which the terms of *inclusion* can be problematic, disempowering or inequitable … [a focus on] the terms of access' (Hickey and du Toit, quoted in Howson 2012: 200). In contrast to financial inclusion discourse, this approach implies the importance of detailed analysis of the actual (uneven) practices of incorporation:

> While the term 'social exclusion' promises to focus attention on the general socially disabling effects of poverty, this promise is undermined by its failure to come to grips with the precise ways in which poor peoples are actually inserted within broader social and economic formations of power. Part of the problem here is the very simplicity and appeal of the language of social exclusion, and the assumption that it is possible to counterpose 'inclusion' and 'exclusion' in a simple way. What defines marginality is not exclusion (or even imperfect inclusion!) but the terms and conditions of incorporation.
>
> (du Toit 2004: 1003; see also Hickey and du Toit 2007)

The conceptual emphasis of adverse incorporation is imminently concrete and mundane. This focus makes visible specific technologies or mechanisms of incorporation which particular practices encode. Given this focus, what kinds of techniques of incorporation do practices of fringe finance constitute? If the practices of fringe finance do not correspond to the diagram which maps clean and unambiguous lines of insertion, what mechanisms of incorporation do they establish?

Technologies of differentiation

In the remainder of this chapter I argue that fringe finance relies on three particular kinds of technologies of adverse incorporation. This is not an exhaustive typology of forms of adverse incorporation in fringe finance. Rather, I want to note these three forms as relatively important but deeply ambiguous ways in which fringe financial services open 'access' to financial practices. The first of these forms of adverse incorporation are channels of differentiation. Fringe financial practices, albeit in diverse ways, often incorporate those outside of the financial system into formalized financial practices, but in ways that establish differential conditions – that is with greater costs and risks than are often prevalent in 'mainstream' or 'prime' financial markets. What often results are spaces that are both formalized and yet subjected to harsher conditions, risks or costs than those offered through 'core' financial markets.

Micro-insurance extends tangible benefits in certain contexts, but also constitutes differential circuits for micro-clients by offering benefits that are directly related to existing levels of income or asset wealth. Because micro-insurance is increasingly constructed as an investment, it generates 'returns' which are ultimately linked to the initial outlays made via premiums or payments (Wissoker 2013: 403). The most significant way in which micro-insurance establishes differential circuits of incorporation, however, is in the ways in which it exposes micro-insurance clients to risks that are qualitatively different from those that predominate in mainstream insurance markets. Index insurance, for example, a technique discussed in some detail in Chapter 4, is an innovative technique not generally marketed to those in core insurance markets. Because it is based on an index for weather risk, index insurance exposes insured parties to basis risk. Basis risk refers to the possibility that insurance may not protect against actual losses in specific locations if the index and actual conditions that prevail in those locations differ. As Johnson argues:

> [the] partial nature of index insurance, which covers only the losses estimated by the index, inevitably requires farmers to bear the remaining so-called 'basis risk' – the chance that their own individual experience could substantially differ from that estimated by the index on which compensation is based.
>
> (L. Johnson 2013: 2665)

Because this type of insurance – modelled on weather derivatives – is not offered in any significant way in mainstream insurance markets, it helps establish a differential circuit which establishes conditions and risks more onerous than those at the 'centre' of the financial system.

There are also striking technologies of differentiation in fringe credit markets. Often justified as a function of the high costs required to provide services to unbanked populations, fringe lending often imposes costly rates of interest which subject micro-borrowers to punishing burdens. For example, the annual nominal lending interest rate charged by MFIs from 2000–2008 was 42% in Africa (Cotler and Almazan 2013: 70). These figures are relatively consistent with levels of interest charged across other contexts, especially by for-profit or commercialized providers which routinely impose rates of credit which range from 30% to 40% expressed as APR (see Taylor 2012). Many micro-lenders however, including some of the largest institutions in the sector, have often imposed costs much higher than this 40% standard. Banco Compartamos funded rapid expansion by charging rates of interest that resulted in real costs of interest that exceeded 100% (Aitken 2010: 234). Moreover, research now suggests that rates of interest are not directly linked to high costs of loan provision (or loss) but to the increased pressures associated with commercial and financial exposure. Recent studies, for example, note that as many as 75% of MFIs charge rates of interest designed to maximize profit rather than reduce poverty (Gonzalez 2010b: 1–6). As the discussion in Chapter 3 indicates, evidence is accumulating that high interest rates are often pursued as an *explicit* strategy designed to attract global capital (Aitken 2010: 232).

Moreover, because loans are formally designed to support micro-enterprises (although research now suggests that micro-loans are often used for a variety of purposes in practice), the costs of loans need to be paid from revenue generated through these enterprises. Credit extended at rates of interest ranging from 25–35% (and often peaking at much higher levels) requires micro-enterprises to achieve significant returns on equity in order to repay loans and realize any 'profit'. Many micro-enterprises struggle to return enough revenue to cover interest which is often their most costly input (Taylor 2011: 492).

Because micro-enterprises are fragile and operate on very thin margins, the relative weight of these costs are compounded. As Taylor has noted, the problem has been particularly pressing in India where MFIs often borrow lending capital from banks at priority sector rates of 11–15% but extend this credit back to micro-borrowers at much higher rates of interest (Taylor 2012: 608). Because micro-credit loans are extended to an already vulnerable population, the differentiated circuit of capital they help inscribe is particularly pronounced.

In slightly different, but equally pronounced terms, payday lending has also established differential circuits of credit to those least able to afford it. At the heart of the political and social controversies associated with payday lending are the relatively high rates of interest they impose. Although figures vary, rates of interest charged by payday lenders almost always reach over 300%, sometimes much higher. The Consumer Financial Protection Bureau (CFPB), for example, notes that the mean APR of large lenders is 339% and the median 322%, although a 'typical' APR among all sizes of payday lenders is 491% (CFPB 2013a: 17). Because Canadian payday regulators all allow for fees higher than that, rates of interest charged in the Canadian sector are substantially higher than American fees. In some cases anti-poverty activists, and even some lenders, have reported 'typical' APRs that can exceed 1000% expressed as APR.[12] Given this diversity, and range of fees, Fourcade and Healy rightly suggest that the bulk of payday lenders now extend credit at costs that most frequently range between 400% and 700% (Fourcade and Healy 2013: 568).

These differential rates, moreover, intersect with other factors that help situate most borrowers within deeply segmented economic circuits. Although lenders often frame fringe lending as a service consumed by 'average' or 'middle class' borrowers, evidence now suggests that payday borrowers occupy the lower reaches of the income scale (CFPB 2013a: 18). This often means that differentiated circuits of financial inclusion impose costs on those least able to afford it. Melzer, for example, suggests that payday borrowers, are encumbered by differentiated costs which are magnified by existing vulnerabilities – vulnerabilities which often trigger the need for short-term credit in the first place. 'Contrary to the view that improving credit access facilitates important expenditures', he argues, 'the empirical results suggest that, for some low-income households, the debt service burden imposed by borrowing inhibits their ability to pay important bills' (Melzer 2011: 550). Differentiated circuits, in their widest sense, are not points of financial inclusion, but pathways to worsening financial fragility or deepening forms of vulnerability (Langley 2008: 183).[13]

Differentiated circuits of capital, however, not only impose higher costs, but also facilitate a kind of 'social sorting'. Social sorting entails the practices designed 'to classify people and populations according to varying criteria, to determine who should be targeted for special treatment, suspicion, eligibility … and so on' (Lyon 2002: 41). The differential forms of credit enabled by practices of fringe finance are, in many important ways, sorted by race (Fourcade and Healy 2013; Ashton 2012). 'A disproportionate number of these borrowers are elders, African Americans, Latinos, women and rural residents' (Calhoun and Bailey 2006: 195). Payday lending, for example, has often targeted neighbourhoods populated by ethnic minorities. In doing so, it is only one of a suite of credit practices – predatory mortgages, credit cards, pawns – explicitly targeted to racial minorities but in ways that clearly mark out those populations as 'risky'; a designation which imposes exceptional costs and conditions on those populations (Dymski 2009a: 150).

Although, as this book has argued, the practices of fringe finance are enormously diverse, they often share a certain entanglement in technologies of differentiation. These are technologies which simultaneously enmesh populations within formalized financial relations *and* expose them to differential conditions of access. This implies that these practices are not implicated in any simple form of inclusion but in forms of market incorporation which are simultaneously marked by deeper stratification *within* those expanded markets. There has been, suggest Fourcade and Healy (2013: 565), 'increased inclusion at the boundary, and increased segmentation within the market'. Differential forms of inclusion, however, do not only impact points of access to financial markets, but also the possibility of ongoing currents of movement, or *immobility*, within those spaces.

Technologies of immobilization

Techniques of (adverse) incorporation not only enrol populations into financial spaces, but also shape, enable or limit movement within those spaces. The ways in which bodies move through financial spaces it not guaranteed in advance but is conditioned by the kinds of techniques with which incorporation is achieved. This implies the importance of im/mobility. Mobility is a trope often at the heart of the ways in which we imagine finance. For Watson, 'markets are a less important subject than the multiple ways in which capital can be conceived as being mobile' (Watson 2007: 12). This language places mobility as a kind of norm at the heart of global finance, an assumption that frames unimpeded movement as both 'normal and desirable' (Jonsson 2011: 4).

Mobility, however, is far from a 'normal' condition in the spaces of global finance broadly conceived. 'The claim that we live in a world of easy and increasing mobility', argues Turner, 'is overly optimistic … the majority live in a world where mobility is sticky and problematic' (Turner 2010: 243). For Turner, contemporary processes of globalization are definitively characterized by their ability 'to contain and immobilize flows of people, goods, and services … Rather than increasing mobility, we can perceive the emergence of an immobility regime' (Turner 2010: 244). In these terms, immobility cannot simply be understood as a kind of residue or absence – a kind of failure to achieve movement – but is an actively constituted condition that is itself produced in complex kinds of circumstances (Larson, Urry and Axhausen 2006: 91).

Mobility and immobility are relational categories deeply implicated in each other. 'Understanding movement and its impact on people and places', argues Jonsson, 'requires [at the same time] an understanding of the absence of movement' (Jonsson 2011: 14). To develop a more relational conception of im/mobility in the practices of fringe finance, I draw on work in anthropology and in migration/refugee studies which situates immobilization as a primary and irreducible condition in its own right. Carling (2002), for example, emphasizes the importance of 'involuntary immobility', external obstacles or barriers to movement that systematically restrict people seeking movement. (See also Aitken 2012: 212.)[14] Contemporary images of migration, he notes, 'evoke immediate associations of fluidity and permeability of borders … [However] one of the most striking aspects of today's migration order … is the degree of conflict over mobility and the frustration about immobility' (Carling 2002: 5). There is a striking inconsistency, however, that arises between this definitive importance of immobility and accounts of globalization which emphasize movement and fluidity. Even accounts of the darkest edges of global politics – war, chaos, disaster – are enunciated in a language which stresses movement; a language of displacement, removal and exile. Although certainly an apt characterization of some dimensions of global politics, this language nonetheless renders invisible processes that immobilize. 'In a world in which social reproduction is often realized "in motion" … it may well be the processes of "involuntary immobilization" that proves most analytically relevant' (Lubkemann 2008: 468). In general this focus on immobility as a constituent dimension of the global economy upends narratives that place mobile subjects as a kind of singular hallmark of globalized practices. As Cresswell (2012: 39) notes, 'while there is a temptation to think of a mobile world as something that replaces a world of fixities … we need to constantly consider the politics of obduracy, fixity and friction'. This entails developing fine-grained analysis of the actual techniques and practices that produce and shape forms of fixity in particular settings.

The practices of fringe finance often immobilize the populations that they incorporate. The very differential costs they impose contribute to forms of immobility in fringe lending markets. Because the costs in these markets are relatively high, borrowers are unable to leverage initial access to credit into broader forms of financial mobility. Even though advocates frame payday lending as a mechanism which can ease financial difficulty, research now suggests that it can immobilize borrowers by presenting them with costs that require additional credit. These additional costs prevent borrowers not only from retiring initial loans, but also from meeting immediate financial requirements. 'The expansion of payday credit', argues Melzer, 'exacerbates financial difficulties … [and] their difficulty in paying mortgage, rent and utilities bills' (Melzer 2013: 3). The immediacy of high costs can often precipitate an immobilizing cycle in which costly debt becomes a prerequisite for additional indebtedness, all of which prevents borrowers from improving their conditions. Put baldly by Fourcade and Healy (2013: 568), 'those who are offered rotten terms in the market because they are riskier prospects are more likely to remain so when the terms on offer are rotten to begin with'.

Practices of fringe finance, however, often inscribe limits on mobility in ways that exceed the immobilizing effects of high costs. Fringe lending, for example, is not linked to formal switching mechanisms which would allow indebted borrowers entry into mainstream circuits of credit (Ramsay 2006: 5; see also Aitken 2012: 214). Because payday lenders neither make use of nor routinely access formal credit reports generated by credit reporting agencies, the successful repayment or retirement of payday loans does not allow borrowers to access more affordable credit streams. This means that payday lending is not integrated into mainstream credit reporting, leaving borrowers without any mechanism that would record their credit histories. In short, 'because payday lenders generally track prior payday advance defaults using databases independent from the major credit bureaus, approval decisions and prior defaults do not affect borrowers' credit reports' (Stango 2012: 27; Bhutta, Skiba and Tobacman 2013: 2). ACE Cash Express, which explicitly refers to its offerings as 'Payday loans without credit checks', notes in a warning to its customers that payday loans do not require 'lengthy paperwork or an extensive credit history … Do not apply for a payday loan to rebuild your credit. These short-term financial tools are not designed to restore ailing credit histories' (https://www.acecashexpress.com/payday-loans/payday-loans-without-credit-checks). Designed only as a source of short-term and unsecured credit, payday lending offers no meaningful channels of financial mobility.

The disconnection between payday lending and established forms of credit reporting is a circular relation. Because lenders often appeal directly to borrowers with impaired or unknown credit histories, they do not consult (expensive) credit reporting records. This disconnection, in turn, becomes an important and attractive pull for borrowers without established or positive credit credentials. What is constituted in these practices, however, is an immobilizing circuit of credit available to subprime borrowers with little prospects of transcending the onerous costs it facilitates.

> Because payday lenders do not usually check a borrower's credit or report to the major credit bureaus, payday loans may be an attractive option to those with poor credit history or who are concerned that a depository institution may deny them a traditional loan. According to payday lenders, they generally assume their customers have unfavourable credit histories and therefore do not typically pull credit reports.
>
> (Cackley 2011: 4)

The obstacles to mobility which confront payday borrowers are often applied unevenly. For example, although payday borrowers are unable to access formal credit reporting processes when taking out or repaying loans, they are routinely subjected to these processes when they default or fall behind on loan payments.[15] Further complicating the immobilities established in payday lending are new credit scoring experiments within the spaces micro-lending. Although most payday lenders are not integrated into credit reporting systems, there have been recent experiments in credit scoring in these sectors. As Paul Langley has aptly noted, the wide spectrum of subprime borrowing is increasing subject to the credit scoring and assessment techniques associated with mainstream financial institutions (Langley 2008). Recent experiments in credit scoring for payday lending actually offer unique forms of assessment which, in some important ways, can have coercive effects.

The most active institutional presence in the scoring of payday borrowers is Teletrack, a risk assessment service managed by the large global financial consulting firm, CoreLogic. Not integrated into mainstream credit reporting bureaux, Teletrack's credit scoring techniques offer 'statistical risk models … a faster, more predictive way to assess risk' than conventional storefront methods and provides a way to 'objectively consider the likelihood of early payment default on short-term loans' (CoreLogic 2013). Teletrack's scoring, in part, resembles mainstream 'risk models', but using a condensed scale and method not commensurate with mainstream credit reporting protocols; a financialized technique adapted to the narrow requirements of payday lenders.

Models like Teletrack offer an abstracted form of credit scoring divorced from broader processes of credit reporting. This package encodes its own specialized language – its own credit assessment scale, a narrowly constituted inventory of factors – legible *only* in webs of fringe lending. Equally immobilizing, however, are recent experiments designed to assemble broader credit scores that could circulate widely within subprime spaces. Corescore, for example, essentially assembles data about fringe borrowers and sells it to subprime mortgage and home equity lenders. In its own terms, the product seeks 'to provide lenders increased visibility into borrower credit behaviour and future credit risk … producing a sharper, predictive view of the consumer' (CoreLogic 2011). This is a sharper form of visibility, however, that circulates within fringe and subprime financial spaces, amplifying the ways in which borrowers are made visible in but not beyond those spaces. CoreScore is framed as a 'new type of credit file', a 'predictive view of the consumer' assembled by mining all forms of public information that might help identify credit risk: 'missed rental payments that have gone into collection, any evictions or child support judgements, as well as any applications for payday loans along with … repayment history' (Bernard 2011).

This type of experiment has also been extended by Experian, one of the established global credit bureaus central to global financial markets. In 2011, Experian launched *Extended View*, an explicit attempt to generate credit reports for approximately 80 million unbanked Americans. Extended View is an explicit attempt to target and score the un/underbanked, a population which 'are unscoreable by most traditional credit score models' (Experian 2013: 2). An 'advanced *scoring and segmentation tool,* Extended View scores are powered by traditional and alternative data sources … and new analytic techniques, driving exceptional predictive power for the risk assessment of the underserved and formerly unscoreable consumer segment' (Experian 2013: 2, emphasis added). The 'alternative data sources' harnessed by Experian include both proprietary and public information relating to loan repayment history (generated via Teletrack), rental payment history, and a wide range of public records (New 2012).[16] Experian has put particular emphasis on public information generated from criminal and legal proceedings in a vast array of settings. To assemble these credit reports, Experian harnesses '600 million unique criminal records … [public information gleaned from] an expanding number of civil cases, bankruptcies and eviction records … data from more than 1,400 different government municipalities at the county, state and federal levels … [and] rental payment data from … property management and collection companies' (New 2012). Expansively incorporating data from petty legal proceedings, Extended View assembles credit profiles projected from an immense web of data, most of which is often only indirectly related to credit practices.

Because the data at the heart of these calculations is often generated in coercive settings, the credit reports they create risk further immobilizing those without formalized or positive credit histories. In some important ways, riskiness is programmed as a kind of norm in these scoring experiments; constituting the under/unbanked population as bodies with inherent credit riskiness. The director of Experian's project has noted, for example, that their new scoring models assume payday lending as a signal of *inherent* financial risk. 'Generally speaking', notes Deuchars, 'just the presence of a payday loan is a sign of financial difficulty and treating this credit like any other piece of mainstream finance can lead to scorecard irregularities' (Deuchars 2013: 7). Moreover, placing emphasis on payday loans (via Teletrack scores) may not so much reflect inherent credit riskiness as much as high costs of credit. 'Reporting high cost credit', notes one consumer activist, 'actually decreases a credit score because the high interest rates on those loans hamper the consumer's ability to repay … using high cost loans as a score of credit reporting information could simply mean bad credit scores instead of no credit scores' (National Consumer Law Center 2009: 1).

The data assembled in these scores may also be incomplete. Because they incorporate data from collections agencies and legal proceedings associated with defaulted credit, and because they do not have access to data related to retired credit from many sources (pawns, auto loans, other fringe lenders), the scores generated in these experiments over-sample negative credit outcomes. Chi Chi Wu, an American consumer legal advocate, notes that 'there is evidence that all it could do for a substantial portion of low- and moderate-income consumers is make their credit files worse' (quoted in Bernard 2011). In launching the new service, officials from Experian noted that 30% of the un/underbanked its new score addresses are 'low risk' at levels that could potentially allow greater access to mainstream credit (Experian 2013). This signals, however, that the vast majority of borrowers scored by Extended View are constituted (or reconfirmed) as risky subjects. These scoring experiments are designed in relatively narrow ways, not as self-consciously crafted pathways into mainstream credit but as instruments which efficiently surveil and quantify what are often perceived by financial institutions as risky borrowers. Risk assessment and scoring methods, however, constitute and shape the risky bodies they purport merely to document. As Experian itself suggests, these models are attempts both to score *and* segment; a form of knowledge designed as much to categorize borrowers into particular grades as they are to push them out of those categories. Because they draw on public information which emphasizes default and riskiness, these models simultaneously render visible *and* immobile the risky bodies they classify (Fourcade and Healy 2013: 566).[17]

Most importantly, these experiments constitute risky subjects in ways that are shaped by the patterns of profitability and value that characterize fringe lending. Because they are a service directly marketed to fringe lenders, (as a scoring device) and not widely taken up by a wider universe of financial institutions (as a reporting mechanism) these experiments often place the profitability of lenders at the centre of their concern. Experian's method for assessing credit risk in payday lending, for example, is definitively shaped by the unique conditions for profitability in that sector. Experian's model dispenses with the standard assessment of delinquency, defined as those accounts not paid in full by the due date. Because many payday loans are routinely extended beyond the initial repayment date (or rolled over), and because this practice is a key source of profitability for lenders, Experian adopted a revised method which scores ultimate long-term default (as opposed to short-term repayment failure) as a key variable in the determination of credit-worthiness. This technique inscribes credit distress as a normal and endemic feature of payday lending; an accepted and stabilized source of profit. 'Many of these cases', notes Experian in its explanation of a method which insulates short-term repayment difficulties from negative credit scores, 'repay in full, and end up being profitable for the lender' (Deuchars 2013: 12). Although payday borrowers face financial distress from fringe loans, and are often constituted as a risk across long-term horizons, their short-term credit burdens are enabled and legitimized as an important source of profit and value.

To the extent that the frontiers of credit assessment and reporting now address payday and fringe lending, they do so in ways that are often too narrow to actually facilitate transition to more affordable forms of credit. The small number of alternative models which do take transition to mainstream markets seriously, place that transition in the context of additional interventions designed carefully in ways which both reconstruct positive credit histories but also ensure that borrowers who enter mainstream circuits of credit do so without financial distress. ZestFinance, for example, has begun to experiment with a much wider stream of data to assess credit capacity of unbanked populations more broadly. Noting that 'all data is credit data', Zest mines a broad range of public information (including information related to social network usage) in order to generate more positive outcomes for those without access to conventional banking services. 'A lot of data for the underbanked is inaccurate or missing', Zest founder Douglas Merrill argues, 'a heavy weight is placed on a small number of signals – bankruptcy, credit card default' (quoted in Crossman 2012; see also Clark 2013). Zest is experimenting in broader forms of credit scoring and partnering with lenders, such as LendUp, which employ that data in more carefully sculpted lending programmes (Quinton 2013).

Long-term immobilization is now a condition built into the very techniques that make fringe lending possible and profitable in the first place. In constructing its credit scoring experiment, Experian sought to make visible, to give calculative form, to a unique tension at the heart of payday lending. This tension emerges from a practice that ties profits to the longer-term stream of interest that accrues when borrowers routinely fail to meet initial loan payment conditions. These initial repayment failures, scored in ways that secure their continuation, enable additional layers of indebtedness and deepening interest payments. 'For a significant volume of cases in a payday loan environment … this is expected, the consumer repays in full with additional interest, remaining profitable for the lender' (Deuchars 2013: 16). This 'expected' outcome is not indicative of a practice which opens greater access to more affordable financial services. Rather, it signals a web of escalating costs as borrowers are converted into immobilized, but stabilized, sources of profit and value. It is in these terms that payday borrowers become, for lenders, a long-term income stream, although one constituted in and out of short-term – *serialized* – pieces.

Technologies of sustained/serialized use

> Payday lending doesn't solve a financial crisis, it creates a new one every second week.
>
> (King 2012)

Forms of fringe lending are formatted into narrowly conceived devices. Payday lending is explicitly framed as a short-term mechanism designed to respond to immediate financial exigencies. At one level, this is simply a recognition of the very design of payday lending as a form of credit extended for the duration of a single pay period. At a broader level, however, payday lenders have mounted a particular discourse – in regulatory submissions, in legal proceedings, and in their own marketing material – which delineates payday loans as a short-term practice. Lenders consistently explain the high costs they extend as a function of the inefficiencies associated with servicing loans over short terms. This has often entailed the mobilization of a certain kind of expertise capable of delineating payday loans as costs that need to be recovered quickly. Lawrence Gould, for example, testified on behalf of lenders in Canadian regulatory hearings by arguing that payday lending, and its costs, are uniquely conditioned by the short life span they occupy. 'It's really misleading', argued Gould, 'to calculate these annualized or effective annual rates of return. There's no question that these loans are high-cost because of their design as short-term, small loans' (Gould 2007: 220; see also Aitken 2012). Payday loans are constituted not as a set of long-term entanglements but as brief, even exceptional, arrangements.[18]

Fringe lending, however, is used in ways that exceed these formal framings. Payday lending is often accessed not as a short-term form but as a longer-term requirement. Moreover, these types of (mis)uses are an endemic part of the ways in which fringe lending practices are designed and a direct function of the technologies of incorporation those practices entail. Fringe lending practices often explicitly channel borrowers in ways that contradict or exceed the formal discourses with which they are associated.

Although framed as a short-term mechanism, payday lending is mostly extended as part of longer-term credit relations. Most importantly, a research consensus now emphasizes the ways in which payday loans are used to address 'persistent shortfalls rather than temporary emergencies' (Bourke, Horowitz and Roche 2012: 6). Payday borrowers, for example, are indebted to lenders for an average of 211 days every year, a figure that extends to 372 days over a typical two-year span (King and Parrish 2011: 21).[19] Because payday borrowers often experience this kind of chronic indebtedness – and not short-term financial emergencies – they persistently extend or 'rollover' loans (Center for Responsible Lending et al. 2012). Even in the face of regulatory sanctions, borrowers persistently extend initial loans for an additional two-week period, take out consecutive loans in order to retire an initial loan, or access credit from multiple sources in order to meet the demands of an existing loan. Each of these manoeuvres results in escalating fees. 'Research consistently shows that most borrowers obtain multiple rollovers or loans per years' (Johnson 2012: 393).[20] It is now estimated that 76% of annual loan volume (totalling US $27 billion in loan originations) is generated by repeat borrowers, a level that has kept payday lending losses below 3% (Parrish and King 2009: 11). Recent research indicates that the 'average borrower has 10, 11, or 12 payday transactions per year … revealing a high rate of rollover transactions per borrower' (Francis 2010: 617).[21] The CFPB has similarly concluded that loan rollovers and extensions are now at the very heart of patterns of payday borrowing. Almost half of borrowers conclude more than ten transactions annually while nearly 30% of borrowers become entangled in over 20 transactions (CFPB 2013a: 21; see also Montezemolo 2013: 3). Striking also is the frequency of persistent payday borrowing. An overwhelming majority of extended loans (87%) occur during the very next pay period after a retired loan and almost all renewed loans (94%) are negotiated within a 30 day window, a further 'indication of the serial usage of these loans among borrowers' (Parrish and King 2009: 9; see also Montezemolo 2013: 3; Carter, Skiba and Sydnor 2013: 3).[22] The persistence of this kind of serial loan extension has transformed payday lending into a long-term set of credit relations. This has also enabled a kind of loan 'churning' in which initial credit is extended in ways that unleash longer-term obligations (Parrish and King 2009: 5).[23]

This longer-term use is intrinsic to the design of payday lending. The CFPB, for example, estimates that the majority of fees which payday lenders earn are generated from borrowers who make repeated and extended transactions. 'Three-quarters of all loan fees', they note, 'come from those with more than 10 transactions [per year] … In contrast, loan fees generated by consumers who borrowed six or fewer times over 12 months make up 11% of the total' (CFPB 2013a: 22; see also MPUB 2013: 65). This implies that long-term entanglements, and the fees those entanglements generate, are intrinsic to payday lending profit models. As a CEO of a large payday lender has bluntly noted, serious forms of profit and revenue are most importantly generated from borrowers with long-term requirements. 'The theory in the business', he noted at an industry event, 'is you've got to get that customer in, work to turn him into a repetitive customer, long-term customer, because that's really where the profitability is' (quoted in Johnson 2012: 393; see also King and Parrish 2011: 11).

Long-term entanglement is intrinsic to the very design of payday lending as a practice. Payday loans are a non-amortized form of credit requiring borrowers to retire the debt in its entirety shortly after it is assumed. This confrontation with a single 'balloon payment' often channels borrowers into loan extensions or rollovers. Because borrowers often experience wider forms of economic distress, when faced with repayment pressure they often negotiate extensions to avoid the burden of a single payment. Research now indicates that merely 14% of payday borrowers can afford to regularly retire the full amount of non-amortizing loans (Bourke, Horowitz and Roche 2013: 6). In addition, because these loans are 'secured' by either a pre-authorized cheque or an authorized electronic access to accounts, they assert a certain repayment priority which encourages loan renewal instead of delinquency (Johnson 2012: 392; see also CFPB 2013a: 43–44).[24] A function of their very design, payday lending constitutes costly patterns of 'sustained use'; credit that is channelled not as short-term requirement but a longer-term, often ongoing kind of relation.

It is in this context that payday lending constitutes a technology of *serialized* or *sustained* use. Serialization, in a general sense, refers to the release of an object over time in accordance with a regular rhythm. As consumer advocate Uriah King notes, payday lending often constitutes 'a serial requirement' (King and Parrish 2011), an entanglement with a distinctive, regular and ongoing pattern over time. Serialization, however, has a second related but more specific meaning associated with computer science. Serialization, in this context, refers to the disaggregation of an object into bits or a byte stream. Serialization is the process by which a larger object is encoded into a stream of byte data so that it can either be transferred across a network or, eventually, reconstructed by reading the byte stream (a process referred to as deserialization). Serialization allows an object to be efficiently deconstructed so that it could then be streamed, transported, stored or reconstructed. Payday lending, a mechanism formally organized as short-term credit, but accessed and practiced as a long-term or sustained requirement, operates as a technology of serialization. By channelling long-term credit requirements into a short-term mechanism, payday lending *serializes* credit relations. It does this by converting what is essentially long-term credit requirements into a regular stream of disaggregated short-term credit engagements. Payday lending substitutes longer-term credit arrangements (with amortized conditions) with a *stream* of short-term credit arrangements extended over a longer but regularized series. The regular stream of credit arrangements payday lenders constitute – through regularly extended loans – imposes the costs, rhythm and conditions of short-term credit on top of what is actually a longer-term object.

The serialization of payday lending is now codified as an emergent regulatory concept. Although attention to loan rollovers now preoccupies all major regulatory efforts, the most significant attempt to address serialization now comes from the CFPB. Over the past two years, the CFPB has announced its intention to direct 'much more attention' onto the payday lending sector and has conducted field investigations, launched an extensive research programme and released, in April 2013, a white paper which began to develop its approach to regulation. At the heart of these efforts is a concern for what it terms *sustained use,* the 'repeated, long-term use of payday loans at very high APRs' (Hletok and Kromer 2012: 2). As announced in the white paper, its regulatory efforts entail 'a primary focus on what we term 'sustained use' – the long-term use of a short-term high-cost product evidenced by a pattern of repeatedly rolling over or consistently re-borrowing' (CFPB 2013a: 4). For the CFPB, sustained use exposes borrowers to risks associated with the high costs that can accumulate. 'A pattern of sustained use', the CFPB argues, 'may indicate that a borrower is using payday loans to deal with expenses that regularly outstrip their income' (CFPB 2013a: 24). This damaging pattern may also imply violations of truth-in-lending requirements which prevent lenders from misrepresenting loans and which require lenders to disclose risks to borrowers:

> Payday loans and deposit advances are both structured as products designed to meet short-term credit needs … these products may become harmful for consumers when they are used to make up for chronic cash flow shortages. We find that a sizeable share of payday loan and deposit advance users conduct transactions on a long-term basis, suggesting that they are unable to fully repay the loan and pay other expenses without taking out a new loan shortly thereafter.
>
> (CFPB 2013a: 43; KPMG 2013: 6)[25]

Although the willingness and capacity of the CFPB to address the issue over the long term remains something of an open question, it does appear to be systematically establishing a framework which places loan serialization at the very heart of how payday lending is understood and managed. In its most recent policy intervention, the CFPB has begun to describe payday lending as a form entangled in 'loan sequences'. Loans issued or rolled over by borrowers within the same pay period during which a previous loan was retired form 'part of the same "loan sequence" ... [and] lead to a perpetuating sequence' (Cordray 2014).[26] This assessment is based on a formal analysis developed by the CFPB of loan sequences; 'the series of loans borrowers often taken out following a new loan' (Burke et al. 2014: 4). Paying particular attention to loans that are renewed or followed by an additional loan within the same pay period, the CFPB now estimates that over 80% of loans become part of a continuous chain of borrowing (Burke et al. 2014: 4). A significant number of loans are part of sequences which are stabilized over time – 14% of new loans, for example, initiate sequences at least ten loans long (Burke *et al.* 2014: 4). Perhaps more importantly, these loans are systematically sequenced in ways that remain non-amortizing – in ways that do not reduce the principal outstanding over time. As CFPB research now attests, loan fees and principal size are more likely to increase rather than diminish over the course of long loan sequences (Burke *et al.* 2014: 16).[27] This has resulted in loan sequences, serialized loan chains, which encapsulate the majority of payday loans now issued. A full half all loans exist within sequences of ten or more loans (Burke *et al.* 2014: 12).

The CFPB has identified sustained use as a tension at the core of payday lending and an emblem of the ways in which it incorporates underbanked populations into formalized credit practices. At the heart of these concerns is an incongruity located in a diagram which delineates payday lending as a short-term mechanism and a practice increasingly characterized by sustained use. This incongruity deepens the costs and risks of payday credit for a population largely unable to accept its burdens. As the CFPB notes, 'to the extent these products are marketed as short-term obligations, some consumers may misunderstand the costs and risks, particularly those associated with repeated borrowing' (CFPB 2013a: 44). The gap that marks the space between representations of payday lending as a short-term category and its configured practice as a long-term relation, is indicative of a larger slippage in the broader discourses of financial inclusion with which fringe finance is associated. Although financial inclusion is often imagined as lines of clean and ambiguous insertion, the practices of fringe finance often open channels of incorporation which are more ambiguous. In some important ways, the codification of sustained use as a regulatory concept is precisely a recognition of payday lending not as a form of inclusion but of adverse incorporation. This implies, by extension, the importance of analyses which can make visible finance not only in terms of the abstract maps it claims to occupy. We also need analyses which foreground the actual practices and technologies with which the spaces of finance are constituted and the complexities with which populations are placed within those spaces.

Conclusion: from inclusion to incorporation

Most importantly, placement is a reference to action, indicating the process by which bodies are moved into place and the channels that movement takes. This chapter has framed the practices of fringe finance in terms of the actual practices and techniques with which bodies are enrolled into financial spaces and the ways in which movement through those spaces is opened, closed and channelled. I have placed emphasis on three technologies of incorporation which have been particularly important: technologies of differentiation, immobilization and serialization. In contrast to the pristine maps of financial inclusion, these technologies invoke ambiguous and adverse forms of incorporation which result not in simple forms of access but in forms of coercion, inequality or deepening financial distress.

The impact of these forms of adverse incorporation is distilled in the micro-credit crisis which crested in Andhra Pradesh (AP), India in October 2010. Between 2005 and 2010 the expansion of debt in AP resulted in poor sectors not 'excluded' from credit practices, but systematically 'included' in a complex web of financial and credit relations. 'Households in rural India', argues Taylor, 'are comprehensively "included" in credit/debt relations through a variety of sources … The Indian countryside is therein saturated with relations of debt that are pivotal to the social fabric of rural society' (Taylor 2012: 604). At the heart of this rapid expansion of credit in AP were micro-credit offerings, supported enthusiastically by the World Bank and International Monetary Fund. In the five years from 2005 to 2010, MFIs in the region expanded their loan portfolio from US $252 million to $3.8 billion (Taylor 2012: 608). By the end of this period, and at the height of the credit boom, over 36% of all AP households were entangled in micro-credit (Mader 2013: 51).[28]

This saturation was fuelled in large part by the enthusiasm of private, often foreign, investment in private MFIs (Taylor 2011: 489). As Chapter 3 noted, much of the general boom in micro-credit was fuelled by the development of financial innovations, such as securitization, which helped channel global financial investment into micro-credit networks. Attracted by the relative discipline of micro-borrowers, and the profits that commercial MFIs generated, private finance capital began to flow into MFIs (Taylor 2011: 490).[29] In 2006, for example, there was only US $6.3 million of private investment in Indian MFIs (Mader 2013: 51). Between April of 2008 and July 2010, by contrast, the inflow of global capital into AP MFIs reached $529.6 million (Mader 2013: 51). As investors continued to generate positive returns, their success attracted the attention of both the international development agencies and private capital which, in turn, exerted greater pressure on lenders and brokers to place micro-credit aggressively among poor borrowers.

Although 'included' – even saturated – within credit practices of various kinds, micro-borrowers nonetheless began to experience deeply negative consequences. As pressures to place micro-credit mounted, the costs of that credit began to exert pressures on individual borrowers. In Taylor's assessment, the micro-credit extended in the AP episode 'served to consolidate rather than undermine existing trends toward social differentiation' (Taylor 2011: 499). This adversity stemmed, in part, from coercive collection techniques which were predominant among both traditional moneylenders and MFIs (Taylor 2012: 608).[30] The loans extended in the AP credit bubble were also accompanied by deceptive, undisclosed or non-transparent terms and conditions, often confronting borrowers with unanticipated costs or terms (Mader 2013: 50). Most importantly, the AP bubble extended credit which was both immobilizing and serialized. At the core of mounting defaults was a widespread practice among borrowers of assuming multiple loans from different lenders or MFIs, often in a regular and ongoing pattern (Taylor 2012: 607). As the average borrower's debt doubled, individual indebtedness was compounded by 'multiple borrowing' (Mader 2013: 52). As Mader reports, for example, it became a standard practice for MFIs to both hide and delay rising default pressures by '"rolling over" loans, replacing older non-performing loans with new ones registered as performing' (Mader 2013: 55). This crude serialization of loans greatly compounded levels of personal debt and eventually left many borrowers exposed to unsustainable levels of indebtedness. By 2010, levels of debt in AP consistently measured as much as ten times the national average (CGAP 2010: 3).

Although the claims of borrower suicides have been disputed by lenders, it is now widely acknowledged that at least 54 suicides can be linked directly to levels of debt (Rai 2010; see also Results UK 2012). These suicides occurred in a wider context in which Indian farmer suicides have been occurring at a rate of six suicides per day during the period between 2003 and 2011. All of these farmer suicides are deeply implicated in the 'dynamics of vulnerability that have risen in the context of severe cost pressures stemming from liberalized agriculture [and] rising levels of household debt' (Taylor 2013: 691–692). Moreover, the spike in borrower suicides, whatever the actual figures, dramatically prefigure a range of broader social costs: physical deprivation, intensified forms of domestic violence, and all variety of mental illness (Husain 2011; Chakraborty 2012; Garud 2013).

The AP crisis underscores the tragic importance of the kinds of incorporation which immobilize the individuals they simultaneously include, which enrol individuals in differentiated financial spaces or which establish long-term commitments to high-cost forms of credit. As Taylor argues, 'attention needs to be focused on the circumstances in which financial inclusion … acts as a form of "adverse inclusion", i.e. incorporation into a cycle of indebtedness with potentially catastrophic results' (Taylor 2012: 608). Both this chapter, and the larger argument of the book as a whole, have been preoccupied with these questions of incorporation – with the practices which transport bodies into formalized financial services.

Michael Denning, however, has argued that conventional forms of political economy have, in their own way, often privileged analysis of incorporation by training analytical attention onto the populations who have, in whatever ambiguous form, been inserted to some degree into capitalist relations. This focus on incorporation, however, ignores those who are left *fully* outside of the reaches of capital, neither useful as a latent or residual source of labour nor visible in any manner within the structures of capitalist development. This 'bare' or disposable life is made visible only at its moment of incorporation, only when it is swept over the lines that separate lives useful for capital and those which are discarded. For Denning this is most fully evident in the ways in which 'wageless life' is rendered invisible in accounts preoccupied with waged work as a key signifier of capitalism and its inequalities. This ignores, however, the complex web of human life fully refused by capitalist relations:

> Understandings built upon wage labour cannot … account for the reality lived by the most numerous and wretched of the world's population: those without wages, those indeed without even the hope of wages: bare life, wasted life, disposable life, precarious life, superfluous life: these are among the terms used to describe the inhabitants of a planet of slums. It is not the child in the sweatshop that is our most characteristic figure, but the child in the streets, alternately predator and prey.
>
> (Denning 2010: 70)

Although Denning is preoccupied with the wage/wageless dichotomy, something of his argument impinges upon the claims advanced in this chapter and across the arc of this book. In focusing on the processes by which un/underbanked populations are brought into the spaces of global finance, I have made visible only those populations addressed in whatever meagre and adverse manner by organized forms of financial capital. The bodies addressed in this book only become objects of analysis, only become visible to me, when they become objects of interest for financial institutions. Although this approach does address a wide range of populations – the middle and working class subjects of payday lending, the undocumented workers addressed by micro-insurance innovations, the poor bodies assembled by micro-credit programmes – it does not make visible those left fully surplus to the reach of finance capital, the bare life not rendered valuable to capital in any form. My concern with the 'outside' of capital takes the form of an interest in the unstable and changing border that marks that outside from the spaces of inclusion. These borders, as I have indicated in this chapter, are best understood not as abstract or pristine lines, but as imminently concrete and relational practices. Understood in this concrete manner, the borders of finance are fluid and ambiguous – subjecting some to forms of inclusion which are simultaneously adverse or differentiated. This is not to dismiss those left unaddressed by capital but, rather, to reflect more concretely on the borders that mark these separations. These borders, of course, are more ambiguous for those brought across their width than for those left fully on their exterior.

Nonetheless, articulating a sense of the ambiguities associated with incorporation is not simply a recognition of the ways in which fringe finance is often lived and experienced, but also a disruption of the pervasive diagrams of financial inclusion. The politics of this ambiguity seem particularly urgent in the face of the kinds of distress generated in the AP episode. At the very least, there is now some possibility that ambiguity might be emerging as a formal presence in policy discussions as articulated, for example, in the CFPB's concerns for sustained use. What becomes of this discussion is, of course, an open question worthy of political reflection. The ambiguity of fringe finance is itself complex, however; a description not only of the incorporations fringe finance enables, but also of the contestations which it attracts, the focus of Chapter 7.

Notes

1 'Once relegated as permanent surplus', notes Yates, 'these populations are little more than human waste, excreted from the capitalist system' (quoted in McIntyre and Nast 2011: 1470; see also Tyner 2013: 703).

2 There has been a wave of research which has made significant progress in mapping the geographically and historically contingent ways in which 'the "surplus" is being produced, ordered, segmented and racialized' (Arnold and Pickles 2011: 1599; Pye et al. 2012).

3 The idea of social inclusion emerged out of policy discussions in France in the 1970s in relation to *les exclus*.

4 Social exclusion relates to 'the lack or denial of resources, rights, goods and services, and the inability to participate in the normal relationships and activities, available to the majority of people in a society, whether in economic, social, cultural or political arenas' (Levitas *et al.* 2007: 9).

5 'Exclusion', notes Seckinelgin, 'is seen as a function of the existing institutional relations rather than as a function of individuals' characteristics' (Seckinelgin 2009: 208; Oxoby 2009: 1134).

6 As Soederberg (2013: 609) has forcefully noted, the 'financial inclusion agenda is not a neutral project, but one that is part of longer, neoliberal-led development strategies'.

7 See also Isaac 2014: 3; Shaul 2012.

8 Financial inclusion is, in these terms, an attempt to allow the financially exlcuded 'to manage her day-to-day life more productively, shield her against risks, and support her in achieving major life goals, like education, home and business growth' (Center for Financial Inclusion 2013: 2).

9 As Stein et al. note: 'Low-income families own assets, both social and physical, movable and immovable. The right financial infrastructure can help with recognition of these assets by the formal sector' (Stein, Randhawa and Bilandzic 2011: 11).

10 As Andrijasevic puts it, adverse incorporation is a challenge to the 'currency and adequacy of the exclusion-based interpretative model' (Andrijasevic 2009: 391).

11 As Philips notes: 'Adverse incorporation instead constructs an explanation based on the *terms* on which people are incorporated into particular economic and social processes and structures' (Philips 2013: 174 emphasis in original).

12 Wonga, for example, a notable British lender recently made news by shifting its 'typical APR' up 1600% to over 5800%, in anticipation of stricter disclosure rules which might not allow firms to list certain fees in particular ways (Osborne 2013).

13 As Paul Langley (2008: 183) suggests, 'the demarcation and differentiation of anomalous, specialist and excluded spaces of finance populated by low-income, high-risk, and sub-prime borrowers actually contribute to the charging of relatively high rates of interest by lenders present in those realms'.

14 Note that this paragraph draws upon and extends an argument developed in Aitken (2012: 212).

15 The Financial Consumer Agency of Canada (2013: 5) notes, 'since payday lenders are not currently members of the main credit-reporting agencies, getting a payday loan and paying it off on time will *not* improve your credit score. However, if you do not pay your loan back on time and it is sent to a collection agency, this will likely be reported to a credit-reporting agency and could have a negative impact on your credit report'.

16 Experian notes three pockets of information particularly important to Extended View: all available credit data, rental information and public record data including missed child support payments (Experian 2012).

17 As Fourcade and Healy (2013: 566) note, 'by enabling and facilitating the differential pricing of people, scoring has expanded the reach of the market while opening the door to new forms of classification with stratifying effects'.

18 See www.zippycash.ca.

19 As King and Parrish (2011: 21) note, borrowers are indebted, on average between 59% and 63% of the time.

20 As the Pew research has suggested, 'payday loans are frequently described as short-term credit for unexpected expenses … [yet] repeat borrowing is the norm. Prior research indicates that borrowers are indebted for an average of five to seven months of the year … the profitability of payday lenders depends on repeat borrowing' (Bourke, Horowitz and Roche 2012: 15).

21 As Francis goes on to note, 'the striking feature of this data is that the CFSA study, which should be most favourable to the payday-lending industry, shows that almost a majority of all borrowers are rolling over their loans multiple times' (Francis 2010: 617).

22 As commentators have noted, most borrowers will roll over each loan an additional two times before paying it off (Carter, Skiba and Sydnor 2013).

23 Parrish and King note that 60 % of business is generated by borrowers with 12 or more loans per year. This kind of loan churning now accounts for 76% of overall payday loan value and at least US $2.6 billion in excess fees (Parrish and King 2009: 5).

24 The CFPB's research (2012a: 43–44) has also noted this relationship between sustained use and the very nature of credit extended in payday loans: 'many consumers are unable to repay their loan in full and still meet their other expenses … they continually re-borrow and incur significant expense … the high cost of the loan or advance may itself contribute to the chronic difficulty such customers face in retiring the debt'.

25 Sustained use patterns have become a key signal at the heart of the CFPB's regulatory efforts; to 'evaluate whether options for sustained use (rollovers or back-to-back transactions) are disclosed '"accurately" and "non-deceptively"' (Hletok and Kromer 2012; CFPB 2013b; KPMG 2013: 6).

26 As Cordray (2014) notes, 'From this finding, one could readily conclude that the business model of the payday industry depends on people becoming stuck in these loans for the long term.'

27 Burke *et al.* (2014: 16) report that 'most borrowers do not self-amortize their payday loans'. The data that forms the core of this analysis was mobilized by the CFPB in and through the supervisory process it manages.

28 This saturated inclusion was not only accomplished by MFIs but also by traditional moneylenders that MFIs were thought to have displaced (Mader 2013: 52).

29 As Taylor (2011: 490) notes, the 'emergence of for-profit, shareholder-driven micro finance within Andhra Pradesh created a new logic of competitive rural credit provision'.

30 As Taylor (2012: 608) notes, in these coercive techniques, formalized micro-credit resembles informal practices: 'formalized micro-credit embeds informal coercive practices deep within its internal workings, even as they are represented as its opposite'.

References

Aitken, R. 2010. 'Ambiguous Incorporations: Microfinance and Global Governmentality'. *Global Networks.* Vol. 10, No. 2: 223–243.

Aitken, R. 2012. 'Assembling the Immobile Subject of Fringe Finance'. *Mobilities, Knowledge and Social Justice.* Ed. Suzan Ilcan. Montreal and Kingston: McGill-Queen's University Press: 207–226.

Alliance for Financial Inclusion. 2012. *A Quick Guide to the Maya Declaration on Financial Inclusion.* Bangkok Thailand: Alliance for Financial Inclusion.

Andrijasevic, R. 2009. 'Sex on the Move: Gender, Subjectivity and Differential Inclusion'. *Subjectivity.* Vol. 29: 389–406.

Arnold, D. and J. Pickles. 2011. 'Global Work, Surplus Labor, and the Precarious Economies of the Border'. *Antipode.* Vol. 43, No. 5: 1598–1624.

Ashton, P. 2012. "Troubled Assets': The Financial Emergency and Racialized Risk'. *International Journal of Urban and Regional research.* Vol. 36, No. 4: 773–790.

Bernard, T.S. 2011. 'A Credit Score the Tracks you More Closely'. *New York Times.* 2 December 2011.

Bhutta, N., P. Skiba and J. Tobacman. 2013. *Payday Loan Choices and Consequences.* Washington: National Bureau for Economic Research.

Bourke, N., A. Horowitz and T. Roche. 2012. *Payday Lending in America: Who Borrows, Where They Borrow, and Why.* Washington, DC: Pew Charitable Trusts.

Burke, K., J. Lanning, J. Leary and J. Wang. 2014. *CFPB Data Point: Payday Lending.* Washington: Consumer Financial Protection Bureau.

Cackley, A. 2011. *Payday Lending: Federal Law Enforcement Uses a Multilayered Approach to Identify Employees in Financial Distress.* Washington, DC: Government Accountability Office.

Calhoun, M. and N. Bailey. 2006. 'Predatory Lending: Undermining Economic Progress in Communities of Color'. *Poverty and Race.* Vol. 15, No. 1: 190–204.

Carling, J. 2002. 'Migration in the Age of Involuntary Immobility: Theoretical Reflections and Cape Verdean Experiences'. *Journal of Ethnic and Migration Studies.* Vol. 28, No. 1: 5–42.

Carter, S., P. Skiba and J. Sydnor. 2013. *The Difference a Day (Doesn't Make): Does Giving Borrowers More Time to Repay Break the Cycle of Repeated Payday Borrowing?* Madison: University of Wisconsin-Madison.

Cash America. 2014. *Form 10-K: Cash America International, Inc. 2013 Annual Report.* Forth Worth TX: Cash America International, Inc.

Center for Responsible Lending, Consumer Federation of America, National Consumer Law Center, Americans for Financial Reform, Center for Digital Democracy, Consumer Action, Consumers Union, Insight Center for Community Economic Development, Leadership Conference on Civil and Human Rights, National Association of Consumers Advocats, National People's Action, Neighbourhood

Economic Development Advocacy Project, Public Citizen, California Reinvestment Coalition, Community Legal Services Inc. and New Jersey Citizen Action. 2012. *Comments to the Consumer Financial Protection Bureau on Payday Lending Abuses.* Washington, DC: Center for Responsible Lending.

Center for Financial Inclusion. 2013. *Seizing the Moment: On the Road to Financial Inclusion.* Washington, DC: Center for Financial Inclusion.

CFPB. 2012. *Subject Providers.* Washington, DC: Consumer Financial Protection Bureau.

CFPB. 2013a. *Payday Loans and Deposit Advance Products: A White Paper of Initial Data Findings.* Washington, DC: Consumer Financial Protection Bureau.

CFPB. 2013b. *Short-Term, Small-Dollar Lending Examination Procedures.* Washington, DC: Consumer Financial Protection Bureau.

CGAP. 2010. 'Andhra Pradesh 2010: Global Implications of the Crisis in Indian Microfinance'. *Focus Note* 67. Washington, DC: CGAP.

Chakraborty, S. 2012. 'MFI Sector Will Take Years to Recover: Philip Vassiliou'. *Business Standard.* 27 March. http://www.business-standard.com/article/finance/mfi-sector-will-takeyears-to-recover-philip-vassiliou-112032700042_1.html.

Chatterjee, A. 2012. 'Access to Insurance and Financial-Sector Regulation'. *Protecting the Poor: A Micro-insurance Compendium, Vol. II.* Eds. C. Churchill and M. Matul. Geneva: International Labour Office: 548–572.

Clark, L. 2013. 'ZestFinance CEO: "We Need Data Artists to Save Zombie Borrowers"'. *Wired Magazine.* 15 August.

Collins, J. 2011. 'What Difference Does Financial Expansion Make?' *Identities.* Vol. 18, No. 1: 39–46.

Cordray, R. 2014. *Prepared Remarks of Richard Cordray, Director of Consumer Financial Protection Bureau.* Nashville, Payday Field Hearing, 25 March.

CoreLogic. 2011. *FICO and CoreLogic to Develop New Credit Risk Scoring Solutions.* Santa Ana, CA: CoreLogic Inc.

CoreLogic. 2013. *The Value of an Objective Risk Model to Storefront Lenders.* Irvine, CA: Core:ogic Inc.

Cotler, P. and D. Almazan. 2013. 'The Lending Interest Rates in the Microfinance Sector: Searching for its Determinants'. *JCC: The Business and Economics Research Journal.* Vol. 6, No. 1: 69–81.

Cresswell, T. 2012. 'Towards a Politics of Mobility'. *Routes, Roads and Landscapes.* Eds. M. Hvattum and J. Larsen. Farnham: Ashgate: 163–178.

Crossman, P. 2012. 'ZestFinance Aims to Fix Underwriting for the Underbanked'. *American Banker.* 19 November.

Deleuze, G. 2006. *Nietzsche and Philosophy.* New York: Columbia University Press

Demirguc-Kunt, A. and L. Klapper. 2012. *Measuring Financial Inclusion: The Global Findex Database.* Washington, DC: World Bank Policy Research Working Paper 6025.

Denning, M. 2010. 'Wageless Life'. *New Left Review.* Vol. 66: 79–97.

Deuchars, I. 2013. *Credit Scoring in the Payday Loan Sector: Credit Scoring and Credit Control.* Dublin: Experian.

Dollar Financial. 2013. *Investor Presentation – November 2013.* Berwyn PA: DFC Global Corporation.

Du Toit, A. 2004. "Social Exclusion' Discourse and Chronic Poverty: A South African Case Study'. *Development and Change.* Vol. 35, No. 5: 987–1010.

Dyer, C. 2012. 'Formal Education and Pastoralism in Western India: Inclusion, or Adverse Incorporation?' *Compare: A Journal of Comparative and International Education*. Vol. 42, No. 2: 259–281.

Dymski, G. 2009a. 'Racial Exclusion and the Political Economy of the Subprime Crisis'. *Historical Materialism*. Vol. 17: 149–179.

Dymski, G. 2009b. 'Afterword: Mortgage Markets and the Urban Problematic in the Global Transition'. *International Journal of Urban and Regional Research*. Vol. 33, No. 2: 427–442.

Experian. 2012. *Experian Announces its Extended View Score*. Costa Mesa: Experian.

Experian 2013. *Extended View Score*. Costa Mesa: Experian.

Fanon, F. 1963. *The Wretched of the Earth*. New York: Grove Press.

Financial Consumer Agency of Canada. 2013. *The Cost of Payday Loans*. Ottawa: Financial Consumer Agency of Canada.

Fourcade, M. and K. Healy. 2013. 'Classification Situations: Life-Chances in the Neoliberal Era'. *Accounting, Organizations and Society*. Vol. 38, No. 8: 559–572.

French, S. and J. Kneale. 2012. 'Speculating on Carless Lives'. *Journal of Cultural Economy*. Vol. 5, No.4: 391–406.

Francis, K. 2010. 'Rollover, Rollover: A Behavioural Law and Economics Analysis of the Payday-Loan Industry'. *Texas Law Review*. Vol. 88: 611–638.

Garud, K. 2013. 'Microfinance in Andhra Pradesh, Indian in the Wake of Government Sanctions: A Look at Institutions and Borrowers'. *Sigma Iota Rho: Journal of International Relations*. 10 January 2013.

Gidwani, V. and R. Reddy. 2011. 'The Afterlives of 'Waste': Notes from India for a Minor History of Capitalist Surplus'. *Antipode*. Vol. 43, No. 5: 1625–1658.

Global Partnership for Financial Inclusion. 2013. *Report to Leaders Summit*. St Petersburg: Global Partnership for Financial Inclusion.

Goggin, J. 2012. 'Regulating (Virtual) Subjects'. *Journal of Cultural Economy*. Vol. 5, No. 4: 441–456.

Gonzalez, A. 2010a. 'Analyzing Microcredit Interest Rates'. *Mix Data Brief*. No. 4. Washington, DC: Micro-Credit Information Exchange.

Gonzalez, A. 2010b. 'Is Micro-Credit Growing Too Fast?' *Mix Data Brief*. No. 5. Washington, DC: Micro-Credit Information Exchange.

Gould, L. 2007. 'Testimony Before the Manitoba Public Utilities Board'. Winnipeg: Public Utilities Board, 19 November.

Hall, S. and L. Appleyard. 2012. 'Financial Business Education: The Remaking of Gendered Investment Banking Subjects in the (post-Crisis) City of London'. *Journal of Cultural Economy*. Vol. 5, No. 4: 457–472.

Hickey, S. and A. Du Toit. 2007. *Adverse Incorporation, Social Exclusion and Chronic Poverty*. Manchester: Institute for Development Policy and Management, University of Manchester, CPRC Working Paper 81.

Hletok, V. and J. Kromer. 2012. *Minifinance: CFBP Supervision of Short-Term, Small Dollar Financial Products and Services*. New York: LexisNexis Research Solutions.

Home Credit. 2014. *Consolidated Annual Accounts for the Year Ended 31 December 2013*. Amsterdam: Home Credit B.V.

Howson, C. 2012. 'Adverse Incorporation and Microfinance Among Cross-Border Traders in Senegal'. *World Development*. Vol. 42, No. 1: 199–208.

Husain, A. 2011. *Microfinance in India: A Crisis at the Bottom of the Pyramid*. Dubai: Legatum Ventures.

Isaac, W. 2014. 'Why Payday Loans are Good for Millions of People'. *American Banker*. 15 January.

Johnson, C. 2012. 'America's First Consumer Financial Watchdog is on a Leash: Can the CFPB Use Its Authority to Declare Payday-Loan Practices Unfair, Abusive, and Deceptive?' *Catholic University Law Review*. Vol. 61: 381–428.

Johnson, L. 2013. 'Index Insurance and the Articulation of Risk-Bearing Subjects'. *Environment and Planning A*. Vol. 45, No. 11: 2263–2681.

Jonsson, G. 2011. *Non-Migrant, Sedentary, Immobile, or 'Left Behind'?: Reflections on the Absence of Migration*. Oxford: International Migration Institute Working Paper 39.

Kelly, S. and E. Rhyne. 2013. *Growing Income, Growing Inclusion: How Rising Incomes at the Base of the Pyramid will Shape Financial Inclusion*. Washington, DC: Center for Financial Inclusion.

King, U. and L. Parrish. 2011. *Payday Loans, Inc.: Short on Credit, Long on Debt*. Washington, DC: Center for Responsible Lending.

KPMG. 2013. *Regulatory Practice Letter RPL 13–11: Payday Loans and Deposit Advance Products – CFPB Report; FDIC, OCC and Federal Reserve Guidance*. Wilmington, DE: KPMG LLP.

Langley, P. 2007. 'Uncertain Subjects of Anglo-American Financialization'. *Cultural Critique*. Vol. 65: 67–91.

Langley, P. 2008. *The Everyday Life of Global Finance*. Oxford: Oxford University Press.

Langley, P. and A. Leaver. 2012. 'Remaking Retirement Investors: Behavioural Economics and Defined-Contribution Occupational Pensions'. *Journal of Cultural Economy*. Vol. 5, No. 4: 473–488.

Larson, J., J. Urry and K. Axhausen. 2006. *Mobilities, Networks, Geographies*. London: Ashgate.

Lazzarato, M. 2012. *The Making of the Indebted Man: An Essay on the Neoliberal Condition*. Tr. Joshua David Jordan. Amsterdam: Semiotext(e).

Levitas, R. 2004. 'Let's Hear it for Humpty: Social Exclusion, the Third Way and Cultural Capital'. *Cultural Trends*. Vol. 13, No. 2: 41–56.

Levitas, R., Pantazis, C., Fahmy, E., Gordon, D., Lloyd, E. and Patsios, D. 2007. *The Multi-dimensional Analysis of Social Exclusion*. London: Department for Communities and Local Government.

Li, T. 2009. 'To Make Live or Let Die? Rural Dispossession and the Protection of Surplus Populations'. *Antipode*. Vol. 41, No.1: 66–93.

Li, T. 2013. 'Insistently Seeking Social Incorporation'. *Journal of the Royal Anthropological Institute*. Vol. 19: 252–253.

Littlefield, E., B. Helms and D. Porteous. 2006. *Financial Inclusion 2015: Four Scenarios for the Future of Microfinance*. Washington, DC: Consultative Group to Assist the Poor, Focus Note No. 39.

Lubkemann, S. 2008. 'Involuntary Immobility: On a Theoretical Invisibility in Forced Migration Studies'. *Journal of Refugee Studies*. Vol. 21, No. 4: 454–475.

Lyon, D. 2002. 'Surveillance as Social Sorting: Computer Codes and Mobile Bodies'. *Surveillance as Social Sorting: Privacy, Risk, and Digital Discrimination*. Ed. David Lyon. London: Routledge: 13–51.

Maclean, K. 2012. 'Gender, Risk and Micro-Financial Subjectivities'. *Antipode*. Vol. 45, No. 2: 455–473.

Mader, P. 2013. 'Rise and Fall of Microfinance in India: The Andhra Pradesh Crisis in Perspective'. *Strategic Change: Briefings in Entrepreneurial Finance*. Vol. 22: 47–66.

Magnani, E. 2013. 'From Financing Labour to Labouring Finance: Subjectivity in Financial Times'. *Cosmopolitan Civil Societies Journal*. Vol. 5, No. 2: 129–142.

Manji, A. 2010. 'Eliminating Poverty?: 'Financial Inclusion', Access to Land and Gender Equality in International Development'. *The Modern Law Review*. Vol. 73, No. 6: 985–1025.

Marx, K. 1999 [1887] *Capital: A Critique of Political Economy, Vol. 1: Book One: The Process of Production of Capital*. Moscow: Progress Publishers/Marx-Engels Internet Archive. https://www.marxists.org/archive/marx/works/1867-c1/ch25.htm.

McCarthy, J. 2010. 'Processes of Inclusion and Adverse Incorporation: Oil Palm and Agrarian Change in Sumatra, Indonesia'. *The Journal of Peasant Studies*. Vol. 37, No. 4: 821–850.

McIntyre, M. and H. Nast. 2011. 'Bio(necro)polis: Marx, Surplus Populations, and the Spatial Dialectics of Reproduction and "Race"'. *Antipode*. Vol. 43, No. 5: 1465–1488.

Melzer, B. 2011. 'The Real Costs of Credit Access: Evidence from the Payday Lending Market'. *The Quarterly Journal of Economics*. Vol. 126, No. 1: 517–555.

Melzer, B. 2013. *Spillovers from Costly Credit*. Washington, DC: Center for Economic Studies Research Papers.

Mezzadra, S. and B. Neilson. 2012. 'Between Inclusion and Exclusion: On the Topology of Global Space and Borders'. *Theory, Culture and Society*. Vol. 29, Nos. 4/4: 58–75.

Mitchell, T. 2007. 'The Properties of Markets'. *Do Economists Make Markets: On the Performativity of Economics*. Eds. D. Mackenzie, F. Muniesa and L. Sui. Princeton, NJ: Princeton University Press.

Montezemolo, S. 2013. *The State of Lending in America and Its Impact on U.S. Households*. Washington, DC: Center for Responsible Lending.

Mosse, D. 2010. 'A Relational Approach to Durable Poverty, Inequality and Power'. *Journal of Development Studies*. Vol. 46, No. 7: 1156–1178.

National Consumer Law Center. 2009. *Using Nontraditional Credit Information: Boon or Bane?* Washington, DC: National Consumer Law Center.

Nelson, S. 2011. *Sovereignty and the Limits of the Liberal Imagination*. London: Routledge.

New, C. 2012. 'Experian Debuts New Credit Scores, Helps Bring 'Underbanked' Into Lending Fold' *Huffington Post*. 14 June.

Osborne, H. 2013. 'Wonga Increases its Typical APR by 1,600%'. *The Guardian*. 21 June.

Oxoby, R. 2009. 'Understanding Social Inclusion, Social Cohesion, and Social Capital'. *International Journal of Social Economics*. Vol. 36, No. 12: 1133–1152.

Parrish, L. and U. King. 2009. *Phantom Demand: Short-Term Due Date Generates Need for Repeat Payday Loans*. Durham, NC: Center for Responsible Lending.

Philips, N. 2011. 'Informality, Global Production Networks and the Dynamics of "Adverse Incorporation"'. *Global Networks*. Vol. 11, No. 3: 380–397.

Philips, N. 2013. 'Unfree Labour and Adverse Incorporation in the Global Economy: Comparative Perspectives on Brazil and India'. *Economy and Society*. Vol. 42, No. 2: 171–196.

Polgreen, L. and V. Bajaj. 2010. 'India Microcredit Faces Collapse from Defaults'. *New YorkTimes*. 17 November. www.nytimes.com/2010/11/18/world/asia/18micro.html (accessed 17 November 2010).

Pye, O., R. Daud, Y. Harmono and Tatat. 2012. 'Precarious Lives: Transnational Biographies of Migrant Oil Palm Workers'. *Asia Pacific Viewpoint*. Vol. 53, No. 3: 330–342.

Quinton, S. 2013. 'The Online Lenders that Could Break the Payday Loan Racket'. *National Journal*. 28 March 2013.

Radermacher, R., H. McGowan and S. Dercon. 2012. 'What is the Impact of Micro-insurance?' *Protecting the Poor: A Micro-insurance Compendium, Vol. II*. Eds. C. Churchill and M. Matul. Geneva: International Labour Office: 59–82.

Rai, V. 2010. 'India's Microfinance Crisis is a Battle to Monopolize the Poor'. *Harvard Business Review*. Blog2 November.

Ramsay, I. 2006. 'Consumer Law, Regulatory Capitalism and the "New Learning" in Regulation'. *Sydney Law Review*. Vol. 28, No. 9: 2–35.

Results UK. 2012. *Microfinance in India: Re-Examining the 2010 Andhra Pradesh Crisis and Considering the Indian Government's Response*. London: Results UK.

Schwittay, A. 2011. 'The Financial Inclusion: Assemblage: Subjects, Technics, Rationalities'. *Critique of Anthropology*. Vol. 31, No. 4: 381–401.

Seckinelgin, H. 2009. 'Global Social Policy and International Organizations: Linking Social Exclusion to Durable Inequality'. *Global Social Policy*. Vol. 9, No. 2: 205–227.

Shankar, S. 2013. 'Financial Inclusion in India: Do Microfinance Institutions Address Access Barriers?' *ACRN Journal of Entrepreneurship Perspectives*. Vol. 2, No. 1: 60–74.

Shaul, D. 2012. *Testimony Before the United States Senate Special Committee on Aging*. 24 July 2012.

Smith, G. 2011. 'Selective Hegemony and Beyond Populations with 'No Productive Function': A Framework for Enquiry'. *Identities: Global Studies in Culture and Power*. Vol. 18, No. 1: 2–38.

Soederberg, S. 2013. 'Universalising Financial Inclusion and the Securitisation of Development'. *Third World Quarterly*. Vol. 34, No. 4: 593–612.

Spector, M. 2008. 'Payday Lonas: Unintended Consequences of American Efforts to Tame the Beast'. *The Future of Consumer Credit Regulation: Creative Approaches to Emerging Problems*. Eds. M. Kelly-Louw, J. P. Nehf and P. Rott. Aldershot: Ashgate: 107–128.

Stango, V. 2012. 'Are Payday Lending Markets Competitive?' *Regulation*. Fall: 26–23.

Stein, P., B. Randhawa and N. Bilandzic. 2011. *Universal Access: Addressing the Global Challenge of Financial Inclusion*. Washington: International Finance Corporation.

Taylor, M. 2011. '"Freedom from Poverty is Not for Free": Rural Development and the Microfinance Crisis in Andhra Pradesh, India'. *Journal of Agrarian Change*. Vol. 11, No. 4: 484–504.

Taylor, M. 2012. 'The Antinomies of "Financial Inclusion": Debt, Distress and the Workings of Indian Microfinance'. *Journal of Agrarian Change*. Vol. 12, No. 4: 601–610.

Taylor, M. 2013. 'Liquid Debts: Credit, Groundwater and the Social Ecology of Agrarian Distress in Andhra Pradesh, India'. *Third World Quarterly*. Vol. 34, No. 4: 691–709.

Todman, L., S. Taylor, K. Cochrane, J. Arbaugh-Korotko, J. Berger, E. Burt, M. Caponi, E. Houston, A. Hahn and D. Mandeleew. 2009. 'Social Exclusion Indicators for the United States'. *The Journal of Individual Psychology*. Vol. 65, No. 4: 330–359.

Turner, B. 2010. 'Enclosures, Enclaves and Entrapment'. *Sociological Inquiry.* Vol. 80, No. 2: 241–260.

Tyner, J. 2013. 'Population Geography 1: Surplus Populations'. *Progress in Human Geography.* Vol. 37, No. 5: 701–711.

Watson, M. 2007. *The Political Economy of International Capital Mobility.* Basingstoke: Palgrave Macmillan.

Wissoker, P. 2013. 'From Insurance to Investments: Financialization and the Supply Side of Life Insurance and Annuities in the USA (1970–2006)'. *Cambridge Journal of Regions, Economy and Society.* Vol. 6, No. 3: 401–418.

7 Economies of social practice

Creating alternative circuits of financial incorporation

Every day, several times a day,
A thought comes over me.
I owe more debts that I can ever pay back
More money than I'll ever see …
I think of what I thought this cold morning,
I think of what I'm thinking at three.
At ten and at midnight the same damn thing,
I wish this debt was about money.
(Woody Guthrie, *The Debt I Owe*)

In 2010, Paolo Cirio, an Italian artist launched a unique piece of tactical art entitled *P2P Gift Credit*. In mounting *P2P Gift Credit* Cirio essentially issued 'counterfeit virtual money' by producing thousands of credit cards with readable numbers (all with the prefix 4007 99) technically compatible with the global credit and payments system. These cards were conceived as an attempt to constitute what Cirio describes as Gift Finance, a system of 'person to person gift credit sharing' in which each new peer is freely issued a basic allocation (denominated as GBP 100) which is then used as a basis of an expansive system of credit generated as p2p card holders exchange and trade with each other. 'Since 2010', he notes, 'I've issued illicit Visa credit cards … [which] enables a decentralized peer-to-peer network of social relations sharing and building value based on engagement in the system of democratic money creation' (Cirio 2012). Upon reaching critical mass, Cirio envisions a widespread expansion as 'basic credit' comes to operate as a virtual currency. By expanding the use of credit within a network of peers (consisting not of financial elites but of everyday populations), the basic gift finance system generates a new kind of capital rooted in the interactions we have with each other as peers and the social obligations that animate those interactions (see Figure 7.1). 'The project', Cirio argues, 'was born from the idea of universal Basic Income directly regulated by the network of relationships that link people together at local and global levels' (Bazzichelli 2011). A direct reaction to the kinds of abstract financial relationships key to the 2008 financial crisis,

Cirio's intervention longs for a mode of financial practice governed not by instrumental calculation but by social relations.

Although Cirio stopped issuing p2p credit cards in 2012, partly as a result of legal action mounted by credit card issuers, the resonance of his work remains. Most striking are the ways in which the launch of *P2P Gift Credit* in 2010 echoes the emergence and consolidation of actual experiments in peer-to-peer (p2p) financial arrangements. Emerging in serious form in 2004 and 2005, there has been a prolonged boom over the past decade in disintermediated p2p financial practices offered explicitly to everyday populations. Self-consciously designed as spaces outside of mainstream financial institutions, p2p lending initiatives seek to construct direct linkages between everyday borrowers and lenders. Although still relatively small in relation to global capital markets, p2p lending has nonetheless grown rapidly over the last number of years. In the 12 months which ended 30 September 2013, the two largest American p2p lenders (Prosper and Lending Club) loaned almost US $1.9 billion, a 173% increase on loan capital placed over the preceding 12 months (Renton 2013a: 6).

In this proximity to real p2p experimentation and growth, *P2P Gift Credit* foreshadows something of the limits *and* enormous momentum of fringe finance. As I suggest in this chapter, and building on Cirio's gesture, p2p lending networks make visible fringe finance as a deeply contested space, the boundaries of which are often marked by alternative credit practices and counter-diagrams which emphasize finance as a social practice. At the same time, the recent trajectories of p2p networks also highlight fringe finance as a deeply innovative force capable of absorbing even those practices it incites as alternatives. As I argue in this chapter, the most pronounced recent trajectory for p2p networks include efforts which convert loan receivables into investable assets.

It is in this context that I argue that p2p lending is caught between two contending impulses. On one hand, p2p financial networks, especially as initially formulated as a form of 'social lending', entail what Zadie Smith describes as a *refusal* – a demonstration of the ways in which we are 'not content to slot our energies into the smooth running of the present order' (Smith 2013). On the other hand, however, I also argue that p2p networks make visible the expansive diagram at the heart of fringe finance – a diagram which emphasizes the innovative absorption of those on the very edges into mainstream financial arrangements. P2P networks have themselves become increasingly absorbed within the mainstream financial circuits from which they seek a certain distance. These countervailing tendencies punctuate both the fragility of fringe finance – a diagram which is contested and sometimes outmanoeuvred – but also its expansive innovation. P2P networks are situated in the contested pressure of two different kinds of creativity; the creativity, on one hand, of those engaged in shaping networks that seek to limit, overturn or render 'social' the logic of financialization, and the creativity, on the other hand, of mainstream financial agents keen to innovate new sources of value,

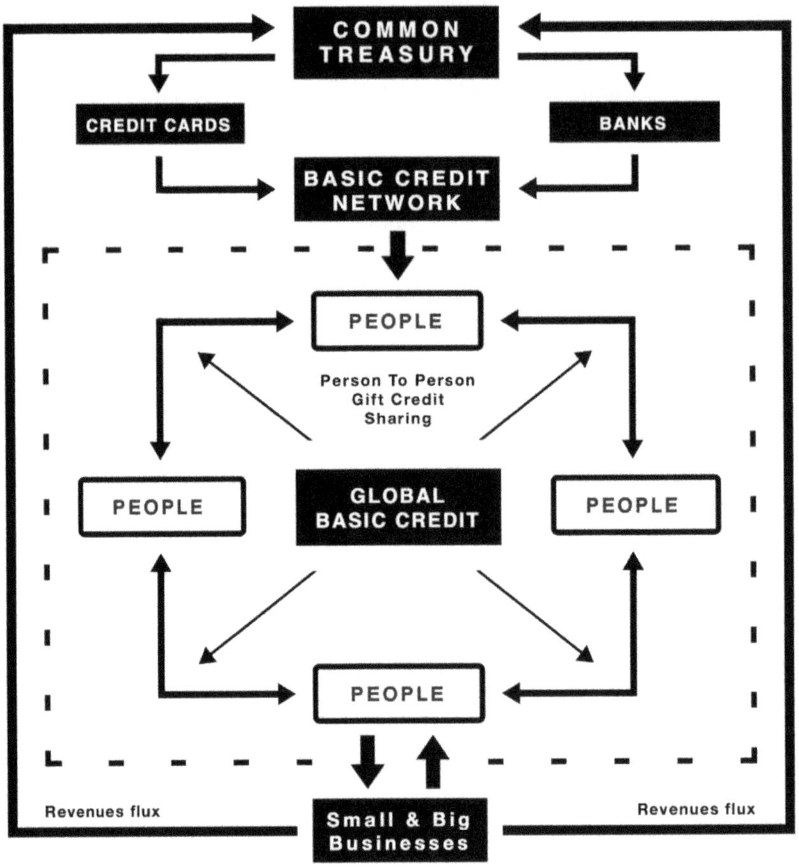

Figure 7.1 P2P Gift Credit Card
(Cirio 2010)

even from those sites of contestation themselves. In this chapter, as a punctuation to the argument the book develops, I claim that p2p networks make visible both the fragility *and* innovation now associated with fringe finance. The futures of fringe finance are bound up in these contests and in the political and economic forces that animate them.

To make this argument that the recent emergence of p2p networks distils some of the antinomies of fringe finance more broadly, this chapter is divided into four sections. The first section describes, in general terms, some of the diverse efforts to craft what Zelizer has referred to as alternative economic circuits. These alternative circuits are often built around a kind of 'social' relationality that is counterposed to the instrumental rationality or abstraction that governs mainstream financial networks. A second section addresses one of these alternative circuits of incorporation that has grown rapidly over the past decade – p2p financial networks. As this section claims, p2p networks are designed as financial webs that evade financial institutions and that constitute disintermediated financial relationships reworked as 'social' practices available to a wide population including those on or beyond the reach of mainstream financial institutions. A third section examines, by contrast, the ways in which these networks have also become the object of attention by mainstream financial agents: in the bundling and securitization of loans, in the involvement of large capital market investors and hedge funds in the p2p sector, and even in the role of banks in circulating their own capital through p2p lending networks. The conclusion argues that this recent trajectory reveals the kinds of expansive innovation which often lie at the heart of fringe finance. A fourth and concluding section returns to broader issues by noting the ways in which p2p networks emblematize fringe finance as practices which embody a certain innovation *and* fragility. This section extends this observation by addressing broader questions about the possibility of refusals in a world seemingly gripped by the 'financialized imagination', and with what Simmel referred to as the 'character of calculability' so core to the practices of financial rationality.

Finance and circuits of social incorporation

> In our individual vulnerability to precarity, we find that we are social beings, implicated in a set of networks that either sustain us or fail to do so, or do so only intermittently, producing a constant spectre of despair and destitution. Our individual wellbeing depends on whether the social and economic structures that support our mutual dependency can be put into place … As bodies, we suffer and we resist and together, in various locations, exemplify that form of the sustaining social bond that neo-liberal economics has almost destroyed.
>
> (Butler 2011a: 13)

Despite the intensifying growth and innovation of fringe financial services, there has been a range of experiments in financial incorporation from outside of the logic of fringe finance. Many American credit unions, for example, have experimented in crafting alternatives to payday loans and in extending themselves into 'unbanked/underbanked' populations. One scheme promoted by the National Credit Union Foundation in the USA entails a lending mechanism which, in lieu of high fees, creates a pool of capital generated by mandatory borrower contributions which can compensate loan issuers in cases of loan defaults. This establishes a kind of pool with which borrowers insure and secure their own access to credit (Real Solutions 2008). Variants of this model have now been adopted by the Pennsylvania Credit Union Association, which has created a large pool of capital from which credit unions are reimbursed for 50% of loan losses (PCUA 2012). From a more radical direction, *Occupy Bank* has initiated a discussion about the possibility of a range of alternative financial practices. A longer tradition of alternative or local currencies has also contributed to alternative financial experiments through the establishment of trading networks in which value, wages and credit can be extended along egalitarian or democratic lines (North 2007).

Although diverse, these experiments seek what Zelizer has referred to as the creation of alternative economic circuits. For Zelizer, economic circuits refers to the complexity of ways in which economic practices are constructed 'from the bottom up'. In contrast to the conventional language of economic sociology or political economy (which emphasizes units such as firms or production), economic circuit implies relational social patterns that govern a wide range of economic activities. Circuits, she notes, are characterized by 'shared economic activities carried on by means of social relations ... the creation of common accounting systems ... [and] shared understandings concerning the meaning of transactions within the circuit, including their moral valuation' (Zelizer 2011: 304). Circuits, grounded in the crucible of everyday life, are constructed in order to provide care, enact norms of social obligation, and engage in reciprocity, often in the face of commercial relationships that undermine those practices. Circuits are 'the means by which people bridge the apparently unbridgeable gap between social solidarity and commercialized transactions' (Zelizer 2011: 336–337). Zelizer puts emphasis in particular on circuits constructed by everyday populations 'from below' as they seek out economic and social relations using methods of exchange and modes of calculation not reducible to the instrumental logic of the market.

The past decade has witnessed a resurgence of interest in mechanisms that enact alternative modes of economic exchange and incorporation. Recent alternative circuits have been assembled in diverse locations from a range of distinctive rationalities but have often coalesced around two particular frames. The first of these frames is an imaginary which stresses the possibility of a *collaborative* economy. This includes a range of businesses, enterprises and non-profit initiatives which orbit around the possibilities of public sharing, common property or direct peer-to-peer relationships: open source software, car/house sharing arrangements, forms of shared consumption and all variety of p2p mechanisms. Both enabled and modelled by the kinds of social networks at the heart of the internet, collaborative economic circuits provide a space 'in which autonomous agents can freely determine their behaviour and linkages without the intermediary of obligatory hubs' (Bauwens 2006: 38).[1] Because they are dispersed, these networks operate across space by enmeshing distant strangers in forms of solidarity, social cooperation or participation. These kinds of networks, one advocate notes, 'now present an unprecedented opportunity to link previously disconnected populations ... [and] create participatory communities of interest that link the poor and wealthy and defy the traditional limitations of geographically-bounded space' (Alexander 2013: 312). Collaborative mechanisms are both efficient and broad in scope, allowing for the construction of novel economic circuits not bound by place but animated by widely distributed common interests in shared resources.[2]

P2P networks have formed outside of the control or previously dominant players – firms, state bureaucrats or large institutional bureaucracies. 'Peer to peer', notes Bauwens, 'is a form of relationally between human beings whereby people can connect to each other without permission' (Bauwens 2012: 158). Sharing circuits organize 'collaboration among large groups of individuals … who cooperate effectively … without relying on … managerial hierarchies to coordinate their common enterprise' (Benkler and Nissenbaum 2006: 394–400). Although disintermediation is only partial in the sense that networks are deeply constituted through the complex of human and non-human elements that form digital relationships, they have emerged in ways that are largely outside of traditional forms of hierarchical control.

Finally, collaborative networks also emphasize a certain granularity of economic practice. This entails the division of economic practices, assets or resources into small fragments or modules that could then be shared among a wide public and reassembled in multiple ways. Granulation is a strategy that both allows widespread participation and facilitates the reassembly of common resources or assets in diverse combinations. Collaborative consumption programmes, such as p2p car-sharing programmes allow the use of assets to be divided into small units which can then be consumed and shared widely in ways that reduce the collective costs of owning and maintaining those assets in the first place. In doing so, these types of sharing mechanisms allow for the consolidation of a certain kind of value derived from common assets. As Benkler has noted, these types of arrangements

> provide a new way of imagining who we are, and who we can be; a cluster of practices that allow us to experience and observe ourselves as cooperative beings, capable of mutual aid, friendship, and generosity, rather than as the utility-seeking, self-interested creatures that have occupied so much of our imagination.
>
> (Benkler 2013: 215)

A second frame which animates recent alternative economic circuits relates to the possibility of *sociality*. This entails, in a most general sense, a recognition not of our essential individuality but of our basic entanglement with other social beings. Emerging from the ongoing street movements associated with Occupy Wall Street (OWS) and anti-austerity politics, there is now a growing call for a reconsolidated social economy. This mode of sociality, however, does not, in any simplistic manner, seek a return to conceptions of the 'social' rooted in practices of social citizenship. Rather, this form of sociality is rooted in the conditions of precarity. Precarity is a broad term designed to address a range of seemingly complex trends which undermine the security and well-being of everyday populations across diverse settings. 'In its broadest sense, it can be described as insecurity and vulnerability, as uncertainty and endangerment' (Lorey 2011)[3]; 'the multiple forms of nightmarish dispossession and injury that our age entails' (Muehlebach 2013: 298). Precarity refers, in particular, to the shifting and deepening forms of inequality and vulnerability associated with welfare restructuring, heightened border controls, neoliberal economic reforms and all variety of social and economic upheaval (Lorey 2010: 3).

At the same time, precarity has a kind of double inflection, not only a diagnosis of our political-economic present, but also, at the same time, an opening for new forms of social engagement. 'Precarity', argue activists, 'might be reinvented as a tactical form of productivity that resists the destructive initiatives of global capitalism' (Critical Art Ensemble 2012: 50).[4] Most importantly, in this sense, precarity signifies a kind of shared fragility, an inescapable but shared insecurity that exceeds us as individuals.[5] This common vulnerability binds us into each other – *exposes* us to each other – because our lives are, in some ultimate form, dependent on the complex range of ways in which others, and the care they provide, make our lives possible in 'livable' forms. 'Precariousness is by no means individual; it denotes the common existential vulnerability that is *shared with others* … the condition that exposes us to others, that makes every life fundamentally dependent on others' (Lorey 2011). At the heart of this sense of shared precarity is a recognition of the sociality that binds us to each other in our common susceptibility (Maurer 2012: 415).

The 'social' used in this context, is a deeply relational category, emblematic of our common fragility. In this formulation, our common vulnerability is also an inescapable point of our social connection with each other. Precarity signals 'a relational condition of social being that cannot be avoided' (Berlant *et al.* 2012: 165), a kind of social relationality built into the existential conditions of our lives. In contrast to neoliberal conceptions of an individualized self, precarity implies a deep reliance on each other and, by extension, our obligation to each other in light of that precarity. 'We have to start', argues Judith Butler, 'from this shared condition of precarity … a conception of ethical obligation that is grounded in precarity … it is, we might say, our common non-foundation' (quoted in Berlant *et al.* 2012: 170; Kearns 2013: 191).

Precarious obligation is shared but not uniform. Although precarity throws us into, exposes us to, deep webs of relation with each other, it also orbits around divides of inequality. This implies 'a notion of relational difference in interdependency with others. If we say 'we are all precarious', then the precariousness that is shared with others is always something that separates us from others' (Berlant *et al.* 2012: 171; Kearns 2013: 191).[6] This conception of relational vulnerability *and* difference establishes a complex sense of social being. We are, in this vulnerable way, constituted outside of ourselves, in the grids of sociality in which we, and our life chances, are conditioned. 'Liveable lives', by extension, are only made possible in social arrangements and institutions which acknowledge the constitutive conditions of our precarity. This entails:

> a different social ontology [which] would have to start from the presumption that there is a shared condition of precarity … our thinking

> gets nowhere without the presupposition of that very corporeal interdependency and entwinement … We are in this way, even as located, always elsewhere, constituted in a sociality that exceeds us. This establishes our exposure and our precarity, the ways in which we depend on political and social institutions to persist.
>
> (Butler 2011b)[7]

Finance has occupied an important location in these discussions of precarity. Although finance is often associated with the forces that constitute precarious lives in the first place, it is also an important source of metaphors of mutual regard and interdependence. As Martin suggests, 'we can look carefully at the ruination that the compulsory drive of finance leaves in its wake to see what else arises from it' (Martin 2012: 71). For him, the language of derivatives offers a useful point of departure for the reconstitution of social interdependency. The 'dynamics of the derivative', he notes, 'engender mutual indebtedness, interdependencies … What we call identity is certainly an attribute of self that gets bundled, valued, and circulated beyond an individual person' (Martin 2012: 65). Derivatives become an emblem of identity itself, a circulation of the self in ways that exceeds itself within webs of mutual exchange.

Most important to the rehabilitation of social being, however, is the language of debt. As Andrew Ross notes, 'loan-service payments that stretch out to an ever-receding horizon are a new element of the condition of precarity' (Ross 2013: 27). Recent organizing around debt, however, has also refigured debt as a set of claims related to our mutual entanglement. In ways that directly echo precarity as a form of mutual vulnerability and regard, debt resistors simultaneously refuse *and* embrace certain forms of debt. As OWS declared, 'to the financial establishment of the world, we have only one thing to say: We owe you nothing. To our friends, our families, our communities, to humanity and the natural world that makes our lives possible, we owe you everything' (Strike Debt/Occupy Wall Street 2012: 10).

If precarity is about the vulnerability we share, then debt exists as one of our basic points of common and shared fragility. 'Our whole system runs on debt and credit', notes the debt resistors manual, 'the whole world has become indebted … We are all debtors now' (Strike Debt/Occupy Wall Street 2012: 52). Because it is both extensive and shared, debt also is formative of our identities; a kind of shared foundation for our sense of being and how we might relate to each other. Debt is all-encompassing, often tracing a kind of limit within which our lives are rendered legible. 'All you have is debt' notes key Occupy organizer Amin Husein (Husein 2013), echoing Woody Guthrie's much earlier contention that 'all of us owe everybody. The amount that we owe is all that we have got' (see Aitken 2008: 450). Debt is both an intimate and unshakeable presence key to our own precarity and the seemingly emasculated sense of self that precarity constitutes.

The shared vulnerability of debt implies, however, not only a pressure exerted on our very sense of self and identity, but also, more radically, a larger social obligation. For many activists concerned with precarity, debt is not reducible to its financialized form, but encodes more resonant meanings. Alongside, and in opposition to the forms of financial debt there is a conception of debt as a rich metaphor of sociality, of belonging to each other. This mutual vulnerability is what Amin Husein refers to as *generative* debts, forms of social obligation to each other that might serve as the basis of new forms of 'positive common'; an explicit attempt to 'open up' the language and practice of debt as a way to 'fulfill the debts which are horizontal' (Husein 2013). 'By dissolving the bonds which bind us to the 1%, we seek to forge new and equitable bonds with one another' (Strike Debt/Occupy Wall Street 2012: 106). In this formulation debt is not a calculation that can be settled and retired but a *relational* category deeply generative of new forms of common obligation and mutual aid.

If we are social beings, vulnerable – *indebted* – to each other, then we are in need of economic arrangements which give substance to that sociality in concrete form. As Butler notes, our mutual exposure to each other demands concrete mechanisms of economic and political arrangements which address our common fragility. It is 'important to call "precarious"', she argues, 'the bonds that support life … forms of political organization that sustain living beings on terms of equality' (Berlant *et al.* 2012: 169). These precarious bonds have not been abstractions, but have animated a range of experiments in 'social and economic structures that support our mutual dependency'; experiments often deeply 'invested' in the possibilities of p2p arrangements.

'Communities of financial interest': collaborative capital in p2p circuits

Among the most ambitious of recent attempts to constitute a relational – indebted – form of finance are modes of social lending made possible through p2p platforms designed 'to connect lenders and borrowers in ways never before imagined' (Verstein 2011: 447). The first commercial p2p lender of note, Zopa, was launched in the UK in 2005 backed by a network of funders with deep connections to key 'web 2.0' ventures (Ashta and Assadi 2009; Slavin 2007: 10).[8] Zopa, and the two large American p2p lenders who have followed in its wake, Prosper and LendingClub, have now marked out a rapidly growing space in which borrowers and lenders negotiate their own credit arrangements largely outside of the purview of mainstream financial institutions. In idealized form, p2p lenders are web portals which allow prospective borrowers and lenders to connect with each other directly, sometimes in personalized ways, and make their own decisions regarding the extension of credit. P2P platforms are designed to aggregate lending capital from small contributors, allowing individual lenders to float as little as US $25 toward particular loans.[9] P2P arrangements 'have become online marketplaces where individuals, rather than institutions, work collaboratively to form capital'

(Collins, Swart and Zhang 2013: 3). In doing so, p2p networks allow borrowers (including those deemed too risky by mainstream banks) to access credit more widely and at costs cheaper than those charged by conventional lenders.

P2P financial arrangements are now a significant source of innovation. Over the past couple of years, for example, there have been viable attempts to establish p2p currency exchanges – spaces which allow everyday populations to exchange directly small amounts of foreign currency outside of conventional foreign exchange institutions.[10] Insurance has also become an important site of p2p innovation. *Friendsurance* allows friends (or social network contacts) to form into self-appointed risk pools. Friends in the pool essentially insure each other for small amounts of liability or general insurance, covering the deductible amounts of claims not covered by general insurers (see Economist 2012). Building on this success is jFloat, a British insurance experiment 'aims to side-step the insurance industry by allowing individuals to develop their risk pools in the absence of major insurers' (Langlois 2013). The scheme allows groups of 100 people, consisting of friends or contacts mutually selected through the website's networking portal, to constitute their own risk pools. Supported by reinsurers, each pool receives and manages 80% of all premiums generated by their members and is governed, at least in part, by rules its own members generate.

The most significant set of p2p arrangements, however, are credit networks which facilitate collaborative arrangements negotiated by borrowers and lenders outside of the scope and reach of financial institutions. In aggregating capital from many small lenders, and allowing direct collaboration between borrowers and lenders, p2p platforms attempt to reconcile a kind of mutual aid with forms of individualized self-regard (Hulme and Wright 2006: 46). This is a form of mutual advantage, moreover, which has grown rapidly since 2005. In the UK, for example, the p2p credit market grew by 91% from 2012 to 2013, a rate of growth just marginally higher than the 75.1% growth rate it experienced over the past three years. It is now estimated that 9.4 million 'investors' are involved, in one form or another, in p2p financial schemes in the UK (Collins, Swart and Zhang 2013: 4). The American p2p lending scene has grown even more rapidly. The largest and most dominant p2p lender globally, Lending Club, issued US $2 billion in 2013, up from $780 million in 2012 (Gelman 2013). Since its inception in 2007, LendingClub has issued over 95,000 member loans (LendingClub 2013: 2; Gelman 2013; Marketline 2013).

Although framed by its advocates as a form of disintermediation – a foundational contention that 'individuals, rather than institutions, stand on *both* sides of the transactions' (Chafee and Rapp forthcoming)[11] – p2p platforms are not simple vehicles for direct contact and exchange. Rather, p2p platforms shape the relations they claim merely to relay. On the one hand, in p2p networks, conventional forms of financial intermediation (especially the calculation and distribution of risk) are managed not by financial institutions but by lenders more directly. 'Lenders', Verstein notes, 'ultimately finance borrowers without banks interposing their own credit risks and guarantees' (Verstein 2011: 452). Put simply, lenders both extend capital and carry risk in p2p exchanges in ways that evade the normal role in which banks mediate credit contracts.

On the other hand, however, p2p platforms shape both the access to credit and the terms with which that credit is extended. P2P platforms, for example, establish important rules and benchmarks for borrowers in ways that increasingly resemble lending criteria enacted in mainstream credit markets (Bachmann *et al.* 2011: 8; Government Accountability Office 2011: 11). Lending Club now requires a FICO (Fair Isaac Corporation) score of at least 660 (generated by mainstream credit agencies), a debt-to-income ratio which sits below 35%, a minimum formal credit history which spans 36 months, six or fewer credit requests over the preceding six month period, and the existence of at least two currently active revolving accounts (Gelman 2013; LendingClub 2013: 3). In this vein, all of the major p2p exchanges now extensively grade the loan requests they receive, effectively setting the rates of interest for loan requests by categorizing potential loans along conventional financial and credit scoring criteria (LendingClub 2013: 14). In addition, p2p exchanges now offer a range of mediating web tools for prospective investors designed to allow them to construct loan portfolios. In these various ways, p2p lenders significantly shape the credit extended through their platforms; forms of intermediation which are a key source of revenue (Ashta and Assadi 2010: 8; Ortega and Bell 2008).[12]

The kind of reintermediation that p2p platforms accomplish is actually made possible through standard financial techniques. The technical mechanism which enables p2p networks, for example, is a system of basic securitized notes. Platforms like Prosper and LendingClub do not actually allow borrowers and lenders to consummate loans directly. Once a loan request has been fulfilled by lenders, p2p platforms actually execute the loan themselves (sometimes through a third party institution, such as WebBank) and then issue a note to all of the investors/lenders who have agreed to fund the loan (Chafee and Rapp forthcoming). These notes are unsecured and transfer the risk (and return) of the loan directly onto lenders (Verstein 2011: 459).

Although they exist as an exchange of securitized notes, the large American p2p platforms initially refused to define their loans as securities. In 2005 and 2007 both Prosper and LendingClub offered loans without registering them as securities offerings. After a prolonged investigation, the Securities and Exchange Commission issued a cease-and-desist order against Prosper, the oldest of the American platforms. Prosper resumed selling notes when its formal registration statement became effective in July 2008. LendingClub, in turn, suspended sales of notes to lenders from April to October of 2008 in order to complete the registration process which included the extension of a formal prospectus as well as other requirements (see Government Accountability Office 2011: 23–24).

For advocates, p2p lending platforms are most significant because of the horizontal axes they establish outside of the intervention of banks and other mainstream financial institutions. In the words of Occupy Wall Street's own endorsement, p2p networks are 'an industry that brings together individual savers and lenders on online platforms … filling a vacuum left behind by the banks' (Alternative Banking/Occupy Wall Street 2013: 115). Relational financial arrangements offer, in addition, a kind of reversal of the processes of demutualization which, over the past decades, have generally resulted in the privatization of all variety of funds and insurance arrangements. In doing so, p2p arrangements have revitalized mutual aid arrangements by establishing financial arrangements in which our own interests reside collectively or in common financial assets. 'Peer-to-peer communities', one advocate argues, 'are emerging with mutual aid solely in mind, bypassing classical banking value chains altogether' (Balnaves 2012: 143). In this formulation, p2p lending constitutes 'mutual aid in social networks' opening up a *social* field marked by our deeply relational obligations to each other.

The sociality of p2p lending is not, however, the space of the social associated with mid-twentieth century conceptions of social insurance or the welfare state. That form of social governance enacted a kind of mandatory mode of social solidarity by pressing citizens into the space of the social through mandated programmes of social security. In contrast, the social field encoded in p2p lending schemes implies a more voluntaristic ethos, requiring an active commitment from borrowers and lenders to enter into freely negotiated relations:

> Social lending initiatives are founded on a horizontal structure of power relations … providing a foundation and utility for community formation and social interaction … Social lending schemes can be understood as specifically 21st century communities of financial interest based on an intersection of individualism and community and a system of opting-in or voluntary participation in the community.
>
> (Hulme and Wright 2006: 9)[13]

This promise of horizontal relationality is also associated with a claim about broader access. In its initial framing, p2p lending was designed to open credit to those communities which had historically been denied access to mainstream financial institutions. This entailed a kind of balanced framework in which borrowers would lend to historically disadvantaged lenders but in ways that would secure for them relatively robust returns on their lending capital (Government Accountability Office 2011: 18). Because p2p platforms explicitly exist outside of the traditional authority invested in banks and other formal financial institutions, they have been able to avoid the ways in which those institutions have traditionally marginalized (or 'redlined') certain populations of borrowers. In this way, p2p networks became 'an attractive alternative option for borrowers who are unlikely to qualify for a loan from a traditional bank' (Larrimore et al. 2011: 21; Alexander 2013: 336–337). At its most ambitious p2p networks are conceived and constituted as a kind of novel source of capital made available more widely than the kinds of finance capital which flows through instrumental circuits. 'P2P lending' argue Chafee and Rapp, 'has allowed capital to flow to communities that were underserved by the credit markets … allowed capital to flow into economically depressed communities' (Chafee and Rapp forthcoming).[14] In this formulation, p2p lending is both an extension of and an alternative to the diagram of fringe finance which forms the core of this book. On one hand, like other forms of fringe lending, p2p credit holds out the prospect that financial innovation might remap the spaces of capital in ways that could draw in those currently outside of mainstream circuits of finance capital. At another level, however, it makes this claim by standing as a kind of alternative to those very forms of mainstream fringe finance – an extension of capital not (primarily) as a profitable but collaborative form.

It is in this way that p2p networks stage what Zadie Smith terms a kind of creative refusal. As Smith notes, 'at the heart of creativity lies a refusal. For a genuinely creative piece of work always declines to see the world as others see it or as it is commonly described … it "makes new"' (Smith 2013). Refusal, in these terms, involves the constitution of genuinely novel approaches to any particular object, a refusal to adopt pre-existing codes, practice or rituals. The 'making new' that p2p lending attempts is a kind of displacement of traditional banks; a process which will result in a gradual erosion of the power, scope and presence of banking institutions. In its most expansive form, this vision entails a refusal of finance more broadly. It also imagines p2p lending as a space in which the reckless world of disembodied and abstracted financial speculation could be contained or rendered social. As Lenz argues,

> the web-based transferal [of credit] enables the mobilization of high capital volume by bringing together numerous savers. The credit default risk … is broken up into small amounts and spread throughout the mass of capital providers … [in this manner] the economy's credit supply is withdrawn from the daily speculation of the bond market and therefore receives a long-term stabilizing element.
>
> (Lenz 2011; see also Haldane 2013)[15]

Because they form capital in incremental amounts across distributed networks, p2p networks help both to disperse capital widely and to stabilize global credit markets outside of mainstream financial institutions.

The space between this refusal and the actual trajectories of p2p networks, however, is widening in important ways. Although the cyberspaces created in p2p networks 'connect previously disconnected individuals, facilitate repeat transactions, and allow social networks to rate and evaluate participants', they are becoming increasingly distant from their initial social intentions (Alexander 2013: 313). The growth which each of the large p2p platforms experienced, for example, has resulted less directly from their idealized commitment to horizontal financial relationships and more immediately from the financial value that p2p networks have managed to instrumentalize. Most importantly, p2p lending networks have become a mechanism capable of efficiently harnessing the 'bank margin'; the difference between rates of interest on basic deposits and the rates charged on loans extended by banks and other financial institutions. Because p2p networks operate outside of mainstream financial institutions, the price of credit they establish allows p2p creditors and debtors to share this margin in mutually advantageous ways (Lenz 2011).[16]

Inserted into this margin, p2p networks have managed to harness value within what has become an innovative financial instrument. At one level, p2p notes are a somewhat limited investment – essentially unsecured assets[17] which cannot be exchanged in any kind of secondary market. Notes, once sold, can only be exchanged through an exclusive resale trading platform operated by a private brokerage, FOLIO*fn* Investment Inc. (LendingClub 2013: 12). Moreover, most p2p platforms allow borrowers to pay off the loan early without penalty (Steinisch 2012). This combination of factors creates a financial instrument with risk weighted onto investors. At another level, however, by providing capital to borrowers outside of the mainstream financial system, lenders frequently earn rates of return higher than typical deposit instruments. Over the long-term many LendingClub and Prosper investors have commonly realized returns on investment of 10% on many of the graded loans they have extended (Renton 2013a). Prosper has exceeded returns of 11% annually since its formal securities registration in July 2009 (Government Accountability Office 2011: 9).

The shift of p2p networks into a space measured in terms of investor returns has been a diverse accomplishment involving the work of both p2p advocates as well as regulators. As p2p lending platforms have tightened their own lending criteria, they have collapsed some of the space in p2p networks that had been available for borrowers with limited or fragmented credit histories. This tendency to privilege investor preferences has also been echoed in regulatory processes. In the USA, in particular, the protracted process by which p2p platforms came under the purview of the Securities and Exchange Commission formalized a series of new responsibilities to investors, including specified reporting requirements and a suite of investor protections. These measures, notes Alexander, 'are privileging lenders' and investors' interests over those of borrowers' (Alexander 2013: 375). Combined, these trends have resulted in a kind of 'weblining' of populations already distant from mainstream lending or credit practices (Alexander 2013: 374).[18]

The absorption of p2p lending into the realm of securities regulations is an echo of what these broader trends announce; the recasting of p2p credit not as a horizontal relation but, more formally, as an 'investment contract'. 'The current regulatory system provides ... person-to-person lending platforms with protections consistent with those afforded to conventional bank borrowers and investors in registered securities' (Government Accountability Office 2011: 47). In doing so, these developments signal a certain departure from the initial goals of social lending. Initial experiments in social and p2p lending privileged access to credit for a wide group of borrowers, including those on or beyond the fringes of the mainstream financial world. However, 'as these markets evolved and courted more mainstream economic actors, they created benefits for lenders and investors and restricted marginalized actors' access' (Alexander 2013: 376; Alloway 2013). This 'evolution', moreover, has been recently punctuated by the arrival of even larger financial agents and the threading of even denser lines into mainstream financial webs.

Financializing social relationality

As Butler has noted, we are constituted in a 'sociality that exceeds us'. The version of social relationality mobilized in p2p networks, however, is quickly itself becoming a financialized object. Investors have, for example, been attracted to the conventional financial advantages of p2p loans as a financial asset, including significantly lower operating costs than traditional lenders. LendingClub entails operating costs of only 2%, a level that makes it attractive to investors of all sorts (ABS 2013).

Most importantly, the remaking of p2p lending into an asset stream has centred around the possibilities of harnessing financial value from the kind of relational webs it enacts. Relational webs allow a certain kind of efficiency leveraged from the ways in which p2p networks pry open access to assets or resources which are held privately or under-utilized. In some important ways, p2p networks constitute capital by unearthing it in everyday networks where it lays inert. The kind of relationality enabled by p2p platforms 'enables people to more efficiently use their assets, in this case money … by investing with peers to get more value' (Forbes 2013). It is this extraction of value from inert places, however, that often creates the conditions for financialization.

The efficiencies gained in and through p2p lending models have now become the serious object of formalized and mainstream financial attention. The largest p2p lending platforms, for example, are now becoming more closely integrated into the financial mainstream in both interpersonal and material ways.[19] The most prominent initiation of LendingClub into mainstream financial circles, however, is related to recent rounds of financing, all of which are likely to culminate in a widely rumoured IPO that could be staged as early as 2014 (Crowder *et al.* 2013: 5). A series of recent secondary transactions have now valued LendingClub at US $2.3 billion involving a $57 million financing packaging arranged by DST Global (Calvey 2013a; Crowder *et al.* 2013: 5). Punctuating this financing was an investment made by Google which 'led a $125 million deal to buy a [7%] stake in' LendingClub (De la Merced 2013).

Prosper has had its own similar moments of enfolding into mainstream finance. In January 2013, Sequoia Capital led a takeover and refinancing of

Prosper that essentially relaunched its management approach. The new management structure is fronted by Steve Vermut and his son Aaron who were closely associated with Merlin Securities and Wells Fargo and have important connections to a series of prominent hedge funds (FinAlternatives 2013). This latest round of financing for Prosper includes a large capital investment by BlackRock, 'the world's biggest money manager' (Salmon 2013).

Moreover, both of the large American p2p platforms have initiated formal relationships with banks. LendingClub has negotiated a loan origination programme with a series of community banks which allows those banks to purchase loans that LendingClub originates and services (Alloway 2013; Aspan 2013). British p2p lenders have also tried to cultivate ties into mainstream retail finance. After intense lobbying, the UK Chancellor of the Exchequer announced his intention in his Autumn 2013 financial statement to allow p2p loans as a permissible investment for Individual Savings Accounts, a tax deferral mechanism used widely for retirement savings (Euromoney 2013). This closer alignment with the spaces of mainstream finance has resulted in rapid growth which has cemented p2p lending as a legitimate presence in financial markets. LendingClub, for example, announced in December 2013 that it had originated US $3 billion in total loans, only six months after marking $2 billion in loan originations (Calvey 2013a; Collins, Swart and Zhang 2013; Euromoney 2013b; Shah 2009; Ende *et al.* 2013).

This growth of p2p lending platforms and their increasing entanglement in the world of mainstream finance are mutually implicated. As p2p lending has grown in both scope and volume, it has attracted the attention of financial interests keen to harness the kinds of efficiency and financial value it constitutes. As a consequence, however, p2p lending platforms are increasingly characterized not by the web of social relations they enact, but by the innovative financial value those webs can generate. As I argue in the remainder of this section, the financialization of p2p networks is accomplished via three clusters of innovation. A first cluster of innovation involves mechanisms designed by p2p platforms which make them accessible to large institutional investors. Increasingly, p2p lenders rely on hedge-funds and other institutional investors to finance lending that initially came from everyday individuals. As one analyst puts it, p2p loans are 'an entirely new asset category … [attracting interest among] hedge funds, pension funds, mutual funds and wealth-managers requiring better returns on their capital' (Lee 2012). In responding to this interest, lending platforms have tightened their own credit screening and grading mechanisms in an explicit attempt to attract investors. One analyst, for example, approvingly notes that 'Lending Club says that it now has a two-step vetting process that weeds out 90 percent of applicants, making the remaining pool safer' (Feldman and Pinsker 2013). This initiative, which has been echoed by other platforms, has helped lenders develop loan portfolios which are attractive to investors.

Most importantly, p2p networks have widened channels of access for institutional investors. The core of these efforts has been the construction of 'whole loan programmes'. Most social lending networks initially operated using a 'fractional ownership' model which prevented investors from holding more than a fixed percentage – often 75% – of any particular note. This was designed mainly to ensure the continued dispersal of loans across a wide body of peer-investors. In the past two years, however, many of the large p2p networks have initiated 'whole loan' programmes which allow 'institutional investors to buy up complete notes in bulk before they ever reach the public market' (Loper 2013). American p2p platforms, for example, have established two distinct pools of loans; one populated by whole loans available to institutional investors and a second "fractional pool', in which loans are divided up among lenders, mostly retail investors' (Economist 2013). Because these whole lending programmes have been very successful, nearly 65% of recent total loan originations are fully funded before individual investors have a chance to access them (Loper 2013).

Whole-lending programmes have been instrumental in making p2p loans accessible to large funds in an efficient manner. 'Investors are increasingly hedge funds, or high-net-worth brokerage clients or other pools of money highly redolent of the Wall Street of old' (Salmon 2013: 4).[20] The adoption of whole lending approaches has also spurred the development of new funds specifically oriented to p2p investing opportunities. The most prominent of these is a series of closed-end funds launched by Marshall Wace LLP, one of the largest London-based agents in global markets. To cement this arrangement, Marshall Wace bought a controlling interest in PSP Capital Solutions, a firm with deep ties to City-based investment houses, which has launched a suite of funds listed on the London Stock Exchange 'that will … invest direct onto peer-to-peer lending platforms' (Faes 2013: 17). Noting that the launch of the new funds 'has the potential to transform … lending practices worldwide', Marshall Wace framed its investment as an attempt to integrate p2p lending into the heart of the global financial system (quoted in Larson 2013).

A second cluster of innovation which has ushered in financialized p2p lenders relates to securitization. In ways that replicate the securitization of subprime mortgages (and the securitization of micro-credit receivables examined in Chapter 3), p2p loans have recently been assembled into broader packages of securities (see Dachille 2013).[21] The first experiment in broad-based p2p securitization was launched in the fall of 2013 by Eaglewood Capital, a New York based firm that has raised over US $150 million investment directly in p2p lending platforms; a leader in what one key industry figure calls the 'institutionalization' of p2p lending (Faes 2013).[22] In 2013 Eaglewood Capital packaged some of its LendingClub loans and 'sold them in a $53 million securitization deal, with the buyer understood to be a large insurance company' (Euromoney 2013b: 42; Financial Times 2013). In some ways a conventional securitization, the Eaglewood offering allowed a point of access for institutional investors to a particular selection of p2p loans, effectively providing 'institutional investors exposure to a high-yielding asset class that banks cannot provide' (Euromoney 2013b: 44). The Eaglewood securitization was divided into two tranches, a senior trench worth $40 million sold to an unnamed insurance company and a $13 million junior tranche that was kept by Eaglewood itself (Alloway 2013). On one hand, this bundle of p2p loans was assembled into a 'securitized structure similar to the vehicles that sparked the US sub-prime crisis' (Euromoney 2013a: 6).[23] On the other hand, however, by retaining the junior tranche Eaglewood will take losses of up to $13 million before anyone else, effectively creating a 25% loss buffer. Eaglewood's offering both parallels the innovative experiments in micro-credit securitization detailed in Chapter 3, and responds to criticisms mounted during the subprime crisis during which firms who did securitizations did not keep any portion of loans on their own books (Eavis 2013).

In many important ways, both the whole loan programmes and securitization are important not only because they facilitate a certain kind of flow of capital into p2p webs, but also because they enact a kind of symbolic presence as a practice fully enmeshed within the sophisticated world of mainstream finance. Advocates of securitization often frame it as a key artifact of financialization itself. Securitization is a marker of what Knorr Cetina and Bruegger refer to as the 'global microstructures' – the 'patterns of coordination' – that link financial markets across global space (Knorr Cetina and Bruegger 2002: 907).[24] Because it is closely associated with the rituals that make up contemporary finance writ large, securitization is often conceived as a kind of prelude to deeper and more complete forms of integration within global finance. Matt Burton, for example, the founder of Orchard, a key investment advisor at the intersection of p2p networks and institutional investors, notes that the 'next major development is a secondary market. There will then need to be credit ratings, exchange traded funds, a Bloomberg-like terminal, everything you see today in a mature financial market' (quoted in Alloway 2013; see also O'Donnell 2013).[25]

This deeper connection to 'mature' financial markets continues apace with the first ever rated securitization of p2p loans. SoFi, a p2p platform which originates student loans, recently completed a US $152 million senior note securitization rated Single-A by DBRS (Dominion Bond Rating Service) which was sold to 'top tier institutional investors'. The loans were pooled and assembled by Morgan Stanley and sold to a small cluster of pension funds and insurance companies (Renton 2013b). The formal rating that attended the securitization was partly possible because SoFi offers student loans which are both longer in duration than typical p2p loans and immune to bankruptcy, guaranteeing a high level of quality (Alloway and Massoudi 2013). Nonetheless, the successful rating has widely been viewed as a significant achievement by p2p lenders.

A third cluster of mechanisms which have facilitated financialization has emerged out of experiments by lending platforms themselves in creating their own financial instruments. LendingClub has advanced its own web of financial instruments designed to help hedge funds or high-net-worth clients construct portfolios of p2p loans. LendingClub's ultimate objective is to constitute its own 'publicly available closed end mutual fund' consisting of p2p loan receivables (Feldman and Pinsker 2013). In the short term, and as an attempt to build momentum, LendingClub formed its own financial arm, LC Advisors, in 2011. LC Advisors now offers a series of funds for those who want to invest in p2p loans but who do not have the interest or capacity to assemble and purchase notes themselves (Wang 2013).[26] LC Advisors, to date, has launched three major funds, the Broad-Based Consumer Credit Fund (consisting of notes graded mainly in the B to D range), the Broad-Based Consumer Credit Fund (which is the qualified purchaser version of the same fund) and the Conservative Consumer Credit Fund (which consists mainly of notes graded in the A and B range). Since inception, the conservative fund has achieved annualized returns in the 5.5% to 7.5% range while the broad-based funds, which in 2012 had invested in 16,000 unique consumer loans across all credit grades, had achieved an annualized return of 9.36% (Wang 2013).

In the wake of these mechanisms of financialization, the language and identity of p2p lending continues to change. Although initially envisioned as the basis of alternative economic circuits constituted directly by everyday populations, p2p networks are increasingly framed in the language and practices of mainstream finance. Like other financial offerings linked to the financial edges, p2p loans have now taken up an important role in strategies of investor diversification. P2P loans are unmediated by larger financial institutions (at least in the processes of origination) and are often framed as a valuable source of portfolio diversification. As one financial analyst has noted, in p2p products, lenders/investors 'get a whole new asset class which is neither a savings account nor an investment … independent from anything else in the existing portfolio' (Slavin 2007: 17; Prosser 2013).[27] Because they are rooted in relational webs, and because they are often constituted as fixed-term investments, p2p instruments are often marketed as a device designed at a remove from the uncertainties of mainstream financial markets. 'These are tumultuous times for investors', notes one analyst, 'with risks and volatility inflicting pain across most investment classes and around the global economy … [p2p notes] have outpaced other common investments or indexes' (Javelin Strategy and Research 2009: 9). Although some critics question the degree to which p2p loans are autonomous from cyclical trends (see Stevenson 2013)[28], many analysts now promote p2p investment instruments as assets which are valuably detached from other financial trends or assets (Economist 2013).[29]

As a result p2p platforms are now populated, on the lending side, not by individuals (enmeshing themselves in social relations) but by institutions (seeking forms of financial value). As Prosser notes, p2p lending 'is at an inflection point where the investment in Notes is shifting from individuals making their own investing decisions to professionally managed money' (Prosser 2013). The proportion of total investment in LendingClub from individuals, for example, dropped from 78% to 56% in 2013 although the absolute numbers of individual lenders does continue to increase. Although no p2p loans were purchased by financial institutions as recently as 2012, 16%

of all notes in 2013 were owned by institutional investors. By 2014, it is estimated that the majority of investment in p2p lending sites will come not from self-directed individuals but from institutions (Prosser 2013; Salmon 2013). In this trend, the antinomies of p2p lending are revealed with a certain clarity. On one hand p2p platforms still frame themselves as a radical and even democratic way of organizing credit – a method by which economic circuits can be constituted by those not well served by existing modes of financial incorporation. As one key advocate has noted, p2p networks are 'using the internet to reshape the financial system and profoundly transform the way people think of credit and investment' (quoted in De la Merced 2013). On the other hand, however, p2p networks increasingly resemble – or at least give shelter to – the financial agents they seek to transcend.[30]

In this context, p2p lending is a practice in motion. In some spaces, the attempt to mobilize a kind of creative, collaborative and relational web at the heart of how finance might work, remains important to the overall identity of social lending. In these spaces, p2p platforms are vehicles for alternative economic circuits, places where, in Zelizer's terms, everyday populations negotiate the requirements of social solidarity even in the face of commercialized or financialized transactions. In its most prominent locations, however, the meaning and intentions of p2p lending have been modified by the kinds of financial innovation it has attracted. Increasingly the object of experimentation and innovation initiated by mainstream financial agents, p2p lending has become ever more enfolded into the kinds of institutional financialization it was initially committed to overcome. Situated in the midst of these contending pressures, p2p lending is emblematic of fringe finance more broadly – a diagram which relies upon innovative methods designed to draw fringe populations into mainstream finance but which can also be disrupted by those opposed to its expansive reach.

Conclusion: Is there an art of not being financialized?

> I know we're gonna meet someday in the crumbled financial institutions of this land
> There will be tables and chairs
> There'll be pony rides and dancing bears
> There'll even be a band
> Because listen, after the fall there'll be no more countries
> No currencies at all, we're going to live on our wits
> We're going to throw away survival kits
> Trade butterfly knives for adderall
> And that's not all
> Woah! There will be snacks, there will
> There will be snacks, there will be snacks!
>
> (Andrew Bird, *Tables and Chairs*)

On 15 November 2012 a diverse assembly associated with OWS and a campaign known as Strike Debt staged *The People's Bailout*, an event that has become a signature moment in the campaign for a renewed form of indebted social life. Staging, and mimicking, the kitsch of a fundraising telethon, *The People's Bailout* sought to raise money for the *Rolling Jubilee,* an attempt to buy 'bad' debt in order to cancel it, 'all of it organized by ordinary people' (Ross and Ackerman 2012). The 'telethon', held at Le Poisson Rouge in New York City, was designed to solicit small donations in order to fund purchases of debt in the secondary market (see Figure 7.2). At one level, the intent of the *Rolling Jubilee* was deceptively simple, to 'buy up defaulted personal debt and then instead of collecting it, 'abolish it' through crowdsourced donations' (Burns 2012). Because debt can be bought in the secondary market for a fraction of its face value, the *Rolling Jubilee* has been able buy over US $15 million in medical debt from $400,000 it raised from widely dispersed contributions averaging $40. It has raised an additional $200,000 with which it will make another ambitious debt buy in 2014 (Gokey 2013a). A unique tactic, the *Rolling Jubilee* essentially constitutes its own unique financial instrument capable of harnessing a dispersed pool of small contributions. These contributions are assembled into and instrumentalized as a packaged fund active in secondary debt markets in ways that targets particular forms of distressed debts.

At another level, however, the *Rolling Jubilee* is a dense and complicated intervention. Although it is the result of an immense current of collective and organized effort, one its most important initial tributaries came from the experiments conducted by artist and activist Thomas Gokey. Although the general idea of a mechanism that would intervene directly into debt markets had long circulated in activist circles, and especially at OWS, Gokey was the first to engage with how it might work in specific terms. Guided by important conversations with David Graeber and Mica White at Adbusters, Gokey began his effort at constructing a jubilee intervention; what he describes as his own 'small scale experiment to understand the mechanism' (Gokey 2013a) by simply making contact with local debt buyers in and around Syracuse New York and trying to learn details about how the market operates. Using US $466 of his own savings, he managed to purchase (and then abolish) $14,000 worth of debt owed by 11 Americans, to Wells Fargo. From this experiment, the outline of the basic *Rolling Jubilee* mechanism was constituted. Strike Debt, based in New York and deeply connected to OWS, both adopted the *Rolling Jubilee* as a signature action and began to assemble a much wider team, including a range of experts (accountants, tax lawyers, financial specialists) who could assist in technical and practical concerns: constructing a suitable debt portfolio, establishing purchase and cancellation procedures, registering the action as a legal entity capable of intervening in debt markets, negotiating lower prices with debt sellers, and sorting out legal and tax issues related to debt cancellation. What has resulted is simultaneously a piece of complex financial engineering and what Gokey and others have referred to as a kind of 'social hack', an attempt to disrupt the logic of the financial system by intervening into the very codes, practices and mechanisms that make that system function. These interventions – these forms of social hacks – repurpose actual financial mechanisms, or what Gokey calls the '*little exploitable parts*' of those mechanisms, for critical intent, a kind of use of financial leverage 'in reverse' (Gokey 2013a; 2013b).

In establishing a mechanism in which everyday populations can intervene into and cancel the debt of others, the *Rolling Jubilee* encodes a certain kind of relationality often gestured at but not fully realized in p2p lending networks. At the heart of the initiative is a practice of social indebtedness. The *Rolling Jubilee* both addresses the crushing debt in which we are all enmeshed, but also allows, at the same time, a different kind of debt as obligation. On one hand, debt is often conceived as a particular form of violence and dispossession. 'A debt', notes David Graeber in a formulation that has been influential among debt resistors, 'is just the perversion of a promise. It is a promise corrupted by both math and violence … just as no one has the right to tell us our true value, no one has the right to tell us what we truly owe' (Graeber 2011: 392; see also Strike Debt/Occupy Wall Street 2012: 106). On the other hand, however, debt is also refigured as a kind of obligation. The *Rolling Jubilee* is, according to Gokey, a recognition in practice that 'society requires social bonds' and a consecration of 'debt as a social obligation' (Gokey 2013b). The *Rolling Jubilee* is a deeply affirmative practice which, according to organizers, helps constitute a broader sense of social relationality, what Amin Husain refers to as the 'generative debts' that implicate us in the precarity of others (Husain 2013).

For those closely associated with the *Rolling Jubilee*, debt is a kind of relationality worked out over time. In resisting debt, and in affirming our own indebtedness to each other, we might also begin to discover and specify the kinds of obligations we could make on and for each other. It is in the crucible of debt refusal, that a different sense of obligation and entanglement can be constituted. 'We need', argues Gokey,

> to build … [a] debtors movement to really question what our true obligations are *to one another* … a debt is a promise we make to one another. It's a kind of bond, a way we bind ourselves to one another … we should be able to determine for ourselves what kind of obligations we have to one another.
>
> (Gokey 2013b, emphasis in original)

In these terms, the *Rolling Jubilee* is a site where the determination of those very bonds can be clarified, discovered and affirmed.

The *Rolling Jubilee* was never envisioned as a discrete mechanism but as a catalyst for a broader politics of debt refusal that begins with a certain kind of visibility. In a string of conversations organized loosely around OWS, debt

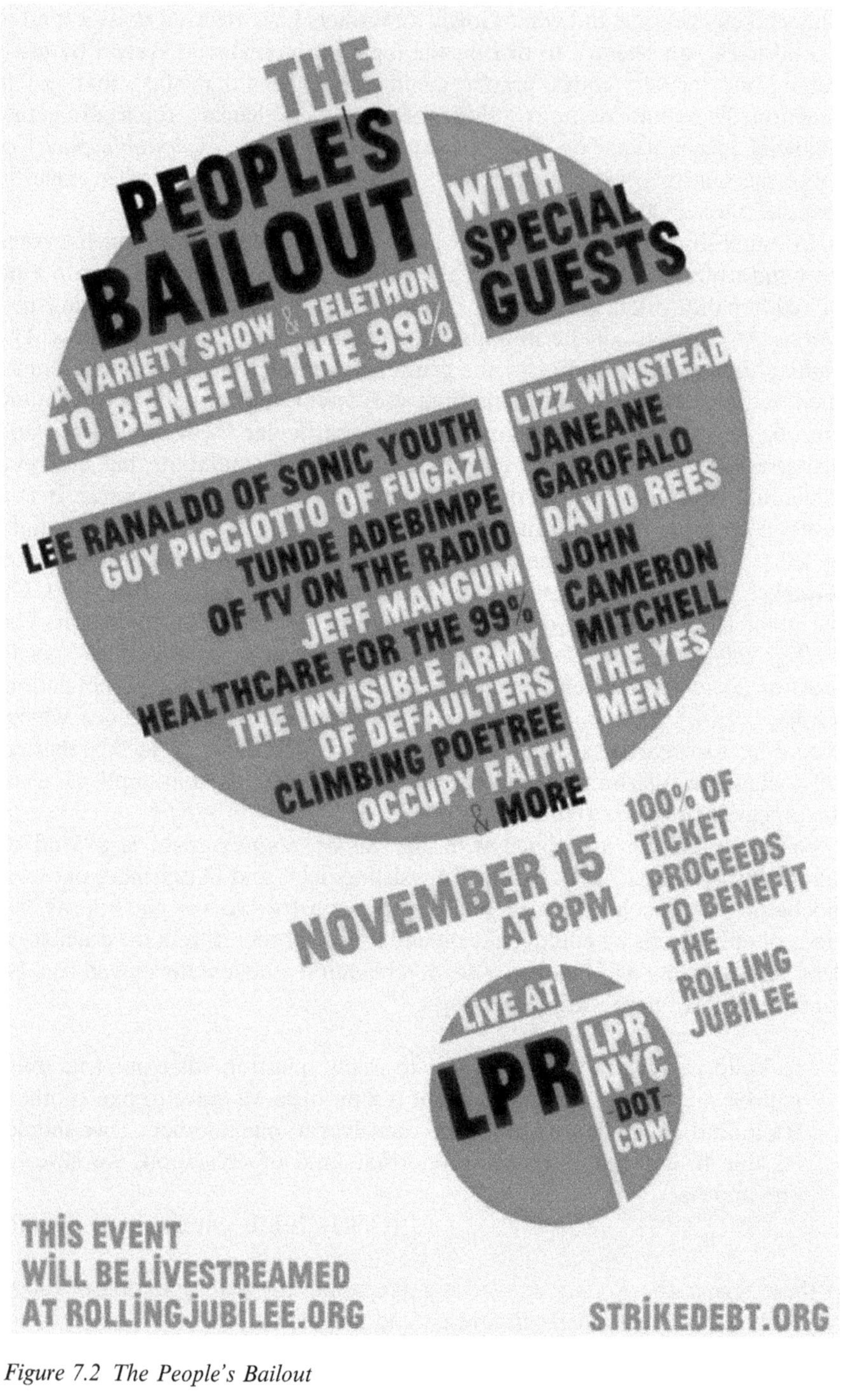

Figure 7.2 The People's Bailout

refusal campaigns became animated by various attempts to make personal debts of all kinds visible. The '99 percent tumblr', for example, became an online space in which indebted individuals could reveal the extent of their debt burden. This was echoed in conversations across other settings including the Occupy Debt Assembly. By 2012, on the first anniversary of OWS, making debt visible – and using that visibility as a basis of a broader solidarity – became an important form of political action. Noting debt as a widely shared condition, activists framed debt as both a ubiquitous but also potentially unifying force. In the words of one declaration issued at the first anniversary of OWS, 'we are the invisible army of defaulters … We are everywhere … In Year II, we step out of the shadows' (quoted in McKee 2012: 6).

Because we are all encumbered by debt, and because debt is the basis of both our precarity and our vulnerability to each other, it is the basis of a broader movement for political-economic change. As Andrew Ross has put it, 'the struggle over debt will be the front-line conflict of our times, just like the struggle over wages in the era of high industrialization' (Ross and Ackerman 2012). Debt refusal becomes a basis for both a much broader movement and larger networks of mutual aid; 'ushering in an entirely new tactical model for bringing together cultural capital, collective resource-mobilization and the principle of mutual aid' (McKee 2012: 3). The *Rolling Jubilee* was not designed as a completed achievement as much as an opening to larger possibilities. In Gokey's terms, it was an experiment in a certain kind of action as well as an invitation to 'see past' itself to a longer-term suite of interventions (Gokey 2013a). 'The dream', one activist summarizes, 'is to create a global, nonviolent, non-cooperation campaign focused around debt' (Tepper 2012).[31] This larger movement would attempt not only modes of global debt refusal, but also forms of positive obligation to each other on a much larger and more concrete scale. The *Rolling Jubilee* becomes, in this vein, a kind of model itself for the broader forms of life and mutual regard that might, if expanded, reverse the grounds of precariousness; 'an infrastructure where we could actually sustain each other' (Burns 2012).

The *Rolling Jubilee* sits in striking counterpoint to the story told in this chapter about p2p lending networks. Although they orbit around an original claim that economic circuits could be constituted by everyday borrowers themselves, p2p lending networks have become more fully an outlet for financial capital than an unmediated site of financial relationality. The *Rolling Jubilee*, however, is an important reminder that economic circuits built around relational practice are still a resonant possibility. At the heart of the *Rolling Jubilee* is a kind of mutual aid generated not through any mediated presence but through the relations we ourselves constitute with each other. 'Strike Debt', notes one of its organizers, 'opens a space for imagining and enacting … ways of living without relying on existing authorities … in which people bail out one another' (McKee 2012: 12). Although the radical political possibilities associated with p2p lending platforms are now refracted through a more complex series of tradeoffs associated with its relationships to the world of mainstream finance, Strike Debt's experiments imply a lingering hunger for relational financial mechanisms capable of inserting us into each other's indebted lives.

At the same time, the *Rolling Jubilee* also implies that fringe finance more broadly is a field constituted in contestation. The story of p2p networks, and its juxtaposition to more radical experiments like the *Rolling Jubilee*, reveals a field not settled in its own trajectory but shaped by a series of ongoing contests. I have concluded this book with a discussion of p2p lending because it seems particularly emblematic of fringe finance more broadly – a diagram which maps out serious financial innovation but is ultimately implicated in a certain fragility. On one hand, p2p lending has become an important site of innovation in the ways in which the edges of the financial system might be converted into forms of financial value. In some ways p2p lending is an immaculate emblem of the kinds of financialization that continue to shape the global political economy – a site where innovation has facilitated the reach of financial agents into a practice not only distant from, but constituted in opposition to, mainstream financial networks.

On the other hand, however, both the origins of p2p lending as a form of social lending and the ongoing experiments in more radical forms of relational financial webs, like the *Rolling Jubilee*, highlight the fragility of fringe finance. This book has argued that fringe finance is both an elegant diagram of the financial edge *and* a set of practices which often encounter more friction, ambiguity and contestation than that diagram implies. The future of fringe finance, and the pressures it will exert over everyday populations across the global economy, will be determined, in ultimate form, by the ways in which these ambiguities and contests either persist or become resolved.

Perhaps more importantly, however, the *Rolling Jubilee* offers a unique critical strategy aimed at disrupting finance and the logic of instrumental rationality so often at its core. This critical strategy, I want to note by way of conclusion, renders its own complicated map of the topography of financial power and resistance. The *Rolling Jubilee* occupies a complicated space in relation to the financial markets it seeks to address. Although, at one level, it seeks to constitute a kind of relationality *outside* of the logic of financialization, it is, at another level, an intervention *within* those markets. In some ways, the *Rolling Jubilee* is neither fully inside nor outside of the markets it seeks to disrupt. Rather it seeks a kind of tactical repurposing of finance by working within those markets and with what Gokey has referred to as the 'little exploitable parts' of finance. The *Rolling Jubilee*, although understood by its organizers as a 'public education' action aimed at a much longer and more radical rethinking of debt (Ross 2014), is also consistently described as a kind of *mechanism*; a reworked tool that could intervene into those markets as currently constituted (Gokey 2013b). In these terms, initiatives like the *Rolling Jubilee* operate across a complex space – both inside and outside of the markets, both fundamentally mundane and imminently short-term in focus, both critical and practical in orientation.

By contrast, the dominant topography of financial power and resistance invoked by critics of finance is one that often maps an outside to finance. In various forms – in calls for a finance once more re-embedded within the social, in projects that aim at a kind of counter-hegemonic movement – our most common critical language of finance orbits around claims that are often exterior to finance or which require a kind of detachment. The most common logic of resistance in IPE, for example, often implies a 'move/counter-move' logic in which dominant social and economic forces are contested by forms of critical agency which 'step back from the world as it is' and construct alternatives outside of the reach of dominant institutions (see Cox 1987). These topographies insist on a kind of inside/outside logic in which alternatives are grounded in constellations of social action located outside of the centres of power they refuse. Although not without resonant value as an image of political strategy or intervention, this topography of power and resistance does not exhaust the ways in which contestation might disrupt or constitute 'alternative' practices. The *Rolling Jubilee* is important, in my view, not because it occupies a location outside of finance (or because it exists as an exterior platform for critical intervention) but precisely as an intervention enabled by a deep knowledge of the interiority of financial markets (the mundane financial, legal and accounting practices and techniques at the heart of secondary debt markets) and the ways in which those markets might be repurposed.

So, is there a way of imagining an outside of finance, a meaningful limit to the reach of financial rationality? More relevant to the discussion of this book, is there an art of not being financialized?[32] If there is a way of refusing finance, I want to suggest, one of its paths is relational; that is, a path that might be expressed not in terms of the separations between finance and its alternatives but in terms of their mutual implication. This book has examined the 'inside' and 'outside' of finance not as two discrete spaces, but as deeply interconnected zones which are not so much bounded from each other as implicated in and along shifting and mutually constitutive edges.

This implies that 'alternatives to finance' might not exclusively exist in ways separate from finance. Rather, some of the most resonant forms of activism opposed to mainstream finance exist in complex relation with (sometimes tactically internal to) the dominant tendency they seek to disrupt. As Maurer suggests, it might be critically productive to ask 'how participants make alternatives and how those alternatives, once specified and rendered objects of reflexive knowledge, oscillate in and out of phase with the central tendency, and what aspects of them continue to produce dissonant vibrations even when in phase with that mode' (Maurer 2012: 415). This is not to suggest that there is no 'outside of finance' nor any value to imagining a world untouched by financial abstraction as in Andrew Bird's evocative *Tables and Chairs*. Indeed, in some ways, this book has been precisely about the 'constitutive outside' of finance; about the ways in which finance, even finance 'writ large', is constituted in the uneven ways in which it confronts its own edges and those on the other sides of those edges. Rather this is to suggest the some of the strategies most resonant in our present are those that are, at least in some sense, internal to finance and which seek to render those internal spaces knowable.

Cirio's evocative form of tactical art, for example, is a disruption of finance that makes use of the very technical infrastructures which enable finance in the first place. In his view this involves not an assault on finance from the outside but a kind of social 'hacking' of its interior space. Cirio describes this as a longer-term intent to create 'social algorithms' which both use but also rework the mathematical systems at the heart of contemporary financial practices. Social algorithms, according to Cirio, are interventions which are both within, but which also strike at the deepest core of, finance. 'They are not', he suggests, 'malicious hacks, they are not sabotaging viruses, nor are they speculative aesthetics, funny hoaxes or simple slogans … They propose new realities … activate political evolutions' (Cirio 2011). This does not involve establishing an external critical perch, but engaging deeply with and within existing financial arrangements and the actual mundane tools that make those arrangements possible in the very first place. Cirio's art speaks an insistence that we, as critics of neoliberal finance, begin to learn in more intimate terms the complex practices that enable finance and the ways in which those tools might be asked (or repurposed) to meet other ends. 'We can develop a new design for our money', notes Cirio, by 'taking over and democratizing these tools' (Cirio 2011). This is not to suggest a kind of reduction of politics to the merely technical. Rather, I am suggesting that if there is an art of not being financialized, then it lies not in any single or 'grand refusal' but in fragmented refusals operating across various scales and locations, including those aimed at or situated within the most mundane or technical corners of contemporary finance (see Amoore 2007).

This type of critical gesture mirrors the focus in this book on the fluidity or ambiguity of boundaries. Where are the borders of finance? What demarcates the spaces, practices and interventions that are 'inside' or 'outside' of finance? What I have tried to suggest in this book is that even though they are often conceived as fixed or unproblematic, the borders of finance are both constantly shifting (often, as this book has suggested, in an outward direction) and yet also permeable. As Rob Walker notes, although borders are often imagined as if they occupy 'zero width' (simply given bounds to some already-existing or unproblematic body) they 'nevertheless host the most intense practices' (Walker 2010: 52). The practices of fringe finance reveal the edges of finance as, indeed, the host of 'intense practices': practices designed to incorporate those beyond the reach of finance into mainstream financial practices. These borders, as Walker's contentions implies, are not clean lines, but intense zones of ambiguity, contestation and complexity. Put a bit different, the borders of finance are neither fixed nor unproblematic but the site of complex and ongoing political manoeuvres. In this sense the borders of finance are not strict lines, but what Edward Casey has referred to as edges (Casey 2008: 9–10). In ways that takes Casey's argument seriously, this book has argued that the borders of global capital should not be assumed as given, or for that matter, uninteresting. Rather, the edges of finance are shifting objects with immense impact on the populations which inhabit them.

At the turn of the twentieth century, during a moment when the reach of financial rationality was still crystallizing, Simmel penned his famous assessment of the 'character of calculability' as it crested across the spaces of everyday ('practical') life.

> The calculating exactness of practical life … which has resulted from a money economy corresponds to the ideal of natural science, namely that of transforming the world into an arithmetical problem and of fixing every one of its parts in a mathematical formula. It has been money economy which has thus filled the daily life of so many people with weighing, calculating, enumerating and the reduction of qualitative values to quantitative terms.
>
> (Simmel 2002 [1903]: 13)

As this book argues, attempts to 'transform the world into an arithmetical problem' remain an important part of the 'practical life' of our political-economic present. In important ways, the practices of fringe finance require the conversion of the spaces and populations at the edges of finance into quantifiable sources of value calculated in ways legible to mainstream financial institutions. I want to note, however, that the practices of fringe finance do not form any kind of completed or unambiguous achievement; a 'fixing of every one of its parts in a mathematical formula'. Although not in equal measure, the emergence of fringe finance has been subject to its own version of *double movement*. In noting this, I am not suggesting the kind of broad rhythm of social embeddedness invoked by Polanyi in which the self-regulating market becomes subject to its own inevitable limitation, recaptured by the social in which it could be contained and rendered manageable. Rather, I am suggesting fringe finance as a field simultaneously drawn in two different but mutually implicated directions; a kind of double movement fuelled by creativity on both sides. The creativity of those who have innovated novel ways of instrumentalizing the edges of the financial system – and the vulnerable bodies that inhabit those edges – runs up against, at least in some fashion, the creativity of those who seek to disrupt that 'character of calculability'. This implies a kind of inescapable relationality between forces often conceived as distinct – a recognition of conditions that simultaneously separate *and yet* link incorporation and dislocation, innovation and fragility, centres and edges.

Notes

1 As one key sharing advocate has put it, the collaborative economy is constituted out of 'mobile, location-based capabilities, Web and social network growth, changing consumer attitudes, and the historically understood market benefits of share platforms' (Gansky 2011: 14).
2 As one advocacy group notes, collaborative economic circuits have 'been made possible by the emergence of new, networked social tools and a cultural shift toward peer-to-peer commerce that makes trust and efficient exchange between strangers possible' (Spur 2012).
3 It is important to note that precarity is, itself, a complex and intersectional location – often deeply connected with environmental and ecological vulnerabilities. See Weston 2012.
4 In other words, precarity offers a kind of 'rallying cry for a thriving new world of interdependency and care that's not just private' (Berlant *et al.* 2012: 166).
5 As Judith Butler notes, 'precarity exposes our sociality, the fragile and necessary dimensions of our interdependency' (Berlant *et al.* 2012: 170).
6 Note that this focus is also deeply related to a normative commitment to forms of life that might exist outside of the logic of neoliberal markets (Lorey 2010: 5). Or as put by a group of critics closely associated with Occupy, there is 'need to construct collective forms of life and social cooperation, beyond the market and the profit system' (Midnight Notes 2009: 11).
7 As Butler notes elsewhere, 'at the most intimate levels, we are social; we are comported toward a "you";we are outside ourselves, constituted in cultural norms that precede and exceed us, given over to a set of cultural norms and a field of power that condition us fundamentally' (Butler 2004: 45).
8 Prosper, the second largest American p2p financial marketplace, also has deep ties to web 2.0 networks and funders. Prosper was founded by Chris Larsen who confounded E-Loan and John Witchel (associated with Red Gorilla). Prosper is backed by the Omidyar Network established by Pierre Omidayr of ebay (see Slavin 2007).
9 As Hulme and Wright note, 'Social lending schemes are in the process of constructing new ways of using and interacting with financial services … a direct response to social trends and a demand for new forms of relationship' (Hulme and Wright 2006: 7).
10 Currency Fair is the most well known p2p currency exchanges but other recent entrants include MoneyTwins (see Slavin 2007: 14).
11 The reference here to 'foundational' is explicit. For Collins *et al.* the 'socio-economic foundation of alternative finance is built upon financial disintermediation, direct interaction and exchange between individuals without the need for orthodox institutions' (Collins, Swart and Zhang 2013: 12).
12 See Ashta and Assadi (2010): 'The Peer-to-peer lending site is an intermediary.'
13 Hulme and Wright go on to note that 'Social Lending schemes are based on a horizontal power structure, which, although implicated in a set of power relations enable the formation of ties between members. Importantly, Social Lending schemes interface the individual with the community' (Hulme and Wright 2006: 19).
14 In their own way Hulme and Wright agree, noting that 'Social Lending schemes are not that much more amenable to giving the financial excluded access to credit in comparison with mainstream banks … [but still are] more empowering for the disenfranchised for various reasons' (Hulme and Wright 2006: 50; see also Galloway 2010: 19).

15 As Haldane (2013) notes: 'A more diverse, decentralized financial system could improve financial resilience for bank regulators. And higher banking productivity coupled with greater stability would be a prize we could all enjoy.'

16 Although some investors mistake p2p platforms as either a 'surrogate for saving … [or] a near cash financial instrument' (Stevenson 2013).

17 Although the assets are unsecured, defaults have been relatively low, especially over the past couple of years. The GAO report, for example, notes defaults of 1.2% for Prosper and 2% for LendingClub over the recent past (Government Accountability Office 2011: 21).

18 As Calvey has noted, 'even peer-to-peer lenders like Prosper and LendingClub have given up early ambitions to lend to the masses in favour of credit to those with a strong track record of repaying loans' (see Calvey 2013b).

19 The LendingClub Board now includes several prominent financial luminaries: former Morgan Stanley CEO and Chair John Mack, former Visa President Hans Morris and Lawrence Summers a former key player in the Obama White House. There have also been important links between LendingClub and key figures at tech giants Google and Facebook (Blaney 2013).

20 Salmon (2013: 32) continues, to note, that the 'borrowers are still individuals. But they're being lent money by the very Wall Street institutions that the peer-to-peer system was designed to circumvent.'

21 Dachille (2013) notes that p2p lending replicates many of the conditions that created the subprime crisis: 'If you reflect on some of the causes of the recent financial crisis, the parallels to peer-to-peer lending are striking'.

22 According to its own website Eaglewood is an investment advisor 'specializing in online lending strategies … online credit selection' (Eaglewoodcapital.com).

23 The analogy to subprime mortgages is limited given how unique p2p loans are as assets. Shibata notes that p2p loans are unique in many ways including the ways in which the price is determined not through an open market mechanism or auction but by the intermediary itself (Shibata 2013).

24 For Knorr Cetina and Bruegger (2002: 907) the fields of finance 'although geographically distant, are oriented, above all, toward one another and, at the same time, disengaged from local settings are spanned and bound together by global microstructures – that is, patterns of relatedness and coordination that are global in scope but micro social in character and that assemble and link global domains'.

25 O'Donnell (2013) argues that there is 'a need for secondary markets, which also would require third party pricing, ratings, etc. that would help make this asset class more attractive to institutions'. Alloway (2013) confirms this point, noting 'there is talk of more securitizations to come, as well as exchange traded funds and secondary markets where large investors can trade the peer-to-peer loans they have already bought'.

26 Note that in some American states financial suitability regulations have been established. These rules, for example, prohibit investment from investors who do not have an annual income of at least US $70,000 and a net worth of at least $250,000 (LendingClub 2012: 84).

27 Prosser (2013) notes: 'The value of this investment is that it is uncorrelated to any of the other asset classes that … clients hold in their portfolios'.

28 Stevenson (2013) quotes one critic who notes, that the 'hope that the p2p market is countercyclical strikes me as highly naïve … If anything I would believe that they'd withdraw from the market even faster than banks – after all, banks have an institutionalized lending structure in place … p2p lenders on the other hand are just one click away from investing their money somewhere else.'

29 Some have noted, for example, that LendingClub's largest monthly inflow of retail money came in August 2011 when Standard and Poor's downgraded America's

credit rating, 'Investors pulled money from the stock market and put it into what they regarded as the safer option' (Economist 2013).

30 Perhaps this logic is laid bare most succinctly by LendingClub CEO Laplanche who notes, simply, that 'We haven't used the term "peer-to-peer" for the past three years' (Economist 2013; see also Salmon 2013).

31 This ambition has also initiated a range of other concrete projects, including proposals for a kind of mutual-aid check cashing services, what Gokey describes as 'a mutual aid project, a coordinated way for people to cash their pay checks … this is about mutual aid, and alleviating suffering' (quoted in Tepper 2012).

32 This is a reference to the evocative work of James Scott who rightly notes, in a much different context, the ongoing arts of evasion in which those historically conceived as powerless have often sought to exist outside the logic of the state (see Scott 2009).

References

ABS. 2013. 'Goliath Investors Join the Davids of Peer-to-Peer Lending'. *Asset Securitization Report*. 27 November.

Aitken, R. 2008. 'Embedded Liberalism in Counterpoint: Reading Woody Guthrie's Reciprocal Economy'. *Millennium*. Vol. 37: 437–461.

Alexander, L. 2013. 'Cyberfinancing for Economic Justice'. *William and Mary Business Law Review*. Vol. 4: 309–383.

Alloway, T. 2013. 'Big Banks Muscle in on Peer-to-Peer Lending'. *Financial Times*. 28 October.

Alloway, T. and A. Massoudi. 2013. 'Peer-to-Peer Lender Looks to Secure Credit Rating'. *Financial Times*. 14 November.

Alternative Banking/Occupy Wall Street. 2013. *Occupy Finance*. New York: The Alternative Banking Group of Occupy Wall Street.

Amoore, L. 2007. 'There is no Great Refusal: The Ambivalent Politics of Dissent'. *International Political Economy and Poststructural Politics*. Ed. M. De Goede. Basingstoke: Macmillan: 255–274.

Ashta, A. and D. Assadi. 2009. *Does Social Lending Incorporate Social Technologies: The Use of Web 2.0 Technologies in Online P2P Lending*. Brussels: Solvay Brussels School of Economics and Management/Centre Emile Bernheim, CEB Working Paper No. 09/056.

Ashta, A. and D. Assadi. 2010. 'An Analysis of European Online Micro-Lending Websites'. *Innovative Marketing*. Vol. 6, No. 2: 7–17.

Aspan, M. 2013. 'Lending Club Courts Small Banks as Personal-Loan Partners'. *American Banker*. 12 December.

Bachmann, A., A. Becker, D. Buerckner, M. Hilker, F. Kock, M. Lehmann and P. Tiburtius. 2011. 'Online Peer-to-Peer Lending – A Literature Review'. *Journal of Internet Banking and Commerce*. Vol. 16, No. 2: 2–18.

Balnaves, M. 2012. 'The Australian Finance Sector and Social Media: Towards a History of the New Banking'. *Media International Australia*. No. 143: 132–145

Bauwens, M. 2006. 'The Political Economy of Peer Production'. *Post-Autistic Economics Review*. No. 37.

Bauwens, M. 2012. *Synthetic Overview of the Collaborative Economy*. London: P2P Foundation.

Bazzichelli, T. 2011. 'Paolo Cirio: When Stealing Becomes Art'. *Digicult*. 63. http://www.digicult.it/digimag/issue-063/paolo-cirio-when-stealing-becomes-art.

Benkler, Y. 2013. 'Practical Anarchism: Peer Mutualism, Market and the Fallible State'. *Politics and Society.* Vol. 41, No. 2: 213–251.

Benkler, Y. and H. Nissenbaum. 2006. 'Commons-Based Peer Production and Virtue'. *The Journal of Political Philosophy.* Vol. 14, No. 4: 394–4919.

Berlant, L., J. Puar, J. Butler, B. Cvejic, I. Lorey, A. Vujanovic. 2012. 'Precarity Talk: A Virtual Roundtable'. *The Drama Review.* Vol. 56, No. 4: 163–177.

Blaney, M. 2013. 'The Cool Kids of Finance Join the Peer-to-Peer Bandwagon'. *American Banker.* 17 December.

Burns, R. 2012. 'Charity or Mutual Aid? A Conversation with Organizers of the "Rolling Jubilee"' *In These Times.* 15 November.

Butler, J. 2004. *Precarious Life: The Powers of Mourning and Violence.* London: Verso.

Butler, J. 2011a. 'For and Against Precarity'. *Tidal.* Vol. 1, No. 1: 12–13.

Butler, J. 2011b. 'Bodies in Alliance and the Politics of the Street'. Venice: Public Lecture, State of Things, Office of Contemporary Art Norway.

Calvey, M. 2013a. 'Lending Club Hits $3 Billion Milestone'. *San Francisco Business Times.* 9 December.

Calvey, M. 2013b. 'Debt Consolidator Freedom Financial has Big Backers for New Lending Platform'. *San Francisco Business Times.* 12 December.

Casey, E. 2008. 'Keeping Art to Its Edge'. *Rethinking Facticity.* Eds. Fr. Raffoul and E.S. Nelson. New York: SUNY Press.

Chafee, E. and G. Rapp. 2012. 'Regulating On-Line Peer-to-Peer Lending in the Aftermath of Dodd-Frank: In Search of an Evolving Regulatory Regime for an Evolving Industry'. *Washington and Lee Law Review.* Vol. 69, No. 2: 485–533.

Chemin, M. and J. De Laat. 2013. 'Can Warm Glow Alleviate Credit Market Failures? Evidence from Online Peer-to-Peer Lenders'. *Economic Development and Cultural Change.* Vol. 61, No. 4: 825–858.

Cirio, P. 2011. *Social Algorithims.* http://www.paolocirio.net/press/text_social_algorithms.php. Accessed 17 November 2013.

Crio, P. 2012. 'P2P Gift Credit Card – Gift Finance'. *Origin.*

Clarke, G. 2013. 'Peer-to-Peer Lending: Bypassing the Banks'. *FtAdvisor.* 31 May 2013.

Collins, L., R. Swart and B. Zhang. 2013. *The Rise of Future Finance: The UK Alternative Finance Benchmarking Report.* London: Nesta.

Cox, R.W.1987. *Production, Power and World Order: Social Forces in the Making of History.* New York: Columbia University Press.

Critical Art Ensemble. 2012. 'Reinventing Precarity'. *The Drama Review.* Vol. 56, No. 4: 49–61.

Crowder, D., M. Moe, L. Pampoulov and L. Jiang. 2013. *EFinance is New Again.* New York: GSV Media.

Dachille, D. 2013. 'The Newest Bubble: Peer-to-Peer Lending?' *PBS Newshour/The Business Desk.* 27 November.

De la Merced, M. 2013. 'Leading Web Site Gains a Shareholder in Google'. *New York Times.* 2 May 2013.

Deleuze, G. 2006. *Nietzsche and Philosophy.* New York: Columbia University Press

Drake, D. 2013. 'Crowdfunding in Europe: The Top 10 "Peer-to-Peer" Lenders'. *Forbes My Say.* 23 April.

Duarte, J., S. Siegal and L. Young. 2012. 'Trust and Credit: The Role of Appearance in Peer-to-Peer Lending'. *The Review of Financial Studies.* Vol. 25, No. 8: 2455–2583.

Eavis, P. 2013. 'A Step Toward "Peer to Peer" Lending Securitization'. *New York Times.* 1 October 2013.

Economist. 2012. 'Friends with Benefits'. *Economist.* 15 July.

Economist. 2013. 'End of the Peer Show: Peer-to-Peer Lending Needs a New Name'. 1 June 2013.

Ende, J., S. Hodges, J. Kibbe and R. Suber. 2013. *Peer to Peer Lending: Why Institutional Investors are Flocking to this Emerging Asset Class.* San Francisco, CA: LSTA.

Euromoney. 2013a. 'Peer-to-Peer Lending Enters the Financial Mainstream'. *Euromoney.* November 2013.

Euromoney. 2013b. 'UK Peer-to-Peer Lenders Eye Institutional Investors; New Crowdfunding Products'. *Euromoney.* December.

Faes, C. 2013. 'Have you Considered Peer-to-Peer Finance?' *International Advisor.* 20 November.

Feldman, A. and B. Pinsker. 2013. 'P2P Lending Pulls in Big Investors – Should you Bite?' *Thomson Reuters.* 25 June.

FinAlternatives. 2013. 'Hedge Funds and Institutional Investors Tiptoe into P2P Lending'. *FinAlternatives.* 8 April.

Financial Times. 2013. 'Wall Street v P2P: The Bankers Start to Recolonize the Disintermediators'. *Financial Times.* 14 November.

Flannery, M. 2007. 'Kiva and the Birth of Person-to-Person Microfinance'. *Innovations* (Winter/Spring) Vol. 2, No. 1: 31–56.

Forbes. 2013. 'With IPO in Sight, Lending Club Looks to Upend Banking Industry'. *Forbes.* 18 October.

Galloway, I. 2010. 'Peer-to-Peer Lending and Community Development Finance'. *Community Investments.* Vol. 21, No. 2: 18–39.

Gansky, L. 2011. *The Mesh: Six Reasons Why the Sharing Society will Trump the Ownership Society.* New York: Change This.

Gelman, I.A. 2013. 'Show us Your Pay Stub: Income Verification in P2P Lending'. Social Science Research Network. http://papers.ssrn.com/sol3/papers.cfm?abstract_id=2288037.

Gokey, T. 2013a. *Interview with Author.* 16 December 2012.

Gokey, T. 2013b. 'As Debt Sloshes Higher, Gokey Calls for Jubilee; the Rage for Redemption'. *Nooganomics.* 20 April.

Government Accountability Office. 2011. *Person-to-Person Lending: New Regulatory Challenges Could Emerge as the Industry Grows.* Washington, DC: United States Government Accountability Office.

Graeber, D. 2011. *Debt: The First 5,000 Years.* New York: Melville House.

Haldane, A. 2013. 'Banking May Be on the Cusp of an Industrial Revolution'. *Wired.* September 2013.

Hulme, M. and C. Wright. 2006. *Internet Based Social Lending: Past, Present and Future.* London: Social Futures Observatory.

Husein, A. 2013. *Interview with Author.* 10 December.

Javelin Strategy and Research. 2009. *Lending Club Investment Analysis.* New York: Javelin Strategy and Research.

Kearns, G. 2013. 'The Butler Affair and the Geopolitics of Identity'. *Environment and Planning D: Society and Space.* Vol. 31: 191–207.

Knorr Cetina, K. and U. Bruegger. 2002. 'Global Microstructures: The Virtual Societies of Financial Markets'. *American Journal of Sociology*. Vol. 107, No. 4: 905–950.

Langlois, C. 'Insurance Innovation: "jFloat", New UK P2P Insurance Platform Coming Soon'. *Visible Banking*. 17 April 2013.

Larrimore, L., L. Jiang, J. Larrimore, D. Markowitz and S. Gorski. 2011. 'Peer to Peer Lending: The Relationship Between Language Features, Trustworthiness and Persuasion Success'. *Journal of Applied Communication Research*. Vol. 39, No. 1: 19–37.

Larson, C. 2013. *Hedge Fund Marshall Wace Invests in Peer-to-Peer Lender*. New York: Bloomberg, 29 October.

LendingClub. 2012. *Member Payment Dependent Notes (Prospectus)*. San Francisco, CA: LendingClub Corporation.

LendingClub. 2013. *Form 10-K: Annual Report 2012*. San Francisco, CA: LendingClub Corporation.

Lee, A. 2012. 'Peer to Peer Lending: The Murky Future with American's New Consumer Protector'. New York: Reuters Thomson/Business Law Currents. http://blogs.reuters.com/financial-regulatory-forum/2012/01/25/peer-to-peer-lending-the-murky-future-with-america%E2%80%99s-new-consumer-protector.

Lenz, R. 2011. *Get Rid of Banks and Build up a Modern Financial World!* Vienna: Paper prepared for the 17th Workshop on Alternative Economic Policy in Europe, 16–18 September.

Liu, D., Y. Lu and D. Brass. 2013. *Friendship in Online Peer-to-Peer Lending: Pipes, Prisms and Social Herding*. Louisville: University of Kentucky.

Loper, N. 2013. 'Is Peer-to-Peer Lending Over?' *The College Investor*. 11 December 2013.

Lorey, I. 2010. 'Becoming Common: Precarization as Political Constituting'. *E-Flux*. No. 17: 1–10.

Lorey, I. 2011. 'Governmental Precarization'. *Transversal*. http://eipcp.net/transversal/0811/lorey/en.

Ly, P. and G. Mason. 2010. *Individual Preferences over NGO Projects: Evidence from Microlending on Kiva*. Tacoma: University of Puget Sound.

Marketline. 2013. *Lending Club Corporation – Mergers and Acquisitions, Partnership and Alliances and Investments*. London: Marketline Analysts.

Martin, R. 2012. 'A Precarious Dance, a Derivative Sociality'. *The Drama Review*. Vol. 56, No. 4: 62–77.

Maurer, B. 2012. 'The Disunity of Finance: Alternative Practices to Western Finance'. *The Oxford Handbook of the Sociology of Finance*. Eds. K. Knorr Cetina and A. Preda. Oxford: Oxford University Press: 413–430.

McKee, Y. 2012. 'OWS Debt Resisters Mobilize Arts, Education and Media for 'People's Bailout''. *Waging Nonviolence*. 25 October: 1–13.

Midnight Notes. 2009. *Promissory Notes: From Crisis to Commons*. New York: Midnight Notes Collective.

Muehlebach, A. 2013. 'On Precariousness and the Ethical Imagination: The Year 2012 in Sociocultural Anthropology'. *American Anthropologist*. Vol. 115, No. 2: 297–311.

North, P. 2007. *Money and Liberation: The Micropolitics of Alternative Currency Movements*. Minneapolis: University of Minnesota Press.

O'Donnell, C. 2013. 'Helping Big Get Small'. Thisisgoingtobebig.com. Accessed 10 December.

Ortega, A. and F. Bell. 2008. 'Online Social Lending: Borrower-Generated Content'. *Proceedings of the Fourteenth Americas Conference on Information Systems.* Toronto: 14–17 August.

PCUA. 2012. *The Credit Union Alternative to Payday Loans.* Harrisburg PA: Pennsylvania Credit Union Association.

Prosser, C. 2013. 'The Evolution of P2P Loans into Consumer Loans'. *Forbes.* 22 October.

Real Solutions. 2008. *Solving the Financial Needs of America's Working Families.* Washington, DC: Real Solutions/Filene Research Institute.

Renton, P. 2013a. *Peer to Peer Lending.* Denver, CO: Lend Academy.

Renton, P. 2013b. *Sofi Securitization.* Denver, CO: Lend Academy.

Ross, A. 2013. 'Occupy, Debt, and the Wages of the Future: A Response to Guy Standing'. *Public Culture.* Vol. 15, No. 1: 25–28.

Ross, A. 2014. *Interview with Author.* 10 January.

Ross, A. and S. Ackerman. 2012. 'Strike Debt and Rolling Jubilee: The Debate'. *Dissent Magazine.* 13 November.

Salmon, F. 2013. 'Kickstarter for Hedge-Funders'. *New York Magazine.* 29 September.

Scott, J. 2009. *The Art of Not Being Governed: An Anarchist History of Upland Southeast Asia.* New Haven, CT: Yale University Press.

Shah, A.M. 2009. *P2P Lending – A Threat to Traditional Players.* Bangalore: Finacle/ Infosys.

Shibata, M. 2013. *The Case for P2P Lending as a Fixed-Income Asset.* Denver, CO: Lend Academy.

Simmel, G. 2002 [1903]. 'The Metropolis and Mental Life'. *The Blackwell City Reader.* Eds. G. Bridge and S. Watson. Oxford: Wiley-Blackwell.

Slavin, B. 2007. *Peer-to-Peer Lending – An Industry Insight.* Chicago, IL: Brad Slavin Analysts.

Smith, Z. 2013. *Creativity and Refusal.* Rome: Festival Internazionale di Roma.

Spur. 2012. 'A Policy Agenda for the Sharing Economy'. *The Urbanist.* Issue 517.

Steinisch, M. 2012. 'Peer-to-Peer Lending Survey: Online Alternative to Bank Loans, Credit Cards'. *Action News.* (Summer 2012).

Stevenson, D. 2013. 'P2P Bad? Really?' *alt finance news.* 13 December.

Strike Debt/Occupy Wall Street. 2012. *The Debt Resistors' Operations Manual.* New York: Strike Debt/Occupy Wall Street.

Tepper, F. 2012. 'The 'People's Bailout' was Just the Beginning: What's Next for Strike Debt?' *Yes!* 13 December.

Verstein, A. 2011. *The Misregulation of Person-to-Person Lending.* New Haven, CT: Yale Law School Center for the Study of Corporate Law.

Walker, R.B.J. 2010. *After the Globe, Before the World.* London: Routledge.

Wang, J. 2013. 'Lending Club Offers Hedge Funds'. *Bargaineering.* November 2013.

Weston, K. 2012. 'Political Ecologies of the Precarious'. *Anthropological Quarterly.* Vol. 85, No. 2: 429–455.

Zelizer, V. 2011. *Economic Lives: How Culture Shapes the Economy.* Princeton, NJ: Princeton University Press.

Index

2008 financial crisis 74; subprime crisis 68, 77, 78, 81, 85, 86, 215, 227
2010 Andhra Pradesh crisis 72, 82, 84–85, 87, 186–87; adverse incorporation 186–87; borrower suicide 84, 85, 187; differentiation, immobilization, serialization 187; indebtedness 186, 187; MFI 84–85, 186, 187, 191; rapid growth in commercialized micro-credit 84, 186; securitization 72, 82, 84, 85; SHG 84, 87; *see also* India

accumulation: accumulation by dispossession 86; capital accumulation 12, 37, 86, 160; for elite and powerful financial agents 71
ACE Cash Express 177
ACH (Automated Clearing House) 42, 59
Advance America 51
adverse incorporation 13, 22, 162, 163, 170, 171–86, 189; 2010 Andhra Pradesh crisis 186–87; deepening economic fragilities/inequalities, exposure to risk 162, 171, 174; differentiation 162, 163, 172–75, 186; economic disenfranchisement 13, 22; fringe finance 172–86; immobilization 22, 25, 162, 163, 175–81, 186; indebtedness 187; inequality 13, 171, 186; marginality 13, 171, 172; poverty 171; serialization 162, 163, 181–86, 190, 191; *see also* differentiation; immobilization; incorporation; serialization
AFI (Alliance for Financial Inclusion) 163–64
agency 19; *agencements* 19, 26, 144
AIC (agricultural insurance agency) 108, 109
Alborn, Timothy 96, 102, 119
Alexander, Lisa 211
Allianz 100, 119
Alloway, Tracy 227
Andrijasevic, Rutvica 170, 189
anthropology 22, 143, 162, 171, 176
Aoul, S. 112
Appleyard, Lindsey 26, 167
ASIC (Australian Securities and Investment Commission) 137, 147
Austin, John Langshaw 19–20, 26, 132, 133
Australia: fringe lending 11, 129, 137, 147–48, 155; payday lending 45, 147–49, 151, 155

Badiou, Alain 170
Banco Azteca 50–51
Banco Walmart 47, 50
Baptist, Edward 8
Baragar, Fletcher 58
Barnett, Barry 105
Barry, Dean 101
Basix 108, 109, 120
Bassett, Thomas 65–66
Bateman, Milford 70–71
Bauwens, Michel 203
behavioural economics 104, 144–46, 155, 167–68
Benkler, Yochai 203
Berndt, Christian 144, 155
Besley, Timothy 119
Bevir, Mark 26
Bird, Andrew 217, 223
Blackburn, Robin 58
BlackRock 213
BlueOrchard 73, 75, 79

Boeckler, Marc 144, 155
Borges, Jorge Luis 56–57
borrower *see* population
Borscheid, Peter 99
Brassett, James 134–35, 137, 154
Brazil 47, 48, 50, 51
Breslau, Daniel 133, 134
Bruegger, Urs 215, 227
Buck-Morss, Susan 33, 35
Bulmore, Richard 59
Burchell, Graham 101
Burke, Kathleen 190
Burton, Matt 215
Butler, Judith 152; performativity 20, 132–33, 134–35, 146; precarity and sociality 201, 204–5, 206, 212, 226
Bystrom, Hans 82

Cackley, Alicia 177
Callon, Michel 20, 134, 143, 152
Canada: *Criminal Code* 138, 139; formal legitimacy 11; fringe lending 129, 136, 138–41, 154, 155; Manitoba order 139–41; MPUB 139, 140, 155
capital: capital accumulation 12, 37, 86, 160; capital/ordinary people relationship 12, 161; capital/vulnerable population relationship 11–13; concept of 3, 15–16; an expansive force 2, 35, 56, 65; map of expansion and exploration 56; spaces of capital 24, 33, 163, 167
capitalism 152, 160, 188; financial capitalism 7, 23, 39; global capitalism 134, 204
Carling, Jørgen 176
Casey, Edward 23, 153, 224
Cash America 48, 59–60, 166
Cash Converters International 45, 49, 50, 60
Cash Store 45, 57
Castaneda, Ernesto 112
CFI (Center for Financial Inclusion) 164, 168
CFPB (Consumer Finance Protection Bureau) 57, 148, 155, 174; serialization 182–85, 189, 190, 191
Chaffee, Eric C. 210
Chatterjee, Arup 165
Chen, Zern-shun Adam 83
Chernomas, Robert 60
China: remittance insurance 120
Christophers, Brett 134
Churchill, Craig 112
Cirio, Paolo: *P2P Gift Credit* 198–99, 200, 224
Citi Financial 164
Clarke, Chris 134–35, 137, 154
Clarke, Geoffrey 93
Cole, Shawn 120
collaborative economy 202–3, 225–26; p2p arrangement 202–3, 206, 209, 210, 226; *see also* economies of social practice
Collier, Benjamin 105
Collins, Liam 226
Compartamos 72, 75, 173
Consultative Group to Assist the Poor 164
consumer protection: fringe lending 11, 130, 143–46 (cooling off period 145, 146; disclosure 145, 146, 150; risk warning 145, 146)
contestation: contestation/innovation tension 25; formalization 11, 130; fringe finance 4, 11, 17, 18, 22, 222; fringe lending, regulation 11, 21, 131, 146–51; insurance 93, 95, 96, 101; payday lending, regulation 147–51, 155–56; regulation 146; topography of power and resistance 223
conversion 7–9, 11, 19, 23, 26, 225; financialization 7, 23, 39; micro-credit 19, 68; micro-insurance 19, 92–93, 94, 102–3, 106, 107, 115; payday lending 19, 35, 41, 58; prospecting 7, 23, 36, 39, 40, 56, 93, 111; *see also* micro-credit; micro-insurance; payday lending
Cordray, Richard 137, 191
CoreLogic 178
CoreScore 178
CPLA (Canadian Payday Loan Association) 139
Crediamigo 49–50
credit card 1–2; *P2P Gift Credit* 198–99, 200, 224
credit reporting 177–81, 190
Credit Suisse 75
Credito Real 47
Cresswell, Tim 176
CS Financial 149, 154
Currency Fair 226

Dachille, Doug 227
Dalal, Aparna 104, 119
De Bock, Ombeline 119
De Goede, Marieke 3, 16–17, 95

Deblon, Yvonne 117
debt 205; 99 percent tumblr 221; 2010 Andhra Pradesh crisis 186, 187; adverse incorporation 187; borrower 182, 190; CDO 79; chronic indebtedness 182; debt refusal 220–21; Mexico 46; micro-credit 69; normalization of indebtedness 58; *The People's Bailout* 218; *Rolling Jubilee* 218–23; shared fragility/social indebtedness 205–6, 220–21; sociality 206; stigmatization of over indebtedness 58
decommodification 68
Deleuze, Gilles 10; borders 169; diagram 5–6, 7, 13, 17, 24, 25, 35, 55
Denning, Michael 188
deposit advance 35, 41, 42–43, 184; *see also* payday lending
deregulation 20, 70
DFC Global Corporation/Dollar Financial 43–44, 51–55, 59; credit quality standards 53; global credit analysis 52–53; network 52; population 52–55, 60, 166 (ALICE demographic 53–54); shareholder valuation 57, 60
diagram 5–6, 13, 23, 55; an abstract machine 5, 23, 24; ambiguity and instability 6, 25; definition 5; diagram of expansion 56, 67, 85; diagram of occupation 67; relations between forces 5, 6, 55, 57; spatial relationships 26; *see also* Deleuze, Gilles; diagram of fringe finance; mapping
diagram of fringe finance 5–14, 23, 135; actors 6; centre/edges relationship 4, 6, 24, 26; clusters of practices 7–14; complexity 25; contestation 24–25, 131, 200; diagram of expansion 56, 67, 85; diagram of occupation 67; diversity 23, 24; expansiveness 7, 35, 200; innovative absorption of those on the edges into mainstream finance 200; micro-credit 23, 68; micro-insurance 23; p2p lending 200, 210, 217, 222; particular diagram of financial power and practice 6; payday lending 23, 41–42, 57–58; regulation 151; shifting lines 7, 11; spatial metaphor 5, 6; *see also* conversion; edges; formalization; fringe finance; incorporation
differentiation 162, 163, 172–75, 186; micro-insurance 172–73; micro-lending 173–74; payday lending 174, 175; social sorting 174–75; *see also* adverse incorporation
Dollar Financial 43, 149
Doyle, Aaron 101
Du Toit, Andries 13, 171, 172

Eaglewood Capital 214–15, 227
economies of social practice 14, 22, 25, 198–232; alternative economic circuits 200, 202, 203, 216, 217; American credit union 201; circuits of social incorporation 200, 201–6; collaborative economy 202–3, 225–26; sociality 201–6, 226; *see also* p2p arrangement; p2p lending; *Rolling Jubilee*
edges 25, 58, 224; ambiguity 22, 41–42, 169, 188–89; financial edges as fertile sites 6, 7; hosting intense practices 4, 23, 26, 224; idealized mapping of the edges 23, 24; lines of zero width 1, 2, 26, 224, 230; problematic edges 23; shifting edges 5, 7, 18, 223, 224, 225; *see also* diagram of fringe finance; fringe finance
Edney, Matthew H. 65
El Salvador: remittance insurance 114–15
EMB (Empire Marketing Board) 66
empire 65; Borges' map of empire 56–57; *Highways of Empire* 67, 68; map of empire 65–66
Enova International 48, 57, 59–60
Epstein, Gerald 58
Equitas 80, 81
Ericson, Richard 101
European Union 129
Ewald, François 91, 92–93, 95
exclusion 163, 189; financial exclusion 168, 189; social exclusion 163, 172, 189; *see also* inclusion
Experian: Extended View 178–80, 181, 190
EZCORP 49–50, 57, 60

FCA (Financial Conduct Authority) 42, 144–45, 150, 151, 155
Feehan, Daniel 166
Fernandes, Kshama 86
Fernando, Jude L. 69–70
FICO (Fair Isaac Corporation) 208
finance: alternatives to finance or the art of not being financialized 223–24; concept 3; critique of 222–23;

expansiveness 17–18, 35, 39; gambling and finance 10, 129; genealogies of 14–18, 94–95, 129; legal/illegal distinction 9–10; legitimacy 3, 16–17, 95, 129; a scientific endeavour 16–17, 94, 95 (codification of risk as scientific practice 95–96); a social practice 18–22, 25, 200; a socially controversial practice 16
Financial Consumer Agency of Canada 190
financial subjectivity 21, 22, 166–70
financialization 37–40; conversion 7, 23, 39; debates on 35, 36, 37–40; definition 37–38, 56, 58; expansiveness 39, 40; innovation 39–41, 56; micro-credit 67, 68–73, 76, 85–86; p2p lending 25, 200, 212–17, 222, 227; payday lending 19, 36, 41–43, 56, 58, 59; privileged population 40, 59; processes of accumulation taking financial form 37; shareholder value orientation 37–38; spacing of financialization 5, 40, 59 (unevenness/inequalities 40, 59); USA 37
FinnFund 73
FOLIO*fn* Investment Inc. 211
formalization 9–11, 23, 25, 26, 118, 152; contestation 11, 130; diagram of fringe finance 131, 136, 146; formal legitimacy 10–11; fringe lending 130–31, 132, 136, 151, 152 (objectives 136, 154); legal/illegal distinction 9–10; regulation 130, 132, 136–51 *passim*; unevenness 131, 132; unfinished project 130; *see also* fringe lending, regulation of; payday lending, regulation of; regulation
Foucault, Michel 5, 22, 57, 146; diagram 6; genealogy 14–16; neoliberalism 94, 102
Fourcade, Marion 174, 175, 176–77, 190
Francis, Karen 190
French, Shaun 5, 40, 59, 167
Friendsurance 207
fringe finance 3, 118; contestation 4, 11, 17, 18, 22, 222; creativity 225; definition 4; increasingly in flux 4; innovation 200, 201, 222, 225; objects of financial knowledge and intervention 6; population 4, 135–36; profitable financial intervention 23; under-examined practices 4; variety of techniques 7–8; *see also* diagram of fringe finance; edges; fringe finance/mainstream finance link
fringe finance/mainstream finance link 225; insurance: transferring risk from the edge 110, 116, 117; micro-credit 71, 73; micro-insurance 94, 105–6, 118; *see also* p2p lending and mainstream finance; payday lending and mainstream finance
fringe lending, regulation of 11, 130–31, 132, 135–46; activism 131, 132, 153 (performative activism 153–54); Australia 11, 129, 137, 147–48, 155; authorization mechanisms 130, 137–41, 146; Canada 129, 136, 138–41, 154, 155; consumer protection 11, 130, 143–46; contestation 11, 21, 131, 146–51; debates on 129–30, 152; formal legitimacy 21, 129, 130, 132, 141, 146, 150, 151; formalization 130–31, 132, 136, 151, 152 (objectives 136, 154); immobilization 162, 177, 181; interest rate 136, 138–39, 149–51, 154, 155–56; mechanisms of 137, 146, 149, 154; misuse of 182; national/global dimensions 131, 153–54; performative regulation 130, 131, 152, 153; performativity 20, 131, 132–35, 137, 141, 152–53; politics 130, 131, 137, 139, 141, 143, 146, 151–54; predatory, unfair, racialized practice 11, 130; price mechanisms 130, 141–43, 146 (consumer price requirements 141; pricing calculation 142; truth-in-lending requirements 141–42, 145); reform 149–51; South Africa 129, 138; UK 129, 145; USA 11, 137–38, 141, 142, 145, 155; *see also* payday lending, regulation of

gambling 96, 97, 129; Gambling Act 97, 119; gambling and finance 10, 129 (codification of risk as scientific practice 95–96); insurance and gambling 95, 96–97, 111, 119
gaming 95, 97–98, 111, 129, 132
Gelade, Wouter 119
genealogy 14–18, 26; decomposition 14–15; finance 14–18, 94–95, 129; fringe financial practices 17; insurance 93, 94–99, 116
Germain, Randall 59
Germany 143

Gibbons, Damon 59
GIIF (Global Index Insurance Facility) 109, 120
global finance 3; expansive size and scope 2, 12; global financial governance 26, 27; *see also* finance; fringe finance/mainstream finance link
Gokey, Thomas 218, 220, 222, 228; *see also Rolling Jubilee*
Google 212, 227
Gould, Lawrence 182
Graeber, David 218, 220
Grant, James 33
Grupo Elektra 50–51
Guthrie, Woody 198, 205

Haldane, Andy 210, 226
Hall, Sarah 26, 59, 167
Harley, Brian 56
Harvey, David 86
Haueter, Niels Viggo 99
Healy, Kieran 174, 175, 176–77, 190
Hecht, John 45
Helleiner, Eric 37
Henriksen, Lasse F. 134
Hershman, Lynn 1–2
home-credit 4, 41, 49
Home Credit 48, 165–66
Hook, Derek 16
Hoyle, William 129
Hulme, Michael K. 209, 226
Hungary 11
Husein, Amin 205, 206

ICICI Bank 78, 108
IFFCO-Tokio 108
IFMR Capital 80–82, 83, 84, 86; IFMR Capital Mosec-1 81, 82; IFMR Trust Pioneer II 80
im/mobility 175–76; involuntary immobility 176; *see also* immobilization; migration
immobilization 22, 25, 162, 163, 175–81, 186; fringe lending 162, 177, 181; payday lending 176–78, 179, 181; *see also* adverse incorporation
IMWIP (Indonesian Migrant Worker Insurance Program) 113–14
inclusion 13, 23; financial inclusion 160, 163–64, 168, 189 (neoliberalism 189); G20 Principles of Innovative Financial Inclusion 163; inclusion and belonging 170; inclusion and financial subjectivity 166–70; 'inclusion/exclusion' ambiguous borders 169; 'inclusion/exclusion' simplistic formulation 13, 22, 25, 161, 162, 169–70; Maya Declaration 164; MFI 164; micro-credit 160, 164–65; micro-insurance 160, 165; payday lending 165–66; placement 21, 22, 162, 168–69, 186; social and economic enfranchisement 163; social inclusion/exclusion 163, 189; spaces of capital 163, 168; un/underbanked population 165–66; *see also* adverse incorporation; exclusion; incorporation
incorporation 11–14, 23, 25, 26, 160–97, 225; ambiguity 189; capital/vulnerable population relationship 11–13; complexity 13; financial subjectivity 21–22; population (surplus population 11–12, 160–61, 188, 189; vulnerable population 25); *see also* adverse incorporation; inclusion
India: micro-credit 72, 78, 79–82, 174, 186; micro-insurance 107–9; *see also* 2010 Andhra Pradesh crisis
Indonesia: remittance insurance 113
inequality 117, 161, 204; adverse incorporation 13, 171, 186; financialization 40, 59
innovation 200; financial innovation 8, 39, 57, 79, 210, 217, 222; financialization 39–41, 56; insurance 96; micro-credit 68, 79–80, 81–82, 83, 186; micro-insurance 19, 94, 106, 110, 111, 112, 116, 117, 119; p2p arrangement 201, 207, 210; p2p lending 213–17, 222; payday lending 48, 52, 56
insurance 91–93, 111; actuarial science 24, 98, 99; contestation 93, 95, 96, 100; entrepreneurial approach 98, 119; framing of 97, 102–3; gambling, fraud, murder 95, 96–97, 111, 119; genealogies of finance 93, 94–99, 116; growth of 99; innovation 96; insurable interest 97–98; internationalization of 99; investment 97, 98, 102; *Life Insurance Map* 91–92, 93; p2p arrangement 207; security is a commodity 91; uneven financial practice 94, 99; welfare state 101, 117, 118; *see also* insurance/micro-insurance and risk; micro-insurance

insurance/micro-insurance and risk 24, 92–93, 95–96; actuarial science 24, 110; codification of risk 95–96, 97, 98; collectivization/individualization of risk 100; insurance/risk link 95–96, 102–3, 115; risk management 24, 102, 116, 118; risk mitigation 110, 117, 119; transferring risk from the edge 110, 116, 117; *see also* micro-insurance; risk
interest: adverse incorporation 174, 190; fringe lending and interest rate 136, 138–39, 149–51, 154, 155–56; micro-credit 84, 86, 173–74; payday lending 142–43, 147–48, 174, 190; USA 136, 142–43
International Finance Corporation 72, 100, 109, 164
International Labor Organization 119
investment 38; insurance 97, 98, 102; micro-insurance 100, 104–5, 115, 116, 117, 119; p2p investment instruments 215–16, 227; *see also* MIV
IPE (International Political Economy) 2, 15, 16
IPF (International Personal Finance) 49
IPOs (Initial Public Offerings) 43, 47, 72, 84
Irving, N. 138

jFloat 207
Johnson, Leigh 173
Jonsson, Gunvor 176
Joseph, K. 45
JP Morgan 79, 100

Karl, Alissa G. 152
Kaufman, Alex 154
Keppler, Joseph 9
King, Uriah 183, 190
Kirsten, Marié 138
Kiva Microfunds 33; *Intercontinental Ballistic Microfinance* 33, 35
Kneale, James 167
Knorr Cetina, Karin 215, 227
knowledge: 'collateral' knowledge 26–27; finance as knowledge of information 58; shaping 'economic' objects 20
Kobzar, Olena 140
Kodar, Freya 154
Krippner, Greta 37
Kunz, Rahel 115, 120

Lake, Walter 155
Langley, Paul 41, 169–70, 178, 190; calculation/calculative device 7, 134, 146, 154; financial subjectivity 21, 167–68
Latin America 4, 47, 51
Lazzarato, Maurizio 166
LCICI-Lombard General Insurance Company 108
Leapfrog Investments 100
Leaver, Adam 167–68
legitimacy 21; finance 3, 16–17, 95, 129; formalization 10–11; fringe lending 21, 129, 130, 132, 141, 146, 150, 151; UK 11; USA 11
lender: formalization/regulation 130, 132, 136–51 *passim*; payday lender 43; profitability for 70, 180, 181
LendingClub 200, 206, 207, 208, 211–16 *passim*; LC Advisors 216; mainstream finance 212, 213, 216, 227
LendUp 181
Lenz, Rainer 210
Leyshon, Andrew 5, 9, 111; financial capitalism 7, 23; financial subjectivity 21; financialization 36, 38–39, 40–41, 56, 59
Li, Tania 12, 13, 161, 171
liberalism: classical liberalism 163; micro-insurance 94, 99–101, 116, 118, 119
Lobo-Guerrero, Luis 97, 105–6, 116
Loewe, Markus 117

Mackenzie, Donald, 18, 19, 26, 73, 133–34
Maclean, Kate 167
mapping 33, 56–57; genealogy 16; *Life Insurance Map* 91–92, 93; map of expansion 65, 67; map of flow 67, 85, 86; map of occupation 45, 86; mapping the economy 33–35; *see also* diagram; empire
marginality 13, 163, 171, 172
market: market *agencement* 19; materiality of market 18–19, 26
Marshall Wace LLP 214
Martin, Randy 38, 205
Marx, Karl 11–12, 86, 160–61
Maurer, Bill 223
McFall, Liz 97, 100, 119
Melzer, Brian 174, 176
Mexico: consumer credit 46–47, 59; debt 46; EZCORP 49–50, 60; micro-credit

72; micro-insurance 120; payday lending 46–47, 49–51, 59, 60
Mezzadra, Sandro 151
MFI (micro-credit institution) 69–71, 73–82 *passim*; 2010 Andhra Pradesh crisis 84–85, 186, 187, 191; financial inclusion 164; interest rate 84, 85, 86, 173, 174; MIV 73–74, 76; securitization 78–79; solidarity 70
MFRC (Micro Finance Regulatory Council of South Africa) 155
micro-credit 4, 24, 67–90; accumulation for elite and powerful financial agents 71; anti-poverty practice 67, 68, 167; conversion 19, 68; critique 69–71, 86; deregulation 70; diagram of fringe finance 23, 68; financial valuation 71–72; financialization 67, 68–73, 76, 85–86 (market governance 69); growth of 69, 164, 186; inclusion 160, 164–65; India 72, 78, 79–82, 174, 186; innovation 68, 79–80, 81–82, 83, 186; interest rate 84, 86, 173–74; intermediation 67, 68, 73–76 (private intermediation 75); Mexico 72; micro-credit/mainstream finance connection 71, 73; micro-credit network 24; neoliberalism 69, 70–71, 167; risk 68, 76, 77, 85 (individualization of risk 69–70); securitization 19, 24, 67, 68, 76–82, 83, 93; population 68, 71, 174; World Bank 69, 85; *see also* MFI; MIV; securitization
Micro Credit Rating International 72
micro-insurance 4, 19, 24, 91–126; agricultural insurance 19, 94 (crop insurance 107; weather index insurance 94, 107–11, 173); conversion 19, 92–93, 94, 106, 107, 115 (human life into risk/asset 102–3, 115); definition 92–93; diagram of fringe finance 23; differentiation 172–73; fringe finance/mainstream finance link 94, 105–6, 118; growth of 100, 103, 117–18, 119; inclusion 160, 165; index insurance 109–11, 116, 120, 172–73; India 107–9; innovation 19, 94, 106, 110, 111, 112, 116, 117, 119; insurance network 117–18; investment 100, 104–5, 115, 116, 117, 119; liberalism 94, 99–101, 116, 118 (insurance as thrift 101, 119); Mexico 120; micro-insurance education 103–5, 119 (*Treasure Pot* 105); neoliberalism 101, 104–5, 115–16, 120 ('enterprising' self/entrepreneurialism 94, 101–2, 104, 106, 116); population 94, 116, 117, 119; prospecting 93, 111; remittance insurance 19, 94, 111–16; self-insurance 110, 120; social protection 117; *see also* insurance; insurance/micro-insurance and risk
micro-lending 4, 25; differentiation 173–74; immobilization 162, 177, 181; regulation 130, 132; *see also* fringe lending, r egulation of
Microrate 72
migration 111–12, 176; irregular migration 111, 112; *see also* remittance
Millo, Yuval 133–34
Mitchell, Timothy 16, 20, 137
MIV (microfinance investment vehicle) 68, 73–76, 79, 86; MFI 73–74, 76; public sector participation 75; success 74, 86; *see also* micro-credit
MoneyTwins 226
Montgomerie, Johanna 38, 40
Morduch, Jonathan 104, 119
Morgan Stanley 164, 215
MPCI (Multiple Peril Crop Insurance) 107
Murphy, Sharon 96, 98

National Credit Union Foundation 201
Neha Malhotra, 59
Neilson, Brett 151
neoclassical economics 144
neoliberalism 201; entrepreneurialism 70, 101–2, 167; financial inclusion 189; financial subjectivity 21, 166–67; Foucault, Michel 94, 102; insurance, entrepreneurial approach 98, 119; micro-credit 69, 70–71, 167; micro-insurance 101, 104–5, 115–16, 120 ('enterprising' self/entrepreneurialism 101–2, 104, 106, 116); performativity 20; remittance insurance 115, 120

O'Donnell, Charlie 227
O'Malley, Pat 102, 103
Occupy Bank 201
OFT (Office of Fair Trading) 46, 149–50, 155–56
Oikocredit 73, 74, 75
Omidyar Network 73, 226

OWS (Occupy Wall Street) 203, 205, 209, 220–21, 226; *The People's Bailout* 218

p2p arrangement 199, 200–201, 206–12; collaborative economy 202–3, 206, 209, 210, 226; disintermediation 201, 203, 207, 226; innovation 201, 207, 210; insurance 207; p2p car-sharing programme 203; p2p currency exchange 207, 226; UK 206; web portal 206; *see also* economies of social practice; p2p lending

p2p lending 4, 14, 25, 199–200, 207–8; alternative mode of incorporation/economic circuit 25, 217; diagram of fringe finance 200, 210, 217, 222; finance as a social practice 200; fringe finance, fragility and innovation 200, 201, 222; growth 207, 210–11, 213; innovation 213–17, 222; population 209–10, 212, 216, 226, 227; social practice 25, 200, 209, 212, 217; sociality 209, 217, 226; UK 207, 213; USA 207, 208, 211, 214, 227; *see also* economies of social practice; p2p arrangement; p2p lending and mainstream finance

p2p lending and mainstream finance 200, 201, 208, 221–22, 227; banks 201, 213; capital market investors and hedge funds 201, 213–14; converting loan receivables into investable assets 200, 211, 212; financialization 25, 200, 212–17, 222, 227; p2p investment instruments 215–16, 227; refusal of mainstream finance 200, 201, 209, 210; securitization 201, 208, 211, 214–15, 227; whole-lending programme 214, 215; *see also* p2p lending

Pani, Erica 39

Parrish, Leslie 190

Pathak, Pathik 58–59

payday lending 4, 24, 40–64, 137, 181–82; Australia 45; cognate practices 35, 41, 47; conversion 19, 35, 41, 58; CPA 42; credit reporting 177–81, 190; definition 35, 41; deposit advance 35, 41, 42–43, 184; diagram of fringe finance 23, 41–42, 57–58; diagram of occupation 67; differentiation 174, 175; expansion 67, 85; globalized networks of credit provision 36–37, 45–55, 56 (financialized global networks 36, 48–49); growth and consolidation 24, 36, 44–45, 46, 137; illegal payday lending 59, 136, 154; immobilization 176–78, 179, 181; inclusion 165–66; innovation 48, 52, 56; interest rate 174; Mexico 46–47, 49–51, 59, 60; misuse of 182; non-amortized credit 42, 47, 183, 185; payroll loan 35, 41, 47; population 36, 41, 52, 54, 165–66, 185; serialization 181, 182–84, 190; shareholder value 57–58, 60, 67, 85; short-term loan 19, 42–43; UK 45–46, 50, 59; USA 44, 45, 51; *see also* payday lending and mainstream finance; payday lending, regulation of

payday lending and mainstream finance 24, 35–36, 42–45, 55, 56; capital recirculation through mainstream markets 24, 57–58; financialization 19, 36, 41–43, 56, 58, 59; reliance on techniques/networks of mainstream finance 36, 40–45, 52, 55, 56; securitization 59; transformation of payday lenders into financialized networks 24, 42, 43

payday lending, regulation of 10, 57, 59, 132, 137–43, 153; Australia 147–49, 151, 155; authorization, mechanisms of 137–41; Canada 138–41; contestation 147–51, 155–56; interest rate 142–43, 147–48, 190; serialization 184–85; UK 149–51, 155–56; USA 137–38, 142–43, 147, 155; *see also* fringe lending, regulation of; payday lending

Pennsylvania Credit Union Association 201

performativity 19–20, 26, 132–35, 137, 154; controversy on 134–35; critique 153; definition 20, 132; fringe lending 20, 131, 132–35, 137, 141, 152–53 (performative regulation 130, 131, 152, 153); performative activism 153–54; versions of 134–35

Philippines: OFWs 113; remittance insurance 113

Phillips, Nicola 171, 190

Pioneer life 113

placement 21, 22, 162, 168–69, 186; *see also* adverse incorporation; inclusion

Planet Rating 72

Polanyi, Karl 225
politics: fringe lending 130, 131, 137, 139, 141, 143, 146, 151–54; micro-lending 25
population 4, 135–36; ALICE demographic 53–54; capital/ordinary people relationship 12, 161; capital/vulnerable population relationship 11–13 (conceptual argument 12, 13; empirical argument 12–13); DFC Global Corporation 52–55, 60, 166; financialization and privileged population 40, 59; fringe finance 4, 135–36; marginal population 6; micro-credit 68, 71, 174; micro-insurance 94, 116, 117, 119; p2p lending 209–10, 212, 216, 226, 227; payday lending 36, 41, 52, 54, 165–66, 185; securitization, risk for vulnerable population 82, 83, 85; surplus population 11–12, 160–61, 188, 189; un/underbanked population 4, 12, 165–66, 178–79, 188; vulnerable population 4, 11–13, 25, 26, 82, 83, 85
poverty 163, 164, 171; micro-credit, anti-poverty practice 67, 68, 167; poverty reduction 70
Power, Michael 118
precarity 203–6, 220, 221, 226
Preda, Alex 3, 8, 95
Profund 73
Prosper 200, 206, 208, 211, 226, 227; mainstream finance 212–13
Prosser, Marc 216, 227
Proudhon, Pierre-Joseph 91
PSP Capital Solutions 214

Rankin, Katherine N. 70
Ramsay, Iain 154
Rapp, Geoffrey C. 210
regulation: contestation 146; micro-lending 130, 132; serialization 184–85; *see also* formalization; fringe lending, regulation of; payday lending, regulation of
remittance 112
remittance insurance 19, 94, 111–16; China 120; El Salvador 114–15; Indonesia 113; neoliberalism 115, 120; Philippines 113; Spain 114
ResponsAbility Investments AG 75–76; Global Microfinance Fund 75–76
Riles, Annelise 18, 26–27
risk 17; fringe lending and risk warning 145, 146; micro-credit 68, 76, 77, 85 (individualization of risk 69–70); *see also* insurance/micro-insurance and risk; securitization
Rolling Jubilee 218–23; disrupting finance and its logic of instrumental rationality 222
Rose, Nikolas 101–2, 104
Ross, Andrew 205
Russell Sage Foundation 159

Said, Edward 91
Salmon, Felix 227
Schwittay, Anke 168, 169
Seabrooke, Leonard 20–21
Seckinelgin, Hakan 189
Securities and Exchange Commission 208, 211
securitization 215; 2008 financial crisis 68, 77, 78, 81, 85, 86, 215, 227; 2010 Andhra Pradesh crisis 72, 82, 84, 85; India 78, 79–82; MFI 78–79; micro-credit 19, 24, 67, 68, 76–82, 83, 93 (dispersal of risk 77–78, 81, 82, 85, 93; dispersing capital from the edge into diffused investors 68, 77, 83; risk for vulnerable population 82, 83, 85); p2p lending 201, 208, 211, 214–15, 227; payday lending 59; subprime mortgage 77, 78, 81, 83, 86, 178 (p2p lending 214, 215, 227)
SegurCaixa 114
Seguros Futuro 114–16
serialization 162, 163, 181–86, 190, 191; CFPB 182–85, 189, 190, 191; definition 183–84; payday lending: loan rollovers and extensions 181, 182–84, 190; regulation 184–85; *see also* adverse incorporation
SHARE Microfin Limited 78
shareholder value: financialization and shareholder value 37–38; payday lending 57–58, 60, 67, 85
Sherlock, Steve 133
Simmel, Georg 201, 225
Sinclair, Hugh 70
Skees, Jerry 105
SKS Micro-credit 72–73, 79, 86
Smith, Gavin 12, 161
Smith, Zadie 200, 210
social practice: finance, a social practice 18–22, 25, 200; p2p lending 25, 200,

209, 212, 217; *see also* economies of social practice
social protection 112, 117
social studies of finance 3, 18–21, 25, 131
sociality 203–6; p2p lending 209, 217, 226; precarity and sociality 201, 204–5, 206, 212, 226; *see also* economies of social practice
Soederberg, Susanne 46, 47, 60, 77, 152, 189
SoFi 215
South Africa: fringe lending 129, 138; *Usury Act* 138
Spain: remittance insurance 114
Spector, Mary 136
Speedy Cash 44–45, 59
Spencer, Todd 33
Springleaf Holdings 43, 59
Standard & Poor's 71, 227
state: financialization 59; welfare state 101, 117, 118
Stein, Peer 189
Stevenson, David 227
STOC (*Stock Ticker Orbital Comparison*) 33–35, 58
Strange, Susan 2
Strike Debt 218, 221–22; *The People's Bailout* 218
Swiss Re 100, 102, 109, 119
Szymborska, Wisława 55

Taylor, Marcus 6, 36, 136, 174, 186, 187, 191
Teletrack 178, 179
Thrift, Nigel 9, 111; financial capitalism 7, 23; financialization 36, 38–39, 40–41, 56, 59
ticker 8
Townsend, Peter 163
Trivedi, Rohan 79
Turner, Adair 77, 175
Turner, Bryan 175

UK (United Kingdom): formal legitimacy 11; fringe lending 129, 145; p2p lending 207, 213; payday lending 45–46, 50, 59 (contestation on reformulation of 149–51, 155–56)
USA (United States of America): American credit union 201; *Colorado Deferred Deposit Loan Act* 147, 155; Colorado plan 147; *Colorado Uniform Consumer Credit Code* 147; *Credit Reform Act* 138; financialization 37; formal legitimacy 11; fringe lending 11, 137–38, 145, 155; interest rate 136, 142–43; p2p lending 207, 208, 211, 214, 227; payday lending 44, 45, 51 (regulation 137–38, 142–43, 147, 155); Regulation Z 141, 142

Vail, John 68
Van der Zwan, Natascha 37
Verstein, Andrew 207–8
Vickery, James 107
Vogl, Joseph 35

wage/wageless dichotomy 188
Wainwright, Thomas 5, 40, 59
Walker, Robert B. J. 1, 2, 26, 224
Wall Street 9, 129, 214, 227
Walters, William 5, 14–15
Watson, Matthew 175
WBCIS (Weather Based Crop Insurance Scheme) 108
Weber, Heloise 70
White, Mica 218
Williams, Toni 154
Wonga 59, 190
World Acceptance 47
World Bank: Global Findex 4; index insurance 109, 111; micro-credit 69, 85
Wright, Collette 209, 226

Young, Alan 9
Yunus, Mohamed 69

Zapata, Gisela 116
Zelizer, Viviana 96, 98, 99, 119, 200, 202, 217
ZestFinance 180–81
Zopa 206

For Product Safety Concerns and Information please contact our EU
representative GPSR@taylorandfrancis.com
Taylor & Francis Verlag GmbH, Kaufingerstraße 24, 80331 München, Germany

www.ingramcontent.com/pod-product-compliance
Ingram Content Group UK Ltd.
Pitfield, Milton Keynes, MK11 3LW, UK
UKHW011000180926
475701UK00004B/488
* 9 7 8 0 3 6 7 5 9 9 6 4 5 *